China's Rural Industry

China's Rural Industry
Structure, Development, and Reform

Edited by
William A. Byrd and Lin Qingsong

PUBLISHED FOR THE WORLD BANK
Oxford University Press

Oxford University Press

OXFORD NEW YORK TORONTO DELHI
BOMBAY CALCUTTA MADRAS KARACHI
PETALING JAYA SINGAPORE HONG KONG
TOKYO NAIROBI DAR ES SALAAM
CAPE TOWN MELBOURNE AUCKLAND
and associated companies in
BERLIN IBADAN

Manufactured in the United States of America
First printing February 1990

The findings, interpretations, and conclusions expressed
in this study are entirely those of the authors and should not be
attributed in any manner to the World Bank, to its affiliated
organizations, or to members of its Board of Executive Directors
or the countries they represent. The maps that accompany the
text have been prepared solely for the convenience of the reader; the
designations and presentation of material in them do not imply
the expression of any opinion whatsoever on the part of the
World Bank, its affiliates, or its Board or member countries
concerning the legal status of any country, territory,
city, or area, or of the authorities thereof, or concerning
the delimitation of its boundaries or its national affiliation.

The Chinese characters used on the cover and throughout this
book stand for "rural industry."

Library of Congress Cataloging-in-Publication Data

China's rural industry : structure, development, and reform / edited
by William A. Byrd, Qingsong Lin.
   p. cm.
Includes bibliographical references.
ISBN 0-19-520822-6
1. China—Industries, Rural. 2. Industry and state—China.
3. China—Economic policy—1976– I. Byrd, William. II. Lin,
Qingsong.
HC427.92.C46553 1989
338.951'0091'73'4—dc20

89-26665
CIP

Contents

Preface

The emergence and recent rapid growth of rural nonagricultural enterprises (township, village, and private enterprises—TVPs) in China is a striking and in many ways unique phenomenon. Almost overnight, industrial activity has expanded tremendously and enterprises have proliferated. These changes have brought about large increases in rural personal incomes and significant shifts in the structure of the rural labor force.

China's TVP sector has several noteworthy features.

- *Dynamism.* Output has been doubling every three to four years, and hundreds of thousands of new firms have emerged each year on average.
- *Competitiveness.* The sector has gained a large share of the domestic market for many industrial goods and has penetrated some export markets as well.
- *Small scale.* Although enterprises of substantial size exist, especially in the more developed areas, most firms are small concerns with only a few score employees and about Y100,000 in assets.
- *Diversity.* There is great geographic variety in ownership, institutional arrangements, level of development, and degree of industrialization.
- *Outward orientation.* Most output, especially of manufactured goods, is sold outside the community or locality in which it is produced.
- *Community orientation.* Nearly all TVPs are tied in complex ways to their rural communities, and they would not consider relocating.
- *Factor immobility.* Like the enterprises themselves, factors of production and human talent are largely immobile across localities and communities.

These characteristics will be analyzed in detail in this volume.

Despite considerable scholarly work on China's rural industry in the 1970s and later (see chapter 2), little research of a comprehensive nature has been done. In particular, the rapid development of the TVP sector since 1984 has not been adequately documented and analyzed. In late 1985 the Institute of

Economics of the Chinese Academy of Social Sciences (CASS) and the World Bank agreed to undertake a collaborative study of China's industrial TVP sector that would involve extensive data collection, joint fieldwork, shared data processing and analysis, international comparative research, and sponsorship of an international conference. This research followed earlier collaborative work on Chinese state-owned industrial enterprises (see Tidrick and Chen 1987).

The main objectives of the project were (a) to gain a better understanding of how China's industrial TVP sector actually functions, (b) to learn about the rural communal institutional and regulatory framework within which it operates, (c) to ascertain the reasons behind the rapid growth of the sector, particularly since 1984, (d) to identify and analyze the problems and obstacles faced by the TVP sector as it continues to evolve and develop, (e) to evaluate on an informed basis different institutional and policy options for the future, and (f) to shed light on the TVP sector from an international perspective. The main topics covered by the research included the performance of the TVP sector; the TVP ownership system; roles and motivations of rural community authorities; the market environment and business practices of TVPs; the allocation, circulation, and utilization of key factors of production; labor and wage systems; and regional variations in TVP development and rural industrialization. Details on project objectives and research methods are provided in chapter 2.

This volume contains the initial research output of the project. The papers were written by Chinese and World Bank researchers on the basis of an agreed set of topics and were presented at an international conference held in Beijing, November 4–7, 1987. All of the papers were revised and edited in light of conference discussions. In addition to the two introductory chapters there are ten chapters by Chinese authors and seven by World Bank staff and consultants. All of the former and all but one of the latter focus on various aspects of China's industrial TVP sector. Chapter 19 provides an international perspective by looking at firms elsewhere in the world that are similar in some ways to Chinese TVPs. Other fruits of the project have been published elsewhere or have been circulated internally within China and the World Bank. Given the abundant data collected as part of the project, it is hoped that more published papers and longer works will be forthcoming as the materials and data are analyzed in greater depth.

Through this collaborative research project the World Bank has gained a deeper understanding of China's industrial TVP sector. The Institute of Economics of CASS and other participating Chinese research institutions have benefited from organizing and conducting the first comprehensive, systematic research on China's TVP sector—a project that has applied a wide range of analytical techniques to a large, multifaceted, and relatively complete data set. An international perspective on TVPs has also been gained from analysis of existing literature and through field visits to other countries. Finally, this research has provided a basis for analyzing the policy issues that face the TVP sector and for evaluating different policy options. The project represents a further advance in collaboration between Chinese research institutions and international agencies, and we hope that it will lead to similar endeavors in the future.

This collaborative research project would not have been possible without the help and active involvement of many people and organizations. We would especially like to thank the leaders and government officials of Wuxi, Jieshou, Nanhai, and Shangrao counties and the many TVP managers and workers who gave interviews and filled out questionnaires during the field investigations. Their assistance was invaluable and was willingly provided despite the substantial time and effort required. The research team invariably received the warmest hospitality when visiting the four counties. In addition, the help of government officials and of TVP managers and workers in Yuanping County (Shanxi Province) and Taihe County (Anhui Province) during related fieldwork is gratefully acknowledged.

Officials of the TVP Bureau of the Ministry of Agriculture and the State Statistical Bureau also met with members of the research team and provided useful information on the national situation of the TVP sector.

On the Chinese side, CASS and its Institute of Economics covered the bulk of financial expenditures. On the World Bank side, a grant from the World Bank research budget and operational funds from the China Division were the primary sources of financial support. A grant from the Ford Foundation financed international fieldwork and related costs. The financial assistance of all these institutions was essential for the success of this project and is acknowledged with thanks.

Just as important as financing was the time of the members of the research team. In addition to CASS's Institute of Economics and the China Division of the World Bank, the Development Research Institute of China's State Council Rural Development Research Center, the China Economic System Reform Research Institute, and the Sociology Department of Beijing University contributed staff time.

The project was organized under the overall supervision of, on the Chinese side, Liu Guoguang, vice president, CASS, and Dong Fureng, director, Institute of Economics, CASS, and, on the World Bank side, first Fred Levy, senior economist, China Division, and subsequently Gene Tidrick, lead economist, China Department. The respective team leaders for the project were Lin Qingsong, deputy director, Institute of Economics, CASS, and William Byrd, economist, Country Operations Division, China Department, World Bank. Others with major responsibilities for managing the research included He Jiacheng, chief, Development Division, Institute of Economics; Luo Xiaopeng, chief, Macroeconomics Division, Development Research Institute, State Council Rural Development Research Center; and Alan Gelb, senior economist, Financial Policy Division, Country Economics Department, World Bank.

In addition to the contributors to this volume, the following researchers participated in field investigations and other parts of the collaborative research project: Gu Xiulin, Hong Wei, Hou Xueshan, Li Hanlin, Shu Yan, Christine Wong, Yang Xiaodong, and Yang Xiaodong. Their help with research design, data gathering, and other aspects of the work was invaluable. Li Lanting, Li Xiaomei, Lu Xiaoheng, Ma Changshan, Edna Monaghan, Qu Ayang, Wang Shuwen, and Zhang Yi lent administrative and related support to the project, and their help is gratefully acknowledged. The translators of the conference papers were Zhang Ciyun and others from the China Translation Corporation; Zhang Xiaogang and others from the *China Daily*; Dai Rui, He Baoyu, Wang Lina, and Zhang Zhixian. In addition to several contributors to this volume, a number of scholars helped organize the international field visits and related background work for the project: Baburao Baviskar, David Ellerman, Saul Estrin, Derek Jones, Y. Y. Kueh, Nicholas Lardy, Lin Yifu, Virginie Perotin, and Janez Prasnikar. An international panel consisting of Baburao Baviskar, Ronald Dore, Benjamin King, Dwight Perkins, and Martin Weitzman participated in the international conference and contributed valuable comments. Chinese participants not involved with the project who attended the conference included Du Rensheng, Wang Guichen, Bao Youdi, Chen Xihu, Hua Jianchun, Ren Long, Zhang Yi, and Zhou Qiren; their participation and comments are also greatly appreciated.

Abbreviations
and Terminology

Chinese terms, transliterated according to the Pinyin system, are in brackets.

Abbreviations

ABC   Agricultural Bank of China [*nongye yinhang*]

CASS Chinese Academy of Social Sciences

GVAIO Gross value of agricultural and industrial output

GVAO Gross value of agricultural output

GVIO Gross value of industrial output

LMF   Labor-managed firm (Yugoslavia)

LSE   Local state enterprise [*difang guoying qiye*]

PRS   Production responsibility system (in agriculture) [*baochandaohu* or *baogandaohu*]

RCC   Rural credit cooperative [*xinyong hezuoshe*]

TEC   Township economic commission [*xiang jingwei*]

TIC   Township industrial corporation [*xiang gongye gongsi*]. The township government organ that is directly responsible for supervising township enterprises. It has different names in different parts of the country and is sometimes combined with the township economic commission. If the two are not combined, the township industrial corporation is subordinate to the township economic commission.

TVCE Township and village community enterprise [*xiangcun qiye*]. Excludes enterprises run by production teams [*shengchan duiban qiye*].

TVP   Rural nonstate enterprise (township, village, and private enterprise) [*xiangzhen qiye*]. Includes production team enterprises.

Y   Yuan (currency unit). Recent average official exchange rates have been 2.30 yuan to the U.S. dollar in 1984, 2.94 in 1985, 3.45 in 1986, 3.72 in 1987, and 3.72 in 1988. (International Monetary Fund, *International Financial Statistics.*)

Terminology

Bonds [jizi]. Short-term (one to two years) financial instruments issued to workers or local residents by TVPs or community governments; usually non-transferable. Interest on bonds may be fixed, variable with enterprise profits, or a combination of the two.

Community government [shequ zhengfu]. Primarily refers to township [*xiang*] and village [*cun*] community governments but can also include production teams, sometimes termed villagers' small groups [*cunmin xiaozu*].

Enterprises. The types discussed are: state-owned enterprises [*guoying qiye*], community enterprises [*zhengban qiye*], and private enterprises [*minban qiye*]. Under community enterprises are township enterprises [*xiangban qiye*], village enterprises [*cunban qiye*], and production team enterprises [*shengchan duiban qiye*]. Township and village enterprises [*xiangcun qiye*] are referred to as TVCEs. Private enterprises include all kinds of nongovernmental rural enterprises: cooperative firms, partnerships [*lianhu qiye*], and individual proprietorships [*getihu, geti qiye*, or *siying qiye*], which may have 100 or more employees.

Extrabudgetary revenues and expenditures [yusuan wai shouzhi]. Community government incomes and expenditures that occur outside the state budget. Includes profit remittances from community enterprises, management fees paid by TVPs, ad hoc levies on the rural population, and sometimes shared above-quota tax collections that are retained by the community government.

Management fees [guanli fei]. Levies on TVPs by TVP bureaus, industrial-commercial administrative management bureaus, or sometimes community governments, usually calculated as a straight percentage of sales revenue, generally in the 0.5–2.0 percent range.

Units of measure. 1 mu = 0.1647 acres = 0.0667 hectares. 1 jin = 0.5 kilograms.

Counties Surveyed

Jieshou County, Anhui Province
Nanhai County, Guangdong Province
Shangrao County, Jiangxi Province
Wuxi County, Jiangsu Province

Contributors

The affiliations shown are those pertaining at the time of writing.

William A. Byrd	Country Operations Division, China Department, The World Bank
Du Haiyan	Institute of Economics, Chinese Academy of Social Sciences
Du He	Institute of Economics, Chinese Academy of Social Sciences
Alan Gelb	Financial Policy and Systems Division, Country Economics Department, The World Bank
He Jiacheng	Institute of Economics, Chinese Academy of Social Sciences
Lin Qingsong	Institute of Economics, Chinese Academy of Social Sciences
Luo Xiaopeng	Development Research Institute, State Council Rural Development Research Center
Meng Xin	Institute of Economics, Chinese Academy of Social Sciences
Song Lina	Institute of Economics, Chinese Academy of Social Sciences
Jan Svejnar	Department of Economics, University of Pittsburgh
Wang Hansheng	Department of Sociology, Beijing University
Wang Tuoyu	Institute of Economics, Chinese Academy of Social Sciences
Wang Xiaolu	China Economic System Reform Research Institute, System Reform Commission
Josephine Woo	Country Operations Division, China Department, The World Bank

Wu Quhui — Institute of Economics, Chinese Academy of Social Sciences

Xu Xinxin — Department of Sociology, Beijing University

N. Zhu — Department of Economics, Georgetown University

China's Rural Industry

1

China's Rural Industry: An Introduction

William A. Byrd and Lin Qingsong

This chapter surveys the institutional framework, historical background, and present situation and importance of China's township, village, and private enterprise (TVP) sector. It is directed particularly at readers for whom the subject is new or whose knowledge about the sector is not up to date.

We begin with some definitions. There are three levels of rural communities in China. The *township* (formerly the commune), now the lowest level in China's government hierarchy, has an articulated government structure. The typical township has a population of 15,000–30,000. The *village* (formerly the brigade) is not a separate level of government but has governmental functions and a community structure. Villages generally have a population of 1,000–2,000. The *production team* ("villagers' small group") is purely a community structure, having lost most of its administrative functions as a result of the implementation of the production responsibility system (PRS) in agriculture in the early 1980s. The average team consists of about 30 households with a total of 150 people. The general term *community government* is used to refer to authorities at all three levels.

Communities in different parts of the country vary substantially in size and economic power. For example, in Nanhai County, Guangdong Province, the average township has more than 50,000 people and a gross value of industrial output (GVIO) of more than Y35 million. In Shangrao County, Jiangxi Province, by contrast, the average township has only 20,000 people and a GVIO of only Y393,000.

There are some ambiguities in the delineation of the TVP sector, but the broadest definition, which is increasingly popular, encompasses all nonagricultural activities in rural areas and small towns other than those on state farms.[1] Hence the sector includes individual nonagricultural proprietorships and household firms as well as larger concerns.

Enterprises owned by community governments are referred to as *community enterprises,* and firms owned by individuals or partnerships are termed *private enterprises.* Community enterprises owned by townships and villages are referred to as *township and village community enterprises* (TVCES); this category excludes production team firms, many of which have been privatized in one way or another. Occasionally township enterprises and village enterprises are discussed separately. Government organs at the township level responsible for supervising township enterprises are referred to as *township industrial corporations* (TICS).[2]

The Institutional Framework

Since the late 1950s China's rural economy has been organized under rural community structures that are linked to higher levels of government primarily through the Communist party hierarchy. Recent reforms have changed this pattern somewhat by restoring the township as the lowest level of government in rural areas and by allowing much greater scope for economic activities and for the accumulation of assets by private individuals. Nevertheless, community governments retain their cohesiveness and have a significant role in the local economy.

The most important characteristic of China's rural communities has been their stable membership. The household registration system has prevented large-scale rural-urban or rural-rural migration. Most people born into a rural community stay there for their entire lives, and their children belong to the same community. Immobility of population, of course, means immobility of human resources, although "temporary" migration to cities and to other rural areas to seek jobs is increasingly common.

Another key feature is the combination of income sharing within the community with a considerable degree of financial self-reliance in relations with other communities and higher levels of government. Income sharing has taken various forms over time and in different areas. Before the reforms, the work-point system for production teams ensured relatively equal distribution of individual incomes within the team. Allocation of jobs in TVCES has been used to balance family incomes. Even community government decisions on the establishment and location of new firms have taken income-sharing considerations into account. Finally, the relatively equal distribution of agricultural land when the PRS was implemented contributed to maintaining a relatively equal distribution of income within most rural communities. Income sharing has been weakened to some extent by the emergence and rapid growth of private economic activities and the abolition of the commune system.

The degree to which communities, particularly at the township level, are self-reliant has, if anything, increased since the late 1970s. Fiscal revenue-sharing systems have gradually been extended down to the township level, particularly after the township became a separate level of administration and public finance in 1984–86. Most townships depend heavily on extrabudgetary revenues to meet public expenditure needs. These revenues come primarily from TVPs in the form of profit remittances and management fees. (Management fees do not represent payment for services provided; rather, they are extrabudgetary levies by community governments, usually at the rate of 1–2 percent of sales revenue.)

TVPs also generate the lion's share of budgetary tax revenues in the more industrially developed rural communities. Even for poorer, more backward communities, which receive fiscal subsidies, incremental financial resources depend largely on the efforts of the community government and its subordinate economic entities. Reforms in the local banking system have made lending ceilings in a township dependent to a large extent on the generation of deposits within the township.[3] Similarly, because of the immobility of human resources, rural communities must by and large rely on the human capital of their own members, although some better-off areas have been able to attract technical and other skilled persons by offering high wages and other benefits.

Community governments have complex and often conflicting roles and responsibilities. They are essentially ministates that provide a whole range of public and social services and (particularly at the township level) set policies and regulations within their jurisdictions. The instruments available to community governments include the establishment and ownership of TVCEs, decisions on community government expenditures, a considerable degree of influence over the lending decisions of the local banking system in many areas, and encouragement and support of different types of private enterprise. Community governments cannot, however, use certain policy instruments normally available to states. Perhaps most important, they cannot engage directly in deficit financing; that is, their expenditures may not exceed available funds (which include transfers from higher levels of government and from TVPs as well as the portion of locally collected taxes allotted to them). Hence they face a relatively hard budget constraint. Since they cannot effectively impose barriers against trade in goods, they cannot meaningfully protect their enterprises from outside competition. In any case, the markets represented by rural communities, even at the township level, are too tiny to be of much use to local TVPs in most industries.

In addition to being local governments, community governments are profit-oriented economic entities that might be compared with holding companies, investment corporations, or headquarters of loosely controlled multidivisional corporations. Although day-to-day management and business decisions are usually left to enterprise directors, community governments tend to be intimately involved in decisions on important investments, the establishment or dismantling of firms, significant changes in product lines, the appointment of enterprise management, managerial compensation (and sometimes wages as well), and bonuses. Community governments can also absorb risk for subordinate community enterprises and can finance investments, both directly and through arranging other sources of funding such as bank loans. More generally, they represent their community enterprises in an often hostile administrative environment.

Subsequent chapters explore the serious conflicts inherent in this dual role of community governments. But strong fiscal and employment incentives, community governments' role in business development, and the market environment for outputs and material inputs in which TVPs function have combined to generate an extremely powerful push for the development of TVPs.

TVPs fall into several main categories. Traditional TVCEs are under the administrative control of township or village authorities. Firms at the production team level often were not independent accounting units; instead they put their proceeds into the pot for collective distribution to their members. Many production team enterprises were privatized during or in the aftermath of the switch to the PRS. Some township and especially village enterprises have been contracted or leased to individual management. (The contracts typically specify amounts or shares of enterprise profits to be remitted to the community government.) Private enterprises include both individual proprietorships and partnerships owned and managed by several people; many are based on family or kinship ties. Close personal relationships with community government officials are almost invariably necessary for sizable private enterprises if they are to navigate in the complicated administrative environment. Only a few TVPs are owned cooperatively by all or most of their workers, but in small communities where the employees of the main enterprise make up a significant proportion of the population, community ownership has some of the characteristics of cooperative ownership. Finally, there is an increasing number of joint ventures between different forms of ownership, within the TVP sector as well as with urban state and collective enterprises. Joint ventures involving foreign partners are still rare, but especially in Guangdong Province, many TVPs have cooperative relationships with foreign firms.

Recent Changes in Rural Institutions

China's rural communities have been profoundly affected by the reforms that have taken place since the late 1970s. The most important of these was the PRS, which gave individual households partial rights to land that had previously been vested in the production teams. The PRS also greatly reduced the direct supervision of agricultural production by community governments and effectively abolished the system of community work-points and collective distribution of income in favor of a return to primarily household-based generation of personal income. A closely related reform was the abolition of the communes and their replacement by townships, now the lowest level of government in rural areas. An extremely important policy change for the TVP sector was the relaxation of restrictions on the large-scale expansion of nonagricultural activities by rural communities. Although these restrictions were unevenly implemented and were never entirely effective in some parts of the country, their removal in 1978 created a political and administrative climate conducive to the rapid development of TVPs. Similarly, the removal of restrictions against household nonagricultural activities and, more recently, against sizable private firms in rural areas stimulated a great spurt of TVP development.

Finally, the PRS brought about a crucial change in TVP wage systems. In the past many TVCEs paid salaries directly to the production teams of which workers were members—workers received work-points for their labor in TVPs and then participated in collective income distribution by the teams at year's end. This greatly diluted incentives, since the fruits of hard work were shared not only with other workers in the enterprise but also with all members of the production team. Even in TVPs that paid workers directly, fixed time wages were the norm. All this changed with the PRS. TVPs shifted to direct payment of workers, and performance-based pay—in the form of enterprise-based work-points, year-end dividends, profit-related bonuses, and, above all, piece-rate wages—became the norm. The impact on incentives and efficiency in the TVP sector should not be underrated.

Regional Variations in Institutional Structure

Despite its basically uniform organizational framework, China's TVP sector shows a remarkable degree of local and regional institutional diversity. This diversity is partly attributable to differences in exogenous factors—the traditional resource base (especially human capital and agricultural land), proximity to markets and to urban industry, pre-1949 industrial and commercial traditions, delivery requirements for grain and other crops under the agricultural planning system, and prereform rural industrialization. But local authorities and community leaders have sometimes had a great influence on rural industrialization and local institutional structure. In the early 1970s Wuxi County authorities supported the continued development of commune and brigade industries counter to the prevailing national trend. Jiangsu Province (where Wuxi is located) several times successfully ignored national campaigns to shut down and "readjust" commune and brigade enterprises and to concentrate on agriculture. This resistance helped give it a commanding lead in rural industrialization on the eve of reforms in the late 1970s. Nanhai County authorities allowed and protected "underground" private firms even in the prereform period. But in many counties local authorities did not effectively promote development of TVPs until very late, which handicapped the rural industrialization effort.

Areas in which diversity is evident include the ownership of TVPs, the degree to which TVPs are under hierarchical control by townships, the policies of local and community authorities regarding TVPs, and the level of development and industrialization.

OWNERSHIP. In the four counties in which intensive fieldwork was conducted—Wuxi, Jieshou, Nanhai, and Shangrao—striking differences were encountered (see chapters 2, 4, and 7). The 1985 share of private enterprises in the GVIO of TVPs ranged from 3 percent in Wuxi to 51 percent in Jieshou, as against a national average of 17 percent. The relative weight of township and village enterprises also varied considerably; the share of township enterprises was nearly three times that of village enterprises in Jieshou and close to twice as high in Shangrao, but in Wuxi the shares were nearly equal. Only in Nanhai did production team firms account for a substantial part of GVIO in 1985.

CONTROL BY TOWNSHIPS. Villages and teams in Nanhai have been relatively independent and in particular have had freedom to develop their own firms. Wuxi has a highly integrated hierarchical structure of rural communities, and the township rules with a strong hand. Hence, even though village enterprises there are quantitatively important, they are effectively part of the township industrial sector.

The degree of administrative control over wages, the prevalence of profit-related bonuses, the methods of appointment of TVP managers, the allocation of labor, and a host of other practices can differ greatly among regions, localities, and even communities within a locality. These differences can have an important effect on the behavior and performance of TVPs even though in most of them wages and managerial pay are significantly related to enterprise performance.

LOCAL POLICIES. Counties in southern Guangdong Province variously promote large township enterprises, village and production team firms, private firms, and cooperative ventures with outside and foreign entrepreneurs. Wuxi's administrative climate makes it virtually impossible for large industrial private enterprises to emerge. Jieshou County authorities personally sponsor some of the more successful private entrepreneurs, supporting them with bank loans and administrative help.

LEVEL OF DEVELOPMENT. The richest and most industrialized counties, such as Wuxi and Nanhai, have already largely achieved the equivalent of middle-income status. The most backward areas—an order of magnitude poorer and often hundreds or thousands of times less industrialized—are nowhere near the takeoff stage. The industrialized counties face issues of how to organize, finance, and develop the TVP sector most efficiently; the less developed counties are striving merely to get nonagricultural development started. These differences are discussed in more detail in chapter 12.

The diversity of the TVP sector in different parts of China means that reforms and policy measures that work well in some areas may be unsuccessful in others. For example, many poor areas have turned to industrialization based on private enterprise because they recognize that for a variety of reasons the traditional community enterprise system (epitomized by Wuxi) cannot succeed in backward areas. From another perspective, Wuxi's restrictions against private enterprises may not carry terribly high economic costs there because the local TVCE sector is so efficient, but such policies would be disastrous in areas where TVCEs perform poorly.

Historical Background

Before 1949 China was a poor and backward agricultural country, and most of its rural areas had only a few small workshops and some handicraft industries. In 1949 the output value of such household sideline production totaled about Y1.16 billion in fixed 1957 prices. After the founding of the People's Republic of China, sideline production developed rapidly. By 1954 more than 10 million Chinese farmers had taken part-time jobs in the commercialized handicraft industry, which yielded a total output value of Y2.2 billion that year.

During 1955–57 China launched a large-scale agricultural cooperative movement. Farmers who were working part-time in handicraft industry, as well as individual handicraft workers, were organized into specialized sideline production teams under agricultural producers' cooperatives. The excessive emphasis that some cooperatives placed on agricultural production caused their sideline production to stagnate. Remedial measures by the authorities later helped to restore and develop sideline production in cooperatives. In 1957 the total output value of sideline production in China's rural areas reached Y2.29 billion, about 4.3 percent of the total value of agricultural output. Commune and brigade enterprises, the predecessors of the TVPs, subsequently began to emerge and develop on the basis of collective sideline production.

In 1958 the people's commune movement swept across the vast rural areas of China. Dizzy with the "victory of transformation" (nationalization and socialization of the economy), China adopted the Great Leap Forward strategy and attempted to reach the "paradise" of communism by building the "golden bridge" of people's communes. Under the slogan of "mobilizing the whole nation to make great efforts to develop industry," rural people's communes established a large number of commune and brigade enterprises by siphoning manpower, funds, and materials from brigades and teams originally engaged in sideline production and by annexing more than 30,000 handicraft cooperatives that had previously operated in small towns. By the end of 1958 commune and brigade enterprises in China employed 18 million people and yielded a total output value of Y6 billion. In the following year that figure catapulted to Y10 billion.

The communization campaign not only dampened farmers' enthusiasm for production but also precipitated a crisis for the national economy. In 1960 the Central Committee of the Communist party and the central government called for readjustment of the national economy and began to check the communization campaign. As a result, many commune and brigade enterprises discontinued operations. Some were later returned to production teams, some were changed into handicraft cooperatives, and the rest were closed down. In 1961 the total output value of commune and brigade enterprises nosedived to Y1.98 billion, and the figure dropped further to Y790 million in 1962 and Y410 million in 1963. During the following six years these enterprises saw a small rebound in their output value, but they remained basically stagnant.

Development of commune and brigade enterprises resumed during the latter part of the Cultural Revolution period (1966–76). At the North China Agricultural Conference (August–October 1970) the State Council called for efforts to speed up agricultural mechanization. Acting in the spirit of the conference, rural areas began to launch factories to produce agricultural machinery and farm tools. Meanwhile, many urban plants, absorbed in the Cultural Revolution, had stopped work. Market shortages became worse with each passing day, and some rural communities took advantage of this opportunity to set up firms. Although such enterprises were then widely regarded as the "tail of capitalism" and faced all kinds of restrictions and attacks, they still witnessed remarkable development. Their output value climbed from Y9.25 billion in 1970 to Y27.2 billion in 1976, an average annual growth rate of 25.7 percent. After 1976, when the Gang of Four was overthrown, commune and brigade enterprises developed further. In 1978 there were more than 1.52 million such enterprises, and their output value reached Y49.3 billion. Governments at all levels set up administrative bureaus to strengthen management of these enterprises.

In 1978 the Third Plenum of the Eleventh Central Committee of the Chinese Communist party declared that "commune and brigade enterprises should strive for great development" and that

As long as it is in conformity with the principle of rational economic development, commune and brigade enterprises should gradually engage in the processing of all farm and sideline products that are suitable for rural processing. Urban factories should shift part of their processing of products and parts and components that are suitable for rural processing to commune and brigade enterprises and help equip the latter with necessary equipment and technology . . . In addition, the state should adopt a policy of allowing tax breaks or tax exemptions for commune and brigade enterprises in the light of their situation.[4]

In 1981, to reduce discrimination against commune and brigade enterprises, the State Council issued regulations which reaffirmed that "commune and brigade enterprises already constitute an important part of the rural economy, and their growth is in conformity with the comprehensive development of the rural economy."[5] In 1983 the Central Committee further confirmed that "commune and brigade enterprises also belong to the cooperative economy, and great efforts must be made to continue to consolidate and develop such enterprises."[6] A series of such policies and regulations brought commune and brigade enterprises into a new stage of healthy, stable, and sustained high-speed growth. During 1980–83 their total output value jumped from Y65.7 billion to Y101.7 billion; the annual growth rate was 13.5–19.2 percent.

The Central Committee Circular on Agricultural Work of January 1, 1984, stated that, in addition to supporting actively the development of commune and brigade enterprises, governments at all levels should "encourage peasants to invest in or buy shares of all types of enterprises and encourage collectives and peasants to pool their funds and jointly set up various kinds of enterprises by following the principle of voluntary participation and mutual benefit." In a March 1984 circular the Central Committee and the State Council agreed to rename commune and brigade enterprises TVPs, since the people's communes had been abolished and a large number of partnerships and individual enterprises had come into being.[7] The circular also declared,

> Vigorous efforts should be made to guide TVPs in terms of orientation of development and to exercise administration over them in accordance with the relevant state policies to ensure their healthy development. TVPs should receive the same treatment as state enterprises and are entitled to all necessary state aid.

Since then China's TVPs have flourished more than ever. In 1984 the output value of TVPs (including TVCEs, partnerships, and individual enterprises) totaled Y171 billion, and the figure rose to Y273 billion in 1985 and Y354 billion in 1986. Private enterprises grew faster than TVCEs, service activities grew more rapidly than industry, and TVPs in economically backward areas made quicker progress than those in economically advanced areas (see chapter 12).

Present Situation and Importance

The growth of the TVP sector since the late 1970s and particularly since 1983 has been spectacular, whether measured by output, employment, assets, or profits (table 1-1). Nominal gross output value increased at an average annual rate of 24 percent in 1978–86, and GVIO grew by more than 23 percent a year in real terms. (Reliable price deflators for TVP services are not available.) Employment outside agriculture in rural areas grew by nearly 13 percent a year in 1978–86, for a total increase of 124 percent, or more than 30 million people.[8] Data on TVCEs (see table 1-1) indicate that their wage bills, assets,

Table 1-1. Growth of the TVP Sector, 1980–86
(average annual percentage change)

Item	1978–80	1980–83	1983–86	1984	1985	1986	1978–86
Value of output							
Gross (nominal)[a]	16.5	16.5	37.1	34.9	46.8	30.2	23.8
Industrial (nominal)	n.a.	15.0	42.3	40.5	50.7	36.0	27.9[b]
Industrial (real)[c]	16.8	14.9	37.6	38.5	43.0	31.6	23.4
Employment							
Nonagricultural	7.3	5.4	24.2	38.5	20.1	15.1	12.7
Rural industrial	5.8	1.3	15.9	20.0	13.2	14.5	7.7
Number of firms							
All TVCEs	-3.3	-1.9	4.1	22.5	-4.9	-3.3	-0.1
Industrial TVCEs	-2.3	-0.6	5.7	21.1	-5.1	2.7	1.3
Financial indicators (TVCEs only)							
Assets[d]	19.2	13.4	25.8	20.9	30.5	26.2	19.4
Profits[e]	15.0	2.7	13.5	13.4	31.6	-2.1	9.7
Taxes[f]	7.9	31.3	32.7	34.4	37.2	26.9	25.7
Bank loans	n.a.	20.4	61.1	102.6	40.3	47.0	39.2[b]
Gross revenues	19.4	15.9	33.8	36.6	44.1	21.7	23.2
Employment	3.0	2.5	10.7	18.9	7.9	5.8	5.7
Wage bill	17.4	13.8	26.5	36.1	26.0	17.9	19.3
Average wage	14.0	10.9	14.2	14.5	16.7	11.4	12.9
Average wage, state enterprises	11.7	2.5	17.8	19.5	17.3	16.6	10.3

n.a. Not available.
a. Gross output value of rural nonagricultural materials-producing sectors (industry, construction, transport, and commerce).
b. 1980–86 average.
c. Gross output value in current prices was deflated by the implicit price deflator for Chinese industry as a whole (excluding village and subvillage industrial firms). This was done because sector-specific price deflators are unreliable and result in even higher "real" growth rates.
d. Value of fixed assets net of depreciation plus physical working capital.
e. Gross profits before payment of income tax but net of indirect taxes.
f. Includes both direct and indirect taxes.
Sources: State Statistical Bureau (1982, 1985a, 1986a, 1986b, 1987a, 1987c, 1987d).

profits, and tax payments all increased rapidly in line with the growth of output and employment. Profits, however, rose much more slowly than other indicators, suggesting that profitability declined in the TVCE sector. Average wages in TVCEs rose 13 percent a year in 1978–86, considerably faster than the rate of inflation. The stagnant number of TVCE firms probably conceals significant activity in establishments and exits of firms. Moreover, a tremendous number of new enterprises has been created in the private sector in recent years; the number of private enterprises reportedly reached 10.7 million at the end of 1985.

Growth in China's TVP sector has been highly uneven over time, as can be seen from table 1-1. There was a sharp acceleration in 1983–86 compared with 1980–83; real GVIO rose by 15 percent a year in 1980–83 and by 38 percent a year in 1983–86. Growth in 1984 and especially in 1985 was substantially higher than in 1986, and in 1987 the TVP sector again boomed. TVP growth performance has also been unbalanced geographically, with some areas, particularly coastal regions, experiencing more rapid growth than backward, less industrialized interior provinces. Between 1980 and 1985 the nominal value of TVP industrial output rose by 415 percent in Zhejiang Province but by only 37 percent in Nei Monggol (Inner Mongolia). In eight provinces the increase was greater than 250 percent; in seven it was below 120 percent. Many, although not all, of the fast growers were more industrialized from the beginning, and a number of provinces that had lagged in rural industrialization slid further into relative backwardness. Moreover, provincial growth rates mask great differences within provinces.

Table 1-2 provides a more detailed picture of the growth of industrial output for TVPs under different forms of ownership. The GVIO of TVCEs has increased at an average annual rate of more than 20 percent in real terms; it grew especially rapidly in 1984–85. The GVIO of private enterprises (including production team firms) has grown spectacularly from a tiny base in 1980. This may in part reflect the incorporation of economic activities that had previously escaped the statistical network, but it mostly represents real growth. Differential growth rates have led to substantial changes in the composition of TVP industrial output by form of ownership (table 1-2). The shares of township and village enterprises have declined moderately, whereas the share of private enterprises nearly quadrupled between 1980 and 1986.

As a result of the rapid growth documented above, which implies a doubling in size every three years or less, the overall dimensions of the TVP sector have been changing substantially. For example, measured by real GVIO, China's industrial TVP sector was roughly four times as large in 1986 as in 1980. Thus, any attempt to describe its size and characteristics can be only a snapshot of a rapidly changing situation.

Table 1-3 shows the dramatic changes in the composition of gross social product in China's rural areas. The share of crop cultivation dropped from almost half in 1980 to less than one-third in 1986; the share of other agricul-

Table 1-2. *Growth and Ownership Structure of TVP Industry, 1980–86*

Item	1980–83	1983–86	1984	1985	1986	1980–86
Average annual growth of GVIO *(percent)*						
TVCEs						
Nominal	13.8	35.3	38.2	38.8	29.1	24.1
Real	11.4	33.5	38.0	34.3	28.4	21.9
Private enterprises[a]						
Nominal	32.8	93.9	65.4	159.3	69.9	60.5
Real (estimated)	32.7	87.7	63.1	146.1	64.7	57.8
All TVPs						
Nominal	15.0	42.3	40.5	50.7	36.0	27.9
Real	12.8	40.2	40.2	45.8	34.7	25.7
	1980	*1983*	*1984*	*1985*	*1986*	
Nominal GVIO, *by ownership (percentage of total)*						
Township enterprises	52.8	54.5	50.5	45.1	43.5	
Village enterprises	41.8	37.1	39.6	37.9	35.2	
Production team enterprises			—[b]	—[b]		
Partnerships	5.4	8.4	4.6[c]	8.8[c]	21.3	
Individual enterprises			5.3[c]	8.2[c]		

Note: GVIO, gross value of industrial output. Figures are available for nominal total rural GVIO, village enterprises' GVIO, and village-and-below GVIO. From these the GVIOs of township enterprises and private enterprises (including production team enterprises) can be calculated. Figures for GVIO of township enterprises in 1980 constant prices are also available. Real values for other components of rural GVIO were calculated by using the implicit price deflator for China's total GVIO, excluding village-and-below GVIO, for which no deflators are available.

a. Includes production team enterprises.

b. Many production team enterprises were privatized in the early 1980s. Any remaining ones were probably included in the category of partnerships (cooperative firms).

c. Derived from separate statistics compiled by the Ministry of Agriculture, which show higher absolute levels of industrial output value of private enterprises than do the figures of the State Statistical Bureau.

Sources: State Statistical Bureau (1982, 1984, 1985a, 1986a, 1986b, 1987a, 1987c, 1987d); China Economic Yearbook Editorial Board (1981, 1985).

tural activities remained more or less constant; and industry rose from less than one-fifth to more than 30 percent, nearly equal to the share of crop cultivation. In 1987 rural GVIO exceeded the value of agricultural output for the first time. Construction, transport, and commerce rose modestly as a share of the total.

Shifts in the structure of the rural labor force have been less dramatic but nevertheless significant, as is shown in table 1-4. Cultivation declined sharply in 1984 and 1985, but much of the slack was taken up by agricultural sidelines, which more than doubled their share. The proportion of the rural labor force engaged in industrial activities rose only modestly, from 6 percent

Table 1-3. *Composition of Rural Gross Social Product, 1980–86*

Item	1980	1983	1984	1985	1986
Total rural gross social product (billions of yuan)[a]	279.2	412.4	506.8	634.0	755.4
Share of total (percent)					
Agriculture (cultivation)	49.3	47.1	43.3	36.0	33.1
Forestry, livestock, fishery, and sidelines	19.5	19.6	20.1	21.1	20.0
Industry	19.5	20.0	22.9	27.6	31.5
Construction, transport, and commerce	11.7	13.3	13.7	15.3	15.4

a. In current prices. Includes gross output value of the five materials-producing sectors (agriculture, industry, construction, transport, and commerce), excluding nonmaterial services.
Sources: State Statistical Bureau (1986b, 1987a, 1987c).

in 1980 to 8 percent in 1986. Construction, transport, and commerce more than tripled their share, however, rising from less than 2 percent in 1980 to more than 6 percent in 1986. Overall, the movement of labor out of agriculture in rural areas made a strong beginning in 1984–86, but four-fifths of the rural labor force is still engaged in agriculture and sideline activities.

The TVP sector has become increasingly significant in generating fiscal revenues in rural areas and providing a growing proportion of the personal incomes of rural inhabitants. Total tax payments by TVPs in 1985 (including profit tax and indirect taxes) were nearly Y14 billion. These taxes accounted for only 7.7 percent of total national budgetary revenue but for most tax collected in rural areas. (The stagnant agriculture tax generated only Y4 billion in 1985.) Tax payments by TVPs have been rising sharply as earlier exemptions are gradually phased out, although special treatment remains common and private enterprises, in particular, can evade much of their tax liability. The TVP sector remains more lightly taxed than the state sector (the difference is considerably reduced if extrabudgetary remittances of TVPs are taken into account), but its tax burden is much heavier than that of agriculture.

Extrabudgetary remittances by TVPs to community governments are important, especially in the more developed areas. In 1985 TVCEs turned over Y6.8 billion in profits to their supervisory community governments, not including management fees, which may have totaled Y2 billion or more. In comparison, total tax payments by TVCEs were Y10.9 billion. More than half of TVCE remittances to community governments were plowed back into reinvestment, but substantial amounts were used for support to agricultural production, for social services, and for community government payrolls, and a considerable amount (Y620 million) was distributed to community members.

In 1985 the total of wages and distributions to community members by TVCEs was Y31 billion. This represented Y40–Y50 per member of the rural population, or about 15 percent of average per capita rural income. Although

Table 1-4. *The Structure of the Rural Labor Force, 1980–86*

Item	1980	1983	1984	1985	1986
Total rural labor force (millions of people)[a]	318.4	346.9	359.7	370.7	379.9
Share of total (percent)					
Agriculture (cultivation)	82.8	81.5	70.9	67.3	80.2
Forestry, livestock, fishery, and sidelines[b]	6.4	6.4	13.3	14.6	
Industry	6.1	5.8	6.7	7.4	8.3
Construction, transport, and commerce[c]	1.6	2.5	4.4	5.5	6.1
Other[d]	3.1	3.8	4.7	5.2	5.4

a. At year-end. Does not include labor force of state farms.

b. The industrial portion of the sidelines labor force has been included under industry.

c. Commerce includes storage, catering, and other related personal services.

d. Includes real estate administration, public utilities, residential services, consulting, public health, education, sports, social services, scientific research, technical services, banking and insurance, government, Communist party, and the like.

Sources: State Statistical Bureau (1986b, 1987a, 1987d).

private enterprises would add significantly to the figures, the role of the TVP sector in the generation of rural personal income is less important than its role in production. This is partly because the ratios of net to gross output value are much smaller in industry and, especially, in commerce than in agriculture. Furthermore, most TVCE profits go into investment and thus affect personal incomes only indirectly. There is great potential, however, for the TVP sector to become more important in the direct generation of income as well as employment.

The TVP sector has become the most dynamic part of Chinese industry. It is an important actor in most industries and is dominant in a few. Its share in total national GVIO has risen sharply, from only 3 percent in 1971 (when the movement to promote commune and brigade enterprises was getting under way) to 9 percent on the eve of the reforms in 1978, to 12 percent in 1983, and then, rising very rapidly, to more than 21 percent in 1986. The TVP sector has roughly doubled its share of China's industrial output every five years, starting from a tiny base in the early 1970s but continuing to do so even as the base grew large in the 1980s. The share of the state sector declined from more than four-fifths in 1975 to three-quarters in 1980 to only about five-eighths in 1986, while that of urban nonstate firms rose moderately. All segments of the TVP sector have seen their shares in Chinese industry as a whole increase, but private enterprises have shown the most spectacular growth in recent years; they rose from negligible levels in the late 1970s to account for nearly 5 percent of China's GVIO in 1986.

TVPs are active in all but one of the fourteen principal subsectors of Chinese industry; only in petroleum is their share truly negligible. Otherwise the subsectoral coverage is surprisingly broad, and the pattern holds even in a more disaggregated industrial breakdown. The most important TVCE industrial subsectors are machinery, construction materials, textiles, chemicals, and food processing (in that order); together they account for nearly three-quarters of TVCE GVIO. Only for construction materials is the share far higher than for Chinese industry as a whole; shares of other subsectors tend to be no higher or moderately lower than for industry as a whole.

TVP shares in the output of particular industrial products vary greatly, but again the coverage is broad. In 1986 TVPs produced 75 percent of all bricks made in China, 22 percent of the cement, 26 percent of the coal, 26 percent of the silk, 47 percent of the silk textiles, 27 percent of the edible vegetable oil, and 27 percent of the machine-made paper and cardboard. In addition, TVPs accounted for about 30 percent of the national output of phosphate fertilizer and for high proportions of other industrial inputs into agriculture, such as farm tools and implements. Their share of production of metal-cutting machine tools is only about 4 percent, but they are increasingly important in electronics (where they accounted for 6 percent of total national output value in 1986), in many consumer durables, and even in some more sophisticated industries. Only certain basic process industries with substantial economies of scale (for example, petroleum refining) are impervious to entry by TVPs.

In sum, China's TVPs have already become a pillar of the country's economy and are playing a decisive role in rural industrialization and national economic modernization. The TVP sector represents the only hope for moving rural labor into productive employment outside agriculture, particularly as long as restrictions against permanent migration into large cities are kept in place. Without TVP development, much of the gain in efficiency from agricultural reforms would not have been realized. At the same time, the TVP sector is increasingly important in Chinese industry as a whole, both in meeting rising demand for industrial goods and as a competitor and partner of state industry. Reforms and experiments with varied forms of ownership and management in TVPs have already had a great demonstration effect on urban economic reforms and will continue to do so.

From a longer-term point of view, without the transfer of large numbers of farmers to TVPs, China's rural industrialization and national economic modernization will be impossible. The development of TVPs has brought millions of farmers into the competitive commodity economy, and this new environment will instill new values and moral concepts. All these factors will have a far-reaching impact on China's modernization. But the development of TVPs will also inevitably bring a series of new problems for overall strategy and for the management of national economic development. Obviously, thorough and systematic study of problems in the development and operations of TVPs and their influence on the economy as a whole is needed. This book represents a significant effort toward this end, on the basis of extensive new research.

Notes

1. A few TVPs are involved in agricultural production. The definition excludes agricultural production by individual rural households.

2. TICs go under a variety of names, including township industrial corporations, township industry and trade corporations, and township industrial associations. Their functions often overlap those of township economic commissions, which have as one of their main tasks supervision of local industrial development. In some areas the economic commission is directly responsible for township enterprises, and there is no separate TIC.

3. Although there are large (positive or negative) imbalances between the two in many localities, incremental loans to a large extent depend on incremental generation of deposits.

4. "Resolution on Several Questions about Speeding up Agricultural Development," (draft), December 1978.

5. "Several Regulations on Commune and Brigade Enterprises in Implementing the Principle of National Economic Readjustment."

6. "Several Questions on Current Rural Economic Policies."

7. Circular transmitting the "Report on Exploring New Areas for Development of Commune and Brigade Enterprises," submitted by the Ministry of Agriculture and the Party group of the ministry.

8. These figures refer to the nonagricultural, materials-producing sectors in rural areas (industry, construction, transport, and commerce) and exclude nonmaterial services. They may considerably underestimate TVP employment because they appear to leave out large numbers of part-time and seasonal TVP employees and some workers in small private enterprises. Statistics compiled by the Ministry of Agriculture indicate that the total number of TVP employees rose from 22 million in 1978 to 77 million in 1980, an increase of 55 million.

2

Research Design, Methodology, and Data

William A. Byrd and Lin Qingsong

The recent rapid growth, present significance, and great potential of China's TVP sector as outlined in chapter 1 make it an important subject for research. Accordingly, in 1986–87 the Institute of Economics of the Chinese Academy of Social Sciences (CASS) and the World Bank engaged in a major collaborative research project on TVPs. This chapter briefly reviews previous research on China's TVP sector and provides background on how the collaborative research project was initiated and carried out. It then looks at the project's objectives and design, including the approach to data gathering, sample selection, and methodologies. It concludes with a description and analysis of the data set.

Background

China's TVPs (formerly termed commune and brigade enterprises) were the subject of considerable research by foreign scholars in the 1970s. Most of this work, however, dealt with the broader subject of rural small-scale industry, including county-run collective and state enterprises. The main full-length works that emerged from this period were Perkins and others (1977), Sigurdson (1977), and Wong (1979). Of other contributions to the literature on Chinese rural industrialization, Riskin (1978a, 1978b) might be singled out. Research on rural small-scale industry by foreign economists was hindered in the 1970s by lack of access to data, but some scholars were able to conduct careful, detailed fieldwork.

Foreign scholarly interest in the TVP sector continued into the 1980s, although paradoxically the volume of published work has been smaller. Much of the research has appeared in compendiums and journal articles or as part of broader works on rural development in China, including Enos (1984), Griffin and Griffin (1984), and Ho (1986). The World Bank has also done some work on China's TVP sector, most notably as part of an economic study of Gansu Province (World Bank 1988). The astonishing growth of the TVP sector in 1984–85 attracted a great deal of foreign interest, this time more explicitly focused on TVPs, but it has not yet yielded much published output.

Chinese economists have been interested in the TVP sector and in small-scale rural industry for an even longer time. How to view these enterprises, and what were the appropriate policies toward them, were important topics of discussion as early as the Great Leap Forward in 1958. The second wave of TVP development in the early 1970s also engendered considerable research and discussion. But most Chinese research on TVPs before the early 1980s centered on such political and ideological issues as whether rapid development of TVPs was compatible with socialism and whether it would harm the administrative division of labor between agriculture and industry.

Starting in the early 1980s Chinese research on the TVP sector turned from the question of whether the sector should be allowed to develop to how and in what ways it should develop. This shift focused work on more concrete economic questions. Some Chinese research on the TVP sector in the 1980s has been careful, detailed, and high in quality; an example is the work of the Development Research Institute of the State Council Rural Development Research Center.[1] Zhou Qiren and associates have engaged in detailed research on a number of aspects of TVP development (for example, Zhou Qiren and Huang Zhuangjun 1987). Another recent publication, based in part on preliminary testing and research done for this project, is Institute of Economics, CASS (1987). Considerable research has also been conducted on private enterprises in rural areas.

Finally, there has been an extraordinary increase in the available statistical and other source materials on the TVP sector. The Township and Village Enterprise Bureau of the Ministry of Agriculture publishes useful information, as do the State Statistical Bureau (1986b, 1987c, and 1987d) and the Ministry of Agriculture (1986a and 1986b).

Despite the considerable volume of past and ongoing research on the TVP sector, until recently little if any comprehensive work had concentrated specifically on TVPs, as distinguished from rural small-scale industry in general, county-run state enterprises, and so on. Moreover, most of the work, particularly by foreign scholars, was not based on systematic data gathering. Most important, the rapid development of the TVP sector since 1984 has simply outrun past and even much current research. Thus, both the Chinese and the World Bank considered that there was room for a wide-ranging, comprehensive, policy-oriented collaborative project on TVPs.

In September 1985 discussions began on the possibility of a collaborative project on the TVP sector. Detailed work on project and questionnaire design was done in late 1985 and early 1986. A research team was assembled that included representatives of such Chinese institutions as the Development Research Institute of the State Council Rural Development Research Center, the Economic System Reform Research Institute, and the Sociology Department of Beijing University. In early 1986 two counties, Wuxi and Jieshou, were selected as sites for in-depth fieldwork and enterprise samples. Chinese researchers visited each county to discuss logistical and administrative arrangements and to select sample firms. In March 1987 Chinese researchers conducted a pilot investigation, including a test of the draft questionnaires, in Yuanping County, Shanxi Province. The questionnaires were subsequently revised.

In June and July 1986 Chinese and World Bank researchers conducted in-depth fieldwork in Wuxi and Jieshou counties, and some members of the research team also spent several days doing fieldwork in Taihe County. The second main joint fieldwork effort took place in February and March 1987 in Nanhai and Shangrao counties. In October and November 1986 some of the Chinese researchers visited cooperative, labor-managed, and other small-scale firms in India, Yugoslavia, Great Britain, the United States, and Hong Kong and held discussions with scholars during the visits. This trip and supporting work were financed by a grant from the Ford Foundation. In the course of the trip discussions on data processing and analysis for the fieldwork in China were held at the World Bank in Washington, D.C.

The work of processing and analyzing data and preparing research papers began in earnest in April 1987. The International Conference on China's Township and Village Industry, at which the papers in this volume were presented, was held in Beijing, November 4–7, 1987. It was attended by the research team, other representatives of CASS and the World Bank, invited Chinese participants from government agencies and research institutions, and a panel of prominent foreign experts familiar with topics relevant to China's TVP sector.

Project Objectives and Design

The first main objective of the research project was to gain a better, more complete, and more solidly grounded understanding of how China's dynamic TVP sector actually functions. Its institutional and organizational structure needed to be thoroughly explored and analyzed. The second objective was to ascertain and assess the reasons behind the rapid growth of the TVP sector, particularly since the early 1980s.

The third objective was to identify and analyze the problems and obstacles faced by the TVP sector as it continues to develop, especially institutional features of the TVP sector and problems in the administrative and regulatory environment that TVPs face.

The fourth objective was to evaluate future institutional and policy options. Although the research was not intended to generate concrete policy recommendations, it was hoped that the project would improve understanding of policy issues in the TVP sector so that future policy choices can be firmly grounded.

The fifth objective was to gain an international perspective on China's TVP sector through review of relevant literature as well as through visits to foreign enterprises by Chinese researchers. To the extent appropriate, the research was to incorporate methodologies used in similar studies in other parts of the world. In line with its policy orientation, it was hoped that the project could be completed relatively quickly and that at least preliminary findings would be forthcoming in a short time.

These objectives, as well as logistical and budgetary considerations, influenced the design of the research work. The project required considerable in-depth fieldwork that had to be accomplished in a relatively short time and with limited resources. Careful, methodical gathering of both quantitative and qualitative data that could be used in formal statistical analysis was required. With these considerations in mind, it was decided to limit the in-depth fieldwork to four counties, each representative of a different pattern of TVP development (see chapters 4 and 7). The four counties were paired to allow relatively convenient visits on two separate trips, with the joint research team spending ten to fourteen days in each. Logistical considerations hence dictated a focus on China proper; the northeast, northwest, and southwest were not included, and even the northern part of China proper received relatively less coverage (see map 2-1).[2]

The limited number of localities selected made it possible to conduct thorough, comprehensive fieldwork in each, on a relatively large sample of enterprises (an average of thirty in each county), with multiple questionnaires of substantial length. Extensive interviews were held with enterprises and with related local institutions. To ensure maximum reliability of the information gathered, the bulk of the questionnaires had to be administered in person, and responses had to be double-checked in the field to rectify errors and omissions. A relatively large team of researchers (more than twenty) was required to accomplish this work in a short time.

Tradeoffs among the various objectives and constraints affected the sample of enterprises chosen. The bulk of sample firms had to be substantial concerns that kept reasonably good accounts and had at least several years of history to allow a time series. But since a crucial objective was to study the full range of ownership and management patterns in the TVP sector, oversampling of nontraditional forms of ownership and management was considered highly desirable. A difficulty here was that most private enterprises were founded only recently (1984 or later), are relatively small, and tend to keep poor accounts. The sampling of different forms of ownership was further complicated by the great differences in ownership patterns among counties. The samples in two of the four counties contained virtually no private enterprises. The samples in the other two counties included a significant number of private enterprises, but at some sacrifice of the longevity of the firms: 31 percent of sample firms and 53 percent of private enterprises in the sample were reportedly established in 1984–86.

The sample of TVPs was limited to industrial firms, mainly in manufactur-

Map 2.1 *The Location of the Sample Counties*

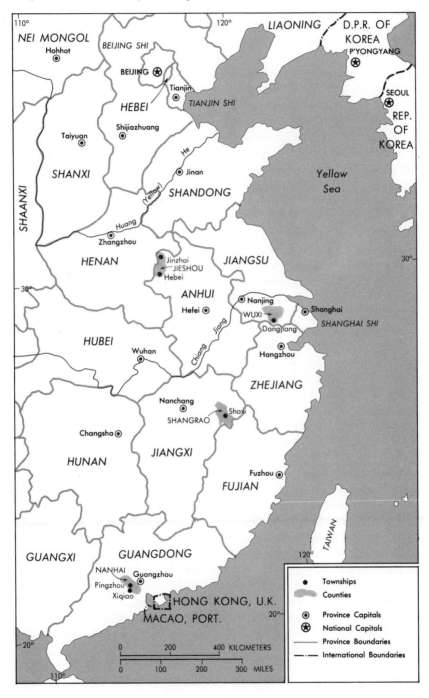

ing. This was done to keep the scope manageable and to maximize compara-bility with previous collaborative research on state-owned industrial enter-prises. Moreover, it was felt that manufacturing is the cutting edge of the TVP sector and holds the key to its future development. This is not to deny that nonindustrial TVPs in commerce, construction, and other services are important, particularly in generating employment, but many of the results of the analysis of manufacturing are applicable to other rural nonagricultural enterprises.

Within manufacturing an attempt was made to ensure that each county sample contained some enterprises in certain key TVP industries such as build-ing materials, textiles, machinery, and food processing. The sample was by no means confined to these subsectors, but it did not attempt to cover all industries in the localities concerned. The intent was to represent as wide a range as possible of such characteristics as size, technology, profitability, and scope of markets (local, regional, or national). These considerations, however, could be subordinated to the need to maximize variation in owner-ship and management forms.

TVP workers were sampled by taking stratified random samples of employees in a smaller subsample of firms, about twelve in each county. A larger propor-tion of employees in smaller enterprises was sampled to ensure a meaningful minimum number of observations for each firm—roughly twelve employees in most cases, although in a few instances workers did not cooperate. Also, management personnel and technical workers were deliberately oversampled so that they would be adequately represented in the data set.

In the survey of township government leaders, an attempt was made to obtain a response from every township where fieldwork was done and also (by mail or in a large group meeting) from every other township in the four target counties. This effort was moderately successful, although in contrast to the other questionnaires, which were administered personally, the re-sponse rate was substantially less than 100 percent.

The information gathered in this research project lends itself to a wide va-riety of analytical methods, as is evident in the chapters that follow. At one extreme, the data permit formal statistical and econometric analysis at almost any level of sophistication. Chapters 11 and 13 make the most systematic use of such techniques. At the opposite extreme are the voluminous inter-view records and related materials, which are often detailed enough to serve as case studies and which can be utilized to paint reasonably clear pictures of the operations, institutional structure, and environment of the TVP sector. Chapter 7 is an outstanding example of this approach.

Most of the chapters fall between these extremes; they utilize both the questionnaire-based data sets and the interview information, as well as avail-able national and regional statistics on the TVP sector. Although hypotheses are generated and supported on the basis of these various kinds of evidence, most of the papers do not contain mathematical models or formal econometric tests. This intermediate approach is appropriate for much of the analysis, which to a large extent is still concerned with building up a coherent understanding of the structure, operations, and environment of the TVP sector. Subsequently, as hypotheses are refined and models developed, it should be possible to utilize the information in the data sets more fully in formal statistical and econometric analysis.

The Data Set

This section first looks briefly at the four counties chosen for in-depth fieldwork and at the townships where extra time was spent on interviews and information gathering. It then describes the five questionnaires and the interviews conducted during the fieldwork.

The Four Counties and the Townships

The TVP sectors in these counties are discussed in some detail in chapters 4 and 7. Here we will briefly describe their main features.

Wuxi County in Jiangsu Province was selected because of its extremely high level of industrialization, both in the prereform period and since the late 1970s. For a long time it has been the most industrialized rural county in China, even though it is by no means the most urbanized. Wuxi is also the quintessential example of the traditional TVP system based on TVCES and tightly controlled under the supervision of township governments. This control is especially evident in wage determination and labor allocation.

Industry in Wuxi is highly efficient by Chinese standards. The TVCES are relatively large, many of them use relatively advanced technology, and they compete effectively with state industry. Private enterprises are severely hampered by administrative restrictions, and sizable ones have not emerged. Markets for labor and land have not developed, but large amounts of financial capital have been brought in by county banks from other parts of the country to support local TVP development, and many enterprises or township industrial corporations have issued bonds to employees and local residents.

Nanhai County in Guangdong Province is also highly industrialized and is more urbanized than Wuxi. It was selected because of the involvement of its TVP sector in foreign trade and in business relationships with the outside world—most notably, through extensive processing arrangements with Hong Kong businesses. Nanhai also has a diversified structure of rural communities, with much greater independence at the lower levels (villages and teams) than in Wuxi (see chapter 7). This diversified community structure has spawned a variegated pattern of TVP ownership. TVCES are important but by no means dominant, and production team enterprises, private enterprises, firms contracted to private management, joint ventures, and even cooperative entities have emerged. The relatively open labor market has stimulated a large influx of migrant workers from poorer areas outside the county, and wage controls are less effective than in Wuxi. Capital flows from outside appear less important than in Wuxi, mainly because the county is well endowed with savings deposits that can be lent to TVPs.

Jieshou County in Anhui Province represents a more or less average level of TVP development. It is much less industrially developed than either Wuxi or Nanhai, and its average rural per capita income in 1985 was somewhat below the national average. The most distinctive features of Jieshou are a lively market in land and the emergence of a substantial number of large private enterprises with the support and even the personal sponsorship of county and community government authorities. Jieshou is also the only county in the sample that has its own county seat (also called Jieshou).[3] This allows county authorities to encourage relocation of successful private enterprises to the town, where infrastructure and support services are more readily available. Private enterprises in Jieshou town are vulnerable to "creeping collectivization" in various forms, however. In the rural areas outside the county seat the level of industrialization remains extremely low, and most community enterprises have gone out of business or have been privatized.

Shangrao County in Jiangxi Province was chosen to represent a level of rural industrialization and TVP development significantly below the national average. Even though the county is endowed with substantial mineral resources, rural incomes depend primarily on agriculture, industrial firms are small and mostly unprofitable, and industrial development is not yet self-sustaining, despite an infusion of capital from the central government. The traditional style of ownership and management of TVCEs has not been successful. TVPs are plagued by such problems as excessive levies by community governments to meet public expenditures, widespread overmanning, poor management, and lack of contact with markets outside the locality.

Within each county one or two townships were selected as places where interviews and questionnaires would be concentrated. In Wuxi, Dongjiang township was chosen because, as measured by gross value of industrial output (GVIO) per capita, it is the most industrialized township in the county and, as of 1985, in China. Otherwise, interview time and data gathering were more or less evenly distributed among a dozen or more other townships scattered throughout the county.

In Jieshou two townships—Hebei and Jinzhai—were chosen. Hebei, which borders on Jieshou town, has become increasingly urbanized and has steadily lost territory to the expanding town. Jinzhai is farther from the county seat and is much less industrialized. But the dominance of Jieshou town in the county's industrial TVP development was reflected in the selection of sample firms, particularly since many relatively large private enterprises are located in the town. Hence in Jieshou County there were really three focal points for information gathering.

In Nanhai the research team spent extra time in two townships,[4] Pingzhou and Xiqiao. The former had long been one of the most industrialized townships in the county, and many of its enterprises have long histories, some under different names and incarnations. Xiqiao is a well-known center for textile production. Both Pingzhou and Xiqiao are somewhat more developed than the average township in Nanhai.

In Shangrao, Shaxi town served as a center for interviewing and data collection.[5] Shaxi probably has the highest per capita income of all the townships in the county and is one of only a handful of townships that have achieved a respectable and stable degree of industrial development. As in Wuxi interview time and data collection were otherwise scattered rather evenly across a number of townships, some of them very poor and backward.

The Questionnaires

Five questionnaires were distributed: a Worker Survey Questionnaire for TVP employees; an Enterprise Survey Questionnaire for management teams of sample firms; an Enterprise Director Questionnaire for directors of sample TVPs; an Enterprise Quantitative Questionnaire, usually filled out by accountants of sample enterprises; and a Township Leader Questionnaire. For comparative purposes some of these questionnaires were also administered to a small number of county-run state enterprises and their employees.

As can be seen from table 2-1, each questionnaire contained many items and required considerable effort to fill out and process. This was especially true of the questionnaires that requested detailed statistical information—the Enterprise Quantitative Questionnaire and the Township Leader Questionnaire. A mix of quantitative and qualitative—factual, perceptual, and attitudinal—information was requested.

Table 2-2 shows the samples generated by the questionnaires. It was intended that the three enterprise questionnaires (the Enterprise Survey Questionnaire, the Enterprise Quantitative Questionnaire, and the Enterprise Director Questionnaire) would be administered to the same firms so that data could be combined. This was largely, although not perfectly, accomplished, as can be seen from the table. The distribution of completed questionnaires among counties was fairly even, although the samples for Wuxi and especially Jieshou tend to be larger than those for Nanhai and Shangrao.

A considerable amount of information was gathered through the questionnaires. Rough calculations indicate that more than 370,000 data items were generated, although some of these are missing values.[6] Only about half of the data contained in the Enterprise Quantitative Questionnaire has been entered in the computer for statistical and econometric analysis.[7] Even so, nearly 250,000 pieces of data have been computerized, and this information serves as the main data base for research.

Table 2-1. Features of the Questionnaire
(number)

Questionnaire	Target	Respondent	Questions	Observations	Observations entered in computer	Main types of questions
Worker Survey	Enterprise employees	Employees	64	112	112[a]	Personal information; attitudes and perceptions
Enterprise Survey	Enterprise behavior	Management team	40	170	170	Qualitative questions, factual and attitudinal
Enterprise Director	Enterprise managers	Director	42	175	175	Personal information; perception of role in firm
Enterprise Quantitative	Enterprise data	Accountant	81	1,477[b]	609[b]	Basic data on firm, 1970–86
Township Leader	Township data, leader's attitude	Township leader and staff	22	316	315	Basic data on township; leader's perceptions

a. A condensed version of this data set, consisting of thirty-six variables, was also generated. It is extensively used in chapter 12.
b. The amount of actual data for most sample enterprises is much less than this because few firms were established early and many of them only in 1984 or 1985.

Table 2-2. *Number of Questionnaires Completed in the Four Counties*

Questionnaire	Total	Wuxi	Jieshou	Nanhai	Shangrao
Worker Survey	1,174[a]	473	297	260[a]	144
Number of firms covered	49	14	15	11	9
Enterprise Survey	115	34	37	24	20
Enterprise Director	117	35	38	24	20
Enterprise Quantitative	122	32	37	23	30
Township Leader	67	19	27	12	9

a. Two completed questionnaires from Nanhai cannot be used in much of the analysis because the firms could not be identified.

WORKER SURVEY QUESTIONNAIRE. The Worker Survey Questionnaire was designed to obtain basic factual information on each employee that could be used to test relationships between various dependent variables and workers' objective characteristics—for example, in wage equations (see chapter 13). It also asked for workers' attitudinal responses on various issues, which could then be systematically related to worker and enterprise characteristics. This questionnaire was drawn up by researchers with extensive experience in questionnaire-based research on Chinese state enterprise employees, and it benefited from ample time for revisions.

The questionnaire was administered to stratified random samples of workers in, on average, a dozen firms in each county. Larger proportions of workers were sampled in small enterprises, and technical workers and managerial personnel were oversampled. Generally, workers were called together to have the questionnaire explained to them and were asked to fill it out on the spot and turn it in before leaving. Chinese researchers administered the questionnaires directly, choosing samples from enterprise payroll lists. They gave the questionnaire directly to workers, explained it, waited while workers filled it out, answered any questions, and collected the questionnaires as they were completed. Workers were assured that their responses would be kept confidential, and the method of administering the questionnaire ensured confidentiality.

ENTERPRISE SURVEY QUESTIONNAIRE. The Enterprise Survey Questionnaire, designed to complement the Enterprise Quantitative Questionnaire, obtained a broad range of primarily qualitative information about the business situation and administrative environment of enterprises. The types of responses included multiple choices, prioritization among alternatives, and, in a few cases, rough percentage shares for enterprise factors, inputs, and outputs. Despite some problems with questionnaire design, most of the data proved useful. The questionnaire was filled out by members of the enterprise's leading group, or management team. This was done collectively or, more often, individually by a deputy director of the firm. Questionnaires were administered in person during enterprise visits and were usually collected on the spot and then checked. Thus there are no serious problems with missing data.

ENTERPRISE QUANTITATIVE QUESTIONNAIRE. The Enterprise Quantitative Questionnaire requested detailed statistical information on the sample enterprises and included a few questions on ownership, location, management systems, profit-sharing methods, and the like. Most items requested data for all years from 1980 and for earlier benchmark years (1970, 1975, and 1978). Only 28 percent of sample firms, however, had been established in 1978 or earlier.

Problems included failure to complete certain items and incorrect or inappropriate information. Data on capital structure turned out to be virtually unusable for these reasons. Even capital stock information is sometimes suspect—for some firms, the reported total value of investment for 1985 or 1986 exceeds the reported figure for the capital stock in the same year. Nevertheless, use of capital stock information in quantitative analysis leads to sensible results for the most part (see chapters 5 and 11). There were internal inconsistencies in some of the data—for example, revenues minus costs minus indirect taxes might not equal reported gross profits. Finally, in some cases numbers were filled in so lightly or were so illegible that data entry was difficult.

Many TVPs, particularly private enterprises and those located in the more backward areas, keep poor accounts, do not have skilled accountants, and hence simply could not provide all the information requested. Private enterprises may also have had stronger incentives than TVCEs to underreport or overreport various statistics, and, unlike the situation with the Worker Survey Questionnaire, it was difficult or impossible to ensure confidentiality. Despite all these problems, a large amount of usable quantitative data was generated.

ENTERPRISE DIRECTOR QUESTIONNAIRE. The Enterprise Director Questionnaire attempted to probe the attitudes and perceptions of sample TVP directors, in particular their views on internal management, on managerial, business, and noneconomic objectives, and on relations with supervisory organizations. Some personal information on the director's background and characteristics was also requested. All of the questions were purely qualitative, although some asked for a ranking of alternatives. The questionnaire is the twin of the Enterprise Survey Questionnaire and shares many of its advantages and drawbacks. Although design problems surfaced in some of the questions, a substantial amount of usable information was generated. In most cases the questionnaire was filled out personally by enterprise directors, but sometimes it was completed by a deputy director—most commonly because the director happened to be out of town at the time. Unfortunately it is not possible to ascertain exactly which forms were not filled out by the director, but the percentage was probably small.

TOWNSHIP LEADER QUESTIONNAIRE. The Township Leader Questionnaire asked for basic quantitative information on the township and its TVP sector, for qualitative perceptions, and for the leader's views and objectives. Unlike the other questionnaires, it was often administered indirectly (by mail), but sometimes research team members met with township accountants or other officials as a group to explain the questionnaire and answer questions. In the townships visited by the research team as part of fieldwork, completed questionnaires were obtained directly and checked.

The basic sampling objective was to reach as large a proportion as possible of the total number of townships in each county. This goal was best attained in Jieshou, where completed questionnaires were retrieved for 82 percent of the townships and towns, and in Nanhai, where the figure was 75 percent. The proportion of townships responding was lowest for Shangrao (29 percent) and in between for Wuxi (53 percent). But in all four counties the share of townships sampled was large enough to be reasonably representative.

The Interview Data

In-depth interviews complemented the questionnaires and constitute a second main source of research data. As can be seen from table 2-3, more than sixty separate meetings were held in each of the four counties.[8] An enormous amount of useful case-study, qualitative, and quantitative information was generated in this way. The 101 TVPs where interviews were done represent a large majority of the sample enterprises. The nearly fifty meetings with township and village leaders also provided useful information, as did the interviews with county government agencies, financial institutions, and government finance entities.

Interviews were conducted with an agenda of basic questions in mind, but the agenda was not rigid, and meetings were allowed to meander in directions that were of interest to interviewers or were suggested by initial briefings or written material provided by interviewees. There was some evolution over time in both the questions asked and the organizations interviewed. More public finance units and financial institutions were interviewed during the second set of field visits (in Nanhai and Shangrao) than in the first (in Wuxi and Jieshou). Enterprise visits declined somewhat after the high reached in Jieshou, in part because of the decline in the size of the samples. Most interviews involved more than one member of the research team. Usually several

Table 2-3. *Types of Organizations Interviewed*
(number)

Category	Total	Wuxi	Jieshou	Nanhai	Shangrao
Enterprises	101	22	33	26	20
Township or village leaders	48	16	8	11	13
Village leaders	8	2	0	4	2
County leaders	8	2	3	1	2
County agencies	52	16	17	8	11
Banks[a]	12	2	2	5	3
Rural credit cooperatives[a]	8	1	1	2	4
Tax bureaus[a]	10	2	2	1	5
Finance bureaus[a]	9	2	1	1	5
Township industrial corporations	8	6	0	1	1
Township economic commissions	15	5	4	4	2
Other township government agencies	11	3	0	7	1

Note: These figures are incomplete because they include only meetings for which formal interview notes were compiled in English.

a. Includes organizations at both county and township levels.

people from the enterprise, community, or county were present, often representing different organizations or levels of government. Generally discussions were open, and interviewees were responsive and forthcoming.

Evaluation of the Data Set

In this section our objective is to point out and assess some of the flaws in the various types of data as well as in sample characteristics. But despite the problems identified here, the data set is very useful and basically reliable, and the sample is in most respects a good one.

Problems in Questionnaire Design

Some flaws in questionnaire design came to light when the data were being processed and analyzed. One example is the inadequate space provided for answers on the Enterprise Quantitative Questionnaire, which made responses more difficult to read and increased the likelihood of mistakes in data entry. Sometimes questions were not worded in a way that permitted unambiguous classification of responses. More commonly, the possibilities given in multiple-choice questions were not conducive to clear assessment of responses. In a few cases permissible responses did not include some alternatives that hindsight revealed to be critical.

The Worker Survey Questionnaire was the best designed of the group; the Enterprise Survey Questionnaire and the Enterprise Director Questionnaire probably had the most severe design problems. A lacuna in the Township Leader Questionnaire was that it did not request any personal information on township leaders. The Enterprise Quantitative Questionnaire perhaps asked for an excessive amount of data, which may have had an adverse effect on the quality of the information provided, at least for certain items.

Despite their flaws, the questionnaires all generated much useful information. Often, suitable manipulation of response categories can ameliorate design problems. Where this cannot be done, especially careful interpretation of responses and cautious use of the data are called for.

Responses to Questionnaires

Owing to the way the questionnaires were administered, the response rate was virtually 100 percent for all except the Township Leader Questionnaire, and even for that one it was respectable. Hence problems concern either possible bias in samples (discussed later in this chapter) or incomplete, incorrect, inappropriate, or inconsistent responses in the completed questionnaires. Overall, response patterns show a considerable degree of logic and internal consistency. This is especially true of the Worker Survey Questionnaire, where the number of nonsensical or inconsistent responses is minimal and compares favorably with similar data in other countries. Broadly speaking, responses to the Enterprise Survey Questionnaire and the Enterprise Director Questionnaire also exhibit logical and consistent patterns.

Nevertheless, there are some problems with responses. For example, many sample firms left certain parts of the Enterprise Quantitative Questionnaire blank or filled them out so poorly that the information is virtually unusable. Another problem is that, according to the Worker Survey Questionnaire, workers in Jieshou County are almost unbelievably content with their jobs, firms, and managers; see chapter 13. (The high degree of satisfaction of Jieshou TVP workers may, however, be related to the fact that virtually all enterprises where the Worker Survey Questionnaire was administered are located in a more urban area, Jieshou town.) Also in Jieshou, private entrepreneurs reported that they feel more responsible toward "the state" than toward themselves, their enterprises, or their communities. Such obvious biases appear in only a handful of questions, but they show the need for caution in interpreting results when it is plausible that a sizable portion of respondents may have felt pressure (explicit or implicit) to answer in a certain way. In general, responses for all questionnaires except certain parts of the Enterprise Quantitative Questionnaire have been more complete and of higher quality than was originally expected.

The Suitability of the Four Counties

Since the counties chosen for in-depth fieldwork in effect constitute a sample of four, their characteristics and their representativeness of the more than 2,000 counties of China are an important determinant of the value of the data set. Do the four counties cover the full range of institutional setups for the TVP sector, or are there many counties with TVP ownership, supervision, and management systems radically different from those sampled? The same question arises for basic features of the economic environment—goods markets, factor markets, relations with the state sector, and the like. Finally, it would be a matter for concern if the four counties were not really representative of the main feature they were selected to typify—if, for example, it turned out that TVP development in Jieshou was considerably above the average for China as a whole or that Shangrao was not significantly below the national average.

The four counties do represent an astonishing range of variation in TVP organization and development, not only in terms of the specific criteria for selecting the counties in the first place but also in several unexpected areas. One example is the dispersion of political authority among administrative levels in Nanhai, in contrast to its concentration at the township level in Wuxi (see chapter 7). Another is the personal sponsorship of large private enterprises by county officials in Jieshou. The lively land market in Jieshou is even more striking. The contrasts in labor market development in the four counties are also instructive and probably cover most of the variation that occurs in the country as a whole (see chapter 14).

One important model of TVP development is not represented by any of the four counties. The famous "Wenzhou model" is characterized by free development of private enterprises (mostly household undertakings), a thriving financial market based to a large extent on private financial institutions, and extensive commercial relationships with distant parts of China.[9] Wenzhou itself was not included in the sample, partly for logistical reasons (travel there is not very convenient) and partly because so many delegations have already visited the area that much information is already available and the receptivity of managers and officials to further in-depth investigations may be strained. Certain elements of the Wenzhou model are, however, present in the four sample counties—the land market in Jieshou, the labor market in Nanhai, ownership patterns in both counties, the "specialized" villages based on household industries in Jieshou's hinterlands, and the movement of temporary migrant labor out of the poorer areas of Shangrao. (In Wenzhou people from the poorer mountainous areas move into the towns in search of better employment; in Shangrao these people move out of the county altogether.) But none of the four counties has a highly developed financial market or private financial institutions. More generally, the four counties may not be able to provide much insight into what happens when all the elements of the Wenzhou model are brought together and allowed to flourish.

It was in the choice of this small sample of four counties that tradeoffs between different objectives were most severe. Inclusion of Wenzhou in the sample would have exacerbated logistical problems and loaded the sample with unrepresentative models, since Wuxi is already included. Substituting another county representative of the Wenzhou model might have skewed the sample too much toward "unusual" counties, since that would have meant dropping Nanhai, Shangrao, or Jieshou. Except for the exclusion of the Wenzhou model, the four counties do seem to provide an adequate range of variation in most dimensions of the TVP sector and cover most of the patterns that are present in substantial numbers of counties. The variety of possible ownership patterns is well represented, and there is a wide range of differences in industrial structure, orientation toward markets, size of enterprises, and so on.

As for the degree to which the four counties are representative of China as a whole, Wuxi and Nanhai are far more industrialized than most other counties, but Shangrao and the rural areas of Jieshou are, if anything, somewhat below the national average (see chapters 4 and 7). Moreover, in the latter two counties some virtually nonindustrialized townships were visited. Since the sample could include only counties with at least a certain degree of TVP industrial development (otherwise there would be nothing to study) and the areas of advanced TVP development also had to be covered, the choice of Jieshou and Shangrao seems appropriate.

Characteristics of Firms

Tradeoffs among research objectives are also evident in the sample of enterprises. There was no attempt to obtain a random sample. Instead, enterprises were chosen according to certain criteria: (a) reasonable size and enough "history" for meaningful research and time-series analysis; (b) the widest possible range of ownership and management forms, with oversampling of new and unusual variants; (c) coverage in every county of such key TVP industries as machinery, textiles, food processing, and building materials; (d) variation in performance (profitability), including some loss-makers; (e) the maximum possible range in firm size, subject to the constraint that firms must be substantial enough to investigate; (f) a range of technologies; and (g) different locations within the county.

Sample characteristics were constrained both by the prior choice of counties and by internal conflicts among the criteria, which could not all be fulfilled completely. Criteria c through g were achieved more or less satisfactorily. Criteria a and b, however, conflicted, since most private enterprises in the TVP sector were established only recently and are much smaller on average than tvces. Criterion b was also severely constrained by the choice of counties, since there are virtually no substantial private enterprises in Wuxi or Shangrao.

These problems are evident in table 2-4, which shows the ownership of sample firms. Private firms make up only 14 percent of the total, and there are no private enterprises in the sample for Wuxi, only one in Shangrao, and only four in Nanhai. Jieshou is thus the only county with a sufficient number of private enterprises (twelve) for many types of statistical analysis. The share of private enterprises in the sample is lower than their share in total numbers of tvps by county but may be reasonably close to the share of large private enterprises in the different counties. Village enterprises are poorly represented in Jieshou, and there are hardly any enterprises run by production teams in any county but Jieshou. Thus, although the sample contains a sufficiently wide range of ownership and management forms, private enterprises are by no means oversampled—on the contrary, there are too few of them. The close relationship between location and ownership in the sample makes it difficult to disentangle county- and ownership-specific factors.

Another question concerns the degree to which the sample firms are representative of tvps in their respective counties. Table 2-5, which looks at township enterprises only, since they constitute more than two-thirds of the total number of sample firms, compares sample means with county averages for several statistical indicators. The most striking feature of the sample is that firms tend to be much larger than average for their counties. In gross

Table 2-4. *Ownership of Sample Enterprises*
(percent, except as specified)

Ownership category	Entire sample		Share of county subsample			
	Number of firms	Share	Wuxi	Jieshou	Nanhai	Shangrao
Township and town	83	68	78	51	57	87
Township	66	54	62	38	48	70
Town	17	14	16	13	9	17
Village	15	12	19	3	22	10
Production team	7	6	3	14	4	0
Private	17	14	0	32	17	3
Partnership[a]	10	8	0	24	4	0
Individual	7	6	0	8	13	3
Total	122	100	100	100	100	100

Note: All sample enterprises originally classified as "other" have been put in one of the regular ownership categories on the basis of a review of interview notes and a judgment as to which form of ownership is the dominant partner in the case of joint ventures. Some firms were reclassified if it was thought that the original questionnaire response was inaccurate; this problem arose primarily in Jieshou.

a. Includes partnerships and family enterprises.

output value the sample mean for Shangrao is 2.5 times the county average, for Wuxi 5.3 times, for Nanhai 7.5 times, and for Jieshou 8.2 times. Sample enterprises are also somewhat more profitable than county averages; the ratio of profits to fixed capital for sample township enterprises is 22 percent higher than the county average in Jieshou, 55 percent higher in Nanhai, 64 percent higher in Wuxi, and 141 percent higher in Shangrao. Profitability varies greatly, however, and in all counties the ratio of loss-making township enterprises in the sample is as high as or higher than the ratio in the county as a whole. Thus, although the sample includes a disproportionate number of firms in the upper tail of the distributions of both size and profitability, the lower tail of profitability is also adequately represented.

Workers and Directors

Despite some problems, stratified random sampling of workers seemed to work reasonably well, and no obvious biases are apparent. In few cases were workers reluctant to fill out forms. Thus the main question concerns the subsample of forty-nine enterprises where the Worker Survey was conducted. In general, this sample seems to mirror the larger sample of firms. For example, the lack of private enterprises in Wuxi and Shangrao is evident, whereas workers were surveyed in an adequate number of private enterprises in Jieshou and a smaller, but still respectable, number in Nanhai. There was some tendency to select larger, more stable firms for administration of the Worker Survey Questionnaire because these had larger labor forces and were less affected when a given number of employees was pulled off the job to fill out questionnaires. Other than this, there is no evidence of systematic bias in the selection of firms within the sample for employee surveys.

The main problem with the Enterprise Director Questionnaire has already been mentioned: in some cases the form was filled out not by the director but by someone else, usually a deputy director. This probably had only a minimal influence on the results: not many forms were affected; even where the deputy director filled out the form, personal information on the director may have been supplied; and in any case, the personal backgrounds and attitudes of directors and deputy directors in the same enterprise may not differ greatly.

Overall Assessment

Although some of the problems mentioned in this section are significant and reduce the usefulness of the data set, none raises doubts about its basic validity and value. The painstaking, careful administration of questionnaires ensured both a high response rate and at least a reasonably high level of quality, as measured by the effort made by respondents. Lack of experience in filling out questionnaires of this kind on the part of enterprise managers, workers, and community government officials created some problems in data gather-

Table 2-5. Comparison of Sample Means with County Averages, Township Enterprises
(millions of yuan, unless otherwise specified)

Average township enterprise	Wuxi		Jieshou		Nanhai		Shangrao	
	Sample mean	Mean for county	Sample mean	Mean for county	Sample mean	Mean for county	Sample mean	Mean for county
GVIO (current prices)	10.081	1.885	2.562	0.314	13.610	1.810	0.246	0.098
Employment (persons)[a]	451	131	131	55	448	123	82	52
Fixed assets[b]	2.245	0.488	0.527	0.068	2.249	0.695	0.161	0.114
Total assets[c]	4.274	0.959	1.022	0.094	5.315	1.194	0.231	0.153
Gross profits	1.780	0.220	0.183	0.018	0.787	0.157	0.022	0.007
Profit tax	0.368	0.040	0.029	0[d]	0.259	0.053	0.004	0.002
Net profits	1.431	0.180	0.137	0.018	0.494	0.104	0.017	0.006
Profit turned over to community government[e]	0.502	n.a.	0.003	0.004	0.123	0.056	0.006	0.005
Ratio of profit to sales[e]	19.0	13.5	8.7	9.2	7.5	8.0	8.9	5.7
Ratio of profit to fixed assets[e]	73.8	45.1	33.0	27.1	35.0	22.6	14.2	5.9
Percentage of loss-making enterprises	12.5[f]	11.7	2.7[f]	0[g]	17.4[f]	18.0	23.3[f]	17.8

n.a. Not available.
Note: Includes enterprises run by towns as well as by townships. GVIO, gross value of industrial output.
a. At year-end.
b. Original value, at year-end.
c. Original value of fixed assets plus quota circulating assets, at year-end.
d. Exact value Y414.
e. Weighted averages were taken for the sample for comparability with county aggregates.
f. Ratio of loss-making enterprises to total number of firms filling out the Enterprise Quantitative Questionnaire (including those who left this item blank).
g. Reported by county authorities, but obviously not accurate.
Source: Information from fieldwork.

38

ing, but it also meant that many of the respondents found the task fresh and interesting and put considerable effort into it.

Shortcomings and biases in the sample should be kept in mind when interpreting results. In particular, it must be remembered that some important segments of the TVP sector are not well represented—small firms, private firms, the most backward areas with few and small TVPs, and nonindustrial enterprises. Some of these gaps can be filled with aggregated local, provincial, and national statistics (see, for example, chapter 12).

An important strong point of the sample is that it includes a significant number of poor performers—backward counties (Shangrao and rural parts of Jieshou), even more backward townships (in Shangrao and Jieshou, and, relatively speaking, several in Wuxi); and poorly performing enterprises. (In all counties a significant number of sample firms had losses in 1985, and some enterprises had obvious management, financial, technical, or other problems.) This inclusiveness was a significant accomplishment, since provincial and lower-level government authorities naturally would prefer to show researchers their "better" localities and firms.

Notes

1. Most of this work has appeared in *Nongcun, Jingji, Shehui* (The Rural Areas, Their Economy, Their Society), published by the China Rural Development Research Group, the predecessor of the Development Research Institute. Four issues of this serial were published.

2. China proper is the term historically used for an area that contains about four-fifths of China's population. Jieshou County, the northernmost of the four target counties, lies on the southern edge of the North China Plain. Yuanping County, Shanxi Province, where an initial test investigation was conducted, is in the far northwest of China proper. Taihe County in Anhui, where some extra fieldwork was conducted, also lies on the North China Plain.

3. A county seat is a town of reasonable size that belongs to the county and serves as its administrative center. As some county towns grew, they were transformed into independent administrative units at an equal or even a higher level in the government hierarchy. In Wuxi and Nanhai the central city is actually in charge of the surrounding counties. In Shangrao the municipality is administratively separate from Shangrao County.

4. In Nanhai County, as in Guangdong Province as a whole, the terms used for rural communities differ markedly from those used in other parts of the country. To avoid confusion and preserve uniformity, we have used the terms that apply to the closest equivalent unit in the other counties. Thus the community entities in Nanhai that were previously referred to as "districts" and were recently renamed "towns" are called "townships" here, since they roughly correspond to townships in the other counties, although they are somewhat larger. (When specific township-level communities in Nanhai are referred to by name, however, we use "town.") Similarly, we use the term "village" for what are called "townships" in Nanhai and the term "production team" for what are called "villages" in Nanhai.

5. In China the term "town" is used to refer to several different kinds of community government entity. Shaxi town and most of the other towns visited during fieldwork are equivalent to townships in their administrative level and population, but they are typically somewhat more urbanized. Jieshou town is a county seat and is hence of somewhat higher administrative rank than a township, although it is still well below county rank. The use of the term "town" in Nanhai was discussed in note 4.

6. Since most firms were not established before the late 1970s, the items for 1970, 1975, and 1978 on the Enterprise Quantitative Questionnaire are usually missing values. Moreover, particularly in the Enterprise Quantitative Questionnaire, some parts were not completed or were completed so poorly that the data turned out to be unusable.

7. This is partly because so many enterprises left some questions blank or responded inappropriately that the information is virtually unusable and partly because some of the questions (for example, in the income statement) asked for redundant or detailed information that was not deemed necessary for analysis.

8. The number of organizations visited exceeds the number of meetings held because many meetings involved more than one organization. This more than counterbalanced the fact that sometimes representatives of the same entity were interviewed more than once.

9. See Wang Xiaoqiang and others (1983) for the first detailed discussion of the Wenzhou model of TVP development. Also see Institute of Economics, CASS (1987), part I.

Part I

Overview

The four chapters in this part deal with a disparate set of topics, but they all provide general descriptions and analyses of various aspects of the TVP sector. Hence they should be read before the later chapters that delve more deeply into narrower topics.

In chapter 3 Du Haiyan analyzes the causes behind the rapid development of China's industrial TVP sector in recent years. He divides the past decade into two distinct periods: 1978–83, when agricultural reforms and the transfer of resources from agriculture provided the motivating force for rural industrialization, and 1984–85, when expanding market demand, policy reforms, and development of the TVP sector itself, particularly private enterprises, gave the impetus for even more rapid growth of TVP industry.

Du notes that both in 1978–83 and earlier, population pressure on limited land resources stimulated the movement of rural agricultural labor into industrial activities. He goes on to show how the resources needed for rural industrialization—capital, technology and equipment, land, materials, labor, and markets—were marshaled in 1978–83. Many resources were supplied directly or indirectly from agriculture, but by 1984–85 the ability of agriculture to sustain this contribution was exhausted. Financial flows began to move from the TVP sector to agriculture rather than in the other direction, and agriculture and industry competed for labor in some rural areas.

But, as Du points out, rather than subsiding, TVP industrial growth accelerated in 1984–85. TVP industrial development had moved onto a self-sustaining path, aided by institutional and policy reforms, the most important of which was the legitimization of private enterprises. As a result, the private sector boomed, with even more momentum in many of the underdeveloped areas than in industrially advanced areas (some of which, like Wuxi County, effectively restricted private enterprises from developing rapidly or becoming large scale). The chapter describes both the measures that localities such as Jieshou implemented to promote development of private enterprises and continuing problems and ambiguities, such as the dependence of private enterprises on local government officials and the conversion of some private enterprises into collective enterprises.

An important element in the 1984–85 TVP boom was the greatly increased supply of bank loans to the sector. When bank lending was subsequently cut back, TVPs turned to other channels, including internal accumulation, for funds. Perhaps even more important for TVP development was the sharp growth of demand for TVP industrial products in 1984–85, which was fueled by credit expansion and by large increases in both urban and rural personal incomes. The strong growth of intermediate demand from the burgeoning industrial TVP sector itself was another key factor.

In the last part of the chapter Du looks at prospects for the future. He sees several grounds for pessimism. Even under conservative predictions of trends in capital-labor ratios, available capital will fall far short of the requirements for generating employment opportunities for the rural people who will need to be shifted from agriculture to industry over the next several decades. Increasingly severe market competition, both within the TVP sector itself and from a reformed, more efficient state-owned industrial sector, will sap the ability of the TVP sector to expand as rapidly in the future. The government's ability to provide resources for the TVP sector will be increasingly limited, and the impact of policy liberalization will be weaker now that the one-time benefits of earlier reforms have been largely realized. The tight linkages between TVPs and rural community governments—which involve administrative intervention by the latter, distortions in investment and employment decisions, and siphoning of TVP profits to meet community needs—will become an increasing liability for TVPs in the future.

In chapter 4 Jan Svejnar and Josephine Woo survey patterns of rural industrial development in the four counties where intensive fieldwork was conducted. After briefly presenting basic data for the four counties and describing salient given, or exogenous, conditions, the authors review the main characteristics of the counties' TVP sectors.

Wuxi and Nanhai counties are far more developed than Jieshou and Shangrao. Industry is the most important part of the TVP sector in all four counties as well as in China as a whole, but the subsectoral structure within industry varies, as does ownership. The growth and performance of the TVP sector also vary greatly in the four counties, although in all cases the past several years have seen rapid increases in industrial output. TVCE labor productivity has been much higher in Wuxi and Nanhai than in Jieshou and Shangrao. But indicators of financial performance (profitability) suggest that the TVCE sector in Wuxi is somewhat more efficient than in Nanhai and Jieshou, whereas Shangrao lags far behind, considerably below the national average.

Svejnar and Woo find dramatic variation in the role of foreign trade and foreign capital in TVP development, although in all four counties the export market is quantitatively much less important than domestic sales. In Wuxi, although exports are substantial, direct contacts between TVPs and foreign customers are limited, and there is little foreign investment. In Nanhai, by contrast, the TVP economy is very open, and firms rely heavily on foreign funds, equipment, expertise, and markets, most commonly through various kinds of compensation trade and processing agreements with businesses in Hong Kong and other places outside China. Jieshou has only just begun to develop foreign economic ties, and in Shangrao there is not one piece of foreign equipment in any TVP or in any other type of firm.

The second part of the chapter analyzes the causes behind these regional patterns. Geographic and historical factors are obviously important, most notably the agricultural resource base and proximity to cities and markets. Each county's endowment of human capital also seems to be significant in explaining the performance of its TVP sector. In both respects Wuxi and Nanhai are much better endowed than Jieshou and Shangrao, and Jieshou is somewhat better off than Shangrao despite the latter's abundant mineral deposits.

Access to financial capital is considered another important explanatory factor in regional variation. Wuxi and Nanhai are able to attract outside funds to support TVP development, and Nanhai has also made considerable use of foreign capital. But in Jieshou and Shangrao, given the relatively low degree of TVP development, it is probably not the lack of local funds but the poor performance of the TVCE sector, especially in Shangrao, that hampers the flow of financial resources.

Still another key factor is county government policy. Svejnar and Woo argue that the county government can play an important, even determining, role in guiding TVP development in areas such as ownership. The timing of the implementation of the production responsibility system (PRS) and related agricultural reforms has varied greatly among the four counties. County government policies can also affect labor allocation and mobility.

The last part of the chapter generates several models of TVP development on the basis of the patterns observed in the four counties. Although the models differ sharply, it is impossible to assert unequivocally that one is better than the others; all have demonstrated at least the potential for supporting successful TVP development under different circumstances. TVPs are able to thrive in a variety of economic and administrative environments. The experience of the four counties suggests that the principal obstacles to TVP development are inappropriate local government policies, a weak economic base, and inability to compete for material resources and for physical and human capital.

In chapter 5 William Byrd and N. Zhu analyze the market environment and industrial structure of the TVP sector. They start by noting some stylized facts about the TVP sector: the primarily market-based allocation of TVP outputs and material inputs; rigidities and administrative intervention in the allocation of factors of production—land, capital, and often labor as well; the dominance of TVCES in TVP-sector industrial output; close ties between all kinds of TVPs and their local rural communities; and the relatively small scale of most TVPs. The ownership and financial structure of TVPs are then examined, and the main characteristics of the product markets that they face are outlined. These characteristics include the tremendous profit and growth possibilities in many markets at the outset; constriction of opportunities in markets for these products over time; and relatively hard market constraints and competitive market conditions for most TVPs.

The second part of the chapter focuses on patterns of competition and market adjustment in the TVP sector. One characteristic pattern is termed "imitative competition with neoclassical adjustment." When entry and exit are easy, an initial profit opportunity leads to widespread imitation by new entrants, and thus to declining prices and profits, until some sort of equilibrium is reached. The "investment competition" pattern is similar but involves activities with higher investment requirements and often a high degree of "asset specificity" as well. As a result, investment competition can lead to large economic losses and may be highly risky. A third pattern, "innovative competition," is emerging in some parts of the TVP sector.

The chapter also reviews competitive and other interactions between TVPs and state enterprises. In industries where controlled prices are artificially low and a two-tier planning and market system has emerged, there may be a niche for TVPs that would not survive in an uncontrolled market environment. But in many industries characterized by buyers' markets, TVPs can hold their own and sometimes even achieve dominance. The state sector serves as an important source of business, technology, and personnel for TVPs. Although cooperative interactions may involve short-term financial and other benefits for state enterprises, in the long run these arrangements may, like international outsourcing, transfer manufacturing capabilities to the TVP sector and threaten the position of state industry. Moreover, the most advanced TVP areas have already moved away from heavy reliance on subcontracting for state enterprises.

TVPs' competitive strategies and methods of adjusting to adverse changes in market conditions are then discussed. Among the former are the "rush to be first" and rapid changes in product lines to take advantage of changing market opportunities. Adjustment to adversity occurs in a variety of ways, some more or less automatic, others discretionary. The authors conclude that TVP markets are for the most part reasonably competitive and that at both the enterprise and the aggregate level the TVP sector shows considerable resilience and flexibility.

The authors next look at industrial structure in the TVP sector, focusing on sectoral composition, firm size, community industrial structure, and economies of scale. The TVP industrial sector is diversified and covers nearly as broad a range of industrial subsectors as does Chinese industry as a whole. Average firm size is small, although firms of substantial scale have emerged in Wuxi and other places. The community ties of larger TVPs, among other factors, probably limit the size they can attain. A preliminary test involving sample firms indicates that there are some economies of scale, but this result needs to be interpreted cautiously. An important finding is that in its community industrial structure Shangrao in most respects resembles the national situation much more than does Wuxi or Nanhai.

The chapter ends with some conclusions and implications. Potential problem areas are the limitations of imitative competition and investment competition, which may further exacerbate gaps between more and less industrialized rural localities; the impact of greater asset specificity on TVP adjustment capabilities and strategies; and limitations on the size of firms. The authors argue in favor of policies to increase the mobility of financial and other resources among communities and localities and against administrative restrictions against entry by TVPs into certain types of industrial activities.

In chapter 6 He Jiacheng takes a broad, long-term look at future development issues and policy choices related to the TVP sector. After describing some overall government objectives for the Chinese economy and for the rural sector during the next several decades, the author discusses the complex and critically important interrelationships between the TVP sector and agriculture. He argues that contradictions between rural industrial and agricultural development are a major obstacle. Of particular concern has been the apparent diversion of resources from agriculture to rural industry, which has led some to argue that the latter sector has been developing too rapidly. The limited resources of agriculture and the inability to get around them through foreign trade call for extreme caution in Chinese agricultural policy.

In discussing policy solutions the author argues that whatever their merits and disadvantages, financial transfers from rural industry to agriculture, price increases for agricultural products, and other macroeconomic solutions are inadequate for addressing the fundamental problems of Chinese agriculture and their inhibiting effects on rural industrialization. A thoroughgoing land reform is needed to rationalize farm sizes, increase agricultural productivity, and promote regional specialization and interregional trade.

The second main area covered is urban-rural imbalances. In addition to the effect of administrative barriers and the antirural bias of China's traditional industrialization strategy, the similar structures of urban and rural industry and the constraints on agricultural development tend to preserve and even exacerbate urban-rural gaps in development and living standards. Still another critical problem is the tension between rural industrialization and urbanization. The small-town urbanization that is occurring as part of TVP development carries benefits but also brings problems, the most important of which are scattered location patterns and the inability to take advantage of economies of scale in urban infrastructure and services.

The author asserts that it is essential to improve human capital, particularly in the more backward rural areas, and he suggests more emphasis on education and training, the introduction of entrepreneurs from more advanced parts of the country, and more appropriate income incentives. In addition, industrial policies should ensure that rural localities focus on activities in which they have a comparative advantage, particularly labor-intensive industries. Finally, a consistent strategy of urbanization for towns and smaller cities should be developed.

In the last part of the chapter the author argues that although in many respects the ownership and institutional structure of TVCEs resemble those of state enterprises, the differences are important enough to have substantial effects on enterprise behavior and performance. But problems in organization and management hamper TVP development. These include the dual functions of township governments; the lack of strong incentives and direct rewards for the ultimate owners of TVCEs—the rural population; insufficient decisionmaking authority for TVCE managers; and shortcomings in labor allocation systems, which lead to excessively high wages and labor shortages alongside overstaffing in many parts of the TVP sector. Private enterprises suffer from external constraints and discrimination, which distort their behavior. To deal with these problems, contract responsibility systems have been instituted for TVCEs in, for example, Jiangsu Province. Although these systems are beneficial, they cannot fully solve institutional and organizational problems, which are inextricably linked with ownership issues and property rights. Reforms in the ownership system of TVCEs, including partial privatization (through sales of assets to workers and other individuals) and better treatment of the private sector, will be necessary.

3

Causes of Rapid Rural Industrial Development

Du Haiyan

The rapid development of China's TVP industry has attracted wide attention both there and abroad. In 1986 there were 6.35 million rural industrial enterprises, and they employed about 47.6 million people. The value of rural industrial output in that year topped Y241.3 billion and accounted for 32.5 percent of the total value of rural social output and 23 percent of the total national value of industrial output. Between 1978 and 1986 the value of rural industrial output increased about tenfold in Wuxi County and nearly twentyfold in Jieshou. Although growth rates differ among regions, TVP development was generally rapid. There were, however, sharp ups and downs (see figures 3-1 and 3-2). The output of TVP industry as a whole—whether in highly industrialized Wuxi County or in more backward Jieshou County— rose and declined twice during 1978–86. The fluctuations were so large and the cycles so short that the stability of the entire urban and rural economy was affected. These swings were obviously related to changes in government policies toward rural industries, to changes in the situation of the urban and rural economies, and to economic reforms.

The development of rural industry in recent years can be divided into two phases: 1978–83 and the period since 1984. There were important changes in government policies, economic reforms, and the urban and rural economies between the two phases.

- The restrictions on farmers' nonagricultural activities were greatly relaxed after the Third Plenum of the Eleventh Central Committee in December 1978, but for some time there were arguments as to whether the unfettered growth of TVCEs would be efficient and compatible with socialism. Government institutions, from the highest authorities down to grass-roots departments, began fully supporting TVPs only in 1984.
- The household production responsibility system (PRS) in agriculture was universally implemented by 1983, and by 1984 new reforms were needed in rural areas.

47

Figure 3-1. *Annual Growth Rate of National and TVP Gross Industrial Output Value, 1978–86*

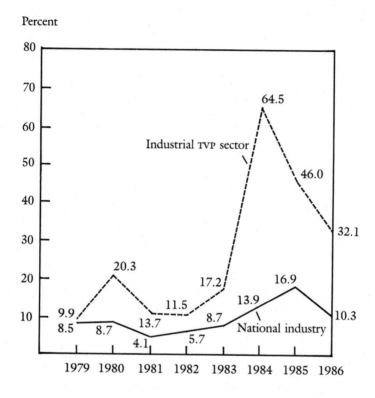

Percent

- After 1978 the output of agricultural products increased greatly, and by 1984 there were even small trade surpluses in grain and cotton. Since 1984 crop production has stagnated.
- Urban economic reforms accelerated in 1984, with some impact on rural areas and the TVP sector.

1978–83: The Initial Stimulus from Agriculture

The growth of rural industry has all along been closely related to conditions in agriculture. For example, in Jiangsu Province, where Wuxi County is located, the growth of TVP industry has been in inverse proportion to the amount of rural arable land per person and the number of surplus agricultural laborers (table 3-1).

It is clear that shrinking agricultural resources were the initial force behind the development of TVPs. In the twenty-five years 1952–77 China's rural population grew by 55.6 percent, whereas the total area of arable land fell by

Figure 3-2. *Annual Growth Rate of TVP Gross Industrial Output Value,*
Wuxi and Jieshou, 1978–86

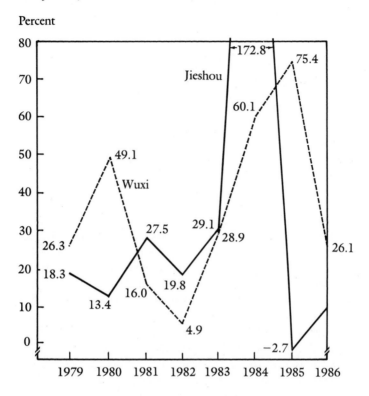

Percent

130 million mu. Arable land per member of the rural population dropped
from 3.29 mu to 1.85 mu. In Wuxi arable land per person declined from 2.52
mu to 1.27 mu and in Jieshou from 2.76 mu to 1.36 mu. During the same
period agriculture's share of national income fell from 57.7 to 37.1 percent.
Yet the proportion of agricultural labor in the national total increased from
82.6 to 84.2 percent, and in 1978 this proportion was more than 70 percent
in Wuxi and more than 90 percent in Jieshou. The net output value created
by each Chinese rural worker fell from Y323 to Y317. The rural economic
situation, as measured by the relation between agricultural inputs and outputs, thus worsened instead of improving.

  Between 1952 and 1977 rural people entered nonagricultural activities in
three great waves. The first came during the First Five-Year Plan, when large-
scale urban industrial construction absorbed a large amount of rural labor.
As rural industrialization did not materialize in this period, the mass transfer
from farming to nonagricultural activities was expressed in cross-regional
population movements and urbanization.

Table 3-1. *TVP Industrial Development and Agricultural Resources in Three Regions of Jiangsu Province*

Counties	Year	Per capita output value of TVPs (yuan)	Farmland per capita (mu)	Farmland per laborer (mu)
Suzhou-Wuxi-Changzhou	1980	585.0	1.10	1.94
	1984	895.9	1.41	2.03
Nantong-Yangzhou-Zhenjiang	1980	258.5	1.20	2.42
	1984	450.1	1.24	2.09
Xuzhou-Huaiyin-Yangcheng	1980	70.0	1.61	4.22
	1984	110.9	1.58	3.47

Source: Information from fieldwork.

The second wave occurred during the Great Leap Forward movement in 1958, when many communes and brigades set up small industries. The shift to nonagricultural activities during this period mainly involved transfer within localities, although there was also some movement into urban industries. Blind development of rural industry created many problems and led to low microeconomic benefits and to macroeconomic imbalances. The readjustment of the national economy that followed not only forced some farmers who had entered urban industries to return to their homes in rural areas but also compelled many commune and brigade enterprises to stop operations.

The third wave occurred in the early 1970s. In 1970 the State Council urged that the mechanization of agriculture be speeded up. Factories producing farm machinery mushroomed, and the total output value of commune and brigade enterprises rose from Y1 billion in 1971 to Y27.2 billion in 1976. But their development was always restrained owing to policies that gave priority to agriculture and especially to development of grain production.

The most conspicuous change in China's rural areas since 1978 has been the adoption of the PRS, a reform that greatly increased farmers' enthusiasm and stimulated agricultural production. Rural productivity increased dramatically without great advances in agricultural production technology. In Wuxi, for example, agricultural productivity increased 1.7 times from 1980 to 1985. This, however, aggravated the situation of surplus agricultural labor. New rural economic policies that encouraged a diversified economy in the countryside were as significant as the PRS. Policies that discouraged rural labor from shifting to nonagricultural activities were basically abolished, and the movement of farmers into nonagricultural activities was accelerated.

The transfer of rural surplus labor to nonagricultural activities involved several important factors: capital, land, labor, equipment and materials, and marketing activity by enterprises.

Capital

Initially, the accumulation of funds for investment in nonagricultural activities was related to the unusual growth of agricultural incomes, which stemmed partly from the growth of agricultural production and partly from procurement price increases that returned industrial profits to agriculture. Before the late 1970s, because of strict price controls on industrial and agricultural products, nearly one-third of the real national income created by agricultural production was transferred to nonagricultural activities, and this seriously affected farmers' incomes. Since 1978 state procurement prices for agricultural products have increased sharply; the purchase prices for the principal agricultural products rose by 50–100 percent during 1978–82 (see table 3-2). In 1978–80 alone the rise in procurement prices enabled farmers to reap Y46 billion in additional net income.

From 1978 to 1983 farmers' average per capita income in China increased from Y133.6 to Y309.8, or 132 percent; in Wuxi during the same period it rose from Y124.4 to Y412.7, an increase of 232 percent. An increase in farmers' bank savings accompanied the rise in their incomes. The saving rate of China's rural residents, as measured by bank deposits, climbed by 7 percentage points during this period. In Wuxi, a county with high incomes, the increase in rural bank savings was all the more striking; between 1978 and 1983 the total amount of rural bank deposits increased by 486 percent, and individual deposits rose by 600 percent. The growth of rural deposits helped expand local banks' supply of funds and has been a positive force in the development of TVPs. For the country as a whole the year-end outstanding balance of loans extended to TVCEs increased from Y1.5 billion in 1977 to Y7.35 billion in 1982, a rise of 390 percent. The growth of farmers' incomes also added directly to the supply of funds for TVP industry. In Jieshou and Shangrao capi-

Table 3-2. *Weighted Average Index of Prices Obtained
by Agricultural Producers, 1978–82*
(1978 = 100)

Product	Index				Annual growth rate (percent)	
	1979	1980	1981	1982	1978–79	1979–82
Grain	126	137	145	149	25.6	5.9
Edible oils	141	151	161	159	40.3	4.1
Pork	137	155	162	166	37.0	6.6
Beef	120	153	174	226	19.7	23.3
Eggs	122	124	134	135	21.9	3.5
Aquatic products	149	176	199	211	48.6	12.3
Cotton	118	139	137	142	17.6	6.5

Source: State Statistical Bureau (1983).

tal was often raised by requiring workers to finance the enterprises they joined—in some enterprises each worker might bring in as much as Y10,000 in capital.

Capital from agriculture was a forceful stimulant for TVP industry in developed counties such as Wuxi but was less significant in, for example, Jieshou. In 1982 the per capita income of rural residents in Jieshou was merely Y99, and per capita bank deposits were about Y4.1—19.4 percent and 2.2 percent of the respective figures for Wuxi. Even so, the growth of agricultural income played a positive role in promoting the development of TVP industry.

The transformation of money capital into real capital also helped rural labor shift into nonagricultural activities. At present, the industrial TVP sector is still a "talent-type" economy; the success of a firm depends heavily on the quality of its manager. This affects the sources of technology for TVPs. But different regions have different characteristics. Well-located Wuxi County received its technology directly from urban industries; workers who returned to rural areas during the early readjustment of the national economy in the 1960s became founders and technical personnel of local TVP industry. In addition, TVPs in Wuxi have established cooperative technological relations with their urban counterparts. By the end of 1985 about 856 enterprises in Wuxi had links with 1,097 firms in large cities for the production of 1,159 products and had established cooperative technological ties with more than 350 institutions of higher learning. At the same time, the county's own technological potential has grown rapidly.

The situation is different in Jieshou, which is far from big cities and has been plagued by disadvantages in developing products and technology, largely because of poor transport facilities. Under these circumstances the county found its own way by purchasing technology and talent at high prices. Production of a sprinkling machine, at one time the county's most important product, began in this way. Another channel for transfer of technology is through relatives and friends. A handful of managers has played a vital role in obtaining technology for the startup of TVPs in Jieshou.

Land

The implementation, beginning in 1978, of the policy of encouraging diversified activities in rural areas brought into the open the existing gap in incomes from land. As the figures below show, industrial income from a plot of land is far higher than the value of its agricultural output. (The data, which were obtained from fieldwork, are in yuan per mu; n.a. = not available.)

	Wuxi	Jieshou	Nanhai	Shangrao
Agriculture	286.7	149.7	195	194.2
Industry	63,359.5	42,711.4	n.a.	n.a.

Hence there is a strong incentive for shifting land to industrial uses. From 1979 to 1984 about 55 million rural residents entered TVPs, which occupied a total of 30 million mu of arable land. Arable land was reduced by another 15 million mu in 1985; 50–60 percent of that was taken by TVPs.

Primitive land markets began to emerge in many places. In Jieshou sample firms paid, on average, Y7,930 per mu to purchase the land they occupied and Y1,962 per mu per year to lease it. Land markets formed in this region because of the concentration of infrastructure and the inflow of TVPs. Many TVPs have moved to Jieshou town to obtain electricity and better transport, causing a continuous rise in land prices. Land markets not only favor the rational distribution of land resources but also give firms not run by community governments an opportunity to survive. If the firms have money, they can get land through land development companies run by local governments.

Labor

According to Todaro (1969), the transfer of labor from rural to urban areas is affected by the urban-rural wage differential and by the opportunities for nonagricultural employment. In rural China the basic unit of economic accounting is the household. When land was contracted according to head count, it did not matter whether a household member was engaged in agricultural activities, since the land could be farmed by other members of the family. As a result, the opportunity cost of a farmer's turning to industrial activities was practically zero. Besides, there were large discrepancies between personal incomes from agriculture and from work in TVPs. In 1980 rural per capita income from agriculture was Y166, whereas per capita income in TVPs was Y398. In 1985 these figures rose to Y351 for agriculture and Y726 for TVPs. Such wide differences made farmers even more eager to get into the nonagricultural sector. TVP industry at this stage thus faced an abundant supply of labor, which promoted its development.

Equipment and Materials

After 1978 planned procurement of agricultural products by the state shrank even as farm output grew, which stimulated the growth of TVPs that used agricultural raw materials; between 1978 and 1983 the output value of such TVPs increased by 254 percent. Meanwhile, TVPs that produced energy and raw materials also grew rapidly and helped form a new chain for the flow of materials in rural areas. For example, in Jiangsu Province the share of township enterprises in the total provincial output of certain key industrial producer goods was already high in 1983, as the figures below, obtained from fieldwork, indicate.

	Percent
Rolled steel	11.3
Metallurgical materials	18.2
Iron ore	8.0
Fireproof materials	28.6
Nonferrous metals	30.0
Copper products	27.4
Aluminum products	21.0

The adjustment of the country's national industrialization strategy also enabled TVPs to receive some materials subject to monopoly distribution under the state plan. The proportion of state-distributed coal in total coal consumed by TVPs in Wuxi in 1980 was 32.9 percent; the figure was 41.3 percent for electricity, 62.7 percent for petroleum products, and 5.3 percent for steel. Some localities, such as Shangrao, have even formulated rules to ensure that a certain proportion of their allocations of materials from the state is distributed to TVPs.

TVPs get their equipment from many sources. In highly developed Wuxi, where equipment is often advanced and up to date, there has been a trend since the early 1980s toward transferring equipment out of the county to economically underdeveloped regions. In backward counties such as Jieshou obsolete equipment makes up a large share of the total. About 38 percent of the county's equipment was made before 1970, and about 79 percent of TVP equipment consists of items handed down from state enterprises. The proportion of locally made equipment is also high in backward regions.

Marketing

All along, TVPs have been sensitive to market trends because they have had no access to state commercial channels, and TVP industry has placed strategic emphasis on sales. Most TVPs have followed the pattern of having one person in charge of production, two in charge of purchases, and three in charge of sales. This has led to a widely held belief that the success of TVPs owes much to their marketing. There are more than 10,000 sales personnel in Wuxi TVPs, and Jieshou has thousands of people who market nylon ropes around the country. Generally, the more irregular the production, the higher the ratio of salespeople.

TVPs use several methods to improve supply and sales work.

- *Widespread participation by enterprise staff in obtaining supplies and promoting sales.* Enterprises in Wuxi use three main methods: they designate permanent supply and sales personnel whose salary is fixed but who receive bonuses and whose hotel, food, and transport costs are covered by the firm; they hire part-time supply and sales personnel who receive a bonus for the amount of work they do but who are not recompensed for travel and lodging; and they hire temporary supply and sales person-nel who negotiate their terms with the enterprises.

- *Large bonuses.* Incomes of supply and sales personnel are generally several times higher than the average for all employees and may even exceed a factory director's salary. Some salespeople earn more than Y100,000 a year. Statistics from sample firms show that incomes of supply and sales personnel are still rising.

- *Ample funds.* In TVPs in Jieshou it is generally accepted that 3–5 percent of the value of purchased inputs or of products sold can be drawn out as operational fees and funds to gain access to supply and sales links. State enterprises, with their relatively stricter financial accounting inspection systems, cannot do this.

- *Exchange of agricultural and sideline products.* Shortages of and high prices for agricultural and sideline products have led TVPs to use them as quasi-currency. This practice enables TVPs to buy raw materials that even state enterprises find hard to get and to sell their substandard but high-priced goods to state commercial departments. In counties where TVPs are highly developed, agricultural and sideline products are often used as a medium for establishing cooperative ties with urban industrial bases.

- *Nonprice competition.* TVPs face an environment in which structural reforms in state enterprises are just starting. The problem of the soft budget constraint in traditional public ownership has yet to be solved. The shrinking of administrative controls and the strengthening of the profit motive for state enterprises under the reforms have led to rampant growth of activities such as barter trade, unplanned sales of products listed in the state plan, and speculation on commodity quotas at state prices. This environment provides an opportunity for TVPs to shift part of state enterprises' profits into their own hands by such means as giving sales commissions, paying sales agents, and making out blank invoices. Hence TVPs, whose backward technology is often coupled with high input costs, can sometimes outcompete state enterprises that have advanced technology and low input prices. Although TVPs have to pay much more for inputs, they boast higher economic benefits (see chapter 18). These factors have enabled TVPs to occupy a substantial share of the market for many industrial goods.

1984–Present: Market Expansion and Self-Supported Progress

TVP development in the early stages depended heavily on financial support from agriculture and on the abnormal growth in the supply of production inputs from agriculture. But by 1984 agriculture could no longer adequately support TVP growth. On the contrary, part of the profits from TVP industry came to be transferred to agriculture, especially in industrially developed regions like Wuxi. With the rapid development of TVP industry, agriculture fell into "sunset industry" status, dropping from its dominant role to secondary importance. In 1979–85 TVP industrial profits used to subsidize agriculture in all of Jiangsu Province totaled more than Y4 billion, accounting for about 30 percent of TVPs' after-tax profits. In the two years 1984 and 1985 in Wuxi, Dongjiang township alone allocated about Y6 million of industrial TVP profits to the construction of farm infrastructure and the mechanization of agriculture. Every mu of the more than 1,000 mu of arable land of Hujia village in Yanqiao township absorbed an investment of Y600 from the profits of TVP industry. In addition, community governments took part of TVP industrial profits to subsidize the prices of agricultural products and so stimulate agricultural production. The subsidy rate in southern Jiangsu was as high as Y0.5 per jin of rice.

Competition for labor also has become a serious problem in Wuxi, where 80 percent of the agricultural labor force is already engaged in TVP industry. In Dongjiang township local enterprises are forced to give ten days of leave to all their workers during the two harvest seasons every year, at a cost of Y7 million of output value and Y700,000 of profits. The impetus given to TVP industry by agriculture has obviously fallen short of needs.

Despite these problems, in 1984 and 1985 TVP industry not only did not shrink but achieved even higher growth rates. The main factors pushing growth during this period were the self-development of TVP industry and changes in microeconomic policies. Local policies in support of TVP industry were instituted. The county government in Jieshou, for instance, used promotion of TVPs as an important criterion for evaluating community government officials and required all townships to have two or three enterprises with an annual output value of Y30,000 by 1984. To supplement this strategy, financial aid, credits, and tax breaks were extended. The burgeoning private economy became an important element in the rapid development of TVP industry, especially in economically underdeveloped regions. The Central Committee's Document No. 1 of 1984 allowed private firms to hire workers and relaxed restrictions on them. This brought about a rapid development of private enterprises (see table 3-3).

New cooperative economic entities—farmers' joint cooperative enterprises ("partnerships")—have emerged. These enterprises are often initiated and financed by several households and hire varying numbers of workers. Farmers who hold stocks are both managers and producers. In addition to their normal wages they are entitled to dividends according to the number of shares owned. Shareholders tend to be relatives or fellow village members. These new firms are actually private in nature.

In underdeveloped regions the momentum for the development of the private economy has been all the stronger. Some local authorities, in drawing up their development scenarios, have pinned their hopes on relaxed political

Table 3-3. *Development of Private Enterprises, 1984–86*
(percentage of total for TVP sector)

Characteristic of private enterprise	1984		1985		1986	
	Number	Share	Number	Share	Number	Share
Number (thousands)	4,202.2	69.3	10,374.6	84.9	13,425.4	88.6
Partnerships	906.3	15.0	1,121.1	9.2	1,093.4	7.2
Individual firms	3,295.9	54.3	9,253.5	75.7	12,332.0	81.4
Employment (millions)	12.26	23.5	26.52	38.0	33.96	42.8
Partnerships	5.24	10.0	7.71	11.0	8.34	10.5
Individual firms	7.02	13.5	18.81	27.0	25.62	32.3
Output value (billions of yuan)	24.40	14.3	67.89	24.9	102.45	29.0
Partnerships	12.65	7.4	24.50	9.0	31.01	8.8
Individual firms	11.75	6.9	43.39	15.9	71.44	20.2

Sources: Information from fieldwork, and Ministry of Agriculture data.

controls and on encouragement of the private economy. The number of private enterprises in Shangrao, for example, more than doubled within one year as a result of such policies (see table 3-4). In Jieshou, of the 6,330 TVPs in 1985, private enterprises numbered 5,604, or 88.5 percent of the total. Underdeveloped regions like Jieshou have adopted four main supportive measures to encourage the private economy.

- *Relaxation of controls on registration.* Usually a person who applies to open a business gets approval within a week.
- *Changes in the residence system.* In Jieshou rural residents can buy urban resident status for Y20,000. Farmers are allowed to establish enterprises in urban areas on condition that they provide a certain amount of employment to urban residents.
- *Financial support.* A private enterprise can obtain bank loans if two well-managed enterprises act as its guarantors.
- *Assistance in making connections and signing contracts.* According to the rules set by the Shangrao County government, a private enterprise with less than Y200,000 annual output value can call itself a village firm, and a firm with more than Y200,000 annual output value can be called a county collective. These measures have increased the credibility of private enterprises.

Policies toward the private economy differ among localities. Wuxi relaxed controls on private enterprises for a short period in 1984, only to discover that private firms posed a threat to TVCEs. It soon reversed the policy. The county industrial and commercial bureau does not allow private enterprises to compete with state enterprises and TVCEs for raw materials, energy, technology, and human resources. Private transport firms are not allowed to hire

Table 3-4. *Ownership Structure of TVPs, Shangrao County, 1984–86*
(percent)

Type of TVP	Share of total number of TVPs			Increase over previous year	
	1984	1985	1986	1985	1986
Township enterprises	8.0	3.6	3.7	−2. 4	4.6
Village enterprises	12.0	5.3	5.4	−3. 8	3.6
Partnerships ⎱ Individual firms ⎰	80.0	91.1	{ 11.1 ⎱ 79.8 ⎰ }	150. 4	1.4
Total	100.0	100.0	100.0	119. 3	1.6

Source: Information from fieldwork.

workers, private construction firms are not allowed to take on public construction projects, and private industrial and commercial households are allowed to hire only one or two helpers and three to five apprentices. These restrictive policies and the predominance of the highly developed local TVCE sector have limited the development of private industry, and as a result it is unstable. In Wuxi in the first half of 1986, 2,120 business licenses were issued to private industrial and commercial households, but during the same period some 1,485 households stopped business operations. In the first six months of 1987 the number of licenses issued was 2,601, and 2,072 businesses stopped operations. TVCEs have always held the dominant position in Wuxi's TVP industry, accounting for more than 90 percent of total output value in 1985.

The second element that spurred the rapid development of TVP industry after 1984 was changes in the supply of funds. The 1984 policy of supporting the growth of TVPs led to a considerable relaxation of restrictions on bank loans and a consequent credit inflation that directly augmented the supply of funds to TVPs. In 1984 and 1985 national rural loans increased by 60 percent. Loans extended by local banks to TVPs in Jiangsu Province reached Y3.39 billion in 1984, an increase of 130 percent over the previous year. Similar increases occurred in Anhui Province. The proportion of loans provided by banks and credit cooperatives in total funds of sample firms in Wuxi was only about 1 percent in 1978 but 23 percent in 1984. For Jieshou's sample firms the 1985 figure was 37 percent, up about 10 percentage points from the previous year.

Controls on bank loan quotas in rural areas in 1985 seriously affected the volume of credit extended to TVPs. In May and June of 1985 a total of about Y300 million in bank loans was withdrawn throughout Jiangsu Province. In this situation TVPs began to search for new sources of funds, including local residents and cooperative investments. In 1985 TVPs all over China mobilized more than Y10 billion from these sources. According to statistics made available by Wuxi's Agricultural Bank, 65 percent of the money pooled by local

TVPs was obtained by squeezing bank savings, meaning that bank funds were still reaching TVPs through indirect channels.

The self-accumulation capacity of TVPs was also expanding. Between 1980 and 1985 total profits used to expand production in TVCEs rose by 68.5 percent, and the share of this investment in total profits rose from 49.7 to 51.4 percent. The share of profits reinvested in expansion by sample firms in Wuxi rose from 47.9 percent in 1980 to 57.5 percent in 1985. Overall, despite the reduction of agricultural funds in the capital of TVPs in 1984 and 1985 and the return of part of the profits of TVP industry to agriculture, the total supply of funds was enlarged owing to improvements in the functioning of financial markets and greater self-accumulation by TVPs.

Changes in product markets were perhaps an even more important factor in the speedy development of TVP industry during this period. As TVPs lack fixed channels for sales, they are susceptible to fluctuations in commodity markets. The loss of macroeconomic control in 1984, which caused an excessive growth of demand for both investment and consumer goods, provided an important stimulus to TVPs. Meanwhile, reforms in the system of mandatory purchases and sales by the state in urban areas allowed TVP products to enter urban commercial channels on a more stable basis.

With the development of TVP industry and the expansion of nonagricultural activities in rural areas, the share of agriculture has shrunk. In Jieshou in 1978 agriculture accounted for 57 percent of the total value of industrial and agricultural output, industry for only 43 percent. In 1984 the value of industrial output exceeded that of agriculture, and by 1985 the proportion of the value of industrial output in the total reached 55.2 percent. In Wuxi, a developed county, the production structure is much more industrialized, and the value of industrial output is more than eleven times as large as the value of agricultural output.

With these changes in the rural production structure, a new process of income generation has emerged in rural areas. TVP industry is increasingly important for the growth of farmers' incomes. During 1981–85, Y7.1 billion was transferred by TVPs to local production teams for distribution, and wages of workers in TVPs were Y123.3 billion. The two figures totaled more than Y130 billion, an average of Y326 per member of the rural labor force. Average per capita rural income, which was Y191 in 1980, jumped to Y397 in 1985. In 1985 wages of TVP workers reached Y47.3 billion, an average of Y675 per worker, accounting for 15 percent of average per capita rural income.

The rise in rural incomes brought about an increase in consumption and changes in the consumption structure. Between 1978 and 1985 the total volume of retail sales in rural areas of China grew by 238 percent. The annual growth rate of the consumption level of rural residents was 4 percent higher than that for urban residents. Meanwhile, there were three significant changes in rural consumption structure. (a) The value of purchased commodities (as opposed to self-produced goods) in the consumption of the rural population in Wuxi increased at about 20 percent a year. (b) The Engel coefficient in the consumption structure dropped by 10 percent. (c) Investment in housing rose; a total of 4.1 billion square meters in housing floor space was constructed in rural areas throughout the country between 1978 and 1985. At Y40 per square meter, this represented an estimated total investment of Y164 billion.

The growth of farmers' incomes since 1978 has enabled them to enter the consumption goods market. Rural demand stimulated the growth of TVPs that manufacture consumer goods, thus creating a new source of income for rural residents and further spurring their demand for consumer goods. Rapid production increases in TVPs that produce consumer goods stimulated the development of firms that manufacture investment goods and further increased rural incomes. While creating income for the rural population, TVP industry was building up an ever wider market for itself. These chain effects have become more and more conspicuous since 1984.

Prospects for the Future

Three basic elements stimulated the rapid growth of China's TVP industry between 1978 and 1985. Policy changes permitted key rural factors of production to shift to nonagricultural activities. Changes in the macroeconomic environment and in market conditions created space for the survival and expansion of TVP industry. And structural changes in TVP industry itself and the chain effects caused by the initial rise in agricultural incomes further spurred growth. At first, policy played the main role, but market conditions and structures assumed greater importance in the second stage of development. In developed regions market conditions have been dominant factors in the growth of TVP industry; in backward areas policy changes have been more important.

This analysis provides a starting point for a preliminary assessment of the prospects for the development of China's TVP industry. But it should first be noted that specific conditions—isolated urban and rural economies and separation of factor markets—gave birth to China's mode of rural industrialization: "leaving the land but not the village, entering the factory but not the city." TVPs have not yet completed the split from their mother—farming—and as a result they keep in close contact with the traditional rural social framework, the community. Most TVP workers still maintain the right to own and control land. Many are still engaged part-time in agricultural production. This incomplete shift of farmers to nonagricultural activities is characteristic of China's rural industrialization. Industrialization has moved ahead while urbanization has lagged behind. The newly created industrial organizations are still clinging to traditional agricultural structures. TVP development, as a realistic path to restructuring the rural production structure and transferring surplus agricultural labor to nonagricultural activities, is only one phase in the process of rural industrialization and is linked to particular historical conditions. With the deepening of economic reforms in urban and rural areas, a generalized market for factors of production will emerge, and TVPS will be included in the modern economic system on the basis of an organized, rapid pace of urbanization. From this long-term perspective, the current rapid growth of TVP industry is not a stable phenomenon.

TVP industry will face the following difficulties in the future:

• *Shortages of funds* (the biggest difficulty). During the eight years 1978–85 TVPs employed nearly 70 million laborers. The plan is for them to hire another 185 million workers in the fifteen years 1986–2000—about 50 percent of the total rural labor force. But the strengthening of the technological structure of TVP industry has brought about capital intensification much too early, and TVPs have paid an increasingly high price for employment generation. In 1979–84 each new employee cost TVCES Y3,361 of fixed assets; in 1985 TVCES had to provide Y5,347 of fixed assets for each new employee. On the basis of the 1985 figure, the transfer of 185 million agricultural laborers into nonagricultural activities would require an investment of Y989.2 billion, but the total net profits of TVPs in 1985 were only Y28.74 billion. Even if 40 percent were invested (which is quite generous), that would be only Y11.49 billion. If profits grew at 10 percent a year, the cumulative total would barely reach Y417.0 billion by 2000. Self-accumulation by TVPs therefore cannot realize the goal, and sufficient state financial aid and a favorable credit policy may not be forthcoming. A wide gap exists between the supply of and demand for funds for TVPs.

• *The progressive decline in the impact of resource mobilization and policy readjustment.* With the reform of state mandatory planning, economic resources in the hands of the central government have been reduced, and the government's ability to support the growth of TVPs by allocating additional resources is disappearing. The effect of policy readjustment will also diminish. The main reason for the unprecedented effect of the government's rural economic policies on TVP industry after 1978 is that the economy had amassed huge amounts of untapped potential during the long period before the reforms. Once policy restrictions were relaxed, this energy was released in a short time. But in the future the effect of policy changes will be progressively reduced.

• *Rapid increases in labor costs.* Much of China's economic takeoff is dependent on cheap labor in the countryside, but this labor cost advantage is dwindling at an alarming rate. Between 1978 and 1986 the total TVP wage bill increased 5.76 times, from Y8.7 billion to Y58.6 billion. Workers' per capita income increased 1.64 times, from Y306 to Y809. In 1978 workers' per capita income in Wuxi sample firms was Y456; by 1985 the figure had risen to Y1,261, higher than the income level of workers in state enterprises in the same area. Wage increases in the relatively developed areas seem excessive. If the national average income of TVP workers could be fixed at the 1985 level, Y172.38 billion in pay—2.65 times the present level—would be needed to enable the nonagricultural sector to absorb 185 million members of the rural labor force. To bear this tremendous labor cost and maintain the present profit rate, TVP industry would have to increase its output value by Y723 billion. Under such circumstances, resource bottlenecks are likely to become even more severe.

• *Worsened market conditions as a result of sharp competition.* The rapid growth of TVP industry in 1984–85 depended partly on a market bloated by the loss of macroeconomic control and conceded by state enterprises owing to their lack of vitality. But reforms in state enterprises will change their organizational form and property relations so as to hold down their demand and build up their competitive strength. TVPs will then no longer be the sole beneficiaries of the expansion of the market mechanism, and their favorable market opportunities will gradually diminish. At present the industrial and product structure of TVPs is highly similar to that of state enterprises. Equal competition in the same market space will be disadvantageous to TVPs, which are plagued by low technological levels and poor product quality.

• *Obstructions in the organization of TVPs themselves.* The most basic organizational characteristic of TVPs is their dependence on the rural community, as reflected in the deep involvement of community governments in enterprise management. With the rapid development of TVP industry, this kind of administrative interference affects firms adversely. Although TVP investments are based partly on the profit motive, the motive of regional development is much stronger. A dispersed regional development pattern will lead to a shortage of working capital and irrational distribution of industries, and TVPs in general will suffer the consequences of being uncompetitive and uneconomically small in scale. Local governments' objective of solving employment problems tends to prevent the rational movement of human resources and leads to the coexistence of overstaffing and shortages of workers in TVPs, especially in developed regions. Furthermore, the system of ownership by community governments gives birth to unreasonable distribution mechanisms. In Wuxi, for example, a township draws, on average, Y1.2 million–Y1.6 million a year in administrative and social welfare expenditures from TVPs' profits—equal to roughly 45 percent of their after-tax profits. With the heavy burden of community government finances on their shoulders, TVPs will be plagued by obstructions to their development.

4

Development Patterns in Four Counties

Jan Svejnar and Josephine Woo

The TVP sector has become increasingly important in China's economic development. But there is great geographic diversity in TVP performance. Our research project looked at four counties: Wuxi in the Yangtze River Delta, Nanhai in the Pearl River Delta, Jieshou, about 500 kilometers inland on the North China Plain, and Shangrao, in a valley to the north of the Wuyi mountain ranges. There is much disparity in their economic conditions, with Jieshou and Shangrao lagging far behind Wuxi and Nanhai (table 4-1).

Table 4-2 shows some of the exogenous factors that influence the development and the relative strength of TVPs in each county. Wuxi and Nanhai are more favorably endowed in many respects than are Jieshou and Shangrao. Nanhai does not have as strong an industrial base as Wuxi, but it has greater access to capital and to foreign technology. Shangrao has some advantage over the other counties in mineral resources, but it is poorly endowed otherwise. The availability of skilled labor and of technical and management skills is linked to the level of local industrial development, and in this respect Wuxi and Nanhai are clearly better off than Jieshou and Shangrao.

Although these exogenous conditions were important for the initial development of TVPs, county authorities have been extremely influential in fostering (or preventing) particular forms of TVP development. Some have been ardent supporters of TVCEs, while others have promoted private enterprise or pursued a more balanced approach toward enterprise ownership. In some cases, mainly because of factors beyond their control, local authorities have been unable to provide any support to TVP development.

In this chapter we undertake a descriptive analysis of the structure and functioning of the TVP sector in the four counties. Our goal is to identify the principal features that have influenced TVP development and to provide a conceptual framework for interpreting the main findings. We describe the characteristics of the TVP sector in the four counties, identify the chief determinants of TVP development patterns, and present some implications of TVP experience.

Table 4-1. County Data, 1985

Item	Wuxi	Jieshou	Nanhai	Shangrao
Population (millions)	1.02	0.57	0.85	0.70
Area (square kilometers)	960	667	1,153	2,490
Administrative divisions				
Townships[a]	36	33	16	31
Villages	586	433	236	343
Teams	9,518	3,981	3,328	3,782
County GVAIO (millions of yuan, 1980 prices)	4,680	257	2,541	211
County GVIO[b]	4,331	148	2,182	50
GVIO of TVPs[c]	3,650	104	1,518	27

Note: GVAIO, gross value of agricultural and industrial output; GVIO, gross value of industrial output.
a. Includes township-level but not village-level towns.
b. Including the output of township, village, production team, and private firms.
c. 1986 data for Nanhai; estimate for Jieshou.
Source: Information from fieldwork.

Table 4-2. Influences on TVP Development

Item	Favorable 5	4	3	Less favorable 2	1
Local manufacturing industries	WX	NH		JS	SR
Proximity to large cities	WX, NH			JS, SR	
Natural resources					
Agricultural		WX, NH		SR	JS
Mineral		SR			WX, NH, JS
Human resources					
Technical and management skills	WX	NH		JS	SR
Skilled labor	WX, NH		JS		SR
Local labor supply (1 = shortage)	WX, NH				JS, SR
Access to capital	NH	WX		JS	SR
Access to foreign technology	NH	WX	JS		SR

Note: WX = Wuxi; NH = Nanhai; JS = Jieshou; SR = Shangrao.

Characteristics of the TVP Sector in the Sample Counties

This section describes the main characteristics of TVPs that are relevant for our analysis: size, sectoral composition, industrial structure, ownership, growth, performance, and experience with foreign trade and investment.

Figure 4-1. *The Relative Sizes of the TVP Sectors in the Four Sample Counties, 1985–86*

Index (Wuxi = 100)

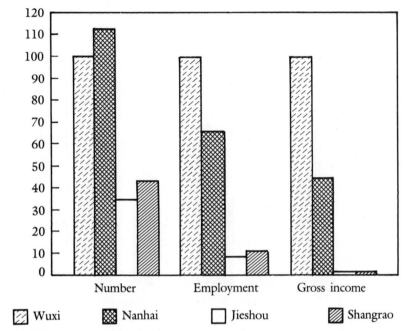

| | Wuxi | | Nanhai | | Jieshou | | Shangrao |

Source: Information from fieldwork.

Size

Figure 4-1 shows the relative size of the TVP sector in each county in 1985–86. In number of enterprises, employment, and gross income, the TVP sector in Jieshou and Shangrao is much smaller than in Wuxi and Nanhai. In terms of industrial TVCEs (figure 4-2) Wuxi is clearly superior to the other counties. Its TVPs contributed 84 percent of the total gross value of industrial output (GVIO) of the county in 1985; in Nanhai and Jieshou the corresponding shares were about 70 percent, and in Shangrao the share was only 54 percent. The average size of TVPs, especially TVCEs, is large in Wuxi and Nanhai compared with Jieshou and Shangrao (see chapter 5 for details).

Sectoral Composition

Industrial activities, as measured by TVP gross output value, are predominant in all four counties, but the service sector has a large number of firms, especially in Nanhai and Shangrao. In Wuxi industrial TVPs accounted for 74

Figure 4-2. *The Relative Size of the Industrial TVCE Sector in the Four Sample Counties, 1985–86*

Index (Wuxi = 100)

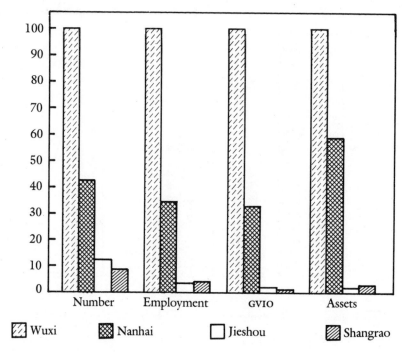

Source: Information from fieldwork.

percent of the total number of TVPs and the same percentage of gross output value in 1984, whereas the service sector accounted for 22 percent of the number of enterprises and the same share of gross output value. In Nanhai industrial firms constituted only 40 percent of the total number of TVPs in 1986, but they contributed 83 percent of total gross output value. By contrast, services have a much larger share in the total number of TVPs (50 percent) than in gross output value (10 percent). In Jieshou in 1985 industrial TVPs accounted for a large share of both the number of firms (66 percent) and the value of gross output (83 percent). In Shangrao in 1986 the share of industry in the number of TVPs (50 percent) was higher than in Nanhai, but its share of the value of gross output of TVPs was only 57 percent. Transport and construction enterprises had a relatively large share in both the number of firms (21 percent) and the value of gross output (32 percent), and other services also had a significant share—30 percent of the number of firms and 11 percent of the value of gross output.

Industrial Structure

The share of heavy industry in the GVIO of industrial TVCEs is much higher in Wuxi (75 percent) than in Nanhai (44 percent). The machinery subsector is the largest in Wuxi, contributing 49 percent of total GVIO, followed by textiles, which accounts for about 17 percent, and chemicals and construction materials. In Nanhai the largest subsector is textiles (29 percent), followed by machinery (21 percent) and construction materials (11 percent)'. In Shangrao the share of heavy industry is high (60 percent), but in contrast to Wuxi it is concentrated in the mining and construction materials subsectors (18 percent and 31 percent respectively), and the machinery subsector is insignificant (2 percent). There is hardly any manufacturing industry in Shangrao, and most light industrial activities are in food processing (11 percent), leather processing (11 percent), and traditional handicrafts. In Jieshou the most important industrial subsectors are construction materials (52 percent, mainly bricks) and food processing (20 percent). Jieshou's machinery and textile subsectors have higher shares than those in Shangrao.

Products of TVPs range from handicrafts to rather sophisticated industrial equipment. In Jieshou, where the industrial base is weak, the main TVP activities are brick manufacturing, traditional handicrafts such as making pottery and weaving bamboo and reeds, simple food processing such as manufacturing beef jerky and imitation protein food, and textile operations such as hand knitting. The skills for such operations are easy to acquire, and in some instances residents of an entire village or district specialize in making a single product. These types of operation have started to appear in Shangrao (for example, comb production in Huangshi township), but much of the nonagricultural labor force there is engaged in coal and other mining and in hydropower generation. There is hardly any local manufacturing activity, and surplus labor goes outside the county to seek work in the service sectors, such as construction and repair. By contrast, many TVPs in Nanhai and Wuxi are engaged in production that requires a higher level of skill and technology. Some produce household appliances (such as electric fans) and electronic equipment (recorders and calculators) for both domestic and foreign markets. Many have contracts with state enterprises or, in the case of Nanhai, with foreign partners. In some areas, such as Wuxi, TVPs have become keen competitors with state enterprises. Some TVP machinery products in Wuxi (for instance, printing and dyeing equipment in Qianzhou) already have won a large share of the domestic market.

Ownership Structure

The ownership structure of the TVP sector in the four counties varies greatly (figure 4-3). In Wuxi TVCEs are predominant: they constituted 36 percent of the total number of industrial TVPs and contributed almost 96 percent of

Figure 4-3. *The Ownership Structure of TVPs, 1985*

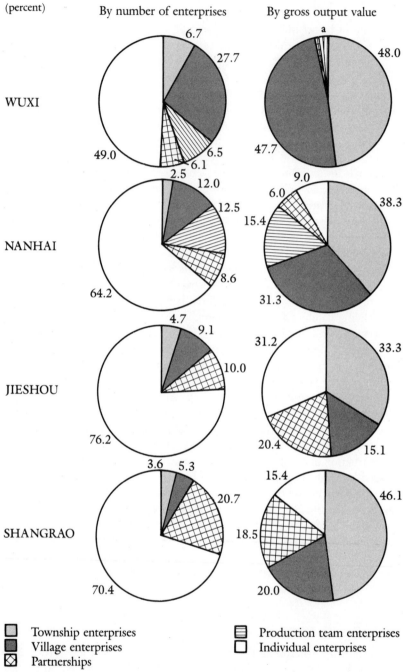

(percent)

By number of enterprises

By gross output value

WUXI

NANHAI

JIESHOU

SHANGRAO

Township enterprises

Village enterprises

Partnerships

Production team enterprises

Individual enterprises

a. Partnerships, 1.0 percent; production team enterprises, 1.6 percent; individual enterprises, 1.8 percent.

Source: Information from fieldwork.

GVIO in 1985. Development in Nanhai is more evenly spread among the various forms of TVPs, and private enterprises have a much larger share in the TVP sector than do their counterparts in Wuxi. In both Jieshou and Shangrao the share of TVCEs in the total number of TVPs is relatively small, although their share in gross income is large, especially in Shangrao. Individual proprietorships in Jieshou have a larger share in the TVP sector than in the other three counties. No production team firms are recorded in the available data for Jieshou and Shangrao, which suggests that privatization of these enterprises has occurred in these counties. Many production team enterprises in Nanhai are actually run like private enterprises, and some are contracted to individuals. (In addition, many private enterprises are registered as community enterprises in all four counties, especially in Jieshou; see chapter 7.)

Growth

In 1980–85 the gross income of TVCEs in China grew at an annual rate of 25.1 percent. With the exception of Shangrao, the counties in our sample registered growth rates above the national average during the same period (see table 4-3). TVCEs in both Wuxi and Nanhai showed continuous increases in employment and gross income, with gross income growing much faster than employment. In Jieshou development has been somewhat erratic: a decline in 1980–81, a sharp increase in 1984, and a drop in 1985. This may be partly attributable to the inconsistency of data over time, especially between 1983 and 1984. In Shangrao data for earlier years are not available, but in 1984–86 both employment and gross income of TVCEs grew steadily, the former faster than the latter.

Private enterprises have also grown rapidly over the past few years. In Wuxi the number of individual enterprises increased sharply in 1983 and continued to rise in 1984, but growth slowed in 1985–86. In Nanhai the number of individual enterprises more than doubled in 1982, almost quadrupled in 1983, and continued to grow at high rates through 1984–86. In Wuxi development of TVCEs is emphasized at the expense of the private sector, whereas in Nanhai development of all forms of TVPs is encouraged. In Jieshou the number of individual proprietorships surged in 1981 and continued to grow at high rates in 1982–85. In Shangrao the number of individual enterprises increased by 15 percent in 1986 over 1985.

In Wuxi the first surge in the growth of TVCEs occurred in 1979–80; a slowdown followed in 1981–82. Another surge, in 1983, was followed by accelerated growth in 1984–85 and somewhat slower growth in 1986. In Nanhai the pattern was roughly the same. Development of the TVP sector in Jieshou and Shangrao did not take off until 1984. The first surge in the growth of the TVP sector in Wuxi and Nanhai coincided with the initial changes that occurred after the Third Plenum of the Eleventh Central Committee endorsed, in December 1978, a program for accelerating growth in rural areas.[1]

Table 4-3. Growth of TVCEs, 1979–86
(annual average percentage growth)

Item	Wuxi	Jieshou	Nanhai	Shangrao	All China
By number of enterprises					
1979	4.6	n.a.	59.0	n.a.	−2.9
1980	11.2	−8.0	−9.6	n.a.	−3.7
1981	−3.4	−22.4	16.6	n.a.	−6.1
1982	−1.0	34.1	11.2	n.a.	1.8
1983	16.1	4.4	−4.9	n.a.	−1.1
1984	35.9	240.3	n.a.	n.a.	22.4
1985	22.2	−6.0	n.a.	−3.2	−4.9
1986	11.4	33.9	−2.2	4.0	−3.8
1980–85	13.0	28.3	13.1	n.a.	1.9
By employment					
1979	17.7	n.a.	4.2	n.a.	2.9
1980	11.1	3.8	6.4	n.a.	3.1
1981	7.6	−25.8	1.3	n.a.	−1.0
1982	7.6	28.9	8.6	n.a.	4.8
1983	18.2	0.8	3.1	n.a.	3.9
1984	22.2	187.6	12.6	n.a.	19.0
1985	23.5	−17.3	12.2	37.0	7.9
1986	31.6	4.9	6.9	2.5	5.8
1980–85	15.6	18.1	7.5	n.a.	6.7
By gross income					
1979	28.9	0.0	16.9	n.a.	13.8
1980	48.6	0.0	22.9	n.a.	21.4
1981	14.6	16.7	43.7	n.a.	12.5
1982	5.9	14.3	11.1	n.a.	15.1
1983	27.9	25.0	16.9	n.a.	20.3
1984	59.4	413.0	n.a.	n.a.	36.6
1985	70.4	−12.1	n.a.	13.2	44.1
1986	17.2	n.a.	21.7	9.3	21.7
1980–85	33.3	49.7	36.4	n.a.	25.1

Sources: Estimates based on information from fieldwork; State Statistical Bureau (1982), pp. 194–95; (1983), pp. 206–07; (1984), pp. 184–85; (1985a), pp. 297–98; (1986a), p. 177; (1987a), pp. 226–27.

Two aspects were particularly significant for the development of the TVP sector: promotion of nonagricultural sideline activities to augment farm households' incomes and the decision to raise procurement prices for agricultural products, which also helped increase rural incomes. These factors seem to have had an immediate positive impact on TVP development in Wuxi and Nanhai, but they did not have any such effect in Jieshou and Shangrao in 1979–81. In 1984, however, there was a surge in TVP development in all four counties after central government directives reiterated support for rural reforms, stressing the need for diversified rural activities and specifically for the development of TVPs as a means of providing employment and raising the living standards of the rural population.[2]

Performance

The overall performance of the TVP sector in Wuxi and Nanhai has been far better than in Jieshou and Shangrao (table 4-4). Labor productivity is similar in TVCEs in Wuxi and Nanhai, but profit per worker is much higher in Wuxi. One reason may be that Nanhai firms are more capital-intensive, as indicated by higher gross fixed assets per worker. Data on enterprises in our sample (table 4-5), as well as aggregate county data, suggest that TVPs in Nanhai rely more on bank loans to finance their operations than do enterprises in Wuxi, and interest payments may eat up some of the profits. Moreover, wages are higher in Nanhai, which adds to production costs. Average production costs for township enterprises in Nanhai were 84 percent of sales revenue in 1985, compared with 65 percent in Wuxi. Both Nanhai and Wuxi are advanced counties in their respective provinces, with profit rates much higher than provincial averages. Their TVCEs also perform much better than the average for China.

Gross income per worker for TVCEs in Jieshou is only about 32 percent of that in Nanhai, and profit per worker is about 35 percent. Jieshou enterprises are below the national average in labor productivity, but in return to capital they seem to do relatively well, even in comparison with Nanhai. In Shangrao gross income per worker is only 19 percent that in Nanhai and profit per worker a mere 10 percent; both are below national averages. In their respective provinces, enterprises in Jieshou perform better than the average TVCE, and enterprises in Shangrao do worse. Data on sample enterprises suggest that TVPs in Jieshou are more capital-intensive than in Shangrao, and profitability is also much higher in Jieshou. Production cost as a percentage of sales revenue is similar in Jieshou and Shangrao and close to that in Nanhai for the enterprises in our samples. Average wages are about the same in Jieshou and Shangrao.

The Role of Foreign Trade and Investment

Foreign trade and investment in the TVP sector are highly significant in Nanhai (table 4-6). In Wuxi they are also increasingly important, but in Jieshou and Shangrao their role is small. In all four counties the contribution of TVPs to total county exports is large—about half of total export procurement volume in Wuxi and Nanhai and even more in Jieshou and Shangrao.

From the perspective of TVPs, however, the export market is far less important than the domestic market. In Wuxi total export procurement from TVPs in 1985 was probably about Y60 million,[3] or less than 2 percent of their GVIO.

Table 4-4. *Performance of TVCEs, 1985*

Item	Wuxi	Jieshou	Nanhai	Shangrao	All China
Gross income per worker (yuan)[a]	10,996	3,439	10,996	2,049	4,401
Gross fixed assets per worker (yuan)	2,496	968	3,396	1,001	1,807
Profits per worker (yuan)[b]	1,337	335	944	95	413
Ratio of gross income to fixed assets	4.4	3.6	3.2	2.0	2.4
Profits as a percentage of fixed assets	53.6	34.8	27.8	9.5	22.8
(Profits + taxes) ÷ fixed assets (percent)[c]	80.1	48.2	49.0	15.4	37.3

a. Wuxi data represents gross output for industrial TVCEs only.
b. Total net profit after deduction of income tax.
c. Total net profit plus sales and income taxes divided by undepreciated fixed assets valued at original purchase prices.
Sources: State Statistical Bureau (1986a), p. 177, and information from fieldwork.

Table 4-5. *Performance of Sample Township Enterprises*

Item	Wuxi	Jieshou	Nanhai	Shangrao
Gross output per worker (yuan)	30,340	17,739	19,015	2,507
Gross fixed assets per worker (yuan)	5,633	3,811	5,526	2,147
Profit per worker (yuan)	4,783	1,450	1,934	293
Ratio of gross output to fixed assets	5.4	4.7	3.4	1.2
Profits as a percentage of fixed assets	84.9	38.1	35.0	13.7
(Profit + taxes) ÷ fixed assets (percent)	108.6	66.2	66.1	23.0
Production cost ÷ sales revenue (percent)	65.2	81.7	86.8	84.0
Bank loans ÷ total funds used (percent)	18.3	25.5	47.3	17.9
Average monthly income of workers (yuan)	102	59	174	62

Note: Includes town-run enterprises. There are twenty-three observations for Wuxi, twelve for Nanhai, seventeen for Jieshou, and twenty-six for Shangrao.
Source: Enterprise Quantitative Questionnaire.

The percentage was the same in Jieshou. In Shangrao the share of TVP exports in the total gross income of TVPs was at most 3–4 percent. In Nanhai the export market is relatively more important; 1986 export procurement from TVPs totaled Y247 million, or about 11 percent of their total gross income. Export procurement as a share of total TVP output in Nanhai actually declined until 1986, when slow sales on the domestic market and tight do-

Table 4-6. Foreign Trade and Investment

Item	Wuxi, 1985	Jieshou, 1985	Nanhai, 1986	Shangrao, 1986
Foreign trade procurement				
(millions of yuan)[a]	100	4.8	477	3.6
From TVPs	29	3.3	247	n.a.[b]
Processing income (millions of				
U.S dollars)[c]	n.a.	n.a.	42	n.a.

a. Value of procurement by foreign trade departments. The estimate for Wuxi includes procurement through channels other than the county foreign trade bureau (for example, Shanghai and Wuxi municipality); the figure for Wuxi TVPs represents only procurement from TVPs by the county foreign trade bureau. The figure for Jieshou TVPs represents output value rather than procurement value. For Shangrao the amount includes exports through Shanghai as well as through the foreign trade departments of Shangrao prefecture.

b. Although the exact amount of procurement from TVPs is not available, information obtained in fieldwork indicates that the exports of Shangrao County depend largely on TVPs.

c. Income received for processing material supplied by foreign partners.

Source: Information from fieldwork.

mestic credit forced firms to look outward for market channels as well as financial resources.

Because of Nanhai's proximity to Hong Kong, the foreign sector has a much more important role than in the other three counties. In 1980–86 foreign investment in the county totaled US$92 million, of which US$27 million went into joint ventures and US$64 million was for processing arrangements. When the central government imposed a tight credit policy in 1985–86, the county government encouraged village and team firms to seek foreign capital through compensation trade and through processing materials for foreign companies. As a result, total processing income increased from US$10.6 million in 1985 to US$42 million in 1986. Many TVPs, including some production team firms, partnerships, and individual enterprises, established direct foreign contacts through relatives or other social connections.

In Wuxi there is some inflow of capital from other parts of the country, but the level of foreign investment has been much lower than in Nanhai. This is partly attributable to administrative restrictions against direct foreign contacts by TVPs. In Jieshou there are a few joint ventures that involve foreign capital; in Shangrao there are none.

The Factors That Determine Patterns of Development

The size, structure, and performance of the TVP sector in each county depend greatly on geographic and historical factors, the availability and types of local resources, the quality and size of the local labor force, access to technology and capital, and the policies pursued by the central and especially the local government.

Geography and History

The size of the TVP sector is closely linked to the level of development of the local economy. Per capita indicators illustrate the disparity among the four counties (table 4-7). In Wuxi and Nanhai there are more market channels, greater access to different types of resources (including physical inputs, financial resources, and technology), and larger demand for manufactured products and for a wide range of services. These counties can therefore make better use of opportunities that arise. This partly explains why the TVP sector in Wuxi was able to take off as early as 1979–80, soon after the central government's policy shift toward diversified economic development in rural areas. To capture the conditions of the TVP sector in each county, we need a historical overview.

Wuxi County is located in southern Jiangsu Province in the hinterlands of Shanghai. The area has been highly developed since the Song Dynasty (960–1279) and has many small cities and urban clusters. It is rich in agriculture and has a strong industrial base. In 1985 Shanghai city and Jiangsu Province together contributed 18 percent of China's gross value of agricultural and industrial output (GVAIO) and 21 percent of its GVIO. In 1985 Jiangsu led all other provinces in China in the GVIO of construction materials, food and beverages, textiles, leather products, furniture, chemicals, plastics, and electronics. It also has an advanced machinery manufacturing industry and many art and handicraft products.[4] Wuxi municipality, located in the middle

Table 4-7. *Per Capita Indicators, 1985*
(yuan, except as specified)

Item	Wuxi	Jieshou	Nanhai	Shangrao	All China
Cultivated land per capita (mu)	0.88	1.2	0.94	0.67	1.39
Average per capita income of rural population[a]	754	285	1,029	322	398
GVAIO per capita[b]	4,588	452	2,989	300	1,164
GVIO per capita[b]	4,246	260	2,567	71	885
GVAO per capita[c]	342	192	422	229	279

Note: GVAO, gross value of agricultural output.

a. Includes income from all sources, including nonagricultural activities and employment in TVPs.

b. Includes the output of TVPs.

c. Excludes the output of TVPs.

Sources: Information from fieldwork; State Statistical Bureau (1986a), pp. 4, 132, 233, 583.

of Wuxi County and since 1983 the supervisory level of government for the county's administration, is an important city in the area.

The county's strong agricultural and industrial base has helped foster development of the TVP sector. Rich agricultural produce supplied the raw materials for many TVP food-processing and textile industries. Advanced industrial development in the surrounding areas provided opportunities for TVPs to engage in processing work for large state or urban collective factories or to pick up products that these factories no longer considered profitable to produce. Moreover, the management and technical skills that had been built up in the area over the years could be drawn on to support the development of TVP industry.

An important impetus for TVP development in Wuxi came from the cadres, workers, and educated youths who returned there during the Cultural Revolution, many bringing skills learned in their previous jobs in Shanghai and other cities. Prompted partly by the need to find work and partly by the shortage of supplies as many urban factories stopped production at the height of the Cultural Revolution, they established TVPs in rural areas.

In the early 1970s, after an intense debate, county authorities decided not to abandon TVPs, even though in accordance with the spirit of the times they stressed the development of agriculture and grain production. By the late 1970s TVP industrial development in Wuxi was far ahead of that in the other counties.

Nanhai County is located in a highly developed and urbanized area about 20 kilometers from Guangzhou. Like Wuxi, Nanhai stretches around a municipality (Foshan) that was given administrative leadership over the county in 1983. The county has several well-developed towns. The area's agriculture produces enough to support its own population and to export a substantial quantity of products to Hong Kong. There were many small factories in the area before 1949, including the first modern silk mill in China, but the industrial base is much smaller than in Wuxi. The GVIO (including output of village industry) of Guangdong Province was only 50 percent of Jiangsu's in 1985, and the output of its machinery subsector was only 42 percent. Light industry, especially food processing and textiles, is predominant. (The proportion of light and heavy industry in total GVIO was 67:33 in Guangdong in 1985 and 56:44 in Jiangsu.) As in Wuxi, the rural areas benefited from the return during the Cultural Revolution of skilled workers who began to set up their own factories in the countryside. Although Nanhai authorities permitted these factories, they apparently took a less active role than their counterparts in Wuxi in fostering TVCEs. Hence TVPs in Nanhai tend to be on a smaller scale. The county enterprise sector is weaker and the private sector is stronger than in Wuxi.

Jieshou County is located on the North China Plain at the western border of Anhui Province, in a less favored area than Wuxi and Nanhai. The region is subject to periodic floods and droughts, with serious consequences for agricultural output. In good years harvests are adequate for export to other regions; in bad years, as in 1985, the area has to be subsidized by grain allocated by the state, and there are severe reductions in personal incomes. (The average per capita income of the rural population dropped from Y345 in 1984 to Y285 in 1985, mainly because of the bad harvest.) The area is much further inland than Wuxi and Nanhai and has hardly any industrial base. In 1984 Jieshou's GVIO (excluding village industry) was only 6 percent of Wuxi's and 10 percent of Nanhai's.

Of the four counties, only Jieshou has its own county seat. During the war with Japan in the 1930s and 1940s Jieshou town, which was not under Japanese occupation, prospered as a commercial center. Although its prosperity diminished after the war, some commercial traditions have been retained. The area has one of the four important livestock markets in China. Local people engage extensively in marketing activities. They are willing to travel long distances to get supplies and sell products, going as far as Nepal, for instance, to sell locally produced nylon ropes. The development pattern of the TVP sector in Jieshou is somewhat similar to that in Wenzhou, a coastal prefecture in Fujian Province; there too, local resources are lacking, but marketing activities have brought prosperity to residents.

The TVP sector in Jieshou seems to have performed better than that of *Shangrao County*. Compared with Jieshou, Shangrao was historically more isolated, being hidden away in a valley among mountain ridges. Although it is now easily accessible by railroad, it is not a commercial center as Jieshou once was, and it is not usually a place where people stop to do business. In 1964 Shangrao County was separated from Shangrao city under the principle, prevalent at the time, that the city should concentrate on industrial development and the county on agriculture. Unlike Wuxi or Foshan cities, however, Shangrao city had poorly developed industries that failed to exert leadership in the industrial development of the vicinity. The share of agricultural output (excluding village industry) in the total GVAIO of Shangrao County exceeded 75 percent in 1984 and 1985. Most of the county's industries are resource-based, tapping rich coal deposits and construction materials. Almost every township has a few hydropower stations, but many are running losses because of poor management. Some of the county's so-called TVPs are administrative establishments set up to manage labor teams that go outside the county to work on construction and repair jobs. Few commercial activities and services are carried out within the county, although a market for ramie fiber thrived in Shaxi town in 1984–86.

Human Resources and Technology

More than 60 percent of the rural labor force in both Wuxi and Nanhai now works in industry. To supplement local labor, both counties have hired workers from outside—about 40,000 in Nanhai and 10,000 in Wuxi. This represents a great achievement in both counties, where until the late 1970s and early 1980s an important incentive for TVP development had been to find jobs for local residents. By contrast, in neither Jieshou nor Shangrao are there enough industrial and other activities to absorb surplus labor from agriculture, and providing employment for the local population is an important consideration for county authorities. The employment problem seems greater for Shangrao's TVPs than for Jieshou's. Many of the former are overmanned, which adversely affects their performance and profitability. In Wuxi, county authorities prefer that TVPs become more capital-intensive rather than increase the number of workers hired from outside, since migrants from outside the county bring with them a number of social problems. Nanhai has a freer labor market and a larger number of workers from outside the county.

As discussed above, TVPs in both Wuxi and Nanhai derived much of their initial technical strength from workers who returned to rural areas in the 1960s and 1970s. These people brought with them not only their technical and management skills but also their networks of social connections, which were essential in obtaining market information and other assistance as the TVP sector expanded in later years. The proximity of these two counties to the large cities of Shanghai and Guangzhou provided TVPs with opportunities to get technical assistance in various ways—for example, by offering short- or long-term employment to workers retiring from city factories or part-time work to technicians in the city and researchers in nearby academic institutions. Nanhai also has easier access to foreign technology, through joint ventures and processing arrangements, than does Wuxi.

Neither Jieshou nor Shangrao has such advantages in access to technical skills and production technology. Many of Jieshou's TVPs are households and small firms that specialize in traditional handicrafts and simple food processing—activities requiring little technical skill. Local residents in Jieshou are rather entrepreneurial, however, and many have taken initiatives to develop new lines of products. They are willing to invest in learning new technology or in sending people to more advanced areas (such as southern Jiangsu and Guangzhou) to be trained. They are also responsive to the market, switching quickly to other products as soon as the market becomes saturated with their old products. Through their connections they obtain information on new technologies and products.

By contrast, people in Shangrao seem more risk averse. Their main industrial activities are tied to natural resources, and only recently have they started to develop handicraft industries. They are less attuned to the market than in Jieshou. Those who work outside the county engage mostly in manual work rather than in marketing. The county also suffers from a severe brain drain; many of its secondary school graduates who go on to college never return to work in Shangrao. In recent years TVPs in Shangrao began trying to obtain technology by striking up joint ventures or other arrangements with entrepreneurs or institutions in nearby Zhejiang Province and in southern

Jiangsu. Unlike Jieshou, the county has no joint ventures involving foreign investment and not a single piece of imported equipment.

Access to Capital

The relatively advanced development and good performance of TVPs in Wuxi and Nanhai offer opportunities for higher returns to capital, and as a result outside financial institutions are willing to invest in them. For instance, in 1984 Wuxi was able to bring in Y40 million in loans from branches of the Agricultural Bank and the Industrial and Commercial Bank in other regions, and a Beijing-based development company came to the county to seek investment opportunities. Moreover, higher per capita incomes lead to an increase in bank deposits, providing a larger base for loans. Some TVCES in Wuxi have issued bonds to finance their investments.

Nanhai has the additional advantage of easier access to foreign capital. The sources of foreign exchange include compensation trade, processing arrangements, and joint ventures, as well as remittances from friends and relatives in Hong Kong and overseas. During 1980–86 the Bank of China lent US$7.8 million, mostly short term, to TVPs in Nanhai. Personal incomes are higher in Nanhai than in Wuxi, partly because government policies in Wuxi have sought to minimize the difference between the incomes of agricultural and industrial labor. Overseas remittances and proximity to Hong Kong also raise incomes in Nanhai. Financial institutions are more flexible, and the banks may be more active in mobilizing funds than in Wuxi. In 1986 Nanhai obtained Y100 million in short-term interbank loans from financial institutions outside the county. Enterprises as well as individuals seem to make more use of banking services than in Wuxi. Personal savings per capita in 1984 were Y588 in Nanhai and Y154 in Wuxi. TVPs borrowed about Y900 million of bank loans in 1986, compared with Y574 million in Wuxi.

In Jieshou and Shangrao the amount of loans available for TVPs is not small in relation to the size of their TVP sectors. In Jieshou many government departments, including the finance bureau, tax bureau, supply and marketing cooperative, and foreign trade department, assist TVPs in meeting their capital requirements. In Shangrao in the past local banks were forced to lend to many unviable TVP projects, especially small hydropower stations. As a result, almost half of the value of outstanding loans in Shangrao in 1986 consisted of bad debts and overdue payments. Banks have become conservative in their lending policies and do not make maximum use of available funds.

TVPs in all four counties complained about the shortage of funds. New loans for TVPs were reduced in 1985 as a result of central government efforts to control investment and consumption in the country as a whole. This somewhat dampened the growth of the TVP sector, but growth continued at a remarkably high rate in all four counties. In Nanhai the tightening of domestic credit induced increased use of foreign capital by TVPs, which seems to have been beneficial to their development.

Government Policies and Strategies

As mentioned above, central government policies have had a significant impact on the growth of the TVP sector. With the Great Leap Forward in 1958 some beginnings were made in rural industrialization, but many of the investments turned out to be wasteful. During the Cultural Revolution grain production was emphasized at the expense of other rural activities; some enterprises, however, were set up in rural areas at the commune and brigade levels, mainly to support agricultural development by providing machinery and tools. Rapid development of the TVP sector occurred after 1978, at first somewhat sporadically as a sequel of rural reforms but later with the encouragement of the central government.

Rural reforms affected TVP development in several ways. The PRS allowed farmers to engage in other activities as long as they fulfilled the terms of their contracts; the reduction of grain procurement quotas relaxed the need for labor-intensive triple cropping and so freed labor for other activities; the increase in agricultural output, especially of cash crops, provided raw materials for TVPs; and the increase in rural incomes helped finance the growth of TVPs. For these reasons the timing of rural reforms in each locality influenced local TVP development.

The first of the four counties to adopt the PRS was Jieshou, in 1981. (Provincial leaders in Anhui Province had endorsed the PRS in the late 1970s and supported its implementation through the initial debates on these issues; see Wu Xiang 1986.) In 1982 individual firms and private partnerships started to develop rapidly. In Wuxi and Nanhai widespread implementation of the PRS began only in 1982, after the system was officially endorsed by the central government.[5] In Wuxi, however, the gradual reduction of triple cropping after 1978 had provided an impetus for the rapid development of the TVCE industrial sector. Partly because of the success of industrial TVCEs, local authorities were reluctant to encourage development of private enterprises that might give community enterprises too much competition. In Nanhai the PRS was initially implemented only in the poorer townships and villages, but starting in 1979 the local government encouraged large-scale development of brigade and production team enterprises. In Shangrao local authorities seem to have been more sluggish than their counterparts in Jieshou in implementing rural reforms. The PRS was not adopted until 1983, and not much effort was made to develop the TVP sector at any level until 1984, when the central government unequivocally promoted TVP development. In the other three counties the central government's clear enunciation of policy in 1984 further boosted the TVP development that had been initiated in earlier years.

The ownership structure of the TVP sector in each county is to a large extent determined by strategies adopted by the county government. (See chapters 7 and 9 for further discussion of ownership patterns and the factors that have shaped them in the four counties.) In Wuxi the community-run economy has a strong base. The government has assumed firm leadership of the TVP sector and is stressing the development of industrial TVCEs. Its strategy is to discourage development of TVPs below the village level (to conserve raw materials and energy) and to protect TVCEs as much as possible from competition for human and financial resources. Private enterprises are tolerated, but their development has been constrained by limits on loans, restricted access to inputs, and environmental and other regulations. Ten percent of the profits remitted by TVPs is used to finance agricultural investment and support services. The government tries to keep the difference between wages of workers in TVPs and in agriculture relatively small, and it imposes wage controls on TVCEs. Hence the Wuxi TVP sector is much stronger at the township and village levels than at lower levels.

In Nanhai, where the government encourages the development of TVPs at all levels, TVCEs are much less predominant. During the past couple of years the government began emphasizing the development of core enterprises at the township level but not at the expense of other types of TVP. Restrictions on loans to private enterprises have been less stringent than in Wuxi, and when macroeconomic control over domestic credit was imposed in 1985, the government encouraged production team firms and even (to a lesser extent) private enterprises to seek financial resources through foreign channels. These measures boosted the development of lower-level TVPs, while the growth of TVCEs was somewhat curtailed by the tightening of credit.

In Jieshou the government has actively promoted the development of individual enterprises by helping them to get loans and inputs and by allowing them to use the name of the community (the township, town, or county). Some individual firms were given loans directly from township government funds. Regulation of individual enterprises is lax; there is no ceiling on the number of workers hired by private enterprises or on wages paid to workers. Hence this sector is relatively large.

In Shangrao the government did not get organized to promote TVP development until 1984–85. There is no obvious indication of government favoritism toward any one form of TVP. Because the township governments in general depend on TVPs to finance their expenditures, they tend to squeeze TVCEs for funds, which harms the enterprises' financial viability and long-term development potential (see chapter 17).

From the foregoing discussion it is obvious that the policies of county and community governments have an immense impact on the performance of the TVP sector. Government requirements for remitted profits reduce the funds available to the enterprises for expansion and harm incentives to workers and managers. In this respect Jieshou is consistently much less demanding than Shangrao, as data on firms suggest (table 4-8).

Local government can also exert considerable influence over the performance of TVPs through labor policy. Wuxi's government, for instance, has a stronger role in the allocation of labor within the county than Nanhai's, and Nanhai allows more workers from outside the county to work in local TVPs than does Wuxi. Wuxi also imposes stricter constraints on wage levels than does Nanhai, which has helped to keep wage costs for TVPs low and to maintain a high level of profits. (See chapter 13 for a discussion of wages and incentives and chapter 7 for details on the factors that affect local government policies on wages and distribution.) In Shangrao the result of government interference in employment and personnel appointments in TVPs has been enterprises that are overstaffed and, in some cases, financially unviable.

Implications of TVP Experience in the Four Counties

Many factors account for the diversity of TVP development and performance in the four counties. The initial conditions are clearly important and account

Table 4-8. *Distribution of Profits in Sample Township Enterprises, 1981 and 1985*

Item	Wuxi	Jieshou	Nanhai	Shangrao
1981				
Total profits (thousands of yuan)	847	35	190	15
Of which (percent):				
Income tax	10.0	20.0	6.8	26.7
Remitted profits[a]	55.0	0.0	29.5	40.0
Retained profits[b]	35.0	80.0	63.7	33.3
Use of retained profits (percent)				
Investment and working capital	98.8	81.8	78.6	88.9
Bonuses, collective welfare,				
and so on	1.2	18.2	21.4	11.1
1985				
Total profits (thousands of yuan)	1,942	161	787	22
Of which (percent):				
Income tax	20.7	18.6	32.9	18.2
Remitted profits[a]	27.7	1.9	15.6	27.3
Retained profits[b]	51.6	79.5	51.5	54.5
Use of retained profits (percent)				
Investment and working capital	87.2	74.2	70.0	91.7
Bonuses, collective welfare,				
and so on	12.8	25.8	30.0	8.3

Note: Includes town-run enterprises. There are twenty-three observations for Wuxi, twelve for Nanhai, seventeen for Jieshou, and twenty-six for Shangrao.

a. Profits remitted to township governments.

b. Total profit less income tax and remitted profits.

Source: Enterprise Quantitative Questionnaire.

for much of the observed difference between the more and less advanced counties. Although such factors as geographic location and natural resources are beyond anyone's control, initial conditions are also significantly affected by endogenous factors—for example, government policies. Hence initial conditions should not be treated as entirely exogenous factors that act separately from the other determinants of TVP structure and performance. Keeping this in mind, and realizing the danger inherent in attempting to generalize from only four cases, we outline four different patterns of TVP development that are exemplified by the four counties in our sample.

General Patterns

Wuxi represents one extreme of community government involvement. Local authorities have stressed the development of TVCES: they have supplied initial funds, shared the risk, and served as a supervisory body, appointing managers and allocating workers. Partly because of the favorable conditions discussed earlier (proximity to Shanghai, the presence of skilled labor, an industrial tradition, and so on), the Wuxi system has worked well. The community governments have ensured that managerial incentives maximize the welfare of the local community, but they have in most cases left managers considerable leeway in making production decisions. Workers enjoy job security but have little say in decisionmaking, and their earnings largely consist of piece rates and profit-related bonuses. Although employment generation was the principal goal of Wuxi TVPs in the late 1970s and early 1980s, the elimination of the labor surplus and the advent of competitive pressures have shifted priorities toward greater capital intensity and modernization. Workers from outside the county are admitted on a temporary basis only. The community government's leadership role includes providing assistance in product selection, marketing, and financing. Financial institutions are important but regulated, and Wuxi TVPs retain a significant part of their profits for reinvestment.

In Nanhai local authorities have been much more even-handed in their treatment of different forms of TVPs. Other characteristics of the Nanhai pattern are a developed banking sector that TVPs use as their primary source of capital, reliance on markets (including the labor market), and significant export orientation with concomitant transfer of foreign technology. Although the government has emphasized development of all forms of TVPs, it is not as directly involved in the operation of these enterprises as in Wuxi. TVPs use a smaller fraction of their profits for investment and rely heavily on banks, which appear to be less regulated than in other parts of China. Through their contacts with foreign (mostly Hong Kong) firms, TVPs have been able to obtain advanced technology and to modernize their production methods. High productivity combined with significant remittances from abroad have contributed to Nanhai's high per capita income. Since Nanhai, like Wuxi, has exhausted its surplus labor, income maximization based on more capital-intensive modern technology has become the principal goal of most TVPs. TVP managers are selected primarily by the community government, but they are given considerable decisionmaking authority. Workers have little say. Layoffs are rare, and most workers are on piece rates or other forms of incentive pay. Workers from other areas are used extensively by Nanhai TVPs.

In Jieshou local authorities have systematically supported the development of large private enterprises, which are important not only numerically but also in employment and output. The government is more supportive of entrepreneurship than in Shangrao and encourages any form of TVP development, including joint ventures that involve foreign capital. Less than half of all enterprise directors are appointed by the local government. TVPs are responsive to changes in the market and, because of the simple nature of their operations, can switch easily to different lines of production. In contrast to Wuxi and Nanhai, employment creation continues to be an important goal, since surplus labor still exists. Despite the obstacles posed by scarcity of capital, of infrastructure, and of skilled labor, TVP development in Jieshou has been successful in recent years.

Shangrao suffers from its remote location and limited industrial base, and community governments there have often been forced to use the TVPs as sources of revenue for public and social expenditures. TVCEs have struggled to survive, while private enterprises have assumed a large share of total TVP output and employment. Community governments control the appointment of community enterprise directors and determine the annual plan in many TVPs. Generating employment to absorb surplus labor remains an important objective, and brain drain has been a significant problem. As in other counties, workers' pay contains an element of individual incentives, mostly piece rates. Shangrao's TVP development started much later than in the other three counties, but county authorities subsequently promoted TVPs and growth rates have been higher since 1984. Improvement in TVP performance may follow the enterprise reforms and restructuring that the county government scheduled for implementation in 1987. Rich resources of coal and other minerals have supported the bulk of TVP activities in the past, but future development, especially of manufacturing industries, will require innovative approaches to identify new products with market potential and to develop human resources.

Implications

TVPs have been able to thrive in a variety of environments. In contrast to state enterprises, TVPs are characterized by great flexibility, harder budget constraints, costs of capital that are more reflective of scarcity, and much heavier reliance on worker incentives. TVPs have clearly demonstrated their ability to grow rapidly under different patterns of local government intervention. Their ability to maintain growth under the restrictive macroeconomic policies of the mid-1980s attests to their viability and superior performance.

Our study also suggests that (except for Shangrao) no particular model is clearly superior to others. The Wuxi case, based on TVCEs, is impressive, but the extraordinary growth record of Jieshou's TVPs, which include a significant private sector, is also remarkable, and the Nanhai approach of balanced ownership combined with market and export orientation has also met with success. The experience of all three counties has drawn significant national attention. Wuxi and Nanhai counties and Fuyang Prefecture, where Jieshou is located, are among the fourteen rural counties and districts selected recently by the State Council for further experiments in various aspects of rural development.

The experience of the four counties indicates that the principal obstacles to the development of TVPs are negative government policies, a weak initial economic base, and inability to compete for material inputs and for physical and human capital. Overall, our study suggests that an important stimulus for the TVP sector will be policies that improve the designed functioning of the capital market and promote the development of infrastructure and the acquisition of human capital.

Notes

1. "Resolution on Several Questions about Speeding up Agricultural Development" (draft), December 1978.

2. Central Committee Circular on Agricultural Work in 1984, January 1, 1984 (*Xinhua Yuebao*, June 1984, pp. 82–86), and circular transmitting the "Report on Exploring New Areas for Development of Commune and Brigade Enterprises," submitted by the Ministry of Agriculture and the Party group of the ministry (*Xinhua Yuebao*, March 1984, pp. 107–11). These directives are also referred to as Documents No. 1 and 4.

3. Procurement by the county foreign trade bureau was Y29 million; in addition, about Y20 million of TVP exports went through Wuxi municipality and another Y14 million through Shanghai and other cities.

4. Jiangsu is close behind Shanghai in the output of the machinery industry; together they contributed 25 percent of the GVIO of the subsector in China in 1985. Jiangsu is a close runner-up to Guangdong in the output value of art and handicraft products; the two provinces contributed 28 percent of total national subsectoral GVIO in 1985.

5. "Minutes on the National Conference on Agricultural Work," Document No. 1 (1982), approved the PRS as an integral part of a socialist economy.

5

Market Interactions and Industrial Structure

William A. Byrd and N. Zhu

China's TVP sector grew rapidly in the 1970s and 1980s and is now a significant force in Chinese industry. The sector accounted for 21 percent of national gross value of industrial output (GVIO) in 1986, compared with 9 percent in 1978 and only 3 percent in 1971. TVPs produce a wide range of industrial goods and have penetrated most of China's domestic markets. They compete not only with each other but also with state enterprises. TVPs have grown extremely rapidly when the economic and political environment permitted, most notably in 1984–85, but they have also shown considerable resilience in the face of adversity. They form the most dynamic and fastest growing part of Chinese industry. This raises a number of questions about the sector's performance, viability, and future. Is its recent growth an aberration? What will happen if state enterprises become more competitive? What are the characteristics of the markets that TVPs participate in (and to a great extent have shaped since the late 1970s)? Is the scale of most TVPs suboptimal? Is the financial structure of TVPs sound, or are many of them engaging in risky, unsustainable, debt-financed expansion? More fundamentally, is the TVP sector efficient?

This chapter explores a number of related topics concerning market environment, enterprise response and adjustment, and industrial structure in the TVP sector. We start by briefly describing some basic features of the institutional structure and market environment of TVPs, looking at patterns of competition and at how firms, communities, and TVP industries adjust to changing business conditions, increasing competition, and adverse developments. We then move on to a preliminary analysis of industrial structure in the TVP sector and a brief exploration of policy issues.

Stylized Facts

China's TVPs operate primarily in a market environment for outputs and material inputs. Table 5-1 shows the share of outputs and inputs of sample enterprises

Table 5-1. *Planned Allocation of Sample Firms' Inputs and Outputs, 1985*
(percentage of sample or subsample)

Item	Share of planned allocation in total [a]				
	0	0–10	10–25	25–50	50–100
Total sample					
Input	63	13	4	11	9
Output	51	8	5	8	28
Input, by county					
Wuxi	52	16	3	19	10
Jieshou	61	17	0	14	8
Nanhai	90	0	5	0	5
Shangrao	55	15	10	5	15
Output, by county					
Wuxi	46	7	7	10	30
Jieshou	57	11	6	6	20
Nanhai	74	5	0	0	21
Shangrao	19	6	6	19	50
Input, by ownership					
Township and town	58	15	3	12	12
Village and production					
team	65	5	5	15	10
Private	75	19	0	6	0
Output, by ownership					
Township and town	40	9	8	9	34
Village and production					
team	80	0	0	0	20
Private	63	13	0	12	12

a. Shares are percentages of firms' annual output value targets specified in plans handed down by village, township, county, and higher-level governments and of principal raw materials allocated by these levels of government. In many cases, the reported plan "target" is not mandatory. Inputs allocated by governments often are priced above the controlled state price.

Source: Enterprise Survey Questionnaire.

allocated by government plans in 1985. For most the share is zero, although there is some variation across counties and forms of ownership. But what sample firms refer to as "planning" more often than not consists merely of reference targets or orders from state commercial units—quite different from government directive planning. In Wuxi the share of mandatory planning by state institutions in the allocation of output of TVCEs is very small, and moreover it declined from 11 percent in 1984 to 7 percent in 1985. Unlike many state enterprises, TVPs buy and sell goods primarily for money rather than through barter.[1] Of 113 responding sample firms, only 8 reported getting any raw materials through barter-like exchanges, and only 7 obtained any electric power in this way. Thus the money economy is well established for the bulk of TVPs. The only partial exception to this pattern is electricity (table 5-2). Most of the power for firms in our samples comes from county government allocations, but self-generation and purchase on the market at high prices are also important. Hence the market is becoming significant in the allocation of electric power.

TVPs, particularly community enterprises, have generally faced rigidities in obtaining the factors of production—land, capital, and, in many areas, labor. For 43 percent of the township enterprises in our sample, local government grants were the most important source of capital at founding. Similarly, 63 percent of sample township enterprises listed the community government as their primary source of labor, through allocation or recruitment. Sample private firms relied very little on the community government for either capital or labor at founding. Most TVPs of any size borrow from local banking institutions, which are subject to community government influence. Table 5-3 shows the sources of land for sample enterprises (also at the time of founding). Except in Jieshou, where the market for land is fairly well developed, the bulk of sample firms relied primarily on the community government. Factor markets are not well developed in the TVP sector, as is true for Chinese industry as a whole (see Byrd and Tidrick 1987), and there is not much movement of factors among rural localities and communities.

Most TVPs of substantial size are owned and controlled by community governments at the township and village level. The community governments often play a critical role in strategic decisionmaking on investment, new product development, breakup and merger, and so on. They also take the lead in establishing new community enterprises, and they pool funds and absorb risk across subordinate enterprises. In fact, community governments can be compared with diversified holding companies or, when tightly integrated as in Wuxi, with headquarters of multidivisional corporations.

Most TVPs are enmeshed in the rural communities to which they belong. Community enterprises belong to community governments and to a large extent

Table 5-2. *Sources of Electric Power for Sample Firms, 1985*
(percentage of total observations)

Item	Share of total power supply (percent)			
	0–25	*25–50*	*50–75*	*75–100*
County government allocations	22	4	9	65
Exchange	95	4	1	0
Purchase at high market prices	70	6	4	20
Self-generation	54	21	16	9
Other	93	0	3	4

Source: Enterprise Survey Questionnaire.

Table 5-3. *Sources of Land*
(points)

Item	Community government intervention[a]	Purchase[b]	Rental	Other
Entire sample	59	26	12	3
By ownership				
Township and town	65	26	5	4
Village and production team	59	19	18	4
Private	21	40	39	0
By county				
Wuxi	75	13	8	4
Nanhai	56	23	21	0
Shangrao	79	14	4	3
Jieshou	29	52	14	5
Jieshou				
Township and town	39	53	4	4
Village and production team	17	50	17	16
Private	19	51	30	0
Nanhai				
Township and town	59	34	7	0
Village and production team	68	12	20	0
Private	84	16	0	0

Note: A point-ranking system based on enterprises' responses was used: 3 points for the most important source of land, 2 points for the second most important, and 1 point for the least important. The ratings were normalized to add to 100.

a. Land acquisition in which the community government served as intermediary; use of land without charge; and land acquisition linked to hiring of local residents.

b. Includes conversion of land contributed into shares in the enterprise.

Source: Enterprise Survey Questionnaire.

further their objectives. But even private enterprises are tied to communities in many ways, and in most cases they would find it difficult to relocate. Virtually all directors of sample firms felt that the advantages of their location outweighed the disadvantages and that the main benefits were administrative protection by the community government and ease of arranging land acquisition.

Most TVPs are relatively small. In 1985 the average industrial township enterprise had fewer than sixty employees and a GVIO of slightly more than Y300,000 (see table 5-5, below), while industrial village enterprises were only about one-third as large. Untrammeled development of TVPs has been going on for only a short time, and administrative restrictions have hindered their expansion. The dependence of the bulk of TVPs on their own retained funds and on funds raised within the township to meet investment needs has also limited their size.

Enterprise Structure

Elements of enterprise structure include ownership, financial structure, and product orientation and structure.

OWNERSHIP. (See chapter 9 for an analysis of TVP ownership patterns and trends.) Traditional community enterprises have a relatively clear ownership structure. They are essentially ministate enterprises, but the "states" to which they belong are community governments, which supervise the enterprises through their industrial corporations. At the opposite extreme, small individual firms also have well-defined ownership. In between are some of the larger "private" enterprises such as those in Jieshou, which may be registered as collective firms and have close personal ties with local government officials. Many larger private enterprises in Nanhai also have close government ties; a few have cooperative forms of ownership. In many private enterprises the capital contributed by enterprise founders is repaid to them fairly early, leaving firms with a growing net worth to which no individual has a clear claim. The many community enterprises that have been contracted to individual management add a further layer of ambiguity.

FINANCIAL STRUCTURE. Nearly all TVPs have much higher leverage (debt-equity ratio) than state enterprises. A study of a sample of 200 large industrial TVPs (Zhou Qiren and Huang Zhuangjun 1987, table 4, p. 48) found that their ratio of total debt to total capital was 0.57 at the end of 1985; the debt-equity ratio was 1.31. Many firms in our sample also have relatively high leverage. Although this might not be considered unusual in other countries, it is far higher than in Chinese state enterprises, most of which got all of their founding capital as state grants. Reliance on internal accumulation by TVPs is also substantial, given the initially high profitability of many TVP activities and tax concessions for TVPs in the past. A certain proportion of the after-tax profits of community enterprises is siphoned off for community expenditures or development of other TVPs. During the startup phase, however, all after-tax profits can be left with the enterprise for reinvestment.

At the community level the industrial corporations responsible for supervising community enterprises function in many ways like financial conglomerates, holding companies, or the headquarters of loosely managed multidivisional corporations. The key financial roles of the industrial corporations include pooling enterprises' after-tax profits for investment and directing other resources (from local banks and credit cooperatives) to particular investment projects; cushioning subordinate enterprises from short-term fluctuations; serving as a short-term financial intermediary by transferring funds from enterprises with surpluses to those with deficits; and facilitating the issuance of short-term bonds to local residents.

PRODUCT ORIENTATION AND STRUCTURE. Traditional community enterprises tend to focus on a single main product or a closely related set of products. Diversification into new product lines often occurs, but it typically leads to discontinuing the old product line or to splitting into several factories. This multiplication of firms is facilitated by the transparency of ownership; any new firms belong to the community government that owns the parent. Private enterprises are less likely to split in this way, and more diversified product lines may emerge over time. For example, a highly entrepreneurial private enterprise in Jieshou started out processing oilseeds, moved into processing soybeans, then began producing soybean-processing machinery, and now plans to ship frozen chickens to Shanghai.

Among rural communities there are examples of both "conglomerate" and "specialized" product structures, as well as cases in which a single dominant firm accounts for a large share of GVIO in the community. The conglomerate pattern is the more common one, but a weaker form of specialization by broad subsectors seems to occur at the township and county levels—machinery production in Wuxi, which accounted for 49 percent of the total GVIO of TVCEs there in 1984, is a good example. Regardless of the precise mix of products, community governments do not set up enterprises that produce the same products and compete directly with each other. Each community enterprise is thus a monopolist within the jurisdiction of its "owner." This is not a serious hindrance to competition, however, since communities are so small that they do not provide viable captive markets for more than a handful of TVP activities. Enterprises belonging to neighboring community governments as well as those belonging to villages nested within townships may compete vigorously, as the flood of entrants into the soft drink industry in Wuxi illustrates. Where private enterprises are encouraged, local competition can be even fiercer.

The Market Environment

The goods markets that TVPs face have only just emerged, largely since the late 1970s. Hence there has been instability and wide, sudden fluctuations, as well as numerous opportunities to make large profits. The state sector left many gaps where latent unfulfilled demand existed. The sharp rise in rural and urban personal incomes starting in the late 1970s also created new demand which state enterprises were, at least initially, not well placed to meet. The progressive liberalization of restrictions on TVPs also helped expand market opportunities. Finally, TVPs may have an advantage in competing with state enterprises because they are allowed to incur much larger selling expenses and to employ salesmen on a commission or consignment basis.[2]

As the TVP sector expanded, existing market niches became occupied, and competition became increasingly heated. Many industrial product markets in which TVPs dominate or are important have thus been characterized by falling or, at most, stable prices and declining profit margins. TVPs that entered the market early, when profit margins were high, could survive and prosper even when margins became narrower, but more recent entrants face greater difficulties. The increasing size and changing structure of the TVP sector itself has created numerous opportunities and market niches for enterprising firms, and continued increases in urban and rural personal incomes and in investments generate additional demand. But the new opportunities are often used to best advantage by the more advanced areas and by well-established firms. The markets in which TVPs in the backward areas can most easily get a foothold are the "old" ones, where profit margins are now narrow. Although these activities provide employment, the long-term benefit to local TVP development is much weaker than for the first group of entrants.

TVPs face a relatively "hard" and often highly competitive market environment that puts great pressure on them to perform well and is relatively unforgiving of mistakes. This environment undoubtedly contributes greatly to the efficiency, dynamism, and flexibility of the TVP sector. Unlike many state enterprises, TVPs have no captive markets for their products. In 1984–85 only 4 percent of the gross sales of all TVCEs in Wuxi were within the home township. Eighty-two percent of sample firms in Wuxi sell less than 20 percent of their output within the county, and 73 percent of those in Jieshou sell less than 40 percent of their output within the county. Large majorities of sample enterprises in all four counties sell at least 40 percent of their output outside the home province. Thus TVPs are largely outward-oriented in their product markets. More generally, given the lax control over TVP output pricing, they are much less likely to face chronic sellers' markets than are state enterprises. The bulk of the output of sample firms is priced by the market, through negotiations with customers, or by the producer. Sellers' markets are similar to captive markets in their impact on producers' incentives and behavior, and they negate many of the benefits of the market mechanism. Hence the weakness of price controls and the near absence of chronic sellers' markets sharply differentiates the market environment faced by most TVPs from that of state enterprises.

The TVP sector's market environment has been unstable and subject to fluctuations because of economic and administrative shocks. This is only natural, since market adjustments had been weak or nonexistent for several decades. Ease of entry, combined with strong pressures in rural communities to develop TVPs as a means of employing surplus labor and generating revenues, can also be a source of fluctuations (see chapter 17). The huge reserve army of rural labor available for relatively simple, labor-intensive activities means that violent downward movements in prices and profits are possible. The weakness of market information networks and the lack of connections between local markets tend to exacerbate fluctuations. Administrative shocks also can engender severe market swings: the national tight credit policy imposed in early 1986 probably had a disproportionately large impact on

TVPs, both directly and indirectly as state enterprises, facing a credit crunch of their own, cut back severely on subcontracting work they had been giving TVPs.

Patterns of Competition and Adjustment

Price competition is intense in many TVP industries, and various forms of nonprice competition occur as well. Brand names are often important in competition—electric fans are an example—and so are product quality and development of new products. Large majorities of directors of sample firms in all four counties considered that they faced "relatively fierce," "very fierce," or "extremely fierce" competition. There are several distinct patterns of competition.

Imitative Competition and Neoclassical Adjustment

In Jieshou, where products are for the most part relatively simple and enterprises are rather small, the dominant pattern can be termed "imitative competition." A resourceful entrepreneur finds out about a new product or process that has been successful elsewhere and earns high profits at first. But since entry is easy, a host of imitators soon springs up, and prices and profits decline sharply. Commonly, the entry of imitative competitors overshoots the appropriate number of members of the industry, and after a certain point widespread exits and a shakedown may occur. Exit is relatively painless because capital requirements are low and assets can easily be shifted to other lines of business.

This pattern involves price and quantity adjustments and entry and exit of firms but little if any innovation in products or technological improvement after the initial entrepreneurial success that opened up the opportunity. The best label for it is "neoclassical adjustment," since it works very much like the neoclassical model of market equilibrium. Price adjustments are fast and often large. Imitative competition ensures that economic profits will be eaten away over time, and the situation tends toward equilibrium.

No product market in Jieshou fits this stylized description exactly, but "soybean meat" [danbairou] and the machinery to produce it [penbaoji] come close (see below). Similar adjustment patterns may be emerging for meat and fruit canning. In many backward areas the brickmaking industry has already settled into equilibrium.

A CASE HISTORY. The penbaoji (PBJ) story is one of backward integration into production of the machinery for making soybean meat, a product that was in great demand all over China in 1982. It affords an interesting case study of how limited market and technological information can permit large initial profits that are rapidly whittled away as information spreads through the market and numerous imitators arise to take advantage of the profit opportunity.

The soybean-processing technique was developed in Changchun, the capital of Jilin Province in northeast China, by a professor at the Jilin Provincial Finance and Trade Institute, who designed the PBJ. Several state enterprises in Changchun began to make the PBJ, but the technology was not released to other machinery producers. The PBJ is simple, however, and any good machine shop can copy it if it has a specimen. In Jieshou a local entrepreneur set up a small enterprise with thirty-five workers to produce soybean meat. The firm bought first one and then seven more PBJs from Jilin and made huge profits in 1982. Competition heated up as other enterprises entered the industry in 1983 and 1984.

Meanwhile, an enterprising private food-processing firm, which had been one of the new entrants into the soybean meat industry, surreptitiously transformed itself into a machinery producer and began to produce the PBJ—a case study of technology transfer and adaptation that cannot be told in full here. It did this without any help from the original purchaser of the machines, which would not let other local factories see its installed equipment for fear that it would be copied. (Producers of soybean meat even tried to prevent other local firms from finding out the name and address of the producer of the PBJ in Jilin.) A state-owned farm machinery plant in Jieshou also got into production of PBJs and became the largest local producer. As technical information on the PBJ spread widely in Jieshou, a dozen or so small machinery plants gained the capability to produce it. By 1985 the market was becoming saturated, and the largest producer cut output sharply in 1986. Many small machine shops simply stopped producing the PBJ.

Price trends clearly show this sharp increase in competition and squeezing of profits. The Jilin producer's original price for a PBJ unit was Y9,500. The central mechanism could be bought for about Y1,400, and the rest of the machine could be made by the user (with some assistance from a machine shop) for a total cost of about Y4,000, less than half the Jilin price. When Jieshou firms began making the PBJ in late 1982 and early 1983, the initial sales price was Y7,500, and profits were huge because the production cost was only about Y2,200. (Machinery plants presumably produced the ancillary parts and covering for the PBJ much more cheaply than most users could.) By mid-to-late 1983 the sales price had fallen to Y5,500. In 1984 the original producer brought out a simplified version that was priced at Y2,800–Y3,500 but could be produced for only Y1,500. In 1985 the price again fell, to about Y2,300 for the simplified version. In 1986 the sales price was Y2,000, but since production costs had risen to Y1,700, profit margins were relatively narrow.

SOME PROBLEMS. The shortcomings of neoclassical adjustment are not in the mode of competition itself. Adjustments clearly go in the right direction—production rises sharply, and consumers or users benefit from the price declines. But where neoclassical adjustment alone is occurring, there may be a certain weakness and lack of dynamism. Market niches are crowded, and margins are squeezed so much that little if any economic profit can be earned, but no further strides in efficiency or product improvement are being made. Markets are functioning well in a narrow neoclassical sense, but they are not very dynamic. The questions about neoclassical adjustment thus relate not so much to what is going on but rather to what may not be occurring. It is too early to tell whether some markets are settling down to static impasses with minuscule economic profits or whether innovations and improvements will subsequently lead to renewed disequilibrium and further industrial development. In the case of the PBJ the introduction of a simplified version as market competition became fiercer is a sign that some producers are trying to improve their products. But in the more backward areas the prevalence of imitative competition may mean that the local TVP sector will continue to lag behind the more advanced areas.

Investment Competition

Investment competition is similar to imitative competition but involves large investments of community resources to build facilities that are capital-intensive and often use advanced, sometimes even imported, technology. It is a means by which latecomers to an industry or to TVP development try to catch up with or leapfrog the frontrunners. In a number of industries many localities have built similar plants with large investment requirements after being shown the way by a few forerunners. State enterprises may become involved as well. General market trends under investment competition are broadly similar to those under imitative competition and neoclassical adjustment. But since the investments involved are large and often involve sunk capital that cannot easily be shifted to other uses, the potential losses from overshooting and excessive entry are much greater.

A good example of investment competition is the aluminum window frame industry. Demand for such window frames rose sharply with the increase in housing construction and the shift from wood to aluminum. This in turn spurred a boom in construction of aluminum extrusion facilities, often with imported equipment. As a result, the market has become saturated, the number of firms in the industry may be excessive, and profit margins are narrow. These trends are reflected in the experience of an aluminum extrusion plant in Nanhai.

In August 1984 the market for aluminum window frames looked extremely good. The enterprise (which had previously produced furniture) and the township government decided to shift to this product. The change required a large investment in imported equipment, financed by bank loans. But by the time the enterprise reached full capacity, the market had been flooded with new entrants, and profit margins were squeezed by falling output prices and the rising market price of aluminum. The enterprise now faces problems in servicing its debts and can do so only with tax concessions.

When the output price was Y17,000 a ton in late 1984, the gross profit margin on aluminum window frames was about Y6,000 a ton. By early 1987 output prices had declined by 30 percent, the market price of aluminum ingots had risen by more than 60 percent, and gross profit margins were only Y1,800 a ton, less than one-third the original level. There are now more than 200 aluminum extrusion plants producing window frames in China, but only about 40 percent of them make profits. Although there is an export market, the domestic price is so much higher than the international price that substantial domestic currency losses are incurred on exports, and the Nanhai plant does not export any of its output.

Investment competition is inherently much riskier than imitative competition, particularly for the community governments that finance the large investments involved or guarantee bank loans. The aluminum plant mentioned is by far the most important enterprise in its township, and its financial performance has a great influence on the financial situation of the township government. Since profit margins are initially high, timing is a crucial determinant of success. Competitors who come on line early can make profits to repay their large investments quickly, whereas those who are a little late may never recoup their investments.

As in the case of imitative competition, the question arises whether there is only a one-time improvement followed by market saturation or whether there can be continuing dynamic change. The greater losses that can occur as a result of the higher requirements for capital investment must be set against any benefits. Moreover, in many cases the equipment is so specialized that switching products in the future may be difficult. But despite the risks, townships in both Nanhai and Wuxi seem to realize that in these kinds of activities success depends on quick decisions and adequate investments. The willingness of county and township officials in both Wuxi and Nanhai to take risks and in particular to invest in large rather than small plants is impressive.

Innovative Competition

Some parts of the TVP sector are experiencing something akin to innovation, which continually disrupts market equilibriums and leads to improvements in products and efficiency. In the TVP sector this form of competition primarily involves not so much genuinely "new" innovations as adaptation and a continual search for new ideas from elsewhere in China and from abroad. This kind of competition is most evident in Wuxi, where an infrastructure is being created to support it. Educational facilities, technical and other training, and importation of experts from the state sector are all part of this strategy. In Nanhai the need to compete in international markets also requires continual improvement and a constant search for better methods and ideas, which to a large extent are brought in from Hong Kong through compensation trade, processing, and other arrangements.

Interactions with State Industry

COMPETITION. State enterprises are significant competitors in many TVP product markets. At the national level the bulk of TVP industrial output consists of product categories in which state enterprises have a dominant share. Because markets for some goods are geographically localized or administratively fragmented, the two sectors may be insulated. But overall, there is considerable competition between state enterprises and TVPs.

For goods that are chronically in short supply at low government-set prices, TVPs may have an artificial market niche. TVPs usually produce these goods at higher cost and sell at higher market prices, but the shortage situation protects them from the full brunt of competition from state enterprises. Under these circumstances TVPs can be viable and competitive even though they are producing goods of lower quality or with more backward technology. The two-tier planning and market system can thus insulate TVPs somewhat from competition with the state sector unless the state enterprises sell a substantial share of their output at market prices. In processing industries subject to the two-tier system—for example, in cement—there are often significant economies of scale. Thus, if prices were decontrolled and state enterprises responded to the higher prices and expanded supply, many TVP producers might have to exit, and some TVPs might survive only because high transport costs allow them to remain competitive in local markets.

In a buyers' market, where demand is no greater than supply at the going price and where there may be some excess capacity, competition with the state sector is different. Typically these industries had relatively high prices, which attracted TVPs and put downward pressure on prices and sales of state enterprises. In industries where TVPs have overwhelming economic advantages because their labor costs are lower, economies of scale are unimportant, and so on, they may take over the bulk of the market, leaving state enterprises in a marginal position. In other industries state enterprises may have a strong advantage because of privileged access to key inputs, better technology, administrative exclusion of TVPs, or other reasons, and they may be able to repel competition from TVPs. More commonly, high-cost state enterprises can keep a niche in the market only by producing higher-quality or more "modern" products or through better access to distribution channels.

Generally, competition with the state sector is more important for technologically more sophisticated, capital-intensive goods, which are produced primarily in advanced areas such as Wuxi and Nanhai. In the case of many low-technology, low-value goods that have localized markets (for example, low-quality cement), direct competition between TVPs and state enterprises may be limited. In industries where economies of scale are not critical and capital requirements are not great, TVPs tend at least to hold their own in competition. More often than not they do better, leaving state enterprises to struggle with declining market shares and financial problems—for example, in low-end textiles and simple consumer durables.

COOPERATION. Production of parts, assembly work, and the like are often subcontracted to TVPs by state enterprises. Sometimes the latter simply market TVP products under their own brand names. Or state enterprises can use cooperation to gain access to raw materials. TVPs can even be a dumping ground for state enterprises' old equipment as it is replaced or retired.

Many subcontracting agreements, joint ventures, and other arrangements are motivated by state enterprises' need to gain access to certain factors of production that they cannot obtain otherwise, notably land and labor. A related motive is to take advantage of lower-cost labor in TVPs. Although in static terms these arrangements exploit the labor cost differential between the two sectors and are financially advantageous to state enterprises, like international outsourcing, they may transfer manufacturing capabilities to the TVP sector and thus threaten the position of state industry over the long run.

The most advanced TVP areas, such as Wuxi, have moved away from heavy reliance on subcontracting for urban industrial state enterprises. The share of Wuxi's TVP industrial output that consists of such subcontracting declined sharply from more than 70 percent in 1978 to only 21 percent in 1985 (Jiangsu Academy of Social Sciences 1981, pp. 5 and 18, and information obtained in fieldwork). This decline may have been related to sectoral shifts in the composition of Wuxi's industrial output, to withdrawal by state enterprises that faced reductions in demand and tight markets, or to development of the Wuxi TVP sector itself to such a point that this cooperation was no longer needed. Nanhai's TVPs, in contrast, have extensive ties with Hong Kong businesses (although their links with local state enterprises are less important).

TVPs' Competitive Strategies

Several distinct TVP strategies can be identified. There is almost invariably a large premium for being first. Early entrants into a newly blossoming activity can earn very high, lightly taxed profits and rapidly grow to substantial size. Then, even when profit margins narrow, these firms can more than hold their own. Hence many TVPs tend to rush into newly discovered profit opportunities as quickly as possible. This is consistent with the imitation strategy because earlier imitators can still make high profits but with less risk than is taken by the first, pathbreaking entrants into the new activities.

Another prototypical competitive strategy is to make rapid changes in product lines to take advantage of changing market opportunities. Both traditional community enterprises and private enterprises have shown great flexibility in developing new products and changing product lines quickly to avoid being stuck too long in industries that face declining market trends. Obviously a key prerequisite for this strategy is low capital intensity or assets that can easily be switched to new activities—in Williamson's (1985) terminology, asset specificity must be low. It is much easier to institute a radical change in product lines for an agricultural machinery plant or a furniture factory than for an aluminum extrusion plant. Given the increasing severity of competition in most TVP markets, established producers may need massive new investments and increasing capital intensity to make substantial improvements in product characteristics and quality. A strategy of high investment and capital intensification in, for example, Wuxi appears designed to achieve and maintain an edge in increasingly competitive markets; it is not merely a response to high labor costs or labor shortages.[3]

At the community level, the strategies followed by community governments parallel those of enterprises but with some additional features. Community governments can choose whether their firms should specialize in a dominant line of business or produce a wide array of products, and they can decide how many community enterprises to establish. These questions are intimately related to the issue of business risk, its impact on the community, and how to deal with it. A "conglomerate" strategy can greatly reduce market risk, but specialization can reap certain economic benefits. Having a large number of enterprises can reduce enterprise-specific risk, but fewer, larger firms may offer economies of scale. In the more developed areas, such as Wuxi and Nanhai, the typical pattern at the township level is ten to thirty township enterprises engaged in a range of activities, with some concentration in one or two industries. Although the biggest firm alone does not account for a large share of a township's GVIO, the top three to five enterprises may contribute a substantial share of both output and profits. Thus most townships appear to follow neither extreme specialization nor extreme diversification.

Adjustment to Adversity

The long-term development of China's TVP sector depends on its ability to respond positively and flexibly to adverse changes in the market. Competition has become increasingly severe in many industries, and there are few if any lines of business in which the TVP sector is protected from competition. How well have the TVP sector and different types of TVPs adjusted? There is now enough experience to give a preliminary assessment. Although the TVP sector boomed in 1978–85, some industries and regions have experienced significant adverse shifts. Moreover, the TVP sector as a whole was squeezed by the national tight credit policy in 1986, which particularly affected advanced areas and machinery production bases such as Wuxi.

At the enterprise level, a number of automatic adjustment mechanisms reflect adverse changes quickly. *Price declines*, as we have seen, can be steep. *Quantity declines* may be forced on firms by lack of demand. Output inventories may increase for a time, but after enterprises adjust production, there may be excess capacity. Because of the rapid price adjustments, forced changes in quantity are probably not as important for TVPs as for state enterprises. These market adjustment mechanisms do not involve active responses by enterprises, but they quickly transmit new signals on supply and demand.

A sphere in which TVPs make positive adjustments is *labor and wages*. Performance-based wages lend themselves to reductions in workers' pay because they fall automatically with declines in output or profits. Some large wage reductions have been observed. For example, in a machinery plant in Nanhai average wages of workers fell from more than Y250 a month in 1985 to Y150 a month in 1986. Such examples are by no means unusual. TVP workers bear part of the burden of adjustment, and the enterprise is to some extent cushioned. The clear linkage between wages and output or profits makes declines more acceptable to the workers. There are limits, however; in Wuxi in 1986 average wages continued to rise despite a sharp decline in profits (see below).[4]

Wage cuts in an adverse situation sometimes lead to voluntary departures by workers and hence to reductions in the work force. In the more developed areas such as Nanhai, high-wage opportunities are available and there is a functioning labor market. In Shangrao, a poor locality, some firms have virtually stopped production owing to management problems as well as market difficulties. Since most of the workers are on piece rates, they would be paid virtually nothing for staying, so they go back to agriculture or engage in small-scale commercial activities. Another common practice is to lay off temporary workers from other areas. Sometimes even regular workers can be laid off, often with the right to return when conditions improve. But in general, downward wage adjustments seem more common than sharp, involuntary reductions in the work force.

More active, dynamic responses to a worsening market situation fall under the general category of *product adjustments*, which include improving quality, changing specific product varieties, cutting costs (often through large new investments), or producing a cheaper product in greater demand. Another adjustment is to improve the product, which may or may not involve an effective price reduction, depending on whether the price is kept constant or is raised. Finally, completely new products can be developed.

Financial adjustments deal with an adverse market situation by permitting different institutions to share the burden of adjustment. A decline in profits automatically cuts profit taxes and, in areas such as Wuxi and Nanhai, profit remittances to the local community government.[5] Another financial response is to build up debts and payables, but this is limited by the tolerance of banks and suppliers. Finally, many TVPs can obtain tax exemptions in times of market difficulties.

Drastic adjustments that affect the very existence of the firm also occur. The work force may decline if workers leave because of low pay, but shrinkage of enterprise assets through sales or otherwise is infrequent. Other common responses for community enterprises involve contracting, leasing, or even selling the firm to private individuals. Exit by small private enterprises is often easy because little capital is tied up in the operation. Shutdowns of township enterprises are rare but not unknown; shutdowns occur more frequently among village and team firms. One reason for the rarity of exits by township enterprises is that in many areas the bank debts of defunct firms become the responsibility of the township government and have to be repaid from the earnings of other township enterprises in that community. In general, exit is much more common in the TVP sector than for state enterprises. In Nanhai, for example, about 4 percent of community enterprises—mostly village firms—and roughly 15 percent of private enterprises went out of business in 1986.

At the community level, the community government can to some extent vary the flow of funds between it and higher levels, but its hard budget constraint (see chapter 17) limits the extent to which this can occur and the length of time over which revenue shortfalls can persist. The ability of community governments to respond to adversity depends crucially on the discretionary funds at their disposal. If these funds are large, as in the better-off townships of Wuxi and Nanhai, community enterprises can be given the leeway to attempt more positive responses. But if most flows of funds from community enterprises to community governments are used to meet essential public expenditures, the community governments cannot help finance adjustment by allowing enterprises to reduce their remittances temporarily. Communities that specialize in certain products face great difficulties in adjusting to adverse changes. Since the financial situation of the community government itself has usually worsened substantially, it is not able to provide much of a cushion for the enterprises. The shortage of funds also hampers positive responses such as establishment of new firms in more promising lines of business. Drastic remedies—shutdowns or at least substantial shrinkage, as well as changes in ownership—may be needed.

Overall, the flexibility and effectiveness of TVPs' adjustments to adverse circumstances are impressive, as some examples illustrate.

WUXI COUNTY, 1986. After extremely rapid growth of TVP industrial output in 1985 (nearly 80 percent in real terms, following close to 60 percent growth in 1984), Wuxi faced a difficult situation in 1986. Demand was stagnant or declining as a result of the national tight credit policy and the increasing market saturation brought on by widespread entry of TVPs in other parts of the country. At the same time, market prices of most raw materials continued to rise. Wuxi's response was to increase TVP industrial output by an additional 21 percent, allow gross profits to decline sharply (by more than 50 percent), reduce total direct and indirect tax payments, but by a smaller margin than the decline in profits,[6] sharply increase bank loans as well as fixed and circulating assets, and, surprisingly, increase the number of TVCEs by more than 10 percent and the number of TVCE employees by more than 30 percent. Moreover, average wages increased by nearly 10 percent.[7] The Wuxi response can be seen as an attempt to keep pushing forward even in the face of adversity, and its success is an indication of impressive flexibility and ability to adjust.

THE XIQIAO TEXTILE INDUSTRY. In the early 1980s Xiqiao's TVCE weaving plants thrived because of processing contracts with local state textile producers, whose own facilities could not meet heavy demand, as well as with commercial agencies. The TVCEs wove raw materials provided by the customer into cloth for a stipulated processing fee. After 1983 private textile factories developed rapidly, also by processing for state units. Increasing competition in textile markets and the national tight credit policy imposed in early 1986 had a severe impact on this industry. State enterprises no longer had extra circulating capital with which to finance processing activities, and market demand for textiles was falling. Thus demand for processing by TVPs declined precipitously. Many private enterprises simply stopped production—80 percent of them did so for several months. But community enterprises did not have this option.

Xiqiao's textile industry had to make the difficult and painful transition to a system under which firms produced on their own account and hence were responsible for supply and marketing. Problems were aggravated by huge losses on inventories as a result of sharp price declines and the unwillingness of many state purchasers to honor contracts. Although the sector now appears likely to survive (only one community enterprise has closed down, although others still incur losses), there have been important shifts in ownership structure, and the private sector has flourished. In the weaving industry private enterprises can outcompete community enterprises because of their lower labor costs (they provide few benefits and rely heavily on young female temporary workers from poorer localities in northern Guangdong) and, in many cases, more modern equipment. (Community enterprises often were given discarded obsolete looms by local state textile mills, whereas private enterprises purchased new equipment from state textile machinery producers, who are now allowed to sell to nonstate firms.) Private enterprises are also better able to adjust to the vagaries of textile production and marketing. Because of their low fixed labor costs, many of them can shut down temporarily when market demand falls off and resume operations when it is profitable

ADJUSTMENT THROUGH OWNERSHIP CHANGES. Xiqiao is an example of adjustment through changes in ownership structure. When village and production team enterprises face adversity, the tendency in many areas is to privatize them in one way or another. The reverse—collectivization of private enterprises in trouble—does not seem to occur because community governments do not want the burden. Some successful private enterprises, however, are explicitly or implicitly transformed into community enterprises of a sort. Cases in which successful TVCEs have been privatized are rare. Thus there is an asymmetry in adjustments of ownership structure in adverse circumstances. The share of private enterprises and of community enterprises contracted to private management is likely to rise, perhaps even sharply. This occurs not only because of privatization of community enterprises but also because more private enterprises may be established and growth of existing private firms may be relatively fast.

Industrial Structure

Market interactions and the institutional and economic features of China's TVP sector have implications for industrial structure. In this section we look at selected topics in this vast area: subsectoral composition, firm size, community industrial structure, and, in a preliminary analysis, economies of scale.

Subsectoral Composition

As can be seen from table 5-4 (which covers TVCEs only), China's TVP sector is diversified and covers nearly as broad a range of industrial subsectors as Chinese industry as a whole. There are some noticeable differences, however. The shares of petroleum and electric power are minuscule for the TVP sector, and the share of metallurgy is much less than in industry as a whole, whereas the share of construction materials is much higher. Wuxi's TVCEs are dominated by the machine-building subsector, which accounted for nearly half of their GVIO in 1984, compared with only about one-quarter for China as a whole. Between 1978 and 1984 the textile subsector more than quintupled its share in the GVIO of Wuxi's TVCE sector, while other subsectors declined moderately. Construction materials are much less important in Wuxi than nationally but are still somewhat more important than in Chinese industry as a whole. The industrial structure of TVCEs in Shangrao is radically different from that in Wuxi. Coal mining and construction materials together account for 54 percent of GVIO, whereas machine building accounts for only 7 percent and there is—surprisingly, considering Shangrao's low wages—no production of textiles or garments. Extractive and processing industries account for 71 percent of total GVIO, compared with 35 percent for the national TVP sector and only 26 percent for the TVP sector in Wuxi.

These differences are indicative of the gap between developed and back-

Table 5-4. *Subsectoral Composition of* GVIO
(percentage of total)

| Subsector | China 1985 | | Wuxi TVCEs | | Shangrao |
	All industry[a]	TVCEs	1978	1984	TVCEs, 1984
Metallurgy	8.0	3.4	0.0	6.7	0.5
Electric power	3.3	0.4	0.0	0.0	5.5
Coal and coke	2.5	3.8	0.0	0.0	21.5
Petroleum	4.5	0.1	0.0	0.0	0.0
Chemicals	11.2	8.4	13.1	11.2	11.1
Machine building	26.9	25.5	56.3	48.6	7.1
Construction materials	4.2	18.9	8.5	7.7	32.2
Forestry	1.6	3.0	0.2	0.6	0.6
Food	11.5	7.9	0.9	1.0	4.5
Textiles	15.3	12.5	3.0	15.5	0.0
Garments	2.4	3.7	1.3	1.6	0.0
Leather	0.9	1.6	0.3	0.5	7.6
Paper	1.3	2.4	0.0	0.0	0.9
Cultural and educational activities	2.6	3.0	0.3	2.5	3.7
Other	3.8[b]	5.4	16.1	4.1	4.8[b]

Note: GVIO, gross value of industrial output.
a. Excludes TVPs at the village level and below.
b. Residual.
Sources: State Statistical Bureau (1986a), pp. 227–28, and information from fieldwork.

ward regions. The former have a high share of manufacturing and, more generally, of subsectors such as machine building that take on increased importance during economic development. The latter have a high share of transport-protected and extractive industries and of industries that serve primarily local markets. The subsectoral composition of Gansu Province's industrial TVP sector also fits this description (World Bank 1988, chapter 3 and annex B). The potential of these industries for stimulating dynamic industrial development in backward areas is limited.

Firm Size

Table 5-5 shows the average size of TVCEs (in output and employment) for China as a whole, for a few industrial subsectors, and for Jiangsu Province and Wuxi County. Average firm size is relatively small, although many if not most industrial TVCEs are of medium size and a few are even large by international standards.[8] Differences among subsectors reflect not so much economies of scale as the ease with which small firms can enter the industries concerned. For example, the largest average firm size is in textiles and the smallest is in electric power (primarily hydropower).

Table 5-5. *Average Size of Industrial TVCEs*

Locality	Township enterprises		Village enterprises	
	GVIO (millions of yuan)	Number of employees	GVIO (millions of yuan)	Number of employees
All China (1985)	0.334	56	0.107	24
Textiles	1.275	135	0.423	59
Machine building	0.465	54	0.229	34
Food	0.153	22	0.027	6
Power	0.051	12	0.010	3
Jiangsu Province (1984)	0.616	102	0.192	45
Wuxi (1984)	1.341	130	0.367	51
Wuxi (1985)	1.655	127	0.510	54

Sources: State Statistical Bureau (1986a), p. 182, and information from fieldwork.

The national statistics hide a great deal of regional and local variation. In Jiangsu Province in 1984 the average TVCE was nearly twice the size of the (1985) national average. In Wuxi in 1985 output per TVCE was roughly five times the national level. In more backward areas firm sizes are even smaller than the average. In the more developed regions a few TVPs have reached a considerable size. Per firm averages for a sample of 200 large-scale industrial community enterprises studied by Zhou Qiren and Huang Zhuangjun (1987, pp. 41–42), were GVIO, Y4 million; profits, Y560,000; fixed assets, Y1.2 million; and number of employees, 370. In Wuxi in 1985 more than half of the 700-odd industrial township enterprises had a GVIO of Y1 million or more, and six had a GVIO of more than Y20 million. But there are few if any TVPs in China with gross output values in the Y50 million–Y100 million range and probably none above that level.

The limits on firm size have little to do with restricted local or otherwise captive markets, since TVPs are primarily outward-oriented in both product and input markets. Lack of time to develop has been one limitation. Probably more important, however, large TVPs are tied to rural communities of no more than about 50,000 people with limited financial resources. Risk considerations further limit the size that most TVPs can attain (see chapter 9).

Economies of Scale

One criticism of TVPs is that they are suboptimal in size and are therefore inefficient. If economies of scale are significant, the overall efficiency of the TVP sector could be improved by increasing average firm size. A preliminary test for economies of scale was carried out with the use of 1985 data for sample enterprises. The results reported here are tentative.

A Cobb-Douglas production function was estimated, with GVIO as the dependent variable and with three factors of production (labor, land, and capital) and three county dummy variables as the independent variables (see the appendix to this chapter). The overall fit is relatively good ($R^2 = 0.90$). Differences in productivity among sample firms in Wuxi, Nanhai, and Jieshou are not statistically significant, whereas firms in Shangrao are substantially (more than 60 percent) less productive. The coefficient for land is not statistically significant; a second regression was run without land and the results were broadly similar. The coefficients for labor and capital in both equations (0.81 and 0.44 respectively in the second regression without land) are sensible.[9]

The sum of the coefficients (1.26 in the second equation) is significantly greater than one, and the hypothesis that it is less than or equal to one is rejected at the 99 percent level of confidence. This suggests increasing returns to scale in the sample. The implication that some firms are of suboptimal scale is, however, not necessarily true. It is possible that each enterprise is of optimal scale and that larger firms are engaged in different activities than smaller ones. Efficiency could be improved by shifting capital and labor to larger enterprises that produce different goods, but it might not be possible to improve efficiency by increasing the size of plants that continue to produce the same goods.

Community Industrial Structure

From a number of perspectives the relevant unit in the TVCE sector is the township or village rather than the enterprise. Table 5-6 gives some basic information on the industrial structure of average townships and villages at national and local levels. In China as a whole there must be a large number of nonindustrialized townships, and most villages probably do not have even one industrial community enterprise. The average number of industrial township enterprises per township is less than three, and the average number of village enterprises per village is less than one. Total industrial profits of township enterprises per township in 1985 were only Y81,000, and for industrial village enterprises the figure was only Y8,000. The figures for Shangrao in many respects resemble the national averages, although GVIO, profits, and taxes are lower. Community industrial structure in many townships and villages resembles the pattern in Shangrao more than that in Wuxi or Nanhai.

Townships that have industrialized successfully have a large number of enterprises (up to several score) that generate substantial output and profits and employ large numbers of community residents. Gross profits of township enterprises per township in Nanhai were twenty-five times the national average and in Wuxi, sixty-eight times the national average; the gap at the village level is hardly smaller. Differences in industrial assets and in TVP employment per community are much smaller, which suggests that the more developed regions hold a clear edge in the efficiency of factor utilization.

Table 5-6. *The Industrial Structure of Rural Communities, 1985*
(average per township or village; current prices except as specified)

Item	Number of units	Average population	Number of firms	Number of employees	GVIO (millions of yuan)	Fixed assets (millions of yuan)[a]	Circulating assets (millions of yuan)	Gross profits (millions of yuan)	Total tax payments (millions of yuan)[b]
All China									
Townships	83,182[c]	10,149	2.9	160	0.960	1.078	0.016	0.081	0.107
Villages	940,617[c]	897	0.7	15	0.070	0.023[d]		0.008	0.004
Shangrao									
Townships	34	20,674	3.5	179	0.393	0.283	0.137	0.024	0.015
Villages	343	2,049	0.6	12	0.020	0.007	0.001	0.002	0.001
Nanhai									
Townships	16	53,137	26.1[e]	3,355[e]	35.174	10.182	17.467	2.014	3.133
Villages	236	3,603	8.7[e]	279[e]	1.890[f]	0.476	0.315	0.232	0.111
Wuxi									
Townships	35	29,337	30.3	3,840	50.071[g]	10.22	11.41	5.47	3.16
Villages	587	1,749	5.8	313	2.70[g]	0.49	0.55	0.37	0.17
Township A, Wuxi	1	18,779	12	3,912	104.02[g]	20.87	26.26	18.92	6.92
Villages	13	1,445	6.4	422	8.27[g]	0.84	1.00	1.45	0.50

a. Net value of fixed assets after subtracting accumulated depreciation, unless otherwise specified.

b. Includes both direct and indirect tax payments and hence overlaps gross profits to some extent.

c. Includes Guangdong and Yunnan provinces, where "townships" are really small communities more akin to villages (with another layer of community government, the district—now called towns—between them and the county government), and villages are really comparable to production teams elsewhere in China. Hence all the unit averages are biased downward, possibly by as much as 50 percent.

d. Original value of fixed assets with no subtraction of depreciation.

e. Figures for all TVCEs, not just industrial enterprises.

f. Gross income of village industrial enterprises rather than GVIO.

g. 1980 prices.

Sources: State Statistical Bureau (1986b), pp. 71, 109, 182; (1987b), p. 98; (1987c), p. 3; and information from fieldwork.

Conclusions and Issues

China's TVP sector has developed into a flexible, dynamic, highly competitive, and relatively efficient part of Chinese industry. Its share in national GVIO doubled between 1975 and 1980 and again between 1980 and 1986. If it again doubles by 2000 (a growth rate much slower in relation to the rest of Chinese industry than in the past), it will account for nearly half of national GVIO. Regardless of whether this in fact occurs, the TVP sector today is the most dynamic and competitive part of Chinese industry.

An important factor in the success of TVPs may be that community governments are not able to use certain instruments to promote their development. First, barriers to trade imposed by community governments are not effective in protecting community enterprises. The market represented by a single township or even by a single county is far too small to serve most manufacturing firms adequately, and restrictions against "imports" or other trade barriers are difficult to enforce. Second, community governments have limited financial resources and face a hard budget constraint. TVCEs may be able to draw on community resources to cushion the short-term impact of adverse changes, but this cannot continue very long. Third, community governments with a significant number of firms are typically in charge of a "conglomerate" of different activities and lines of business, even though two or three of them may account for much of total output. This contrasts with the industrial bureaus responsible for state enterprises, which specialize in a particular subsector. The conglomerate industrial structure of many rural communities may preclude detailed regulation or intervention in operations by the community government.

Possible Shortcomings in TVP Competition

The limitations of imitative competition and the dangers of investment competition have already been discussed. To the extent that the TVP sector relies only on these, parts of it may be caught in a rut from which it will be hard to escape. Much competition in other countries, however, also consists of imitating competitors' production activities and making large catch-up investments. And the benefits of investment competition for successful firms and communities are great.

The real question is whether and to what extent more dynamic competitive strategies and patterns are beginning to emerge in the TVP sector. There is already evidence that this is happening in Wuxi, where competitive strategies involve heavy investments, capital intensification, improvements in quality and products, and development of human resources. Nanhai does much less, particularly in the last area (it relies more on Hong Kong), and neither Jieshou nor Shangrao has the resources to do much toward developing managerial, technical, and other needed human capital. Thus the more backward areas may remain caught in patterns of imitative and investment competition.

Regional and Local Imbalances

Various sources of spatial inequality in TVP development are discussed in chapters 4, 9, 12, and 17. Here still another source of regional and local inequality in TVP development has been identified: backward areas may be engaging primarily in imitative competition, which offers limited benefits, or in risky investment competition, which ties up resources and often results in huge losses. Investment competition carries serious risks, particularly in processing industries in which the degree of asset specificity is high. When poorly managed firms have to close down, enterprises and communities bear heavy losses. Since management is weaker in the poorer, more backward areas, enterprise failures and large losses are more likely to occur there than in the more developed regions.

In addition to their much weaker base of human and material resources, backward areas, as latecomers, face a difficult environment with smaller profit opportunities in the activities that are best suited to their skills and resources. The fundamental economic advantage of poorer, more backward areas with little TVP development is their low wage rates. But this is of limited use if capital and entrepreneurs are largely immobile and are not attracted to these areas. Instead, there may be some temporary movement of labor from backward to more developed areas, which may not directly stimulate TVP development in the former. Under these circumstances industrial structure in the poorer, less industrialized areas is skewed toward resource-based industries, agroprocessing, and activities (most notably, production of construction materials) protected from outside competition by high transport costs.

Asset Specificity and Adjustment

The characteristic method by which TVPs adjust to adverse market trends has been to change product lines. This has given the enterprises great flexibility and allowed them to leave stagnating or declining activities and move rapidly into the most profitable activities. It works best for enterprises and industries in which asset specificity is low—that is, in which capital assets can easily be switched to production of other goods. Such is the case in the machine-building industry, since standard machine tools can be used to produce a wide range of goods. In Wuxi the dominant share of machine building makes switching product lines relatively easy and may to a considerable extent explain the great flexibility and efficiency of the TVP sector there. The degree of asset specificity is low in many other subsectors in which TVPs operate.

As it has grown rapidly, the TVP sector has become involved in industries with higher asset specificity. Capital intensification, technological improvement, and acquisition of imported equipment and technology all can involve an increase in asset specificity. If asset specificity indeed increases, it will become more difficult for TVPs to engage in their characteristic method of adjustment. Other ways of adjusting to adversity will have to be relied on to a greater extent, or the flexibility, efficiency, and profitability of the TVP sector will suffer.

Size Limitations, Causes, and Remedies

The existence of economies of scale in the TVP industrial sector has been suggested but by no means conclusively demonstrated. Even if it is true that many TVPs are of suboptimal scale and that in this sense the sector is not efficient, the policy remedy depends on the reasons for suboptimal scale. To the extent that the small size of most TVPs is simply a function of their lack of time so far to grow to large proportions, the problem will solve itself eventually, provided that no administrative restrictions are imposed on the sizes of private or community enterprises.

All large TVPs belong to rural communities which themselves are of limited size and have limited financial resources. If the limitations of their communities are now or potentially the main constraint on enterprise size in the TVP sector, policies are called for that will increase the mobility of financial resources among communities and create financial instruments which successful TVPs or community governments can issue. These instruments would allow communities to diversify their risks and enterprises to grow beyond the limits imposed by the financial resources available in a single rural community.

Administrative restrictions against entry into certain lines of activity by TVPs or against "inefficient" small enterprises are not the answer to suboptimal firm size. TVPs operate in a market environment, and those that are truly inefficient will be weeded out as the functioning of China's markets improves. Exit by private enterprises is already frequent. Clearly specified bankruptcy regulations for community enterprises might facilitate exit by firms that are unviable in the long run, but bankruptcy should not become a means of allowing community governments to wipe out debts that their enterprises incurred to provide funds to those governments for public expenditures.[10]

Appendix. Test for Economies of Scale

A frequently heard argument is that TVP industrial firms, because of their small size, are not fully utilizing economies of scale, that there is great duplication among these small enterprises, and that efficiency would improve if plant sizes increased. Simple regression techniques and quantitative data collected from sample enterprises can be used to make a preliminary assessment.

Data and Variables

The data are taken from the Enterprise Quantitative Questionnaire and are for 1985, which has by far the most observations (122). The variables used in the regressions are

DJS	Locality dummy for Jieshou
DNH	Locality dummy for Nanhai
DSR	Locality dummy for Shangrao
Y	Logarithm of total industrial output value
LB	Logarithm of year-end labor force
LD	Logarithm of land used by plant
K	Logarithm of total capital stock—the sum of the undepreciated value of fixed assets and "quota" circulating assets (inventories of inputs, outputs, and goods in process)
C	Logarithm of annual factory cost

Production Function Approach

A Cobb-Douglas production function was estimated (*t*-statistics are reported in parentheses under the coefficients).

$$Y = 3.74 - 0.14DJS + 0.12DNH - 0.97DSR + 0.51K + 0.81LB - 0.13LD$$
$$\quad (3.65) \quad (-0.69) \quad (0.45) \quad (-3.75) \quad (4.59) \quad (5.40) \quad (-1.46)$$

$$R^2 = 0.90$$

The overall fit, as indicated by R^2, is good. The county dummy for Shangrao is significant (and negative) whereas those for the other counties are not. Land (*LD*) is not statistically significant in explaining output (*Y*). A second regression was run without *LD*.

$$Y = 4.27 - 0.07DJS + 0.34DNH - 0.95DSR + 0.44K + 0.81LB$$
$$\quad (4.89) \quad (-0.33) \quad (1.40) \quad (-3.70) \quad (4.57) \quad (5.43)$$

$$R^2 = 0.90$$

The hypothesis that there are no returns to scale was tested for both of the above-specified regressions:

$$\text{coeff}(K) + \text{coeff}(LB) + \text{coeff}(LD) \leq 1$$

where coeff( ) stands for regression coefficient. This null hypothesis is decisively rejected for both the second equation, without land (probability 99.7 percent), and the first (probability 97.8 percent). This suggests that enterprises are not operating at efficient scale, or at least that shifting factors of production to larger firms in different lines of activity could improve efficiency. But the failure to take into account differences in production techniques among industries gives grounds for caution in interpreting the results.

Cost Function Approach

A look at enterprise total cost and its relationship to size gives some idea of how the former varies with the latter. The following translog function was estimated on the basis of Fuss and Gupta (1981).

$$C = 0.45 - 0.02DJS + 0.14DNH - 0.03DSR + 0.94Y + 0.0003Y^2$$
$$(0.38) \quad (-0.28) \quad (2.08) \quad (-0.46) \quad (5.47) \quad (0.04)$$

$$R^2 = 0.97$$

The output elasticity of cost is less than one, but not significantly.

Notes

1. In China such transactions are not pure barter. Rather, they are "exchanges" that consist of parallel, at least implicitly tied, purchases and sales, often at state-set prices to give the appearance of conformity with price controls.

2. Many state enterprises complain that they cannot compete successfully with TVPs because the latter provide gifts, banquets, and even direct payments to customers.

3. The TVCE sector in Wuxi added a net total of 86,000 jobs in 1986, increasing the total labor force by over 30 percent despite a difficult market situation. Most of the new employees were local residents. Thus, reports of a labor shortage in Wuxi are exaggerated.

4. Conflicting tendencies were at work because output rose substantially even though profits fell; to the extent that wages were linked with output rather than profits, this would tend to push wages upward.

5. In Shangrao community enterprises are often forced to remit a certain amount of funds to the community government regardless of their actual profits (or losses), so this kind of adjustment cannot occur; see chapter 17.

6. Indirect taxes increased in line with the growth of industrial output value and therefore offset much of the sharp decline in profit taxes. Overall, the fall in total tax payments in 1986 was less than 20 percent.

7. In addition to the linkage between wages and output, another factor that may in part explain this paradoxical rise is that the pay of township cadres and factory directors is permitted to exceed that of the average employee by only a certain margin. If average wages had fallen, cadres' incomes also would have declined.

8. Generally, firms are considered very small if they have fewer than ten employees, small if they have ten to fifty, and medium-size if they have fifty to one hundred. See Little, Mazumdar, and Page (1987), p. 8.

9. If the coefficients are normalized to add to one, the capital coefficient is 0.35 and the labor coefficient 0.65. In a sense the results may be almost too good; they may reflect rising capital intensity as enterprise size increases, which would tend to lower the coefficient of capital.

10. This is a real danger in places such as Shangrao (see chapter 17). Given the relationships between community governments, community enterprises, and banks, the issue of whether loans of bankrupt community enterprises are the responsibility of their community government "owners" should be considered carefully.

6

Development Issues and Policy Choices

He Jiacheng

Since the decisions by the Third Plenary Session of the Chinese Communist Party's Eleventh Central Committee in December 1978, China's economic development strategy has consisted of three main steps: to double the country's 1980 GNP and to meet the basic subsistence needs of the population by 1990; to raise China's per capita GNP to at least $800 by the end of the twentieth century and to improve conditions generally; and to bring China's per capita GNP to the level of middle-income countries in the first half of the twenty-first century, so that the life of the Chinese people will be relatively prosperous. China has largely completed the first step and now must focus on the second. The key lies in the expansion of industrialization and the improvement of life in the countryside. Since poverty and underdevelopment in China are mainly confined to the countryside, the second step will have no chance of success if rural per capita income does not increase dramatically.

The transformation of a low-income country into a middle-income one will be accompanied by a shift of labor from agriculture to nonagricultural sectors, including industry. In other countries this shift of labor is often characterized by massive migration from the countryside to the cities—hence the close relationship between industrialization and urbanization. The international experience has been that when the per capita GNP of a large country (one with a population of 20 million or more) exceeds $800, its agricultural labor force falls below 50 percent of its total labor force, and the rural population falls below 60 percent of the entire population. When an extra-large country (one with a population of 100 million or more) enters this stage of development, the percentages of its agricultural labor force and its rural population tend to be even lower (see World Bank 1984).

These considerations are relevant to China's development prospects to the year 2000. If the country's population program is successful and the population can be kept to about 1.2 billion in 2000, China's rural labor force will climb to no more than 450 million. The number of people involved in agriculture should then be fewer than 300 million. Nonagricultural activities in the countryside will have to absorb 150 million people, and the local urbanization process will have to accommodate 180 million. In contrast, the present rural nonagricultural labor force is only 80 million, and the number of people undergoing local urbanization is still relatively small. During the dozen years between now and 2000 China will have to shift 7 million additional workers to nonagricultural activities each year, which means that every year large numbers of people will migrate to towns and townships in the rural parts of the country.

All this boils down to the question of whether nonagricultural activities in rural China will develop as expected during the next twelve years. Judging from past experience, this depends to a large extent on an accurate understanding of the problems and difficulties that face rural industrialization and the choice of workable policies.

Research on China's rural industrialization policies has in the past concentrated on whether rural industries should be allowed to grow. There was some fear that the development of TVPs would undermine state planning and weaken the state economy and that it would not be in conformity with the country's socialist orientation. This issue was basically settled by the Central Committee's "Resolution on Several Questions about Speeding up Agricultural Development" in 1978 and was further clarified by Document No. 4 of 1984. The focus of research on rural industry is shifting to such questions as its further development and, particularly, general rural development policy as the foundation of rural industrialization, the help needed by rural industrialization, coordination of policies governing rural and urban economies, and the reform of rural enterprise management as the driving force of rural industrialization. This chapter looks into these policy issues.

The Foundation of Rural Industrialization: Agricultural Development Policy

Further industrialization in the Chinese countryside will run into problems arising from the conflict between industrial and agricultural development. Grain output has fallen in the past couple of years after hitting a record high in 1984; the harvest in 1987 was no better than the great harvest of three years before. This raises the question of whether rural industrialization has diverted resources from agriculture. There is some concern that the growth of rural industries may have been too fast.

The unsatisfactory situation of rural industry before 1978 was attributable to the traditional industrialization strategy. Conditions had actually long been ripe for developing rural industry, since the agricultural base was capable of supporting industrialization. The nation's average per capita grain supply was 304 kilograms in 1957, 318 in 1978, and 370 in 1986. Naturally this situation was more conspicuous in the relatively developed areas. Wuxi's grain output rose from 214,500 tons in 1949 to 417,000 tons in 1970, grow-ing at 3.2 percent a year. Grain output per farmer, however, increased only from 850 to 880 kilograms. During the fifteen years from 1956 to 1970 output per farmer even fell, from 1,250 to 880 kilograms.

The rapid pace of rural industrialization after 1978 was prompted by the shift of emphasis in the entire national industrialization strategy and by re-lated adjustments and structural reforms. Controls over the nonagricultural economy in rural China were loosened, the production responsibility system (PRS) was introduced in farming, and state procurement prices for agricultural products were raised. The change in procurement prices transferred consider-able amounts of industrial profits to the farmers, which gave them a financial foundation for entering nonagricultural businesses. In relatively developed Wuxi, price rises between 1980 and 1984 generated 81.9 percent of the total increase in agricultural incomes. This ratio, of course, was not as high in underdeveloped counties because of their greater potential for increasing agri-cultural output, but the transfer of part of urban industrial profits to the coun-tryside through higher agricultural procurement prices probably had a higher marginal effect there. Moreover, rural economic reforms in the past few years have greatly promoted the development of agricultural production and so strengthened the base for rural industrialization.

Nonetheless, Chinese agriculture is still far too backward. Several years of vigorous growth on the part of rural industry have left agriculture too weak to provide a stable foundation for rural industry. Rural industries have occu-pied farmland and absorbed able-bodied farm labor to some degree. For ex-ample, the sown area for grain crops fell by 7.73 million hectares during 1978–84 and decreased another 4 million hectares in 1986 alone. The expan-sion of rural industries has led to a relative and even absolute decrease in investment, particularly long-term investment, in agriculture that has jeopar-dized the growth of the sector. Furthermore, the PRS and the rise in state procurement prices for farm products have already brought about a substantial increase in agricultural production and can no longer offer great incentives for continued rapid development.

The areas with more advanced agriculture are usually those where rural industries have experienced more rapid growth, but they are also the areas where the conflict between industry and agriculture emerged earlier and now appears more acute. The conflict is especially noticeable in Nanhai, where the local TVP sector relies more heavily on private ownership, individual op-erations, and associations, but it is also found in places such as Wuxi, where the principal investors in rural industry are township and village govern-ments. In Wuxi agriculture not only has failed to accumulate funds to support industry but also has absorbed a large share of local industrial profits. Thus the more advanced is a county's rural industry, the more its industry is out of balance with agriculture.

Under such circumstances the present rural industrialization process in

China may reproduce the type of relationship between industry and agriculture created by the prereform industrialization strategy. The goal of the earlier industrialization process was to lay the foundation for an independent industrial system in the shortest possible time. The state limited and even forbade the shift of rural labor to nonagricultural activities, established a land management system that gave political power to grass-roots communities, made agriculture accumulate as much as possible for industry by means of the scissors differential between the prices of industrial and agricultural goods, and excluded the rural population from the urbanization process by imposing the household registration system.[1] An independent industrial system was indeed created in a short time but at the cost of a large gap between industry and agriculture and a worsening urban-rural income gap. As in other countries that followed similar strategies, when such a process reached the limits on exacting from agriculture for industry, the countryside became a severe burden on the entire economy. To permit further industrialization, China had to revise its scenario by making industry help agriculture.

The current rural industrialization process is aimed at lifting the countryside out of poverty as soon as possible. The PRS permitted farm labor to undertake nonagricultural activities. The scissors differential in the prices of industrial and agricultural commodities was reduced. Large loans and tax breaks were extended to rural industries, which in turn were asked to aid farming. This program did cause rural industry to mushroom and freed some areas from abject poverty. But it has failed to provide a basic solution to the conflict between industry and agriculture.

Chinese agriculture cannot at present provide rural industry with a reliable foundation. Successful experiences in this regard resemble either the United States, where agriculture has always been a strong base for industrial development, or Japan, where industry and foreign trade can compensate for the deficiency in domestic farming. The United States has abundant natural resources for agricultural development, and Japan boasts the broad competitive edge of its industry in international markets. China's per capita agricultural resources are severely limited—the country has one-third of the world's farm labor but only one-eleventh of the world's cultivated land—and the American approach is thus not applicable. At the same time, China's urban industry continues to face hardships in competing in international markets, and its even more backward rural industries cannot be expected to depend solely on foreign trade to overcome the inadequacies of domestic agriculture, at least in the near future. All this calls for extreme caution in managing the relationship between industry and agriculture in rural regions.

The slackening growth of farm output since 1984 and great frictions over the development of the nonagricultural sector in recent years have forced governments at different levels to put a new phase of rural reform on their agenda. Some practical moves have also been made, such as easing controls on the prices of farm products, stepping up adjustment of the industrial structure in the countryside, and abolishing the state monopoly on the procurement and sale of farm staples. These measures have thus far not led to anything comparable to the remarkable achievements of the first phase of rural reform.

The absence of a proper stress on the development of agriculture in the process of adjusting the rural industrial structure is a grave defect. The second phase of rural reform has failed to pay enough attention to agriculture and to the fact that one of the goals of the reforms is to provide a solid foundation for agricultural development. Agriculture will long remain the ultimate source of the difficulties confronting the advance of China's rural economy. Like it or not, agriculture must still be regarded as the basis of the national economic development strategy.

Some hope that aid to agriculture by rural industry will provide a solution to the agricultural problem. Such aid, as it has been implemented over the past several years, involves the use of part of industrial profits to stabilize and promote agricultural production. It can to a certain degree alleviate the imbalance between industrial and agricultural development and may become more important when it is systematically institutionalized. Industry's aid to agriculture now works on a county or township basis. Some villages that have been champions of development have also included aid to farming among the responsibilities of rural enterprises. There are sometimes rules about how many persons each household can send into rural enterprises; no family may exceed the quota. There are valid reasons for balancing the interests of farm labor and rural industrial labor in this way. Yet for economists this kind of balance represents a sacrifice in many aspects—most important, a sacrifice of specialization and comparative advantage. Thus attempts to make rural industry help local agriculture do not offer a perfect solution to the problem of the long-term development of agriculture.

Others count on reforms at the macroeconomic level to coordinate the interests of industry and agriculture by drastically increasing prices of agricultural goods and the state's investment in agriculture. Reforms at the macroeconomic level, especially improvement of the market system, are significant and deserve support, but increasing the state's financial help to agriculture would be difficult. In any case, these reforms would provide little leverage for stabilizing the agricultural base for the rapid growth of rural industry.

What is fundamental for ironing out the agricultural problem is a thorough land reform to heighten farmers' enthusiasm for investing in agriculture and build up the momentum for continued agricultural growth. In addition, land reform can rationalize the scale of agricultural production and bring land productivity to a new peak. Trade among regions can thus develop according to the principles of geographic specialization and comparative advantage, and rural industries will naturally move toward the most suitable locations, where management will be better and costs lower. At the same time, state procurement quotas for farm produce in the areas where rural industry is more developed should be gradually transformed into monetary forms to enable these areas to take ever quicker steps toward industrialization.

Coordination of Policies Governing the Rural and Urban Economies

China's rural industrialization faces another category of problems: the imbalance between the cities and the countryside. This is a product of the traditional industrialization process, which led to an excessive dichotomy between urban and rural living conditions. The lack of progress in reducing the difference between the rural class and the urban class is conspicuous. In the late 1970s the ratio between per capita income in the countryside and that in the cities was 1:1.7, close to the Indian level of 1:1.8. If one also considers the difference between the two economic systems—for example, China's full employment scheme, its welfare arrangements for urban residents, and its pricing and marketing system for consumer goods, which gives urban people higher real purchasing power—the urban-rural dichotomy in China was actually even wider in the 1970s. The urban-rural income gap decreased markedly following the introduction of rural reforms in late 1978 and reached its narrowest point in 1982. It then widened again, despite the faster growth of rural industries. In 1982 the average income of a rural laborer was 61.8 percent of that for an urban worker, but the figure declined to 58.9 percent in 1984 and to 48.4 percent in 1985.

What is disturbing is not the gap itself. In the primary stage of such a profound social transformation as the Chinese reforms, many factors (some of them transient) can affect the urban-rural income gap. Raising the procurement prices of farm produce, adopting the PRS, and allowing farmers to swarm into nonagricultural trades could significantly boost rural income levels. At the same time, the creation of jobs for millions of unemployed urban youths, pay hikes to compensate for the wage freeze of previous decades, and, especially, urban enterprises' thirst for capital investment could lead to rapid increases in city dwellers' incomes. The evolving new urban economic structure may generate rapid growth led by technological upgrading, which may further widen the income gap. Moreover, agricultural growth is subject to constraints, and farmers' incomes can hardly increase when they depend solely on agriculture. This being the case, it is rural industrialization that has the historical mission of closing the urban-rural gap. Rural industrialization has three key components: reducing the difference between factors of production in the countryside and in the cities, rationalizing the division of labor in the urban-rural industrial structure, and synchronizing the development of rural industrialization and urbanization.

One obstacle to balanced urban and rural economic development is the immense difference between factors of production in the countryside and in the cities. The essential factor of production is not any form of material capital but human capital. Areas with a higher level of rural industrialization are not usually characterized by affluence in natural resources or finances, but they are located where human capital is more abundant. Compared with Wuxi, Shangrao has more natural resources and, relatively speaking, more funds for launching rural industries. Both as an old revolutionary base and as an impoverished area, Shangrao receives sizable financial aid from higher authorities. But its rural industries are underdeveloped, mainly because of the lack of human capital and the poor quality of township economic commission (TEC) officials, entrepreneurs, technicians, and supply and marketing personnel.

In Shangrao the quality of TEC officials, even in the economically most advanced towns, is conspicuously lower than that of their peers in the developed counties. Some are even unacquainted with the basic financial situation of local enterprises or lack rudimentary knowledge of technology, management, and business. Entrepreneurs in the county lack the qualities of modern industrialists and enterprise managers. Since Shangrao has virtually no history of modern industry, it has at best only some craftsmen, not skilled industrial workers. Both the administration and the public in Shangrao tend to underestimate the role of marketing personnel in developing TVPs. Marketing personnel in the county have failed to become an independent interest group or a strong backbone of local enterprises (see He Jiacheng 1987).

Shangrao's shortage of human capital undoubtedly has roots in the county's unfavorable geographic and economic position and its short experience as a market-oriented economy as compared with Wuxi. Yet the fundamental cause of Shangrao's predicament is its failure to augment the local pool of human talent.

Efforts in this area have taken various forms in Wuxi. Qianzhou township has brought in more than a hundred industrial pensioners and administrative personnel from Shanghai and Wuxi cities. The county has been trying vigorously to tap local human resources as well. Promotions go first to talented local residents. There have been 6,000 such cases, including 1,600 managerial staff, 2,000 marketing personnel, and 2,300 technical workers. Wuxi also cultivates its professional manpower. During the past few years it has sent about 200 local personnel to universities and technical schools. Other forms of education that the county has employed include a television university, a correspondence school, radio lectures, exchanges of trainees and technical advisers with enterprises elsewhere, seminars, and encouragement of self-education. Wuxi maintains a social atmosphere conducive to individual creativity through, for example, local policies concerning pay scales, promotions, awards of technical titles, and public opinion. As a result, urban-rural differences in human resources are no longer salient in Wuxi.

Another obstacle to balanced urban-rural economic development is the similarity of urban and rural industrial structures. The industrial structure of

China's rural economy resembles to a surprising degree that of the entire national economy. The correlation coefficient for fourteen subsectors in rural industry and in China's industry as a whole is 0.721, that for eight heavy industrial trades is 0.793, and that for six light industrial trades is 0.923. (For more details see Development Research Institute 1986.) Such great similarity in industrial structure worsens the prospects for rural industrialization, for the technological upgrading of rural industry, and for full utilization of the advantages of urban industry. Urban-rural competition remains on the same low level, making it difficult to institute effective coordination.

A retrospective look is needed to explain the cause of this similarity. In response to Mao Zedong's call for mechanization of farming in China by 1980, the 1970 Northern China Agricultural Conference decided to allow and to support with funds and materials the establishment by communes and brigades of factories for making farm machinery and tools. But production of farm machinery was badly suited to the resources and factors of production in the countryside. Farmers had to rely almost totally on state support, but this support was not adequate for successful development of the farm machinery industry. Few communes and brigades could actually afford to set up a farm tool factory, let alone a farm machinery factory. More often than not, the factories that were established lost money because of the severe shortage of production and management expertise and the relatively low prices of farm machinery. Faced with this challenge, farmers either closed their factories or went beyond the boundaries designated for their business activities. The more advanced localities such as Wuxi shifted to making the general machine tools needed for farm machinery production in hopes of subsidizing the losses incurred by farm machinery with profits from comparatively high-priced machine tools. By 1978 the structure of rural industry had become highly similar to that of industry as a whole.

A significant change came in 1978 with the Central Committee's resolution on speeding up agricultural development. The document declared that all suitable farm products should gradually come to be processed in the countryside, if doing so was economically rational, and that urban industries should allow part of their finished products or components to be processed by commune and brigade enterprises using equipment and technology supplied by the urban industries. Because no timely complementary measures were adopted, and perhaps because the scope of business designated by the state was too wide, farmers entered virtually all industrial fields. This further distorted the rural industrial structure and generated fierce competition for raw materials and markets between commune and brigade enterprises and state enterprises.

The 1981 national economic readjustment program affected commune and brigade enterprises. In Jiangsu Province, where rural industry was most advanced, the main results included:

- The closing of a number of production lines and projects that had been started without considering local economic advantages (as occurred, for example, in calcium carbide, coke, electric furnaces, asphalt felt, asbestos, pharmaceuticals, and activities such as animal bone processing)
- Restrictions on the development of cotton textile manufacturing and processing, steel rolling, flour milling, and firecracker manufacturing
- Controls on activities that required high energy consumption but turned out substandard goods, such as some pesticide manufacturing and boilermaking
- Restraints on the production of commodities that involved high pollution or were not very marketable
- Encouragement of production of parts for state-run industry and of cooperation with state enterprises
- More careful examination of projects based on nonagricultural materials
- Preferential treatment for the processing of farm produce.

The readjustment brought about a substantial change in rural industrial structure and the beginnings of more balanced development patterns.

As imbalances in the national economy were being corrected, the Central Committee stated its rural industrial policy in Document No. 4 of 1984. This document called for further balancing and readjustment and for priority for food, animal feed, building materials, construction, and energy. Again, owing to the lack of complementary policies, especially macroeconomic guidance to the newly mushrooming private enterprises, the similarity between rural and urban industry has become more marked in recent years.

The last obstacle to balanced urban and rural economic development stems from the conflict between rural industrialization and urbanization. The problem with the traditional industrialization process was by and large not one of fast industrialization and belated urbanization but rather of distortions in city size distribution. The share of China's urban population increased from 10.6 percent in 1949 to 17.6 percent in 1978. This was 24 percent lower than the average for low-income countries, but correction for the underestimate caused by the Chinese definition of urban population yields a degree of urbanization at least equal to the average of low-income countries if not slightly higher. The urban structure, however, appeared undesirable; large and extra-large cities accounted for a big percentage and cities with populations of 100,000 or less accounted for only 32 percent, in contrast to 47 percent in India, 42 percent in the Soviet Union, and 41 percent in Brazil.

The acceleration of agricultural development and rural industrialization since 1978 has given rise to urbanization and the growth of towns and has to a certain extent cured the inappropriate structure of urban scale created by traditional industrialization. TVPs are mostly clustered in or close to local commercial hubs and attract a large part of the surplus agricultural labor force. The thirty-five towns of Wuxi have, on average, thirteen factories and 1,600 workers per town, and fourteen of them report that workers from surrounding villages constitute 30–40 percent of their populations. In eight other towns such workers account for 40–60 percent of the population.

At the same time, urbanization as part of rural industrialization has some noteworthy defects. First, the two do not usually keep pace with each other. In some areas the latter lags, in others the former. The sample counties that do not have their own county seats—Wuxi, Nanhai, and Shangrao—are currently engaged in large-scale construction programs to build county centers. Wuxi and Nanhai enjoy a much higher level of industrialization than Shangrao and have both the finances and the need for county seats. Their industrialization cannot realize scale economies and externalities if it is not correlated with urbanization. In contrast, Shangrao cannot justify building a county seat. Its industrialization process has barely begun, its government still operates with state financial subsidies, and it has neither the need nor the capability to undertake the project. If urbanization is divorced from industrialization, it will inevitably lead to inappropriate and high-cost investments, which will retard industrialization.

Second, the construction of small towns often does not achieve economies of scale. Township enterprises are commonly located in the towns that serve as seats of township governments, and village and team workshops tend to be located within the precincts of their villages or teams. In 1984 Jiangsu Province had 1,962 townships and 22,592 industrial township enterprises with a total employment of 2,315,376. If all township enterprises were headquartered in township seats, each town on average would have no more than 11.5 township enterprises and 1,178 workers. Even though some towns are bigger than others, the broad picture is still one of anarchy in developing small towns. In 1983, 2,100 towns were scattered around Jiangsu Province's 100,000 square kilometers. On average, there was one town for every 51 square kilometers, but the density of towns varied in different areas—one for every 70 square kilometers in northern Jiangsu, one for every 42 square kilometers in southern Jiangsu, and one for every 36 square kilometers in middle Jiangsu. The highest density was found in Yangzhou city (Jiangdu County), where there was one town for every 22.6 square kilometers of land area, while in Huaiyang city (Hongze County), which had the lowest density, there was one town for each 108 square kilometers.

The problems that crop up in the development of small towns are caused by erroneous guiding concepts and by defects in the management structure. Traditional industrialization neglected the growth of small towns, and the consequences were harmful for rational urbanization. But now the overemphasis on the construction of small towns and the existing management structure are preventing small towns from expanding into medium-size cities.

Under such circumstances it will be hard to avoid new distortions in the pattern of urbanization. The organizational reforms of the past few years allowed city governments to oversee the counties in their surrounding areas and township authorities to coordinate the affairs of subordinate villages. These reforms have alleviated problems to some extent but are not a basic solution to the barriers separating the countryside and cities and to the conflicts between towns and surrounding rural areas.

The solution to these difficulties is, first, to emphasize the human factor. Financial policies alone (including direct transfer of funds and greater use of urban savings for rural credit) will not resolve the problems. The adjustment of the urban industrial structure in coming years will also bring about a huge demand for finance, and it is both impractical and unreasonable to sacrifice urban economic development. Much should be done to augment rural human capital through expanding the urban technology market and increasing flows of personnel to the countryside. For the poor areas, what is most important seems to be improvement of the quality of intermediate talent.

In addition, the principle that rural industry should be based entirely on local resources has to be repudiated, and the policy of letting rural enterprises supplement large industries should be revised according to the realities in the countryside—its abundant labor force and insufficient finance. Urban-rural industrial development policies should promote the conversion of labor into funds. Only policies of this kind, especially policies to govern the founding and technological advance of rural industries, can fundamentally solve the problem that when state industry grows, rural industry inevitably appears to be lagging, and the other way around. By shaking off noneconomic ties with state enterprises, TVPs can achieve more coordinated industrial development. More important, there must be structural reforms—of the investment structure and of commercial management, for example—to guarantee the functioning of these industrial policies.

There should be a strategic focus on developing existing small cities and towns directly affiliated with county governments into medium-size cities. A long-term development program for small cities and towns should be drawn up as quickly as possible, and the management structure for small cities and towns should undergo reform. First, cities should act as the economic hubs for their nearby counties so as to combine the urbanization efforts of the cities and the countryside. Second, China must strengthen regulation and control of the construction of county seats so that the expansion of old county seats and the building of new ones are covered by an overall program. Third, the construction of towns governed by townships should be more concentrated geographically, and, in particular, the locations of TVPs should be more centralized. But this demands a thoroughgoing reform of the relationship between TVCEs and their governments.

The Driving Force in Rural Industrialization:
The Structural Reform of TVPs

The third set of problems involves the conflict between the development of rural industry and the management system of TVPs. China's traditional mode of industrialization was not as centralized as the Soviet model. From the beginning China let local governments run enterprises taken over from capitalists and individuals. Later, local industries enjoyed further development when local governments were encouraged to take some initiative. But a highly centralized system of planned distribution and allocation was still the main feature. This system, although it promoted rapid industrialization, conflicted sharply with the needs of industrialization. The result was a slowdown of the pace of industrial development, low and declining economic returns, and limited benefits for the people.

The current system of rural industrialization was also determined by conditions created in the past. Since 1978 most TVCEs have maintained their original property relationships, but some smaller firms and those long plagued by poor management underwent changes. Some enterprise assets were sold to individuals at reduced prices or were leased or contracted to them. This kind of transfer of property rights has developed to such an extent that TVCEs enjoy rapid growth both in regions where they originally flourished and in a few localities with backward rural industry. In some other backward areas, privately owned, household, and privately managed firms as well as partnerships have moved ahead. Since 1984, when the privately owned and managed economy was given a green light for development, it has mushroomed and spawned different modes of TVP ownership and management. These include the Wuxi mode, based mainly on TVCEs, the Wenzhou mode, which emphasizes private enterprises, and the Gengche mode, with development of both TVCEs and private enterprises.

Although property relationships in China's rural industry are different in different regions, public ownership is generally dominant. But this dominance is not the same as during the period of traditional industrialization. Not only is the proportion of public ownership currently much lower, but TVCEs are quite different from the state enterprises that were the main form of traditional industrialization.

The proportion of TVCEs is still high. The share of TVCEs in total employment of TVPs is 97.1 percent in Wuxi, 77.5 percent in Nanhai, 96.7 percent in Shangrao, and 64.0 percent in Jieshou. This will restrict future development in many ways and will particularly obstruct the formation and growth of factor markets. For example, the high proportion of TVCEs is closely related to low mobility of labor. In the sample firms the respective shares of workers from the local township, the local county, and other counties are 94, 97, and 3 percent in Wuxi and 51, 85, and 15 percent in Nanhai. In Shangrao the corresponding figures are 81, 96, and 4 percent and in Jieshou 80, 92, and 8 percent. What is more problematic is that like state enterprises, China's TVPS are subordinated to government administrations and are plagued by the problem of egalitarianism among the workers.

But these similarities do not make TVPS and state enterprises identical. In the first place, the number of final owners is comparatively small for TVCES. In Wuxi, for example, each township has an average population of about 20,000, whereas the average population of a medium-size city is 100,000–500,000. Second, the obligations of township governments toward rural workers as members of their communities are relatively weak and are few in number. Township governments can directly regulate enterprises' economic activities through plans, as municipal governments do. But nonagricultural activities in a township are outside the state mandatory planning system, and economic exchanges among all nonagricultural firms in a township account for only a small part of their activities. Hence TVPS are controlled by the market mechanism in a strict sense.

Unlike urban governments, which represent an entire city, township governments cannot shoulder extensive social functions or pursue many noneconomic targets. Since these governments are unable to support long-term or huge losses in their enterprises, losses suffered by TVCES tend to be much smaller than those that plague state enterprises. For instance, in 1985, 11 percent of township enterprises in Wuxi were loss-makers, and total losses amounted to 3.2 percent of total gross profits of township enterprises. But only 0.6 percent of village firms ran losses. In Nanhai 18 percent of the township enterprises were loss-makers, and losses were 9.1 percent of gross profits; for village enterprises the corresponding figures were 1.5 and 0.7 percent. Losses in TVCES last for only a short time; if they cannot be turned into profits, the enterprises have to shift their production or close down.

The TVCE form of enterprise organization has not promoted the best distribution and utilization of resources. If the industrial TVCE sector is not reformed, it could have even bigger conflicts with the further development of rural industry in the future. At present, this problem is most prominently seen in the following features.

• The township government represents the owners of township enterprises, but it also functions as a government administrative unit. Therefore the township government has to take into consideration the interests of both the enterprise and the township. The interest of the enterprise is in maximizing profits; the interests of the township include increasing the incomes of all the people in the township, the percentage of nonagricultural employment throughout the township, and the income of the township government. The two targets may conflict. The principal problem is that the township government adopts policies concerning distribution of enterprise profits that reduce enterprise reinvestment rates and obstruct the rational flow of the main factors of production among townships. To achieve desired social goals, township governments have placed hurdles in the way of the best distribution and utilization of resources that TVCEs need for their development.

• Legally speaking, the entire population of a township is the final owner of the assets of township enterprises, but the local people are not actually entitled to any individual benefits. Hence they will not behave like owners of a typical joint stock firm. First, township residents do not have a strong desire or willingness to invest in township enterprises, since the investment cannot be inherited or returned as dividends and cannot be transferred elsewhere in response to better investment opportunities. Second, since township residents do not hold decisionmaking rights in township enterprises, there are no restraints on the representatives of the owners (the township governments) and no effective inspection of the enterprises' financial status and management. This is the reason behind encroachment on the capital stock of township enterprises by a few people and is also a cause of inefficiency and slow growth of capital stock in the enterprises. It eventually leads to conflicts between community residents employed by township enterprises and those outside the firms.

• Township enterprise directors do not have adequate decisionmaking power, since factories—even those that have adopted contract responsibility systems—are not entirely independent. As a result, enterprise managers are weak and indecisive and are unable to grasp business opportunities. A factory director's decisionmaking authority is strongest for materials, less so for personnel, and weakest for finances. In Wuxi between 1977 and 1984 the proportion of total net profits kept by enterprises was between 14 and 46 percent. The figure was 65 percent in 1985 and 60 percent in 1986, considerably higher than the 40 percent ratio in state enterprises. The decisionmaking power of a TVCE director over the use of profits retained by the enterprise is similar to that of a state enterprise director; the only difference is that TVPs are subject to fewer controls over their financial accounts and cash transactions. For many TVCEs depreciation funds have to be submitted to township governments for general distribution, and the use of retained depreciation funds is also subject to control by township governments. Overall, TVCE directors cannot expand the capital of their firms on the basis of changes in market supply and demand.

• TVP workers have come to have the same behavioral characteristics as state enterprise workers in many respects (see chapter 18). Availability of labor and low wages should have been the biggest advantages of rural industry, but the existing TVP system has led to coexistence of high local wage costs and a surplus of agricultural labor in general, of overstaffing in some enterprises and acute shortages of labor in other places. For instance, in Shangrao rural areas have considerable surplus labor, but the wages of TVP workers are much higher than farmers' incomes. Excessive employment in some firms may account for 60 percent of the total work force. In Wuxi, although many enterprises have already felt the strain of labor shortages over the past several years, most firms suffer from overstaffing, which may account for 10–50 percent of the total number of employees.

The problem goes far beyond this. At present, even private enterprises are not set up for the best distribution and utilization of resources. The reason lies in external conditions rather than internal financial arrangements or structures. Individual enterprises are officially included in the socialist economy, whereas privately managed firms with more than seven employees are considered a supplementary part of that economy. But most local governments have failed to internalize this new attitude. In general, even in places where the private economy is highly developed, such as Nanhai, private enterprises are discriminated against politically. This is best revealed by the way the private economy seeks survival and development.

To develop further, the private economy must expand all the factors of production, including the number of hired workers. But local informal restrictions on hiring workers and pressure from public opinion have often forced private enterprises into joint operations with township or village governments, as in Jieshou. Or, as happened in Nanhai, private enterprises sometimes have to link hands with their own workers to expand. But these options are all the least preferred choices for private enterprises. When they operate jointly with township governments, they often have to, in effect, turn themselves over to the latter, and when they operate jointly with their own employees, they often can obtain only a small amount of capital. There are more failures than successes in the joint management arrangements between private firms and community governments or employees.

A related problem is that China's commodity economy is not yet highly developed, and many people are ignorant of the values needed in a modern commodity economy, such as credibility and contracts. The country's judicial work and legislation have yet to catch up with economic development, and most economic agents do not bear in mind the rules of conduct they have to abide by.

Over the past several years contract responsibility systems have been introduced in TVPS all over the country. The most famous is that of Yanqiao township in Wuxi. A profit contract system gives small or money-losing enterprises the right to retain incremental profits or the proceeds from reductions in losses, and a quota contract system for large and medium-size firms links wages with profits and allows additional profits to be shared with the entire enterprise work force. Yanqiao's system also involves election of managers, the transformation of fixed salaries into floating wages, and employment contracts for workers. This system has spread widely. In 1984, 98 percent of the TVCES in Wuxi and 90 percent of those in Jiangsu Province had adopted this form of contract responsibility system. Results have generally been good.

These reforms, which mainly involve enterprise management, did not and could not eliminate the weaknesses of the system regarding the relationship between owners and producers. This is an area for future reform. Community governments can, on the basis of local conditions, sell part of their enterprises to individuals and implement an internal ownership system in a planned fashion so that part or all of enterprise assets are gradually sold to workers (see Lin Qingsong and others 1987). Enterprises can establish boards of directors accordingly. Aside from this, community governments should create favorable conditions for the birth and growth of private enterprises. In doing this, community governments should publicize the ideological aspects and, more important, should formulate laws concerning private enterprises as soon as possible.

Note

1. The term "scissors differential" refers to the practice of setting procurement prices of agricultural products artificially low and sales prices of industrial consumer goods artificially high so as to generate additional industrial profits that could be used to expand investment.

Part II

Ownership and Related Issues

Ownership is one of the principal areas in which China's TVP sector differs from the state sector, and forms of ownership vary tremendously within the TVP sector itself. Although the effect of ownership on enterprise behavior, efficiency, and overall development is complex and difficult to assess and is often mediated by other factors, different ownership systems are associated with significant differences in outcome. Many of the chapters in this volume deal with ownership in the context of the topics they cover. The three chapters in this part focus on ownership itself and on such closely related issues as entrepreneurship and differential administrative treatment on the basis of ownership.

In chapter 7 Luo Xiaopeng undertakes a detailed historical analysis of ownership in the TVP sectors of the four sample counties. He explains how the hierarchy of government administrative levels and the multilevel public ownership system gave rise to a rigid ranking, or status stratification, of industrial enterprises, including TVPs as well as urban state and collective firms. Historical, geographic, economic, and even political factors have combined to create substantially different ownership and status stratification systems in different regions and localities, and the four counties well illustrate the range of variation.

Luo documents the causal factors that led to significant differences in ownership and status stratification between Wuxi and Nanhai counties despite their roughly similar level of industrial development. In Wuxi economic power, ownership, and management authority are concentrated at the township level of government. A much more dispersed pattern has emerged in Nanhai, where lower-level communities (villages and production teams) as well as individuals have a considerable degree of independence and economic power. In Shangrao and Jieshou, by contrast, until the late 1970s the TVP sector was tiny and "privileged," with relatively high wages.

Luo next examines the differing impact of rural reform, especially the production responsibility system (PRS) in agriculture, in the four counties.

In Nanhai rural reform facilitated the emergence of a diversified mixed-ownership system in which a vibrant private sector and various kinds of TVPs under joint community and private management existed alongside the multilayered community enterprise sector. In Wuxi tight controls over wages and labor movements and prohibitive restrictions against sizable private enterprises persisted and, after a brief period of struggle, consolidation and further strengthening of the traditional rigid, hierarchical TVP ownership and management system occurred. In Jieshou the PRS rapidly brought about the virtual collapse of the small existing community enterprise sector. This crisis stimulated a positive response by local authorities: the creation of an environment in which private enterprises could thrive and the larger private firms could attach themselves to and receive support from local and community governments. In Shangrao too the community enterprise sector was weakened, but it has been able to survive at a very inefficient and financially weak level. This paradoxically held down the overall level of TVP development in the county. The private sector threatens to overtake the ailing community enterprise sector.

The last section looks at new situations and problems that have emerged since 1984–85. In Wuxi the industrial TVCE sector had its best year ever in 1985, but its financial performance declined sharply in 1986, and increasing problems with investment failures and market saturation for many goods emerged. The county's response was to rigidify the labor allocation system even further and to intensify the trend of TVPs' becoming more like state enterprises in other ways as well. In Nanhai numerous mixed-ownership firms with rather clearly defined ownership rights and responsibilities have emerged. In Jieshou the problems stemming from unclear ownership of large private enterprises and personal involvement by community and county officials have become increasingly evident.

With regard to policy, Luo's main argument is that drastically different opportunities and resources for rural industrialization have made it impossible to achieve the goal of rapid industrialization in every locality. Large gaps in rural industrialization and TVP development have arisen between the most developed areas such as Nanhai and Wuxi and the more backward ones such as Jieshou and Shangrao. A crucial lesson is that urbanization must accompany industrialization.

In chapter 8 Lin Qingsong analyzes the rapid recent growth and development of the private sector, focusing on the reasons for the phenomenon and on the problems the burgeoning private sector faces. He reviews prereform TVP development, which laid the foundation for the subsequent emergence of private enterprises. The development of private enterprises since the late 1970s can be divided into two distinct phases: the "nascent" stage, 1978–83, and the "flourishing" stage, since 1984. (This classification is the same as that developed by Du Haiyan for the TVP sector as a whole; see chapter 3.) Some benefits of the rapid development of private enterprises are outlined, including the transfer of surplus labor out of agriculture, more spatial balance in TVP development, more appropriate subsectoral and industrial structure in the TVP sector, and efficiency-improving competitive pressure on community enterprises.

Lin next analyzes the causes of the rapid growth of private enterprises, chief among which were policy changes and systemic reforms. Through the PRS, the opening of urban markets to all kinds of TVPs, and other measures, the government wiped out long-standing obstacles against the free establishment of firms by individuals. Lin goes on to demonstrate how private enterprises obtain resources and factors of production, including financial capital, labor, land, mineral resources (for private mining firms), and technical personnel.

The last section deals with the problems private enterprises face during and as a result of their headlong development. Lin points out that the tiny scale of most private enterprises is a fundamental problem that will hamper efforts to improve their efficiency and argues that the political environment still impedes expansion of private enterprises beyond a certain size. Ideological ambiguity concerning sizable private firms leads to an uncertain policy environment, which blunts the firms' incentives to reinvest and encourages a short time horizon. Private enterprises often respond to their hostile administrative and regulatory environment by devoting excessive resources to sales and procurement and by establishing close relationships with local and community government leaders. Finally, ambiguity and uncertainty in policy lead to weak and unclear property relationships in private enterprises.

The chapter closes with some policy suggestions. State policy toward private enterprises should be further relaxed and liberalized; government macroregulation of the private sector needs to be improved through a better legal framework, unified finance and accounting methods, new tax laws, and better credit policies; trade unions should be established for the private sector to protect workers' legitimate rights and improve state supervision; there should be more regular government monitoring of private enterprises' operations and financial transactions, with severe punishment for tax evasion and other illegal activities; the government should fully respect the autonomy of private enterprises in choosing their ownership system and management practices; and the voluntary transformation of private enterprises into joint-stock cooperatives should be encouraged.

In chapter 9 William Byrd analyzes entrepreneurship, capital allocation and risk-bearing, and ownership, particularly the interactions among these crucial spheres. He starts by deriving a working definition of entrepreneurship suitable for the Chinese context and singling out two important entrepreneurial activities, the creation of new enterprises and the development of new products. He then describes, with the aid of case studies, entrepreneurship in China's TVP sector and under different forms of enterprise ownership. The most salient characteristics of TVP entrepreneurship include alertness to unexploited profit opportunities; personal commitment and risk-taking; the importance of personal connections; the provision by entrepreneurs of a wide range of services in the absence of functioning markets; and the rootedness of most Chinese entrepreneurs in their home communities. Available empirical evidence indicates that there is greater entrepreneurial activity in private enterprises than in community enterprises and in Wuxi than in other counties. Byrd argues that, given the high degree of immobility among communities, the traditional economic and commercial base of a locality is critical in determining the local supply of entrepreneurs. In this respect Wuxi and Nanhai are much better off than Jieshou, which in turn is better endowed than Shangrao, the only one of the four counties that may have an inadequate supply of indigenous entrepreneurs.

Byrd next analyzes the sources and allocation of capital. Three distinct sources of funds for TVPs are identified: household capital, community capital (which includes bank loans, since banks are viewed as highly responsive to community government authorities in their lending decisions), and enterprise capital. Large community enterprises rely almost exclusively on the latter two and, within community capital, increasingly on bank loans rather than on grants from community governments. Private enterprises mainly utilize household capital at the time of their establishment, but as they expand, the successful ones increasingly tap community capital, primarily bank loans. Risk-bearing is closely related to the mechanism for allocation of capital and is an important determinant of TVP performance. The traditional TVCE system in advanced areas such as Wuxi involves risk absorption by village and, especially, township governments. In more backward areas community governments are unable to play this role effectively, and the burden of risk falls by default on the local banking system.

The chapter goes on to examine interrelationships among entrepreneurship, provision of capital, risk-bearing, ownership, and management. Four main models or systems are outlined. (1) The Wuxi system is characterized by communal ownership, risk absorption by the community government, and enterprise-based entrepreneurship and management. (2) Less successful community enterprise systems also have communal ownership, but community governments are forced to take on a more entrepreneurial role (which often leads to costly failures). De facto risk absorption by the local banking system is the norm, and intervention by the community government in enterprise management is widespread. (3) "Small" private enterprise systems are characterized by the concentration of ownership, capital provision, risk-bearing, and management in the hands of the proprietors and, at most, a few other households. (4) "Large" private enterprise systems still have nominally private ownership, but their increasing reliance on community capital (in the form of bank loans) means that banks also bear some risk and that private management may be compromised. Byrd argues that whereas in systems 1 and 3 the different elements fit together harmoniously and consistently, in systems 2 and 4 they do not, which leads to various problems and inefficiencies.

The last part of the chapter looks at emerging trends and issues. The share of the TVP sector in Chinese industrial output has been rising steadily while that of the state sector has been falling—a trend that is likely to continue. Within the TVP sector the share of private enterprises is rising at the expense of community enterprises, and within the community enterprise sector, it is argued, the share of the top tier (township and town firms) is increasing or at least stable, whereas the share of the lower tiers (village and production team firms) is declining. Thus a "hollowing out" of the TVP sector seems to be occurring. Byrd argues that ownership trends can be understood in light of the analytical framework developed earlier in the chapter. The top tier of community enterprises enjoys better access to financial and other resources, greater ability to spread risks (in the more successful areas), and superior administrative connections. Private enterprises, however, may have greater flexibility and stronger incentives for proprietors. Smaller rural communities and those with inadequate resources may lack the advantages of either extreme of the TVP ownership spectrum.

The consequences that greater independence for the local rural banking system and decentralization of bank ownership will have for community governments and for TVP performance are complex and hard to predict. These measures should be embarked on cautiously. As a general principle, banks should not be owned by community governments, and the boundaries of their operations should not coincide with those of rural communities. Byrd also suggests that community governments could issue bond-like financial instruments to mobilize capital and partially diversify risk.

The chapter closes with a brief look at the problems of backward areas and private firms. The need to import entrepreneurial and other human talent into backward areas such as Shangrao is stressed. Byrd also argues that clarification and strengthening of the property rights of proprietors with respect to larger private enterprises are urgently needed.

7

Ownership
and Status Stratification

Luo Xiaopeng

In 1958 the people's commune movement swept over rural China. The economy and administration of a given area were put under a single organ, the commune, within which there were no independent property owners. The average size of a commune was about 4,000 households and 20,000 individuals, but some were much larger. This utopian experiment did not make economic sense and led to disastrous consequences. Unlike Poland and Yugoslavia, however, China did not beat a hasty retreat to family farming but instead launched a prolonged program to readjust property relationships.

The first step was to restore order in the economy while retaining the commune framework. Between November 1961 and February 1962 the basic economic unit, or accounting unit, was changed first from the commune to the brigade and then to the next lower level, the production team, which normally contained twenty to thirty households. The production team became relatively independent in its management of land, labor, and other commonly owned property. Communes and brigades, however, retained economic as well as administrative power because they still organized irrigation projects and other activities that production teams could not handle and because they had the right to acquire and own property. Moreover, communes and brigades sometimes appropriated resources from production teams without compensation. In the nation as a whole, however, production teams became accepted as relatively independent organizers of production and consumption—"relatively" because they could not sell their land, their production was subject to the state plan, they could market only part of their output, and there were no clear-cut legal regulations to protect their property from infringement by their supervisory brigades and communes.

The critical grain shortage after the Great Leap Forward of 1958 led to the en masse banishment of about 20 million people from urban centers to their home villages. From then on, change of domicile from rural areas to cities was severely restricted. Rural people were organized into production teams that were obliged to provide subsistence to their members, who lost their independence and their freedom to change occupations. Skilled workers might, with the permission of the production team, seek gainful employment elsewhere, but their earnings had to be handed over and shared by all members of the team, and the worker was paid according to the work-points recorded during his absence, at the uniform rate for the team. Failure to abide by this rule meant denial of grain rations or even worse. This policy was intended to ensure sufficient manpower for farming and to balance the remuneration for farm and nonfarm jobs in rural areas.

The rural nonfarm sector, chiefly handicrafts, which had been all but wiped out during the Great Leap Forward, was gradually rehabilitated after 1965. Many workshops became part of the commune system and were owned by communes or brigades. Enterprises run by production teams were not regarded as independent accounting units. Initially all these enterprises had an unofficial status. Only after 1970, when the national government decided to use them to promote the mechanization of farming, were they able to obtain bank loans and fiscal support. In 1976, with the founding of the National Rural Industry Administration, the position of rural firms was formally legalized.

The years 1980–83 saw the transition from collective to family farming in China. The production team as an economic entity was almost phased out, communes became townships, and brigades were renamed villages. Since farmers regained the right to choose occupations and to engage in nonfarm activities, a good number of private business firms emerged, with the permission and support of the national government. Thus, in addition to community enterprises run by communes or brigades (TVCEs), a new sector of private enterprise came into being.

In theory, state enterprises belong to the whole people, township enterprises belong to the people of the township, and so on down the line to private enterprises. Since each category of firms is attached to a unit in the administrative hierarchy which has a clearly defined rank, there is also a hierarchy of firms. Although the law is supposedly blind to status differences, government policy and administrative procedures treat firms differently according to their status. State enterprises and their employees enjoy the most privileges—preference in the allocation of material inputs and bank loans at low interest rates, lifetime employment, and so on. Rural community enterprises, especially township enterprises, are treated preferentially with respect to taxes, interest rates, and fiscal assistance. Thus rank is more than a mere classification of ownership types.

This chapter examines the TVP status stratification system, ownership systems in different regions, and possible future trends. Each of the four counties studied (Wuxi, Nanhai, Jieshou, and Shangrao) has its own characteristics and represents a region and a model (table 7-1). Although they operate within the framework of central institutions and policies, TVPs in the four counties differ in status stratification and ownership systems. Describing and

Table 7-1. Basic Data on the Sample Counties

County and year	Population (thousands)	Gross output of agriculture (millions of yuan)	Gross output of industry (millions of yuan)	Per capita grain output (jin)	Per capita savings (yuan)	Industrial output of TVPs (millions of yuan)	Fiscal revenue of local governments (millions of yuan)
Wuxi							
1978	1,008	325.91	667.44	1,253.0	16.6	425.70	83.20
1980	1,009	277.30	1,160.27	986.2	35.1	814.45	91.62
1984	1,025	395.57	2,806.02	1,196.3	153.7	2,163.43	205.54
Jieshou							
1978	508	67.52	39.09	963.0	6.0	8.81	5.11
1980	531	74.95	48.41	484.3	15.5	13.94	4.52
1984	561	127.06	150.19	716.7	46.7	74.16	7.06
Nanhai							
1978	787	363.81	365.29	832.9	66.2	20.51	74.02
1980	804	526.21	467.23	982.8	134.2	98.89	78.39
1984	842	898.29	981.21	886.1	593.5	516.19	109.01
Shangrao							
1978	645	91.31	23.39	587.6	6.7	12.57	6.44
1980	661	103.90	29.65	582.2	9.5	14.81	6.74
1984	695	147.49	70.98	681.7	34.0	23.70	8.56

Source: Information from fieldwork.

136

analyzing these variations and how they emerged are the basic tasks of this chapter.

Status Stratification before the PRS

In 1962, when the production team became the accounting unit, communes and brigades in most areas deteriorated into mere administrative organs. They remained economic entities in name only, since they possessed almost no property of their own and their independent business operations were limited. The emergence of community enterprises, however, created much new wealth for communes and brigades and gave rise to the idea of gradually expanding the public ownership sector through the development of community enterprises, primarily TVCEs. In 1979 the State Council affirmed that the development of TVCEs would primarily serve agriculture but that it could also expand the collective economy of the commune and the brigade.[1]

Opportunities for TVP industrial development were extremely unequal, however, owing to differing conditions across the country. For example, of the four counties in our study, Wuxi and Nanhai are in rich coastal areas close to traditional commercial centers and were among the earliest localities in China to import Western technology. In contrast, Jieshou has suffered from great disadvantages in its industrial development: it is overpopulated and poor, it is located in the hinterlands of the North China Plain, far from railway trunk lines and urban centers, and in the past it experienced many wars and natural calamities. Shangrao, in the northwestern part of Jiangxi Province, is slightly better off because of its relatively fertile farmland and long history of self-sufficient small farming. These varied backgrounds meant unequal opportunities for developing TVP industry and different economic structures under the three levels of community government—the commune, brigade, and team.

Table 7-2 shows the great variation in the conditions for developing TVP industries, as indicated by the total number of industrial establishments and employees in each county. Although per capita income shows a positive correlation with the total number of establishments and especially with the number of employees in industrial community enterprises, the correlation between the composition of the three-level community economy and the per capita income level is not as consistent. TVCEs in Wuxi account for a higher proportion of aggregate income and aggregate assets than do those in Nanhai, yet Nanhai's per capita income is far higher (an average Y330 per year in 1979–81 compared with Y148 in Wuxi).

Industrial Structure and Status Hierarchy

Differences in local industrial structure may partly explain the status hierarchy of the counties. Wuxi was the home of the first modern machinists in

Table 7-2. *Structure of the Rural Economy, by County, 1980*

Item	Wuxi	Jieshou	Nanhai	Shangrao
Per capita rural income from collective distribution (yuan)	146	48	350	58
Number of industrial enterprises, by level	2,306	355	2,784	350
Township	458	102	246	120
Village	1,848	54	575	230
Production team	0	199	1,963	0
Total rural labor force (thousands of workers)	497.2	220.0	357.0	186.0
Workers in industrial enterprises, by level (thousands)				
Township	43.2	4.6	22.5	14.3
Village	39.5	1.0	5.5	8.3
Production team	0	1.5	42.0	0

Source: Information from fieldwork.

China. Retired workers who returned to their home villages in Wuxi provided a tie with machinery-producing state enterprises in Shanghai, which led to close cooperation between the two places and the early development of capital goods production in Wuxi. Since machinery firms require better management, larger-scale operations, and more capital than other enterprises, in Wuxi the industrial TVP sector was dominated by TVCEs.

Nanhai's geographic advantages are similar to Wuxi's, but its history is different. Community enterprises grew on the foundation of traditional handicraft workshops and small-scale industries that traded mainly in nearby markets. Higher personal income levels, the spread of traditional industrial skills, and greater variations in market demand called for a more diversified industrial structure, and community enterprises in Nanhai gravitated toward the lower end—brigades and production teams.

Cultivated land is scarce in Shangrao, averaging less than 1 mu per person, but it is fertile. The county, situated south of the Yangtze River, has less than 300 people per square kilometer, 25,410,000 mu of forestland, rich deposits of coal, phosphorus, and sulfur, and abundant hydropower. Industry is based on the exploitation of local resources. In 1985 Shangrao's TVPs employed 3,466 miners and 3,069 kiln workers—more than half of the total number of workers in the county's industrial community enterprises.

Jieshou is in an area of flat farmland devoid of industrial resources, and before 1979 the extremely bad performance of agriculture left the county with little surplus produce. In 1979 collectives distributed a mere 105 kilograms of grain per person, and even in 1980 the figure was only 168 kilograms. Any surplus was sold to the state under the unified purchasing system. For this reason, Jieshou had practically no industrial community enterprises before 1975 except briefly during the Great Leap Forward in 1958. In 1971 there was only one commune enterprise left, and its gross value of output was less than Y50,000. After 1975 there was a sudden upsurge in the number of TVCES as a result of administrative intervention and financial support from higher levels of government. The catchword of the time was, "Go all out developing three lines of industries" (farm machinery, kilns, and grain and oil processing). These industries were not market oriented but instead served local needs, and they were mostly dependent on funds and credit from higher-level authorities. Thus their number and scale were limited.

The Origins of Community Enterprises

The different ways in which community enterprises emerged in the four counties were more deeply influenced by their status stratification and ownership systems than by the geographic factors discussed above.

THE WUXI MODEL. Wuxi has a highly integrated economy managed by the three levels of administrative organs. The township (formerly commune) is at the head, and the village (brigade) and the production team, although nominally independent in economic affairs, are actually under its strict control. The historical background of this institutional setup is that for a long time Wuxi was under pressure to fulfill high farm production targets and high government grain purchasing quotas. To ensure that these requirements were met, the county banned production teams from engaging in nonfarm activities. Production teams were compensated for this limitation on their activities by payments from TVCES.

The commune, to coordinate all nonfarm operations, controlled the appointment of top managers of enterprises at both the commune and brigade levels. These managers could be shifted around much like middle-level managers in Western corporations. Managers of brigade firms (village enterprises) did not have to be members or natives of the brigade; in fact, brigade officials were often concurrently managers of the brigade's enterprises. TVCES located in the same commune or brigade avoided competing with each other. The commune was obliged to organize efforts to assist brigades in difficulties. And in decisions about industrial investment and labor allocation, no pains were spared to ensure relatively equal income levels for all brigades and production teams. Industrial investment and employment were thus an important means of promoting equity. The county, by transferring wage payments of industrial TVCE workers to production teams, was able to maintain the high-cost triple-cropping (wheat-rice-rice) system. This is clearly shown by the distribution of income from collective sources in Wuxi in 1980 (see table 7-3).

The unique integration of the three levels of community institutions in the economic life of Wuxi was achieved through a special method of labor

Table 7-3. *Average Income of Commune Members, Wuxi, 1980*

Source	Average income (yuan)	Percentage of total
Farming	8.78	6.0
Sidelines	45.39	31.1
Industry	91.89	62.9
Wages transferred	66.89	45.8
Profits transferred	24.11	16.5
Other	0.89	0.6
Total	146.06	100.0

Source: Information from fieldwork.

compensation in the TVCE industrial sector. Factory workers were not paid directly by their employers but by the production teams from which they came. The production team pooled payments transferred from factories with income from farming and paid each member according to work-points earned during the year.

The commune and brigade had a big say in how much money production teams distributed to members or invested. With the growth of the industrial sector, the size of transferred wage payments and profits also grew. To prevent extreme inequity in personal income levels, the commune needed a sizable industrial sector to assimilate surplus labor, distribute profits, and assist brigades in setting up new ventures. All TVCEs of the commune were obliged to subsidize farming, provide new jobs, and balance local income levels. Although TVCEs and brigades were, to a degree, independently managed, the commune had the power to appoint the leading officials of both. These officials therefore had to take the interests of the entire community into account in their operations and defer to the political interests of commune leaders. The dominance of the commune and the unique type of enterprise ownership that developed were characteristic of Wuxi.

I have not yet found an appropriate paradigm for this peculiar system of property rights. It is heavily tinged with Chinese tradition and very different from the Western system under which the individual is the ultimate owner of property. The Wuxi model as it existed before the PRS might be compared with the traditional Chinese clan, in which three generations lived together. The "grandchildren" (the production teams) depended on their "parents" (the brigades) for a living. If the parents were unable to provide, the grandchildren turned to their "grandparents," the commune. The lower levels were nominally independent in financial affairs, but the "eldest generation" had the final say about disposal of property and distribution of income.

The source of this power was not only the social status of the communes but also the property they controlled and its impact on the interests of the lower levels. In 1981 commune enterprises in Wuxi turned over to production teams wage earnings of Y23.1 million, and brigade enterprises transferred another Y41.3 million. Together these totaled Y64.4 million, or about Y60 per person—one-fourth of the total annual income per capita of the county's rural population. In some communes the proportion was much higher. From the early 1970s income generated by commune enterprises continually increased in proportion to total income, and there is reason to believe that commune enterprises attracted better-quality workers as well. These developments further consolidated the political base of the communes.

NANHAI. Nanhai County's community enterprise economy is characterized by relatively dispersed management with villages and production teams as the basic economic units. The township is to a large extent regarded as an administrative organ, and the three levels of the economy are far less integrated than in Wuxi. There are some historical explanations for this pattern. The Pearl River Delta economy was traditionally more diversified and commercialized than that of Wuxi. Farmers involved in cash crops and nonagricultural activities had to rely for their grain supply on the market and even on imports. After 1949, and especially after the commune system was set up, Nanhai was required to produce grain for its own consumption and for sales to the state, but the pressure was not as heavy as elsewhere because the county had to supply fruit, fish, and vegetables to Hong Kong and Macao. Moreover, government policy in Guangdong Province was always more flexible than in the northern provinces. These factors led to higher local income levels. In addition, the county is adjacent to Guangzhou and Foshan and boasts a few big towns of its own. Its greater urbanization no doubt contributed to the diversification of its economy.

Each of the three levels developed its own industrial sector, as the following figures show.

Level	Percentage of total gross sales of community enterprises	
	1973	1982
Commune (township)	12.9	19.3
Brigade (village)	9.7	21.7
Production team	77.4	59.0

The aggregate income and wealth of the county was skewed toward the lowest level. Commune enterprises, although well developed in comparison with the Chinese average, were clustered around the towns and were not as integrated with the production teams as those in Wuxi. For example, in Nanhai commune enterprises did not have to turn workers' earnings over to production teams for final distribution (see table 7-4). Three factors account for this.

- Many of the workers were from urban centers. In 1980, of 80,000 persons employed by TVCEs, about 55,000 were from rural communities and

Table 7-4. *Income Structure of Production Teams, Nanhai, 1978–82*
(millions of yuan; percentage of total distributed collective income)

Item	1978		1979		1980		1981		1982	
	Amount	Share	Amount	Share	Amount	Share	Amount	Share	Amount	Share
Total production team income[a]	250.448	—	206.268	—	338.696	—	396.856	—	685.570	—
Total distributed collective income	177.437	100.0	142.359	100.0	229.101	100.0	238.721	100.0	449.830	100.0
From brigades	39.681	22.4	38.473	27.0	31.880	13.9	34.280	14.4	24.630	5.5
From communes	0.0	0.0	0.008	0.0	0.032	0.0	0.694	0.3	0.010	0.0

— Not applicable.
a. Includes income from private sideline activities.
Source: Information from fieldwork.

the rest were mostly local urban dwellers. Urban residents' wages were paid to them directly.

- The average incomes of production team members were not much lower than the average incomes of commune enterprise workers, thanks to high farm incomes and the wages of team members working in TVCES. In 1980 commune enterprise wages averaged Y640 as against the average rural per capita income of Y559, a difference of Y81. When income from sidelines and the lower living costs on farms are taken into consideration, there was probably a rough equilibrium, even with freedom of choice of occupation. In fact, many farmers earned more than average workers in commune enterprises, which relieved pressures on communes to transfer workers' earnings to farmers.

- The commune imposed a surtax in kind to supply grain rations to its factory employees who were rural residents so that they would not have to go home for grain distribution.

Brigade enterprises were similar to those in Wuxi in that their workers were largely rural residents and had to obtain grain supplies from the teams to which they belonged. These firms had to see to it that earnings in the factories and on farms were approximately equal. Thus a considerable portion of wages was transferred to production teams for distribution—86.4 percent in 1980. It was not 100 percent because some teams had such high incomes that they could forgo earnings from factories and because grain supplies in some cash crop areas were provided by the state. For example, brigade enterprises in Jiujiang township transferred only 21 percent of their payroll to production teams because the area specialized in fresh-water aquaculture, and fish raisers obtained grain supplies as urban residents did instead of from their production teams.

In Wuxi, as people got richer, more wealth became concentrated at the commune level. But in Nanhai the development of community enterprises led to a relatively dispersed pattern of distribution of wealth and power and to a high degree of autonomy and coherence in some brigades and teams. Since natural villages in southern China are mostly populated by members of one clan, a strong clan culture and consciousness survives to this day, and the development of TVPs has no doubt reinforced this traditional feature.

SHANGRAO. TVCES in Shangrao County had a large share in aggregate income, mainly for two reasons. First, incomes at the production team level were so low as to make incomes from TVCES seem relatively high. In 1980, of the 4,867 teams in the county, 86 percent (4,180 teams) had average per capita incomes from collective distribution of less than Y80. Of the total, 61 percent (2,974 teams) were below Y60, 41 percent (2,006 teams) were below Y50, and 20 percent (995 teams) were below Y40. No team had an average per capita income level of more than Y400; only 2 percent, or 102 teams, were above Y100.

Second, proximity to Shangrao city created demand for services, construction, building materials, and so on. Before the PRS, the TVCE sector in Shangrao County was doing quite well, as the figures for 1978 illustrate.

Aggregate gross sales	Y14,720,000
After-tax profits	Y3,530,000
Taxes on business income	Y600,000
Industrial and commercial taxes	Y130,000
Rate of profit on sales (percent)	28.9

Only Y1,060,000 of after-tax profits, however, came from industrial TVCEs, whereas the service sector contributed more than Y2 million, or Y687 per employee compared with Y149 in the industrial production sector.

It is worth noting that in Shangrao, in contrast to Wuxi, most of the earnings of workers were not transferred to production teams for distribution. With the growth of the industrial TVCE sector, the number of workers multiplied, yet the amount of wage earnings transferred actually dropped, from Y1,570,000 in 1978 to Y540,000 in 1981. The extremely low income levels on farms may account for this. TVCE workers were in a good bargaining position, as the sector generated the lion's share of commune revenues. A regular wage system was used to give incentives to workers who had a strong impact on their firms' performance. This practice spread as an increasing number of people sought jobs in the industrial sector. The difference in income between TVCE workers and farmers was more than threefold, and thus the former constituted a privileged group.

In short, the resources and local markets of Shangrao allowed brigades and especially communes, with the aid of monopolistic practices, to develop a profitable and growing industrial sector and a privileged group of industrial workers. This weakened the economic ties among the three levels of rural communities. Although a certain amount of industrial development took place, the elite part of the population was always a small minority. This is the essential difference between the ownership systems of Shangrao and Wuxi.

JIESHOU. The industrial TVCE sector in Jieshou was similar to that in Shangrao with regard to status stratification and ownership. First, the sector's proportion of income looked relatively large only because of the extremely low farm income levels. The two counties were approximately the same in population, but the average income on farms in Jieshou was even lower than in Shangrao, and the number of industrial workers and the aggregate value of output were insignificant. Second, although Jieshou's industries were limited in scale, they too received privileged treatment, and wage earnings were not transferred to production teams for distribution. The more these industries grew, the more they were alienated from the farming population, as transferred wage earnings shrank.

The main difference between the TVCE industrial sectors in these two counties was that in Jieshou profitability was even lower, so the underlying strength of the sector was weaker. Although tax and wage rates were much lower than in Shangrao, most TVCEs in Jieshou made little or no money. In 1980, of the 102 commune enterprises, 32 employed fewer than ten workers. The firms' aggregate output value was Y450,000, an average of Y14,000 per establishment and Y1,500 per worker. This meant that average net output value per employee was only about Y300, barely enough to pay wages, and consequently many of these community-run industries went out of business. The mortality rate was especially high at the commune level. There were forty fewer commune enterprises in 1981 than in 1980—a loss of 260 jobs, or 13.2 percent of total industrial commune enterprise employment in the county. Such fragility was not seen in the other three counties.

The Impact of the PRS

The PRS brought tremendous changes to rural China. The land tiller now by contract has the use-right to a piece of land and thereby the right to dispose of his own time. Moreover, he has the right to sell farm produce and to acquire productive assets with the proceeds, and his right to seek nonfarm employment has been restored to varying degrees. Such changes, however, emerged from localities' expediencies for coping with their economic problems rather than from conscious efforts to win legal rights for individuals. The economic rights and the degree of freedom of rural people vary in accordance with patterns formed in the past. That is why status stratification and ownership in the sample counties retained their palpable distinctions after the implementation of the PRS.

Jieshou: Private Firms under Collective Auspices

In 1979, after a bad harvest, average farm income in Jieshou County fell to a record low of Y28 plus about 100 kilograms of grain (excluding incomes from sideline occupations). The persistent agricultural crisis went from bad to worse. In the towns small state and collective enterprises, which altogether had some 5,000 employees, had little capacity for absorbing the natural increase in job seekers. The troublesome situation was exacerbated by the return of great numbers of people who had been sent to the countryside during the Cultural Revolution period (1966–76) but now by government order came home looking for jobs. The tremendous pressure on the local government forced it to take extraordinary measures, and as a result the county was among the earliest to institute the PRS (in 1981) and to accelerate the development of rural industry through an unusual program.

In 1980 the county's Communist party committee announced temporary regulations covering farming, commerce, and industry. The measures were considered drastic at the time. The policy statement called for expanding the scope of household responsibility in farm areas, facilitating the marketing of local industrial goods, and giving decisionmaking powers in purchasing and marketing to public commercial agencies. Concerning the industrial community enterprise sector, article III of the regulations reads:

> To hasten the development of TVCE industries and encourage extensive cooperation between enterprises, barriers between various trades, ownership forms, and administrative areas are to be eliminated. All firms may associate themselves in various ways, and all businesses should be conducted in compliance with economic laws. Government workers, urban, and rural residents are free to invest in collective industries run by the county and in TVCEs. Terms may be prescribed by contracts with regard to shares and dividends. Jobs may be provided through negotiations. Savings of enterprises at all levels may be invested elsewhere as shares of joint operations, obtaining dividends therefrom. State and collective enterprises and TVCEs may, through compensation trade, attract investment and expand the scope of operations.

These changes were intended to make a breakthrough in the statutory restrictions of the county. Along with related ad hoc decisions, this new policy led to a significant result—the emergence of a number of special types of TVPs. Some typical examples follow.

THE JIESHOU COUNTY COLLOIDAL PRODUCTS FACTORY. In 1980 a farmer applied for permission to establish a factory in the county seat. A private person was then not allowed by law to use land in town, nor could he open an account for his firm with the bank. The law was sidestepped by designating the business a TVP at the commune level under the direct control of the county. This status made the firm eligible for more liberal bank loans than ordinary private enterprises and gave it exemption from taxes. In addition, it obtained easier access to low-cost inputs through the government channels that served rural industries, advantages in obtaining fiscal assistance from the government (such as a Y5,000 interest-free loan for working capital), better credit standing because of being able to use the county's name, and the privilege of selecting a plant site anywhere in the county. At the time of our survey the firm was using this last privilege to relocate its plant from the county seat to a township that offered a better environment for business. We were amazed to find that the firm had just bought 1 mu of land at the new site for Y10,000, although China's constitution forbids private ownership of land. The purchase would have been impossible had the firm not been designated a township enterprise. In return for all these privileges, the enterprise pays

1 percent of its gross sales as a management fee to the county business administration every year.

THE SHUGUANG FOODSTUFFS COMPANY. The predecessor of this firm was
a small-scale partnership that made food products. In 1984 it planned to
start producing canned beef with support from the local district administration, which was the nominal legal owner for registration purposes but invested nothing whatsoever. The firm was actually owned by four individuals
who pooled Y20,000 and borrowed Y320,000 from the bank to start with.
The partners had full management power. In a short time they retrieved their
original investment of Y20,000. Since then, the ownership status of the firm
has been ambiguous, but the founder has consistently claimed the enterprise
as his own. The district administration—the nominal owner—has never interfered with the disposal of the firm's income. Top management was paid
no more than Y150 a month (not much more than ordinary workers), but
the salesmen, who were paid on a commission basis, could make about
Y10,000 a year. Business was so brisk that in its first year the firm recorded
a profit of Y180,000 and in the second a staggering Y400,000, tax exempt.

These nominally public but actually private firms are not exceptional in
Jieshou. (See chapter 9 for another interesting example, that of an elastic
ribbon factory. Numerous other cases were encountered in fieldwork.) A
check by a county organ in 1985 revealed that eighty township enterprises,
or 73 percent of the total, were carrying the "wrong registration," and these
were dropped from the classification. But the real reason that the firms lost
township enterprise status was not so much that their claim was false as that
they were not regularly organized, were unstable, and had no political back-
ing. Large and profitable firms such as the Jieshou County Colloidal Products
Factory and the Shuguang Foodstuffs Company, which also used false identi-
ties, remained township enterprises. Some of the other firms that retained
their status were extremely small. For instance, a furniture producer with only
two employees remained on the township enterprise list, although it was
much like a "ma and pa" store. In spite of such confusion, Jieshou's bold policies achieved what county authorities had intended—the development of a
number of industrial enterprises that could not have emerged under the old
institutional rules.

Before 1984 the position of the central government on private enterprises,
especially on their right to hire workers, was not clear. But after 1984 the
central government openly supported the rural private industrial sector, and
conditions for its development improved. Individual proprietorships and
partnerships mushroomed in the towns and countryside of Jieshou, as in the
rest of China. These were not enterprises in the regular sense of the word;
most were handicraft producers that did not need even a plant or industrial

equipment. The state of these firms in Jieshou as of the end of 1984 was as follows.

	Partnership	Individual
Number of firms	1,151	4,651
As percentage of total TVP sector	17.4	70.0
Number of employees	5,034	10,494
As percentage of total TVP sector	16.0	33.4

The two sectors combined generated a total income of Y35 million, or 40.6 percent of the aggregate income of the industrial TVP sector of the county. These figures are not quite reliable, as private enterprises tend to understate their incomes so as to pay less tax, and tax-free community enterprises tend to inflate their incomes so that managers can get promotions. Yet they do indicate the profound changes in status stratification and ownership composition that followed the introduction of the PRS. Conventional community enterprises are no longer predominant in the Jieshou industrial TVP sector as a whole, and firms that are basically private in nature have become important. The various ownership forms are now so mixed that the true identity of establishments cannot be ascertained from their nominal status. Ownership of many is actually private or undetermined, although all are attached to some administrative organ to facilitate their operations.

Wuxi: The Continued Predominance of TVCEs

If Jieshou is typical of the poverty-stricken areas in which community enterprises failed to withstand the shock wave of the PRS and turned private, were leased out to individuals, or simply closed, Wuxi illustrates the opposite tendency. Its TVCEs did undergo a shock, but the sector recovered and became stronger than ever. Township governments now possess a greater proportion of assets than all other sectors, and their control over other economic entities is even greater than in the past.

The first benefit the industrial TVCE sector gained from the PRS was the abolition of wage transfers from factories to production teams, which eliminated a large disincentive for factory workers. Under the old system a worker's earnings were not determined by performance in the factory but by the income level of the production team to which he or she belonged. The consequences could be ludicrous; for example, a skilled master might be paid less than his apprentice if the master's team was poorer.

In many other areas as well, wage transfers were gradually phased out after the PRS was implemented. This provided greater incentives for the workers but alienated the townships from the production teams and workers from other members of their teams. In Wuxi the problem was not as severe as elsewhere. The county continued to subsidize high-cost grain production and took measures to alleviate the tension between factories and production teams that arose from inequity of incomes. These measures included minimizing income inequalities among production teams (for example, no production team was allowed to engage in factory production of its own); recruiting factory workers and transferring profit disproportionately so as to subsidize poorer production teams; helping poorer villages set up their own factories; and providing liberal bonuses for technicians and skilled workers.

In addition to improving worker incentives, the PRS also resolved some long-standing conflicts between TVCEs and production teams. County officials, recalling life in the old days, stated that before the PRS these conflicts had been rather sharp. When extra compensation was given directly to factory personnel, production teams were displeased because they regarded the labor concerned as their own assets. Some production teams even went to the length of crediting more work-points to members engaged in agricultural work to reduce the average value of each work-point so that workers who were away at factories were rewarded less. This problem vanished with the advent of the PRS. The piece-rate wage system could be introduced in TVCEs only after the PRS was instituted.

The second great benefit that the PRS gave the county's industrial TVCE sector was soaring farm productivity and a great increase in farm incomes. This was most evident in 1983, when average per capita rural income in the county rose to a new high of Y494, up from Y375 in 1982. Growth temporarily alleviated the pressure to equalize personal incomes after the suspension of transfer wage payments. Furthermore, the rise in farm production across the nation helped relieve Wuxi from its obligation to wrest grain from the land through the uneconomical triple-cropping system, and much less labor input was required in land tilling. The brisk market for manufactured products helped lead the expansion of TVCE industries, which provided more jobs. In 1983 and 1984 more than 70,000 persons were added to factory payrolls, a 40 percent rise. The rapid expansion of employment in the industrial TVCE sector sustained the continuing rise in per capita incomes in the county and made it easier to narrow income gaps among farm households through allocation of factory jobs.

County authorities had not anticipated such a phenomenal and effortless expansion of industry. To prevent income gaps between the farm and nonfarm populations from widening, the county nullified the ban on production team factories. In 1984, when private enterprises mushroomed across China, the county government declared its support for the private sector and encouraged all production teams to engage in industrial activities. Meanwhile, TVCEs experimented with a bonus plan keyed to profits and output value to provide stronger incentives. The county's industrial sector was put on "five wheels," with private and production team firms added to the township, village, and county levels.

But it was soon discovered that these "five wheels" did not keep the same pace. Private firms and production team enterprises challenged the supremacy of TVCEs. They competed in hiring technical and marketing personnel, and their higher remuneration for workers broke the old balance of incomes in the county and caused wider gaps in personal incomes. The impact was so tremendous that many skilled and competent personnel demanded to leave TVCEs to set up their own firms, and labor costs were in danger of getting out of control. But the biggest headache for county authorities was the considerable number of bogus production team enterprises that were actually private. These firms, nominally leased to private individuals, could enjoy tax exemptions and other preferential treatment without contributing any savings to the collective, and they were free to compete with TVCEs for markets, personnel, and raw materials.

In 1985 Wuxi authorities took steps to reestablish order and consolidate the position of TVCEs. The principal measures included

- *Penalties for skilled persons who left TVCEs for greener pastures.* The most effective penalty was that members of the person's family were permanently barred from jobs in TVCEs.

- *A thorough check on production team enterprises, partnerships, and individual enterprises.* The status of firms was verified, and bogus community enterprises were cleared out. The criteria for a community enterprise were that the firm's initial investment must come from the savings of a community body, its site must belong to a community, its production equipment must be the property of a community, and its distribution of profits must comply with regulations. These rules require that deductions be made for a production development fund, a common insurance fund, and a depreciation allowance at the prescribed rates and that profits be remitted to the proper authorities. About 500 firms were removed from the category of production team enterprises, and village control over production team enterprises—which generally cannot even have their own bank accounts—was reinforced. Finally, the number of partnerships and individual firms that compete with TVCEs was restricted by requiring them to have permission from the village government to register, although national law requires only the permission of the production team.

- *Restoration of control over TVCE wage levels.* A new remuneration scheme for factory managers and workers allowed personal incomes to differ under the piece-rate system but tied the average wage level to profits and output value. Moreover, average wage rates were not allowed to diverge too much among firms. Enterprise managers' pay was linked to the average wage in their factories; twice the average wage was normal, and three times was the maximum.

After the implementation of these measures, production team enterprises declined to fewer than 1,000 by 1985. Partnerships and individual firms decreased as well. Only in sectors such as commerce, transport, and services, which do not compete with industrial TVCES, have private enterprises been growing rapidly.

Under the PRS the industrial TVCE sector in Wuxi initially suffered a setback, but its underlying economic strength and strong county policies allowed it to regain its dominant position. This is borne out by table 7-5 on the sources of household income; in 1983 private sources were most important, but two years later income from community sources had drawn ahead. The breakdown of fixed assets gives a similar picture. In 1986 the county's rural areas had fixed assets, excluding land, of Y1,208 million, and the share of township organs was 49.5 percent or Y599 million—2.1 times above the pre-PRS value. The share of assets owned by townships and villages in common was 39.9 percent, or Y483 million—2.75 times above the level of 1982. And the share of production teams was 7.6 percent, or Y92 million, only a 9 percent increase. Finally, the share of household-operated firms was a mere 2.9 percent of the total, or Y35 million.

Nanhai: Production Team Enterprises and Their Turn to Private Operation

Before 1979 Nanhai held the same ideological view as Wuxi with regard to production team enterprises, and to ensure adequate manpower for farming county authorities had even ruled that TVCES could not employ more than 10–15 percent of the county's labor force. But in practice the authorities were flexible. They gave quiet approval to some production team enterprises and tolerated the spontaneous emergence of private enterprises. In fact, this has been a significant characteristic of rural economic policy in Guangdong Province as a whole.

In 1980 the county government noted that in one commune that had allowed every production team to set up firms, local farmers' incomes had in-

Table 7-5. Sources of Rural Household Income, Wuxi, 1979–86
(percent)

Year	Community economy[a]	Partnerships	Household activities	Nonproductive sources
1979	62.4	0	25.6	12.0
1980	60.4	0	25.4	14.2
1981	60.7	0	28.1	11.2
1982	60.7	0	31.4	8.0
1983	26.7	0	66.1	7.2
1984	39:8	0	53.6	6.6
1985	47.3	0.9	46.2	5.6
1986	47.6	1.2	44.8	6.4

a. Includes both distributed collective income and wage income from community enterprises.

Source: Information from fieldwork.

creased rapidly. This approach was promoted across the county under the slogan "let three horses draw the carriage." In 1981, 71 percent of the county's production teams started their own industrial enterprises, and the income of the three levels' industrial sector jumped to Y572.8 million, up 1.83 times from 1978. Income generated by industrial production team enterprises was Y166.43 million, and income per person from collective sources rose to twice the 1978 level, or Y374, of which industrial and sideline occupations accounted for 57 percent. Such impressive successes caused county authorities to hesitate in making the transition from collective to family farming, and even many of the farmers were afraid that they would lose income.

Nevertheless, Nanhai, like Wuxi, went over to the PRS in 1983, and farm production increased considerably. Average personal income rose to Y760, double the figure in Wuxi. In the industrial sector great numbers of individual firms and partnerships were set up, and many production team enterprises were leased or sold to private management. In that one year the aggregate value of fixed assets of production teams dropped from Y158 million to Y134 million, whereas the value of privately owned fixed assets rose from Y16 million to Y104 million. The shock wave of the new system hit the TVCE sector of Nanhai hard, as it had in Wuxi. Skilled and competent personnel, even those at the top management level, wanted to leave and run businesses of their own. County authorities, in trying to stem the tide, were compelled to make rules like those of their counterparts in Wuxi, but these turned out to be ineffective because of the different organizational structure of the industrial sector and the more flexible attitude of county leaders. In the end, a relatively open job market came into being, and the private sector evolved into a significant branch of the TVP industrial sector.

There are several explanations for the more flexible attitude on the part of Nanhai authorities.

- Community enterprises, especially township enterprises, were not important sources of fiscal revenue for the county government or important job providers and sources of income for the rural population. When these enterprises were adversely affected, the impact was not as strong as in Wuxi (see table 7-6).

- In contrast to the situation in Wuxi, factory workers in Nanhai were mostly urban dwellers whose wages were not affected by the production teams' income levels, and so the PRS did not create as much of a shock for township enterprises to absorb.

- The remuneration for administrators and managers differed greatly between the two counties. In Wuxi village administrators and managers of township enterprises belong to the same grade. Their salaries are decided by township authorities in accordance with county government regulations requiring that relative equity be observed, with the average income of workers in local TVCEs the most important criterion. In Nanhai no such relationship existed between township enterprise managers, who are professionals hired by the township government, and village administrators, who by convention must be people from the locality and whose salaries are determined by the village's income level. The personal interests of the village administrators were not affected, and they had no strong motives for impeding the growth of the private sector, especially the shift of production team enterprises to private management.

• For the county as a whole, the trend toward private enterprises was beneficial. Private enterprises—most of which were handicraft workshops or contractors that supplied spare parts to larger factories—complemented rather than competed with county and township enterprises, and they provided jobs, which the industrial TVCE sector was unable to do. The thriving private sector greatly expanded the tax base.[2] As the sector grew, so did bank deposits, and banks in turn had more funds to lend to state and community enterprises.

In 1985, the Nanhai industrial TVP sector recorded an aggregate sales income of Y1,782 million, which was 7.5 times the total in 1978. The breakdown was roughly as follows.

	Share (percent)
Township enterprises	38
Village enterprises	31
Production team enterprises	16
Partnerships	6
Individual households	9

The last two sectors employed more than 46,000 people, as many as the township enterprise sector. Private enterprises paid taxes of Y16.83 million, or 12.6 percent of the total fiscal revenue of the county in 1985. Fixed assets owned by rural individuals rose to Y128.43 million, 6.9 times the figure for 1983, higher than the figure for production teams (Y125.63 million, not including land), and almost equal to the figure for village enterprises. Consider-

Table 7-6. *Contribution of Industrial Township Enterprises, Wuxi and Nanhai, 1983*
(percent)

Item	Wuxi	Nanhai
Taxes as share of county's total revenue	34.9	16.1
Workers as share of rural population	13.6	2.9
Transferred earnings of workers as share of total distributed earnings of production teams	41.3	0

Source: Information from fieldwork.

ing that before 1984 banks were not allowed to make loans to private enter-prises, the rate of growth was indeed extraordinary.

Most of the remaining production team enterprises have been leased or contracted out to private individuals. This trend is likely to continue. The private sector, including production team enterprises under private manage-ment, will stand on an equal footing in economic strength with the industrial community enterprise sector.

Average per capita personal income in Nanhai was Y1,029 in 1985, of which only Y114 (11.1 percent) came from TVCEs and the rest came from private sources and production team enterprises. This structure and trend are in sharp contrast with the pattern in Wuxi. The two counties are both well developed, yet their status stratification and ownership structures have be-come immensely different. This is a subject that should be studied in depth.

Shangrao: TVCEs in a Jam

Before the PRS, there was no comparison between Shangrao's economy and that of developed areas such as Wuxi and Nanhai, but the county was consid-erably better off than Jieshou. The gap between the two poorer counties was at its widest in 1979, when Jieshou was hit by serious natural calamities. In that year average per capita distributed collective income in rural Jieshou hit a record low of Y28 plus 105 kilograms of grain. But for Shangrao 1979 was a good harvest year. Average per capita distributed collective income was about Y70 per person, and the grain ration averaged nearly 250 kilograms per person. (The above figures exclude income from household sideline oper-ations, which was equal to about one-third of the distributed income.) Gov-ernment revenues and expenditures for the two counties also differed widely in that year, as is shown in table 7-7. The biggest difference was in profit remittances from TVCEs. For Shangrao the amount was almost comparable to the fiscal revenue and was 5.2 times the figure for Jieshou. The fiscal re-sources of some townships were more than adequate.

After the PRS was implemented, Shangrao's TVCEs, especially township en-terprises, suffered from deteriorating financial performance. Net profits of township enterprises dropped sharply, from Y2.08 million in 1983 to Y1.3 million in 1984 and Y622,000 in 1985. The number of industrial TVCEs fell from 410 in 1979 to 340 in 1985. Of the total, industrial township enterprises went from 120 to 118—practically no change—whereas village enterprises declined from 290 to 222. Industrial employment of TVCEs fell from 11,358 to 10,294. But the value of fixed assets (at original cost) of township enter-prises almost tripled, from Y5.78 million in 1979 to Y15.75 million in 1985, while the total payroll increased from Y7,390,000 to Y8,420,000 and average wages rose from Y590 to Y749. These figures for profits and costs indicate a severe decline in economic efficiency.

Rising labor costs may account for part of the drop in profits, but invest-

Table 7-7. Public Finance, Shangrao and Jieshou, 1979

Item	Shangrao	Jieshou	Ratio, Shangrao/Jieshou
Fiscal revenue (millions of yuan)	6.20	4.03	1.54
Per capita (yuan)	9.4	7.8	1.2
Expenditures (millions of yuan)	10.30	10.59	0.97
Per capita (yuan)	15.6	20.4	0.76
Profits from TVCEs (millions of yuan)	4.68	0.90	5.2
Per capita (yuan)	7.1	1.7	4.1
Profits from township enterprises alone (millions of yuan)	2.84	0.57	5.0
Per capita (yuan)	4.3	1.1	3.9

Source: Information from fieldwork.

ment failures and management weaknesses were more serious; almost Y10 million of new investment in township enterprises showed no return. TVCEs confronted a number of difficulties. First, higher income levels in rural areas following implementation of the PRS forced factory labor costs to increase. Second, since farmers were now free to change occupations and to set up their own businesses, many profitable community enterprises in transport and services went private. Township enterprises in these two sectors employed 1,804 persons in 1978 but only 445 in 1983. Some construction firms, although nominally not privatized, were in a very strong bargaining position with respect to township authorities, so that when they concealed their actual profits there was not much the townships could do. Third, townships did invest heavily in industry, but unwise decisions nullified their efforts. For instance, a food additive factory was set up at tremendous cost, but the product found no market. Fourth, competition from the increasing numbers of private enterprises, especially in some labor-intensive industries such as coal mining, caused the township enterprises to operate at a loss. Fifth, township governments, in trying to solve their own financial problems, forced township enterprises to turn over to them more of their profits and even some of their depreciation funds. This amounted to "drying the pond to get the fish." Finally, considerable embezzlement of public funds and corruption in hiring occurred.

The failures in the Shangrao industrial community enterprise sector may be justly attributed to mistakes on the part of county and township authorities. But these were inevitable for a first generation of grass-roots managers whose experience had been in a dispersed and closed economy. Perhaps their biggest mistake was their failure to recognize the inevitability of problems.

The fatal weakness of the industrial TVP sector in Shangrao was the absence of a sizable urban center as the core. This becomes apparent when

Shangrao is compared with Jieshou, which has such a core. There are thirty-four industrial firms in Jieshou town. If these are ignored, the TVCE industrial sectors in the two counties are similar in number of firms, average value of annual output, and average rate of profit (table 7-8); they differ only in the average capital stock per firm. In Jieshou town many township enterprises are actually private enterprises or are leased to private management, and they are more efficient in their use of funds. The experience of Shangrao also testifies to the importance of towns for developing TVPs. In the areas of Shangrao that we visited, one town, Shaxi, which is served by a railway line, stood out as a profit maker. In 1985 the profits of its industrial township enterprises accounted for one-fifth of the profits of the entire industrial township enterprise sector of the county. Shaxi historically had been a handicraft and commercial center, and it is still the busiest town in the county. One town, however, cannot industrialize an entire county.

Summary

The economic rights and personal incomes of farmers advanced tremendously when collective farming was phased out. But complex variations and problems concerning status and ownership patterns in the rural industrial sector have arisen. The old pattern in Jieshou was completely disrupted, and community enterprises survive only in name. The new de facto private enterprises

Table 7-8. *Main Financial Indicators for Industrial Township Enterprises, Shangrao and Jieshou, 1985*

	Shangrao		Jieshou	
Item	Total (millions of yuan)	Average per enterprise (yuan)	Total (millions of yuan)	Average per enterprise (yuan)
Gross sales revenues	13.35	113,100	14.36	131,700
Gross profits of profit-making firms	1.08	9,100	1.30	11,900
Total losses of loss-making firms	0.28	2,300	0	0
Net total profits	0.80	6,800	1.30	11,900
Original value of fixed assets	13.45	114,000	6.70	61,500
Net value of fixed assets	9.61	81,400	6.24	57,200
Value of circulating assets	2.55	19,100	0.98	9,000
GVIO				
1980 prices	11.62	98,500	17.11	157,000
Current prices	13.37	113,300	18.73	172,000

Note: GVIO, gross value of industrial output. The number of enterprises sampled was 118 in Shangrao (21 were loss-makers) and 109 in Jieshou (number of loss-makers not available).
Source: Information from fieldwork.

can now select the administrative organ to which they wish to be attached, a change that assists the firms in organizing productive factors but that has caused confusion about property ownership and unfair treatment of different enterprises. In the other three counties farmers have not gained such a degree of independence in running industrial activities; the three-level institutional structure has not changed, even though a new stratum has been added.

There are, however, important differences in the industrial organization of these counties. In both Wuxi and Shangrao the private sector is in conflict with the TVCE sector, but the TVCE sector predominates in Wuxi and the private sector in Shangrao. TVCEs in Nanhai are not adversely affected by the growing private sector because of the cushion provided by production team enterprises. They actually benefited from the development of private enterprises, as they can now borrow more from banks and pay less tax or win exemption from tax.

Trends, Problems, and Implications

The most fundamental factors affecting TVPs will be the inconsistencies in China's reforms and the future course of reform. The changes since 1979 have been the result of the interaction of efforts by interest groups and organizations at the county, township, village, and household levels to maximize their incomes as collectivized agriculture disintegrated. TVPs are striving to set new objectives and find new forms of existence and development. The four counties have to tackle different manifestations of this problem.

Wuxi: The Crisis of the TVCEs and Stabilization of Employment

In 1985 the total output value of industrial TVCEs in Wuxi County grew by 78.3 percent over 1984 to reach Y3.66 billion (in 1980 constant prices), and their total profits shot up to a record Y425 million, an increase of 84.5 percent. This rapid rise in profits was accompanied by a sharp increase in average wages and some expansion of employment. The average annual wage for workers in industrial township enterprises rose from Y918 to Y1,068 (a 16.3 percent gain). The increase in the number of rural residents employed and in their average wages brought the income of the rural population in Wuxi County as a whole up to the level of the urban residents of Wuxi city.[3]

In 1985 industry in Wuxi County employed 282,000 workers, or 52.2 percent of the county's total rural labor force. International experience suggests that this share is high even for a highly industrialized city. In fact, after Wuxi County achieved full employment, it experienced a shortage of labor.

Industrial production of TVCEs in Wuxi County continued to grow at a high rate, and in 1986 gross value of industrial output stood at Y4.444 billion (in 1980 constant prices), an increase of 32.8 percent over 1985. Despite the central government's policy of tightening the money supply, the value of fixed assets of industrial TVCEs continued to grow at a high rate. But the net value of industrial output (in current prices) grew by a mere 0.4 percent for township enterprises, and that of village enterprises dropped by 9.1 percent. Even more threatening were decreases in net profits of 49.7 percent for township enterprises and 55 percent for village enterprises. Government revenue and workers' incomes, however, were not affected. Local governments collected less income tax in 1986, but since indirect taxes grew by a big margin, total local revenue increased somewhat. Average wages continued to increase, with wages of workers in industrial township enterprises reaching Y1,283.

Excessive investment in fixed assets and excessive borrowing of circulating funds reduced the rate of capital turnover to the lowest point in local history. Meanwhile, interest payments and their share of net output value both climbed to a record high (see table 7-9).

According to county government reports, the principal problems confronting TVCEs were caused by intensified market competition and the increased rate of failure of capital investments. Some enterprises with capital investments of more than Y1 million began suffering from overstocks of products just one year after going into production. County leaders are only too well aware of the trend toward increased risks and sharply decreased marginal returns on industrial capital, but they see no alternative except to continue to expand TVCEs. The profits yielded by these firms furnish the bulk of local revenue and constitute the only source of funds for subsidizing agricultural production. Local farmers depend mainly on income earned by working in these firms, and township and village government leaders draw power and benefits from them. In short, TVCEs constitute the county's political and economic foundation.

Despite the increasing risks, local banking organizations continue to aid the development of TVCEs. The local agricultural bank strives not for maximum profits but for maximum benefits for the county through cooperation with the local government. It is therefore reducing interest rates on loans (within the limits set by the central government); increasing the supply of funds by such means as lending at least Y100 million borrowed from banks elsewhere to TVCEs at cost; aiding relatively poor enterprises; and helping firms that are in the red to regain profitability.

Table 7-9. *Interest Payments by Industrial Township Enterprises, Wuxi*

Item	1981	1982	1983	1984	1985	1986
Interest payments (millions of yuan)	1.136	2.163	3.137	5.67	16.50	28.42
As percentage of net value of output	0.6	1.3	1.5	1.9	3.3	5.3

Source: Information from fieldwork.

Local banks take this attitude because TVCEs are their largest borrowers and because of the banks' own incentive system (which is not discussed here). At the end of 1986 outstanding loans extended to TVCEs by the Wuxi County Agricultural Bank and the rural credit cooperatives operating under it amounted to Y460 million—64.9 percent of total outstanding loans of these institutions and equal to 178 percent of local rural residents' savings deposits at year's end. In contrast, agricultural loans amounted to less than 3 percent of savings deposits.

The current crisis is forcing county authorities to make significant policy readjustments. The primary reason for such changes, however, is probably the growing problems in the existing employment system. Owing to fluctuations in production and repeated investment failures, many TVCEs are unable to keep their workers fully employed. The instability of employment and of workers' incomes in TVCEs have caused labor movements that are beginning to threaten the traditional pattern of labor allocation and employment.

To ensure stable employment and effectively readjust the distribution of income, county authorities are trying to control the distribution of capital and labor. Measures include restricting the flow of labor into the county; ensuring the stability of sales by increasing the proportion of product orders covered by state planning, especially from foreign trade departments; borrowing large amounts of money to upgrade the technology and equipment of county firms and township enterprises and make their products more competitive; intensifying the vertical integration of county firms and TVCEs so that even the accessories required by an order received by any firm will be produced locally; instituting countywide retirement and unemployment insurance systems; and increasing expenditures on welfare and fringe benefits for workers at TVCEs. These measures suggest that Wuxi TVCEs will tend to become more like small state enterprises.

Nanhai: Joint Public-Private Firms and Widespread Employment of Outside Labor

In 1986 industrial township enterprises in Nanhai had the same problem as TVCEs in Wuxi. Despite a sharp increase in value of output, they suffered a sharp decline in profits, and their gross losses shot up to Y10.42 million, which amounted to 25 percent of their after-tax profits and was three times the 1985 figure. The net income of private enterprises and of village enterprises leased to individual managers, however, continued to grow. Production team enterprises more and more came to be owned by individuals or were turned into mixed economic entities through mergers with private enterprises. The total personal earnings of partnerships increased by 20 percent over 1985, and the corresponding rate of increase was 18.6 percent for individual household firms. Industrial private enterprises alone generated an additional Y24.84 million of income, a 34.9 percent increase. Rising incomes for workers in private enterprises compelled state enterprises and TVCEs to raise the wages of their own workers despite declining profits. This, plus a rapid increase in interest payments, caused the financial situation of TVCEs to go from bad to worse. The hardest hit were town enterprises with work forces made up primarily of urban residents. In 1986 their average ratio of profits to sales was a mere 0.3 percent.

Some successful private industrialists have experienced problems that range from inadequate space for expanding production to difficulties in obtaining loans. Although they have accumulated large amounts of capital—perhaps Y1 million—they will be defeated in competition if they fail to expand their operations in good time.

Against this background a host of enterprises jointly run by township or village governments and private industrialists has emerged. The establishment of these joint public-private enterprises was motivated by a common desire for mutual benefit based on contracts of equality rather than on responses to political pressures. This is an event of tremendous importance in China's rural industrialization. An outstanding example is the Keda Electrical Apparatus Factory in Guanyao town.

Lin Jike and others operated a factory in Yanbu town near Guangzhou that produced electrical apparatus and had fixed assets valued at about Y800,000. Because of its limited space and capital the factory had difficulty competing in the market. As it happened, the Guanyao Industrial and Commercial Company, the town government office in charge of industry, needed managerial and technical personnel. It signed a joint operating contract with Lin under which it provided a factory building and Y680,000 in equipment in return for a 55 percent share of all losses or gains. Lin Jike was appointed director of the factory, but the Guanyao town government reserved the power to make decisions.

Thus the government seems to have annexed a private factory. But the fact is that joint operation enabled the factory to get large bank loans through the influence of the town government, and the total sum of such loans has exceeded the total joint investment in the factory. Moreover, the ownership of assets for each side is clearly specified. The assets each owned before the joint operation were not merged to become common property. The depreciation funds for each side's assets are deducted and the remaining sum is calculated separately to avoid controversies when the value of fixed assets is reassessed. The two sides share the rights to newly purchased assets on a 55–45 percent basis. Because there are separate systems of taxation and management for township and private enterprises, the local tax department and the Industrial and Commercial Administrative Bureau separately assess the income of each side and collect taxes and management fees from them as before the arrangement. Although this practice seems ridiculous, it shows that Lin and others did not enter the joint operation to evade taxes.

Under the current status stratification system for TVPs, there are no rules that specifically cover public-private enterprises of this kind. The current system allows publicly owned firms to become privately owned, and it permits privately owned enterprises to become publicly owned. It tolerates firms that are publicly owned in name but privately owned in reality, as in Jieshou County. But joint public-private enterprises such as the Keda Electrical Apparatus Factory are a profound challenge to the traditional system and practices.

According to Nanhai authorities joint operations of this kind are not accidental but represent a new trend in the making. Another example is a port machinery plant that was started by rural industrialist Liang Yuanzhang in cooperation with the Pingzhou town government. The two sides each invested Y800,000 in the joint project. The immediate motivation was the town government's inability to fill product orders owing to its lack of expertise and funds. This joint enterprise is more formal than Keda, as it operates under a board of directors with Liang as vice chairman and concurrently director of the plant.

Private industrialists are often shareholders in village enterprises as well as in township enterprises. In Foshan city some private industrialists have even established joint operations with state enterprises. The appearance of joint public-private enterprises in Nanhai is nothing strange. Already ten TVCEs have entered into joint operations with private businesses in Hong Kong, Macao, and foreign countries under the policy of openness. That being the case, why shouldn't they be allowed to cooperate with local private industrialists?

Another phenomenon in Nanhai is community enterprises that hire workers from other places. The Ceramics Factory in Shanyuan village, Nanzhuang town, has a labor force of 1,500. When the local labor supply fell short of demand, it hired 450 workers from other places. Two separate reward systems are practiced for local and outside workers who do the same job. Outsiders are paid according to market prices for labor, converted into standard piecework wages, whereas local community members are paid on a work-point basis and their wages float according to the factory's revenue. Outside workers earn an average of Y6 a day, local workers Y11. The latter workers also enjoy additional fringe benefits, including pensions, free education, and medical services. Shanyuan's income averaged Y3,500 per capita in 1986, the highest among all villages in Nanhai for the second year in a row. Another example is a factory run by the Sixth Production Team of Dagu village, Jiujiang town. In 1986 the factory, by employing large numbers of laborers from other places, achieved a per capita income of Y5,000. The emergence of these enterprises is an outcome of the open labor market in Nanhai. The county now has more than 100,000 outside laborers, and there is free labor mobility within the county.

Jieshou: Dealings between Local Governments and Private Industrialists

By the end of 1985, 124 TVCES in Jieshou had closed down or suspended production because of inability to repay bank loans totaling Y489,000. In relatively developed Wuxi and Nanhai, township and village authorities are expected to pay such debts in most cases, but this amount was beyond the capacity of township governments in Jieshou, so factory buildings and land were lying idle. The Jieshou County branch of the Agricultural Bank of China (ABC), seeing potential for repayment if these facilities were well managed, agreed to grant loans to help private industrialists reinvest in the factories, on the condition that they commit themselves to repay the existing debts. This kind of arrangement is also advantageous to community governments, and it has become an important means of liquidating unpaid bank debts of community enterprises.

Tax exemption rights and rents for public land and facilities, as well as their own land and facilities, are often used by Jieshou private industrialists as collateral for bank loans. In Nanhai private industrialists are not only good managers but also have accumulated capital funds on their own. Consequently, the risks are borne jointly by community governments and private industrialists and the bank takes no risk at all. In Jieshou, by contrast, the bank could quite possibly fall victim to deals between community governments and private industrialists. The Jieshou ABC has been more involved in clearing up bad debts than banks in any other county, since it was unable to shift responsibility onto community governments as its counterparts in other regions did.

Three conditions enabled the Jieshou ABC to get directly involved in creditors' rights and clearance of liability for delinquent loans to TVPs. First, enterprises are few in number and small in size. In 1985 Wuxi had 3,622 industrial village enterprises alone, and their average output was triple that of township enterprises in Jieshou. In Jieshou only 273 TVPs had transactions with the ABC in 1986. Altogether 499 loans totaling Y3.11 million were granted in that year—only 1 percent of the figure in Wuxi and Nanhai counties. Second, land and factory buildings constitute the bulk of TVPs' fixed assets, so that there is less specificity of assets. Third, permission for private industrialists to lease TVPs or to run such firms under the name of the county or community government has increased the mobility of fixed assets.

Nanhai has the best developed labor market among the four counties; in Jieshou the development of such a market is hampered by the unlimited supply of labor. The market for real estate, however, is liveliest in Jieshou. For example, in 1987 the Zaolin Township Textile Mill moved to the county seat to get access to an uninterrupted power supply. In response to Jieshou's thriving real estate market, many firms have invested heavily in land.

Dealings between Jieshou community governments and private industrialists involve a distorted pattern of property rights that not only raises transaction costs but also gives rise to corruption. The Zhuanji Paint Factory is a case in point; a top township government official, in collusion with some relatives, cheated the bank of large sums in loans. Jieshou County has a relatively lively and open economy, but many dealings in violation of established rules have led to widespread corruption.

Jieshou also encourages private industrialists to help start or manage firms that are nominally registered as township enterprises. These enterprises, however, have to resolve two problems: the ownership of successful firms and the responsibility for liabilities of money-losing enterprises. Successful concerns started by private industrialists but registered as community enterprises may be transformed into enterprises that actually are collectively owned and that operate directly under county authorities. The Beef and Mutton Processing Factory and the Zhongyuan Canned Food Company have already been taken over by the County Labor Bureau. The Shuguang Foodstuffs Factory and the Chunyan Elastic Band Factory also may be about to become county collective businesses.

Pressure on private industrialists and businessmen to abandon their ownership rights to their firms comes from both the government, which hopes to increase the employment of urban residents, and the employees, who want job security. Improvements have been made in solving the employment problem in China's large and medium-size cities, but in smaller towns urban workers meet competition from rural workers. Private enterprises and even TVCEs want to maximize profits and would rather employ rural workers, since their labor is cheaper and they can be easily dismissed. Urban workers in most areas still hope to be employed by state enterprises or quasi state-owned ("large collective") enterprises that can provide job security. Workers in large collective enterprises not only have more job security but also have access to housing allocated by their enterprises, receive pensions on retirement, and enjoy other important welfare benefits. Therefore all TVPs with fairly large numbers of urban workers face pressure to turn into large collectives.

Private industrialists sometimes also want their enterprises to be promoted to large collective status because they believe they will not be able to maintain true ownership of the assets anyway and because the consequent change in status for the founders and their families is advantageous. The founders become government cadres, and their families are officially recognized as permanent urban residents and are able to enjoy many privileges not shared by rural residents. Of course, the private industrialists also lose many rights: their personal pay is controlled, and they no longer have the power to hire and dismiss workers freely. No doubt this seriously affects the initiative and efficiency of their enterprises. The Shuguang Foodstuffs Factory and the Zhongyuan Canning Company both produce the same types of products and use the same technology, but their efficiency differs greatly, basically because the former is privately owned while the latter has been turned into a large collective enterprise.

Li Huade and the other founders of the Shuguang Foodstuffs Factory have not yet agreed to exchange their ownership rights for more secure positions. Their present income is high, and market prospects are good. Even more important, the local insurance company has provided them with an arrangement that has reduced their risks. In 1986 the enterprise took out various types of insurance (simple personal safety insurance, accident insurance, and family property insurance) for all workers of the factory. In addition, the enterprise took out annuity insurance of Y50,000 for its principal founders and promised to do the same for other employees in important posts. Li Huade and the others were in fact trying to avoid giving up their right of ownership to the government.

But not all private industrialists are able to stand up to the pressures. In neighboring Taihe County an enterprise chiefly composed of urban workers and successfully managed by entrepreneur Li Shanyu earned annual profits in 1985 and 1986 that averaged Y10,000 for each of the twenty-three workers. Yet the firm was transformed into a large collective enterprise in 1986 under pressure from the workers.

Shangrao: An Intractable Dilemma

Shangrao is the only county of the four to possess fairly rich natural resources. Ironically, it is precisely because of this that the county's rural industry is faced with a dilemma. The difficulties involved in developing small hydropower stations are a good example. Shangrao has many such stations, with a total generating capacity of 6,955 kilowatts in 1983. Twenty-one plants, with a total generating capacity of 5,885 kilowatts, were set up by people's communes, and forty-nine, with a total capacity of 1,070 kilowatts, by brigades and production teams. Although the typical investment for a station was only several hundred thousand yuan—far less than investments in large plants—the stations were still highly risky ventures for a poor area like Shangrao. In general, one-third of the investment came from the state, one-third from banks in the form of low-interest loans for equipment, and the remaining one-third from the communities themselves. By 1986 bank loans for hydropower equipment had reached Y4.77 million, and the total investment was estimated at more than Y10 million.

Although small hydropower stations have brought many benefits to residents and enterprises in the Shangrao area, management efficiency has not come up to expectations. Serious problems occurred in design, construction, and management, and many stations run at a loss. More than half of the loans extended for hydropower have not been repaid on time. Many townships complain that the supply of electricity is not stable and that this seriously affects industrial production. Hydropower projects have to be a certain size and be built under certain conditions to be economically efficient. They also require specialized techniques and managerial knowledge and hence relatively unified and specialized management. The organizational structure and form of ownership of TVCES can hardly cope with such requirements.

The small cement plants of Shangrao County have achieved greater success than the hydropower projects. The simplicity and small size of Chinese-made cement machinery reduces the gap between the management ability of community governments and modern technology. As a result, the production of low-strength cement has expanded rapidly. The qualities of cement products are highly standardized, and it is easy to disseminate the methods of testing quality. Moreover, sales techniques are simple. But the county has paid a heavy price for its cement plants in energy wastage and environmental pollution. The small cement plants are adapted to the low investment and management abilities of Shangrao's community governments, and they do not offer a solution to Shangrao's basic problem—its inability to make use of modern technology. Similarly, large numbers of farmers have set up small coal pits and brick kilns; but this use of primitive technology does nothing to stimulate production for markets in other parts of the country, and it cannot help the farmers broaden their mental horizons.

Conclusions

For some time China followed the Soviet model of development and copied that economic system. The intention was to achieve nationwide industrialization rapidly, but the system also favored the town over the countryside and industry over agriculture. Both countries followed the same model, but China, unlike the Soviet Union, has had to cope with the growing pressure caused by its vast population. This has forced it to elevate rural industrialization from a spontaneous activity to a national strategy for providing jobs for surplus rural labor.

China's rural industrialization has occurred against the background of privileged development of town and industry in comparison with countryside and agriculture. This determined the fundamental characteristics of the organizational structure of TVPs and their ownership rights. As far back as the 1950s the government established a state monopoly on the purchase and sale of grain, cotton, edible oil seeds, and other important farm products. The purpose was to ensure supplies to urban industry while restricting migration of rural residents into the cities and, as a first priority, to feed and clothe all members of the Chinese population. The establishment of a well-organized system of status stratification in rural society under the principle of combining government administration with economic life inevitably followed. The system guaranteed the privileges enjoyed by the city and by industry. At the same time, it deprived farmers of their property rights to land and allowed urban industry to establish monopolies under state protection.

The development of TVCES has been the result of a compromise, or "deal," between the city and countryside as the latter faced population pressure. The motives for this deal and its essence were clearly revealed in the early stages of TVCE development in Wuxi County. To this day, the county still links rural industrialization with the fulfillment of state grain purchasing quotas as a general principle. In the 1960s there was a tacit agreement between city and countryside: the farmers received limited permission to run industries and in return committed themselves to continuing to supply the cities with low-priced agricultural products. In other words, farmers were allowed to own some industrial assets independent of the state industrial establishment, to compensate for their loss of property rights to land.

For TVPs this deal had a dual character. On the one hand, in conformity with the rural commune system of combining government administration and economic management, TVPs had to subordinate themselves to communes or brigades. On the other hand, they were not covered by urban industrial planning. These two conditions led TVPs to form institutionalized structures of status stratification but made them relatively independent compared with urban industrial enterprises.

Important Features of the Ownership System

The main features of the TVP ownership system are as follows.

- In general, the property rights of TVPs are defined in a clear-cut and complete manner in comparison with those of urban state enterprises. With state enterprises it is not clear who is responsible for the income yielded by their assets and for the risks from their operations, especially capital investment risks. Such risks can eventually be shifted onto the entire society, and as far as the enterprises are concerned, property rights and liabilities become meaningless. With TVPs, however, community governments are responsible for such income and risks in most cases. Whether all or only some members of a community are directly responsible for the income and risks of a specific firm depends on circumstances, but on no account will it be possible for the enterprise to shift such responsibility, especially responsibility for capital investment risks, onto other communities.

- The ultimate owners of TVPs are individual farmers or groups of farmers. The ultimate owners of TVCEs are all of the farmers in the communities within which the enterprises operate. But as a matter of fact, the forms of ownership are diversified, and in some cases even essentially different, among regions and localities. The rights of individual members of rural communities with respect to TVCEs are not clear-cut. For example, the statement that "a township enterprise is an enterprise owned by the people in a given township" probably has more practical meaning in Wuxi than in the other three counties.

- TVPs with different forms of ownership do not have equal status. Farmers are of lower status than urban residents, members of villagers' committees are lower than township government leaders, and ordinary farmers are lower than members of their own villagers' committees. Township enterprises are of lower status than state enterprises or urban collective enterprises, village enterprises are lower in status than township enterprises, and so on. The higher the grade of a firm, the more preferential treatment and resources it gets from the government and hence the stronger its sense of security. The lower the status of an enterprise, the more directly is the firm's income linked to that of its owners and the clearer are the relations between them.

- Transfers and changes in enterprise ownership forms can vary according to the ranks of the enterprises involved. The ownership of a TVCE cannot be transferred to another firm of the same rank because workers of all enterprises are residents of the same township or village and therefore cannot be transferred. The ownership of an enterprise can be changed, however, by raising its status. For example, a township enterprise may, through transfer of its assets to the state, have its status raised to that of a state enterprise operating under county authorities. Under such circumstances the status of enterprise workers will be raised correspondingly. In general, it is difficult for the government of a given level to prevent an enterprise directly under its jurisdiction from getting upgraded if the upgrading is in the interests of the workers. As a consequence of the PRS, community enterprises in difficulties can now be sold or leased to private industrialists. Owners of private enterprises can sell them or have them raised to community enterprise status. At present, standard methods and procedures for the transfer and change of ownership of TVPs are lacking. Ordinarily these changes are carried out according to unofficial agreements or unwritten local rules or by adapting official rules and regulations.

The Significance and Adaptability of the TVP System

There are three main policy targets for the TVP sector in China: supporting agriculture and augmenting farmers' incomes; consolidating and advancing public ownership by developing TVCEs; and achieving local rural industrialization to prevent large-scale rural-urban migration and the social and economic problems that arise from urban congestion.

Among the four counties covered by our investigation, only Wuxi has met all these targets. In China as a whole, counties like Wuxi are few and are located mainly in suburban areas under the jurisdiction of large industrial cities or in south Jiangsu and the Pearl River Delta, where there are many well-developed medium-size and small cities. In other regions only a small fraction of the total number of townships and villages has attained these objectives.

Nanhai County seems to have achieved the first and third goals, but its efforts to promote the second have not been as successful as expected. Although Shangrao has made some progress toward the first and third targets, it is now laden with too many difficulties to go further. Jieshou has abandoned all three goals. To assist industrial development in its own urban area, it has altered the traditional definitions for the status stratification and ownership of TVPs by removing restrictions against the development of private enterprises and against rural-urban migration. Cases like that of Jieshou are few nationwide; Nanhai and Shangrao are more representative.

Following the introduction of the PRS the Chinese government shifted the focus of its policy for rural industry onto the third target. It is now working to correct price distortions between agricultural and industrial products. At the same time it has begun to back the development of private enterprises while allowing the transformation of existing community enterprises through shareholding and through adoption of cooperative and other modern organizational forms.

In this situation the organizational and ownership structures of TVPs, taken as a whole, have proved to be highly adaptable, allowing alternative policies for areas with different levels of development and different economic conditions. For example, the Wuxi County government is able to intervene in the operations of grass-roots units and in this way minimize competition among local enterprises, ensure maximum equality and security for all of them, and improve the competitiveness of the county as a whole. Within the same basic institutional framework, Jieshou County goes to the opposite extreme through a laissez-faire policy that allows the privileges of community enterprises to be transferred but not abandoned. In Nanhai County official respect for individual property rights and freedom to choose jobs has increased the society's understanding of property rights in general and of individual rights in particular. This new relationship of rights is becoming an important means of coordinating the development of community and private enterprises under freer market conditions.

Contradictions and Problems

There exist deep-rooted contradictions in the organizational structure and the ownership and status stratification systems of TVPs. Preventing excessive migration of rural residents into cities and consolidating the public ownership of the rural economy are two important policy targets. The principal incentives for achieving such targets should be markets and property rights. But such a policy design works only if there are opportunities and capabilities for industrial development everywhere in the countryside. In fact, the distribution of such opportunities and capabilities is extremely uneven. Hence this policy design caused large investment failures in underdeveloped areas such as Jieshou and Shangrao, whereas in Wuxi and Nanhai it led to excessive industrial growth as all villages and townships started factories.

Since the system of community ownership inhibits the flow of labor and capital, communities or regions with full employment ignore the opportunity cost for the whole society and turn to capital-intensive investments, high social welfare, and high consumption, thus reducing the efficiency of capital utilization and making a fair distribution of income impossible. The standard of living enjoyed by people in some of the townships and villages in Wuxi and Nanhai has approached or even exceeded that of local urban residents. This contributes to fair distribution of income within these counties, but it means greater inequality between them and rural regions that lack opportunities for industrial development. Large investments in scattered public facilities and infrastructure reduce the potential economic benefits from urbanization and concentration.

Under the status stratification system of TVPs, many leaders of grass-roots units work as government officials and simultaneously represent the owners of community enterprises. The combination of these two roles in one person inevitably gives rise to serious political and economic interference. Political pressure from the top often causes encroachment on economic interests, which can lead to distortions of economic information, gross violations of law and discipline, and widespread corruption.

The dependence of TVPs on administrative organs and on administrative protection of their interests and property rights gravely hampers the optimal development of their organizational structure and makes it difficult for them to use organizational and technical innovation to benefit from the expanded local economy and specialized production. This pattern also constitutes the source of investment failures and of destructive and excessive competition. Although the pioneering spirit of private industrialists has been important, the institutionalized discrimination against private enterprises inherent in the status stratification system obviously prevents them from doing their best.

These weaknesses were hidden by the high-speed economic growth of the TVP sector in 1983–85, when the market expanded rapidly. But since 1986 the overall economic efficiency of TVCEs has dropped sharply. This suggests that the weaknesses of TVPs may have already become a significant hindrance to rural industrial development.

Seeking New Ways to Advance under Harsh Restrictions

The present TVP system bears the imprint of the utopian fantasy of thirty years ago. With the gradual disappearance of that unrealistic dream, the harsh reality behind it has become clear to the people. But the system of TVPs unique to China was born under restrictions that are impossible to dismantle in a short time.

It is easy to criticize the system's backwardness and the mark of feudalism it bears by making a simple comparison with the organization and property rights of enterprises in Western societies. But China's unique cultural traditions, as well as its population problem, are the legacy of its history. China has no way out but to take these restrictions into account as it seeks the right path and tactics for its advance toward modernization. Moreover, the forces of inertia in the urban economic structure affect the choice of policy alternatives. In particular, the urban employment and welfare system promotes "equality" for urban citizens but is unfair to farmers and is a great obstacle to China's urbanization.

Rural industrial development will, for a fairly long time to come, continue to be an essential part of China's rural development. Nevertheless, as the experience of many other countries shows, urbanization is the only way to modernize. A development strategy that pushes rural industrialization as a substitute for urbanization might prove costly. To smooth the development of rural industry and to make it a harmonious and active factor in the whole process of modernization, it is essential to revise or even redesign the TVP system and its goals. In view of the difficulties and crises that face TVPs, it is necessary to consider how to speed up urbanization over the medium term. A new urbanization strategy is needed as the precondition for reforming urban-rural relationships, the institutional system for urban and rural enterprises, and other systems.

It is impossible in the near future to pull down the barrier between urban and rural areas and effect a relatively free flow of population. Policy should therefore focus on improving the coordination and management of TVPs. A pressing task is to set up new types of investment and monetary institutions to serve as efficient policy instruments and means of coordination. Domestic market conditions have witnessed profound changes, but the craving for investment is still strong in rural areas. Lack of managerial expertise and of ability to make sound investment decisions have created great risks for TVPs. The first priority at present is to prevent unnecessary grave losses, not to seek optimal development for rural industry.

Designing and realizing the TVP system of the future will require a fairly long period of experimentation. China, a big country with a rich cultural heritage, cannot indiscriminately copy the experiences of foreign countries. It will be possible to implant modern organizational principles into the systems of Chinese enterprises only after significant technical and theoretical breakthroughs are made. So far, long-neglected problems have surfaced, new conceptions are being introduced, and systematic studies have been started. Even more important, some innovations are being tried out in practice. We have every reason to anticipate the establishment in China of a modern, unified system of urban and rural enterprises that preserves the characteristics of the national culture.

Notes

1. "Stipulations of the State Council on Some Issues Concerning the Development of Commune and Brigade Enterprises."

2. Nanhai's fiscal contribution to the next higher level of government was required to increase at an annual rate of 7 percent from the 1983 base, and the country was allowed to keep all of the surplus. In Wuxi more than 80 percent of total yearly fiscal revenues has to be handed over to higher authorities.

3. According to sample surveys, the per capita income of urban residents of Wuxi municipality (which includes three counties—one of them Wuxi County—as well as the medium-size city of the same name) averaged Y957.84, compared with Y974.32 (net income, Y818) for people in its rural areas. It is true that some factors that affect the income and expenditures of rural and urban residents are not comparable, but when the more equal distribution of income in the city than in the countryside is taken into account, we can safely say that by 1985 most rural residents in Wuxi County had the same income level and living standards as residents of Wuxi city.

8

Private Enterprises: Their Emergence, Rapid Growth, and Problems

Lin Qingsong

Since 1978, and particularly in the past several years, rural China has seen an unprecedented proliferation and growth of industrial private enterprises, which immediately became fierce competitors with community enterprises. Recognition of the role of the private sector is necessary to an understanding of the historical process of industrialization in China's rural areas. This chapter discusses China's private enterprises, in particular their environment and the characteristics of their operations.

Since the founding of the People's Republic of China there have been three waves of rural industrialization. The first came in 1958, when the people's communes were established and a nationwide industrialization campaign was launched. The second wave began in 1970 when the State Council, at a conference on agricultural development in North China, called on rural areas to speed up agricultural mechanization. Farm machinery factories set up by rural community governments spread all over China, further boosting the development of commune and brigade enterprises. The third wave came after the Third Plenum of the Eleventh Central Committee in December 1978 shifted the nation's focus to the reform of the economic system. Community enterprises entered a new era of rapid growth, but the main difference between the third wave and the first two was the unprecedented magnitude and speed of the development of private enterprises.

The recent development of private enterprises can be roughly divided into two stages: the nascent stage (1978–83) and the flourishing stage (since 1984). Even before 1978 the soil had been prepared to some extent for the development of private enterprise, and a few rural residents had launched some private firms. But under the influence of the ultraleftist policy of the time these firms were regarded as "illegal underground factories" and were strangled in the cradle. Even household sideline production by farmers was banned as the "tail of capitalism."

After 1978 the Chinese government abolished policy restrictions against farmers' entering nonagricultural production. As a result, even as community enterprises continued to grow rapidly, the industrial and sideline production of farm households (a fledgling form of private enterprise) enjoyed speedy development. Between 1979 and 1981 the value of output of farm household sideline production increased at an average annual rate of more than 14 percent. During 1981–83, with the introduction of the production responsibility system (PRS) in agriculture, the value of output of farm household handicraft industry jumped by 105 percent. Meanwhile, a large number of private enterprises began to emerge, including handicrafts in farm households and simple manufacturing enterprises run by individual farmers. Some regions saw the emergence of cooperatives and industrial partnerships jointly run by groups of farm households. During this nascent stage most of the increase in rural industrial production was still contributed by community enterprises.

1984 saw extremely rapid growth of private enterprises. The gross value of industrial output (GVIO) of individually run rural firms catapulted to Y11.7 billion, or 9.4 percent of the GVIO of all TVPS, and the GVIO of partnerships and other jointly run firms grew to Y10.1 billion, or 8.1 percent of the GVIO of all TVPS. To exclude the effect of different methods of collecting statistics, table 8-1 gives figures on the share of private enterprise in the TVP sector for 1984 and 1985 only. Private enterprises account for a large proportion of the totals for number of firms, employment, value of output, and annual growth rate. Since 1984 private enterprises have given a "second push" to the third wave of rural industrialization, as data on industrial TVPS in Jieshou, Nanhai, and Shangrao counties testify.[1]

The Benefits from Development of Private Enterprise

As is true of community enterprises, the development of private enterprises can help speed the movement of rural surplus labor out of agriculture, invigorate the rural economy, raise the incomes and living standards of farmers, increase central and local government revenues, and promote the historical process of rural industrialization and national modernization. In addition, the development of private enterprise has some distinctive economic implications.

The development of private enterprises may help improve the efficiency of resource allocation and utilization. China is a large developing country with an extremely backward economy, a serious shortage of capital, and an abundant supply of labor. The development of TVPS can help promote the substitution of labor for capital and the more efficient utilization of both factors. According to some estimates, during 1979–84 TVPS increased their total value of output by Y83.6 billion. In so doing, they used 6.9 million rural surplus laborers, which in effect substituted for Y28.1 billion of investment in fixed assets (see Development Research Institute 1986, p. 11). Since private enterprises are more likely than community enterprises to employ labor-intensive production techniques, their substitution of labor for capital is even

Table 8-1. *The Share of Private Enterprise in the TVP Sector*

Item	1984	1985
Total number of TVPs (thousands)	4,812	4,930
Of private enterprises	3,911	4,076
Number of private enterprises as percentage of total	81.3	82.7
Increase in private enterprises as percentage of increase in TVPs	—	139.2[a]
Employment in TVPs (millions)	36.561	41.367
In private enterprises	11.072	13.546
Employment in private enterprises as percentage of total	30.3	32.8
Increase in private enterprise employment as percentage of increase in TVP employment	—	51.5
Value of output of TVPs (billions of yuan)	125.44	182.72
Of private enterprises	21.9	36.79
Value of output of private enterprises as percentage of total	17.5	20.1
Increase in private enterprise value of output as percentage of increase of TVP value of output	—	26.0

— Not applicable.

a. The growth of private enterprises outstripped the overall increase in the number of TVPs because 46,300 community enterprises exited during this period.

Source: Statistical materials on China's TVPs.

more evident. In Jieshou County in 1986, for instance, each Y10,000 of output value of private enterprises required 2.63 workers and a fixed asset investment of Y1,615.5, which meant that private enterprises needed less investment and offered more jobs than state and community enterprises.[2] Moreover, private enterprises use scattered resources that cannot be fully utilized by state or community enterprises, such as leftover bits and pieces of industrial materials and small deposits of low-grade mineral resources, and they economize on costly land to a greater degree.

Private enterprises also contribute to geographically more balanced development. The huge gaps in development among regions before industrialization and the prospect that industrialization itself may widen these gaps have long been a headache for China's economic modernization. During 1949–78 the government achieved some results by constantly increasing state investment in backward areas, but it failed to solve the problem. Such "blood transfusions" of investment are usually extremely inefficient and sometimes encourage backward areas to rely on state aid.

In the first few years after 1978 the government depended almost solely on community enterprises to push rural industrialization. But the gaps among regions, instead of narrowing, widened alarmingly as a few relatively developed areas took advantage of their rich financial resources, abundant human talents, and favorable geographic conditions and enjoyed rapid rural industrialization while the backward areas could hardly get off the ground. Since 1984 the blossoming of private enterprises has helped narrow the gaps among regions and has offered new hope for solving the problem of regional imbalances (see chapter 12) as rural industrialization progresses.

Another benefit of private enterprise is the more coordinated development of nonagricultural production in rural areas and the correction of deviations in the structure of nonagricultural production. China's traditional industrialization strategy led to serious distortions in economic structure and low overall efficiency. Until 1984 the same kinds of problems existed in the development of nonfarm activities in the countryside. The surprising similarity between the structure of the nonagricultural sector in rural areas and in the economy as a whole (see Development Research Institute 1986) arose from the efforts of grass-roots rural community governments to boost rural industrialization. The similarity between urban and rural industrial structures has exacerbated the existing structural contradictions in the national economy and has seriously hindered the improvement of the efficiency of the national economy and the further development of rural industries themselves. Since 1984 private enterprises, with their strong market orientation, have begun to break through the limitations that community governments imposed on community enterprises to further the governments' noneconomic goals. Private enterprises are actively seeking favorable investment opportunities offered by the imbalances in the national economy, and to a certain degree they help correct structural distortions (see chapter 12). They thus contribute to the improvement of the efficiency of the national economy. The overdevelopment of manufacturing industries in Wuxi County, where community enterprises dominate, and the more balanced structure of production in Wenzhou city, which sees private enterprise as the principal part of its TVP sector, support this conclusion.

The development of private enterprises poses a new challenge to community enterprises. In the past rural industrialization shared some of the drawbacks of the traditional industrialization strategy. Centralized control and administrative interference by village and township governments sapped enterprises' decisionmaking power and rendered them unable to react promptly to changes in market supply and demand. The "big pot" system of distributing income among firms within a community and among employees of an enterprise dampened enterprises' and employees' initiative and enthusiasm. Community enterprises still often suffer from economic inefficiency and lack the capability to advance their own development. Private enterprises, which can be more flexible, often obtain more favorable economic opportunities and bigger market shares. Their competition in factor and product markets has put great pressure on community enterprises and has forced them to reform their inefficient systems. In recent years Wuxi, where rural industrialization based on community enterprises is far advanced, has felt threatened by the Wenzhou model, in which private enterprises dominate. Wuxi has sent several teams to study the Wenzhou experience and is now busy preparing further reforms in its TVP system. These experiences show that the impact of the development of private enterprise on China's rural industrialization should not be underestimated.

Why Private Enterprise Has Mushroomed

The vigorous growth of private enterprises in China's current wave of rural industrialization is the result of a series of policy readjustments and system reforms. The government took steps to wipe out the systemic and policy obstacles that prevented farmers from freely entering nonagricultural activities and to provide them with the necessary economic conditions for setting up firms. Private enterprises could not have come into being if government agencies at all levels had continued, as during 1958–78, to control production by compulsory means and to force people "to offer nothing but their labor and on the other hand to have nothing as their own property except that for personal consumption." Starting in 1978 the restrictions that barred farmers from freely entering nonagricultural activities were gradually relaxed. In particular, the implementation of the PRS hastened the dismantling of the system of the "combination of government and commune" and the restrictions on farmers' rights to own property and change their status. System reforms in urban areas have broken down the mandatory planning system and the state-controlled distribution system that had long curbed the development of producer goods markets. The reforms thus wiped out some ingrained obstacles to the development of private enterprise.

The recent phenomenal development of private enterprise was possible because of social and economic preconditions brought about by the economic reforms.

Rural Monetary Accumulation

Funds for launching private enterprises usually come from three sources: the founders' own savings; collective funds—including fixed assets (factory buildings, machines, and equipment) and floating capital—that are now at the disposal of individuals who operate commune and brigade enterprises under contracts or leases; and loans from banks and credit cooperatives as well as credit from local residents.

A survey of typical cases shows that founders' own funds usually account for one-third and sometimes all of the total startup investment for private enterprises. During 1978–84 the introduction of the PRS and the rise in procurement prices of farm products increased farmers' incomes remarkably. Average per capita net income jumped from Y133.57 in 1978 to Y355.33 in 1984, an increase of more than 150 percent, and farmers' bank savings rose from Y5.57 billion to Y43.81 billion. (The amount of cash that farmers kept in their own hands might have been three or four times that figure, since some were afraid to make their wealth public by depositing their money.) As rural households specialize in different types of production, the income gap between farmers has widened, and the cash and bank savings of prosperous farmer households may be thousands or even tens of thousands of yuan. These savings can be tapped by farmers to launch private enterprises, and they are the foundation for credit provided to infant private enterprises.

Another important source of startup funds for private enterprises is the collective fixed assets and floating capital to which individuals gain access by becoming managers of TVCEs through contracts or leasing. Around 1978 some of the TVCEs set up during the previous two waves of rural industrialization closed down and others had low profits or chronic deficits. These firms were a heavy burden on rural community governments. Many communes and brigades, particularly those with weak leadership, followed the example of the PRS in agriculture and dispersed their holdings. They sold some or all of their enterprises to individuals at extremely low prices, leased them at a fixed rent, or contracted them out in return for a certain percentage of after-tax profits. Before 1984, according to surveys, such firms accounted for as much as 50 percent of the total number of private enterprises in economically backward provinces. Thus a large proportion of private enterprises were originally TVCEs. Most of the "capable persons" or grass-roots cadres who obtained ownership or management rights to TVCEs under preferential conditions have proved to be successful managers. So, in a sense, failure in the management of the original TVCEs was a factor in the successful development of today's private enterprises.

Loans from banks and credit cooperatives and credit from local residents form a third important source of funds. Since 1978 the Chinese government has gradually relaxed restrictions on loans to individual businesses and other private enterprises, and since 1984, in response to government encouragement of private enterprise, banks and credit cooperatives have sharply increased their loans to private firms. Loans make up a larger proportion of the total funds of private enterprises in advanced than in backward areas and for large firms than for small individually run enterprises.[3] Meanwhile, where the commodity economy is advanced and private enterprise is the main part of the TVP sector, the informal credit business has developed rapidly, and in such places as the rural areas of Wenzhou city informal credit is already the main source of funds for private enterprises.

Labor Supply

Liberating farmers from their dependence on the land and on community governments and giving them freedom over the use of their own labor was the precondition for a dependable supply of labor for private enterprises. After 1958 the people's communes used such coercive means as the household registration and grain ration systems to confine farmers to the limited arable land. The abolition of the commune system to a great extent eliminated the restrictions that curbed farmers' freedom to choose occupations and move from one place to another. The great numbers of surplus rural laborers that were buried in oblivion in the past began to leave agriculture. Farmers with money or technical know-how and managerial ability started or invested in private enterprises, and others swarmed into the labor market. By the end of 1985, 41,521,400 rural surplus laborers in China were employed by community enterprises and 28,268,900 by private enterprises. It is estimated that there are still more than 100 million surplus laborers in agriculture, so the abundant and cheap labor supply brought into being by the rural reforms is still available to be absorbed by private enterprises.

The main reason that large numbers of farmers are attracted to jobs in private enterprises is higher incomes. Of 951 employees surveyed in fifty-two private enterprises in thirteen counties of Shaanxi Province, 90.6 percent said they sought jobs in these firms to earn more money, 6.5 percent wanted to learn techniques and skills, and 1.9 percent had other reasons. Of those who wanted higher incomes, 6.6 percent (mostly technicians and skilled workers) were from areas with relatively high living standards, 71.7 percent were from families that could afford basic necessities but wanted a higher standard of living, and 21.7 percent were from poor families seeking a basic livelihood.

Freer movement of labor means an improved supply of workers for private enterprises. For instance, local surplus labor in Xiqiao town, Nanhai County, has already been almost totally absorbed by TVPs, but private enterprises can still recruit large numbers of workers from backward areas in other regions. In 1986 TVPs in Xiqiao employed 1,469 laborers from other regions, and jobseekers are still coming to the town. Owing to the rapid development of TVPs, Lianxiang village in the town has had no surplus laborers since 1984. Thus when twelve local farmers pooled their funds in 1984 to launch the Lianchang Silk Knitting Mill, they had to recruit half of their 120 employees from other areas. (The rest were family members and relatives of the shareholders.) But in general, workers in private enterprises come mainly from nearby, and in new firms the first group of employees typically consists of the founders' families, relatives, and friends. In more developed areas employees hired later may come mainly from other townships, counties, or even provinces, since local labor is in short supply and workers from other areas are cheaper, more manageable, and more willing to do heavy manual labor than local people.

Land and Natural Resources

In the past most private enterprises were small individual firms or household-run factories that usually occupied founders' homes or private plots or land contracted to them by local communities. But private enterprises that have many employees or engage in mining or in producing building materials face a serious problem of land acquisition.

Most private enterprises consider two factors in choosing factory sites: the cost of the land and distance from the market for their products. They take into account administrative restrictions, where applicable, but not local governments' employment and nonagricultural output goals. Most firms prefer to set up their operations in small towns and accordingly try to rent public or private buildings.

Although the PRS only defines rights to the use of farmland and its output and does not cover the right to transfer and dispose of land, it represents a significant step toward the commercialization of land. In particular, the policy that implicitly allows farmers to make their contract land available to others gives private enterprises easier access to land. But since there is no clear definition of property rights to land, and since farm households cannot formally transfer the property rights to their contract land, private enterprises, rather than purchasing land for new factory buildings, usually lease it or make joint management arrangements under which the land is counted as shares in the firm.

At present, mineral resources are not highly commercialized. In the past few years a state policy that allows all types of enterprise to use mineral resources freely has given private enterprises access to mining. In 1986 China promulgated its law on natural resources and began taxing their use. But because differential rents for the exploitation of resources were not taken into consideration in fixing the tax rate and because the regulations are not properly enforced, the effective fees for the use of resources are still very low.

The case of the Chaoling Coal Mine in Fangshan County, which has the largest employment of any mining TVP in Beijing municipality, is an example of the low fees and high profits in mining. The mine began operating in November 1984 with capital of Y377,000, all in loans. By the end of March 1986 it employed 195 laborers, had an annual production capacity of 40,000 tons, and had produced a total of 23,850 tons of coal with a total output value of Y632,000 (net of Y93,000 in loan repayments). In 1985 the mine turned over to the state Y16,000 in resource taxes (Y1.50 for each ton of coal mined), Y38,100 in income tax (calculated at the rate of 1.5 percent), and Y1,500 for the individual business administration fee, which left

Y44,000 in after-tax profits. The mine was still enjoying exemption from indirect taxes in 1985.

The mines that the state leaves to private enterprises are usually small and scattered. Nevertheless, high product prices and fat profits still make mining attractive to the private sector.

Availability of Technology and of Technical and
Managerial Personnel

Economic reforms have extended the commodity economy to the science and technology sector. The gradual commercialization of technology has offered private enterprises access to the technology market, and many private enterprises have paid to obtain technology for development. Experience shows, however, that whether private enterprises prosper depends less on technology than on the availability of managerial and technical talent. Success depends on such "capable persons" more than on funds, land, labor, and the other technical factors of production because these people can find supplies of the other factors and pull them together to make profits.

Earlier, markets were often less important than the availability of technical personnel in determining private enterprises' choice of activities. In recent years greater job and geographic mobility for technical and managerial personnel has given a strong impetus to private enterprise. The technical and managerial personnel of private enterprises are primarily former commune and brigade leaders, skilled craftsmen and educated youth, and former workers in state enterprises or TVCEs. A sample survey of 103 leaders from fifty-two private firms in Chang'an, Zhouzhi, and eleven other counties in Shaanxi Province showed that 15.5 percent were former commune and brigade leaders, 53.4 percent were technical and managerial personnel from TVCEs, and 31.1 percent were retired workers of TVCEs and state enterprises or skilled rural craftsmen. A similar survey of sixty-three leaders from fifty-six private enterprises in Tianjin showed that 22.2 percent were former leaders of communes and brigades or their enterprises, 42.8 percent were managerial and technical personnel from TVCEs, 30.2 percent were local craftsmen and ordinary farmers, and 4.8 percent were from other backgrounds. Some private enterprises even offer high pay to recruit technical personnel or part-time technical advisers from state enterprises or research institutions. These technical and managerial personnel have played a decisive role in the development of private enterprises.

Problems Facing Private Enterprises

In the first part of this chapter I suggested that the rapid development of private enterprises is helping to speed China's rural industrialization, raise the efficiency of resource allocation, improve the structure and the regional distribution of nonagricultural activities in rural areas, and advance rural economic reform. I now turn to the problems of organization and efficiency that private enterprises confront as they pursue further development.

The impression given by most case studies is that private enterprises have strict control over their property, enjoy autonomy in management, are responsible for their profits and losses, are relatively efficient at decisionmaking, and are economically efficient because of their direct links between rewards and performance. Many survey reports have concluded that the microeconomic efficiency of private enterprises is generally higher than that of state and community enterprises in the same line of business. For example, a comparison of the economic efficiency of three private and seventeen state manufacturers of plastic products, textiles, and construction machinery in Wenzhou city showed that production costs for the private enterprises were 40–42 percent lower than for the state enterprises, the profit rate was 14–40 percent higher, the value of output per Y1 million of total assets was 67–283 percent higher, the profit rate per Y1 million of total assets was 2–25 percent higher, average taxes turned over to the state per employee were 30–1,100 percent higher, and the average income of individual employees was 29–63 percent higher (Lin Zili, personal communication). All of the indexes of economic efficiency were higher for the three private enterprises than for the state enterprises in the same industries.

But figures on private enterprises in other regions and nationwide show a somewhat different picture. In 1985 in nine sample townships of Shangrao County the ratio of profits and taxes to capital, the ratio of value of output to capital, and the ratio of profit and tax to value of output were all higher for private enterprises than for local community enterprises; average value of output per employee and average profit and tax per employee were lower for private enterprises than for community enterprises (see table 8-2). Nationwide statistics indicate that in 1985 average output per employee, average profit and tax per employee, and average wages in private enterprises were 51.8, 62.6, and 77.5 percent respectively of the comparable figures for community enterprises. Only the private firms' ratio of profit and tax to value of output was higher than that of community enterprises. Moreover, firms polled in surveys are relatively large, but private enterprises in Shangrao County are small, with an average employment of 2.9 persons (6.8 percent of the figure for community enterprises), and private enterprises nationwide have an average employment of 2.65 persons (10 percent of the figure for community enterprises).

I do not intend to go into a detailed analysis of the factors that affect the economic efficiency of private enterprises, but their extremely small scale is obviously the most important reason for their low efficiency in comparison with community enterprises. Figures on private enterprises in Nanhai and Jinjiang counties and in Shangrao County support this conclusion. In 1985 private enterprises in seven sample townships in Nanhai had, on average,

Table 8-2. *Size and Performance of Community and Private Enterprises,*
Nanhai and Shangrao Counties, 1985

Indicator	Community enterprises			Private enterprises		
	Both counties	Nanhai	Shangrao	Both counties	Nanhai	Shangrao
Ratio of profit and tax to capital	32.8	35.4	12.4	48.2	56.1	10.8
Ratio of value of output to capital	215.9	229.6	109.8	237.9	266.8	99.3
Ratio of profit and tax to value of output	15.2	15.4	11.3	20.3	21	10.9
Average output value per employee (yuan)	7,007	8,160	2,123	4,174	4,317	2,926
Average profit and tax per employee (yuan)	1,065	1,260	239	846	907	319
Average number of employees per enterprise	56	61	43	9	13	3
Average value of enterprise assets (thousands of yuan)	183	217	83	16	20	9

Note: Production team enterprises are excluded.
Source: Enterprise Quantitative Questionnaire.

12.5 employees—about 4.3 times the figure in Shangrao—and much higher
figures for six indexes of economic efficiency than the Shangrao firms. Three
comprehensive indexes of economic efficiency (the ratio of profit and tax to
capital, the ratio of value of output to capital, and the ratio of profit and
tax to value of output) were higher for private than for community enterprises
in Nanhai (table 8-2). In 1985 private enterprises in Jinjiang County (Fujian
Province) had, on average, 22 employees—660 percent higher than the figure for Shangrao and 76 percent higher than that for Nanhai. Three indexes
of economic efficiency (the ratio of profit and tax to value of output, average
value of output per employee, and average profit and tax per employee) were
much higher for Jinjiang private enterprises than for Shangrao private enterprises and were higher for private enterprises than for community enterprises
in Jinjiang (tables 8-2 and 8-3). The value of output per employee was significantly higher for private enterprises in Jinjiang than for those in Nanhai.
If average employment per private enterprise nationwide can reach the level
of Nanhai or Jinjiang, the economic efficiency of private enterprises can surpass that of community enterprises.

But at present the scale of most private enterprises in China is much
smaller than in Nanhai and Jinjiang, and their low capacity for self-accumulation will inevitably hinder their development. In addition, the social, political, and economic environment in China still impedes private enterprises'
development and expansion. Private enterprises are still in their nascent

Table 8-3. *Size and Performance of Community and Private Enterprises,*
Jinjiang County, 1985

Indicator	Community enterprises	Private enterprises
Ratio of profit and tax to value of output	14.9	15.9
Average value of output per employee (yuan)	3,607	4,873
Average profit and tax per employee (yuan)	537.7	774.8
Average annual wage per employer (yuan)	823	932
Average number of employees per enterprise	62	22

Note: Community enterprises include township and village enterprises. Private enterprises include enterprises run by groups of households with collected funds and private enterprises solely funded by an individual. Other jointly run cooperative enterprises are excluded.
Source: Institute of Economics, CASS.

stage. Every year a great number of small new firms joins their ranks, which slows the expansion of average firm size in the private sector. Moreover, the living standards of most Chinese farmers are still very low, and even owners of successful small enterprises use thousands of yuan of earnings to improve their living conditions, which means that the amount left for expansion is limited. This situation, of course, is understandable and can hardly be avoided.

The main issue is that there is still some fear and concern that the expansion of employment in private enterprises may lead to the unchecked spread of capitalism in China. As a result, policy is ambiguous. Political and social opinion has put great psychological pressure on private entrepreneurs and has created unfair competitive conditions for them. This in turn has caused distortions in their behavior and seriously limited expansion of scale and improvements in efficiency.

In 1983 the government made a rule that each owner of a private enterprise in rural areas could employ one or two hands, and a person with special skills could take on no more than five apprentices. But the government adopted a "wait and see" policy; it gave no encouragement or publicity to violations of the rules but did not immediately stop or punish them either. This wise policy left room for the development of private enterprises. But the resulting uncertainty also had negative effects on the private sector's development.

First, uncertainty about policy blunts private enterprises' desire to reinvest and makes them extremely shortsighted in their operations. In their early stages, most private enterprises have strong motives to make and reinvest profits. But when employment reaches the limit stipulated by state policy, increasing concern about political risks dampens entrepreneurs' interest in growth and shortens their horizons in operations and management. They take every opportunity to profiteer by legal and illegal means and to take advantage of loopholes in the state's regulatory system, and they are ready to quit business at any time. They are unwilling to undertake projects that require long-term investment and especially to expand employment, preferring to spend their earnings on building and repairing houses and purchasing other living facilities. Because of such shortsightedness, most private enterprises continue to operate on an extremely small scale year after year.

Second, the uncertainty about policy causes deterioration in private enterprises' business environment and degradation of their capability for self-accumulation. The surveys found that in the supply of production materials and the sale of products, private enterprises and, particularly, large individual enterprises encounter more discrimination than do other types of enterprise. They have the most difficulty in obtaining bank loans, and when the state decides to tighten credit, loans to private enterprises are the first to be cut. Thus they may be forced to get loans at much higher rates from informal credit organizations. They usually have to pay higher salaries than community enterprises to recruit technical personnel in short supply, and in areas with shortages of labor they have to pay higher wages to attract ordinary workers. When they purchase raw materials from state enterprises, they are subject to exorbitant prices set by the seller. When electric power is in short supply, private enterprises are the first to suffer from power cuts. Sometimes they have to sell their products on credit and receive payment after a delay or not at all.

To cope with such a hostile climate, private enterprises usually have to assign a large number of staff to purchasing and marketing. In Jinjiang County expenditures on purchasing agents and sales staff alone account for 10 percent of the total profits of private enterprises. In addition, when private enterprises operate under the guise of community enterprises, they must make large voluntary social donations or "pay tribute" to the community government. In some areas government departments levy a multiplicity of taxes and fees on private enterprises. All this bloodsucking by force or trickery has drastically impaired private enterprises' capability for self-accumulation and has restrained their development.

The last and most important problem is that policy uncertainty confuses the property relationships of private enterprises and causes retrogression in their development. In the nascent stage the property relationships of private enterprises are relatively well defined and clear. As totally independent commodity producers that are responsible for all their profits and losses, private enterprises have strong incentives for accumulation and development that are fundamentally different from those of community enterprises. But most small private enterprises, to keep a clear right of ownership over enterprise property, will reduce the speed of their development and stop seeking further advancement when their employment reaches the limits stipulated by state policy. Even if they choose to expand, some private enterprises spontaneously blur enterprise property relationships to ward off social pressures, guard against unpredictable risks, and improve their operating climate.

In addition, policy uncertainty and the ensuing disorder and inefficiency in the regulatory environment generate actual confusion in property relationships.

- Some private enterprises operate under other names. Large enterprises funded by only one individual have the most to fear from social and possible political pressures. These firms may turn in part of their profits and pay administrative fees to township and village governments so that they can call themselves TVCEs. This enables them to open a bank account, improves their operating climate, gives them government protection, and reduces the pressure of public opinion. Alternatively, firms may voluntarily offer shares to township and village governments and operate as jointly run cooperative enterprises, or they may provide funds for public investments. They may even declare that the entire assets of the enterprise belong to the state so that they can operate as cooperative enterprises.

- Diversified funding and joint management in some private enterprises confuse their property relationships. By using funds from outside and resorting to joint management, enterprises can spread their operational risks, quickly pool small sums of money from individual farmers and use these monies to expand, and, most important, open a bank account under the name of a cooperative enterprise. Such firms develop relatively quickly. But they will eventually have to confront the confusion in their property relationships because they are not protected by clearly defined policies and laws. These enterprises are often unstable and find it difficult to pursue further development because there are no clearly defined regulations on the ownership of enterprise property and the distribution of profits. The larger the scale of an enterprise's operations, the more confused its property relationships become and the more difficult it is to coordinate the distribution of benefits.

- Enterprise property relationships also become blurred for TVCEs that are leased or contracted to individuals. "Contract enterprises" are firms that were originally TVCEs but are now operated by individuals under contracts or leases in return for payment of a fixed rent or a fixed percentage of their profits to the original owners. These firms usually operate on a larger scale and have better equipment than other private enterprises. The contractors are mostly local community government cadres, and the rents are often so low that they do not cover depreciation and the value of the land. The contractors can use collective enterprise status to enjoy preferential treatment from banks and the state.

TVCEs that were contracted out had previously suffered from chronic inefficiency and losses because of the drawbacks in their management system. Most of them quickly eliminated their deficits and became profitable, but their property relationships are becoming more and more confused. The community governments that have contracted out the firms think that enterprise assets belong to them and should be returned when the contracts expire. The contractors hold that they own the additional assets created by reinvestment from after-tax profits and that they should actually own the enterprises outright when the original assets have become a very small part of the total. As community governments insist on their ownership rights over these firms, contractors' aspirations for reinvestment will wane drastically, and the enterprises will fail to expand.

Moreover, the uncertainty of policy causes confusion in the state's regulatory functions with respect to private enterprise. Some private enterprises use their status as collective enterprises to seek preferential treatment from the state regarding taxation and bank loans. They pay very low natural resource taxes and commonly practice tax evasion. These advantages and the pressure of public opinion encourage private enterprises to try to blur their property relationships. But some private entrepreneurs express concern that since their firms' establishment and development depended mainly on state loans, the firms can be nationalized at any time.

In short, confused enterprise property relationships caused by the uncertainty in state policy have led to the degradation of private enterprises' development potential and have forced them to operate on a small scale. This is the fundamental problem that private enterprises face.

Some Policy Suggestions

In recent years the rapid development of private enterprises has helped speed the transfer of rural surplus labor to nonagricultural activities and has furthered China's rural industrialization. Private enterprises have shown great vitality. This indicates that the government's reform policies for the rural economy are appropriate, and the policies and principles adopted concerning private enterprises in rural areas have already yielded remarkable results. But the development of large-scale private enterprises has outrun government policies and regulations. Recently the Communist party and the government formally affirmed that the private economy as an employer of hired labor is an indispensable and beneficial supplement to the public economy. Now is the right time to sum up past experience and introduce new policies and regulations to deal with the new situation and the problems that have cropped up. Some brief suggestions for state policies toward private enterprises are offered here.

- State policy regarding private enterprise should be further relaxed so that it will not only continue to encourage and support the development of private enterprise in general but will also allow the existence and growth of private enterprises with large numbers of employees. The state should publicly acknowledge these enterprises' legal status through legislation and permit them to make the most of their potential by supporting their legitimate operations and protecting their lawful rights.

- At the same time that complementary economic and political reforms are speeded up, efforts should be made to improve macroeconomic regulation. The government should exercise economic, administrative, and legal supervision over private enterprises in such areas as financial transactions, income distribution, and labor protection and welfare. For example, regulations on individual, cooperative, and private enterprises should be developed along with improved examination, registration, and licensing procedures; unified standards should be set for financial and accounting systems; new tax laws should be promulgated; bank loan policies should be adjusted and interest rates for loans raised; and tax and credit instruments should be used to give enterprises industrial guidance, regulate the polarization of personal incomes, and encourage enterprises to reinvest profits.

- Trade unions should be set up in private enterprises to protect workers' legitimate rights and to help government departments supervise the firms' operations.

- State industrial and commercial administrative departments and auditing and tax organizations should regularly examine enterprises' financial transactions and operational activities, and law enforcement institutions should mete out severe punishment to firms engaged in tax evasion and other illegal activities.

- The government should respect the autonomy of private enterprises in choosing property ownership systems and forms of operation and management. The gradual transformation of private enterprises into joint stock cooperative enterprises should be encouraged, with the understanding that no harm will be done to the basic rights of the original owners and that the principles of voluntary participation and mutual benefit will be followed.

Notes

1. Between 1984 and 1986 the total value of output of TVPs in Jieshou County went from Y103.75 million to Y137.57 million, a net increase of Y33.85 million. During the same period the total value of output of private enterprises rose from Y45.53 million to Y71.12 million. The increase of Y25.59 million accounted for 65.9 percent of the increment in total value of output of all TVPs. In 1986 the value of output of private enterprises accounted for 51.7 percent of the total value of output of TVPs in the county. Private enterprises' share in the total value of output of TVPs in Shangrao County went from 22 percent in 1984 to 50 percent in 1986, and these enterprises accounted for most of the increase in total value of output of TVPs.

2. The comparison is calculated from statistics on sample townships in Jieshou County.

3. According to estimates based on sample surveys of fifty-six private enterprises in Tianjin in 1985, loans accounted, on average, for 38.8 percent of total funds for private firms with a total investment of less than Y50,000, 43.6 percent for those with a total investment of Y50,000–Y100,000, and 69.9 percent for those with a total investment of more than Y100,000.

9

Entrepreneurship, Capital, and Ownership

William A. Byrd

The importance of entrepreneurship in modern economic growth and development is increasingly recognized, although there is much debate about its exact meaning and it does not fit well into the framework of neoclassical economics. Entrepreneurship, broadly construed, may be even more important in developing countries, where markets often function poorly, than in developed countries.

The astonishingly rapid growth and successful economic performance of the industrial TVP sector in China would not have been possible without a host of entrepreneurs and a great burst of entrepreneurial activity. A tremendous amount of creation of new enterprises and production of new goods has occurred, and functioning markets have emerged where none or only very weak ones existed in the prereform era. TVPs, other than the smallest firms, handle long-distance trade and depend largely on markets outside their own localities. Some TVPs engage in technological innovation, and many others successfully adapt advanced domestic and foreign technology. Entrepreneurial performance in the TVP sector has been especially remarkable in an environment in which ownership and property rights with respect to industrial assets are not clear and pure private ownership is rare except in the smallest concerns. Thus the most powerful reward for small-scale entrepreneurs in other countries—the ability to reap large gains from the "capitalization" of entrepreneurial success in their firms—is absent or at least sharply circumscribed.

One of the main bottlenecks faced by entrepreneurs and small-scale enterprises all over the world is getting the financial capital they need to start operations and to expand. The capital allocation mechanism for TVPs is hence of great importance. A related question concerns the absorption of financial risk. Even a relatively dynamic system of entrepreneurship and investment decisionmaking is bound to generate unsuccessful investments and enterprise failures. If failing firms are allowed to continue and to absorb additional resources, as typically occurs in the state sector, the efficiency of investment will suffer. China's TVP sector has evolved mechanisms for risk-sharing and absorption of losses that seem to have worked reasonably well, at least in the advanced areas.

The ownership system is intimately related to entrepreneurship, provision of capital, and risk-bearing. In private-ownership economies small-scale entrepreneurs reap the profits from their activities primarily through ownership of firms. In sizable enterprises the owners ("capitalists") tend to be separate from the entrepreneurs and managers. How the various forms of private and nonprivate ownership in China's TVP sector structure the relationship between capital provision, risk-bearing, entrepreneurship, and management so as to allow relatively efficient operations and decisionmaking on investment is a crucial question.

Entrepreneurship and Ownership

There are almost as many definitions of entrepreneurship as there are scholarly books on the subject (see Hebert and Link 1982). But since a working concept is a prerequisite for analyzing entrepreneurship in China's TVP sector, this section will derive a definition and delineate the scope of activities to be considered entrepreneurial.

A primary theme in the literature on entrepreneurship is that the entrepreneur is an active organizer of the factors of production. Schumpeter (1934), whose work on entrepreneurship and economic development has been extremely influential, stressed that entrepreneurship is associated with innovation and occurs only in the case of "new combinations of the means of production" organized by entrepreneurs. Others view the concept more broadly. Kirzner (1973, p. 35) asserts that the essence of entrepreneurship is alertness to unexploited profit opportunities and that hence it is an essential part of the market process. Related to the scope of entrepreneurship is the question of its effect on markets. The Schumpeterian approach sees entrepreneurial activity as a destabilizing force that starts the process of "creative destruction," the essence of economic development. Hayek (1948, ch. 2), Kirzner (1973, p. 127), and others view it as a stabilizing force that helps markets move toward equilibrium and makes the market process work more smoothly.

An important distinction is that between entrepreneurship and financial risk-bearing. Where there is uncertainty and incomplete information, entrepreneurial activities are inherently risky. Some entity (often the one providing funding for the activities) must bear the financial risk. The entrepreneur himself may take great personal risks and commit his own financial resources, but these resources are generally insufficient except for very small ventures. Thus there is a clear analytical distinction between the entrepreneur (the organizer of entrepreneurial activities) and the "capitalist" (the owner and provider of capital, whether an individual, a group, a public entity, or the state). (This distinction eluded many early thinkers on the subject; see Hebert and Link 1982, pp. 112–13.)

The working definition of entrepreneurship used here cannot hope to be comprehensive. Although it is recognized that entrepreneurship, broadly construed, occurs throughout a market economy, in minor as well as in major decisions and actions, the former will be excluded from the analysis. For the purposes of this chapter, entrepreneurship consists of activities that lead to new combinations of productive factors or otherwise transform the industrial landscape, in accordance with Schumpeter's stress on entrepreneurship as involving truly "new" and innovative phenomena. But in the case of China's TVP sector (as in developing economies in general), "newness" must be seen in a local, microeconomic context. Entrepreneurship need not involve anything new from a global or even national perspective; rather, it may adapt advanced technologies from outside, set up new enterprises to produce goods not previously made in the locality, and so on.

Two activities that clearly fall within this working definition are the establishment of new TVPs and the development of new products in existing ones. These have the advantage of being relatively clear-cut events for which some statistical evidence is available. The analysis will focus on enterprise creation and new product development as quintessential examples of entrepreneurial activity that will provide insights into entrepreneurship in general.

Entrepreneurship in China's TVP Sector

Entrepreneurship is thriving in China's TVP sector, as numerous case studies show. Although the examples presented here are of the more successful and striking instances of entrepreneurial activity, they are not atypical, and many similar cases must be omitted owing to lack of space.

CASE STUDY 1: WUXI PETROLEUM EQUIPMENT PLANT. In the mid-1970s an engineer in the Shengli ("Victory") Oilfield in Shandong Province on the east coast of China, roughly 500 kilometers from Wuxi, was looking for an enterprise that could produce from his rough preliminary design a drill pump for enhanced oil recovery. He had a friend in the Shenyang Aviation Institute in northeast China, more than 1,000 kilometers from Wuxi, who in turn was acquainted with a person in an agricultural machinery plant in the suburbs of Wuxi city. That enterprise trial-produced one drill pump but gave up because it could not engage in batch production, costs were too high, and it did not see a good market for the product. An agricultural machinery plant in Dongjiang township, Wuxi County, found out about the drill pump through its close relationship with the suburban factory. Since it felt that the product had good prospects, it began trial production in 1975. The first pump was completed in October 1977, and in December it was taken to the

Shengli Oilfield for a test in the field. It was then certified by the Shengli Research and Development Institute.

During the first several years only five or six pumps were made each year because of production problems and low demand. (Enhanced oil recovery was not yet widespread in China.) Batch production began in 1982 with 132 units, but only in 1983 did the enterprise start making a profit on this product. Losses in the first years were covered by profits from production of other goods, mainly welded steel tubes. The Communist party secretary for the enterprise pushed development of the drill pump despite the early losses because he thought it had a good future. In 1984 the factory signed a long-term contract with Shengli to deliver at least 500 units a year in 1984–88. This prompted an administrative decision by the Dongjiang township government to split the existing firm into three enterprises: the original agricultural machinery plant, the welded steel tube factory, and the Wuxi Petroleum Equipment plant. Production jumped to 700 units in 1984 (from 450 in 1983), and in 1985 output reached 2,580. The Wuxi plant is the only specialized producer of this kind of equipment in China and accounts for the bulk of total domestic production—perhaps 70 percent.[1]

The Wuxi factory is a good example of successful entrepreneurship in community government enterprises. Entrepreneurial decisionmaking and activity take place largely within existing firms and under their managers. Profits from existing production finance initial efforts to develop new products. When a product has demonstrated its marketability and profitability, large amounts of funds may be needed to bring it into full-scale production. These come from community sources—the township government, the local bank, or both. The decision to establish a separate enterprise is administrative rather than entrepreneurial. Entrepreneurship of this type in community enterprises has been occurring all along, although there were many problems and inefficiencies in the prereform period, as well as a long learning curve.

CASE STUDY 2: AN ELASTIC RIBBON FACTORY IN JIESHOU. This firm was established in 1982 by five people, two of whom provided initial investment capital totaling Y450. Another founder, a farmer-entrepreneur, sold the new venture some used ribbon-weaving machines for Y50 apiece. The firm was established primarily to generate employment for the founders' children and relatives. The initial site was provided rent-free by the farmer-entrepreneur in return for a job for his daughter. Production took off rapidly. In 1982 output value reached Y40,000 and net after-tax profits Y6,000, and both doubled in 1983. Its head start and its efficiency have enabled the firm to do well in an increasingly competitive environment in which prices for ribbons dropped by about 20 percent between the late 1970s and early 1980s and have fallen another 30 percent since then.

In July 1985 the factory director (one of the two initial investors) went to Shanghai to buy some machine parts. In a department store she noticed that people were lined up to buy a certain type of decorated elastic ribbon. In August she went back to Shanghai and found out from the department store where the ribbons were made. She was directed to a township enterprise in Wuxi but was not allowed past the gate. In the local hotel she asked about other producers of the same kind of ribbon and was given the name of a village firm in Shazhou County, also in Jiangsu. The firm, which had 500–600 workers and (in the eyes of the director) the air of a county enterprise, also refused her permission to enter the factory. But some workers who were leaving the plant told her how to find the house of a deputy director, the founder of the enterprise. She went there, struck up a conversation with his wife, and remarked on how beautiful the couple's daughter was. Something like a family relationship was established when the Jieshou firm's director became a kind of "godparent" to the child.

The Shazhou plant arranged for the producer of the ribbon-making machinery to sell six units to the Jieshou firm. A technician was sent from the Shazhou plant to install the equipment, and some people from Jieshou were sent to Shazhou for training. In return, the Jieshou firm provided large amounts of agricultural and sideline products at a low price for the annual spring festival in Shazhou. Production of the new elastic ribbons got under way in early 1986. Initially the Shazhou plant was to provide the necessary raw materials, but the technician who was installing the equipment stayed at the Jieshou director's house for over a month and built up a personal relationship with her. He told her that the Shazhou plant was planning to overcharge her firm for the raw materials and introduced her to the original supplier, who agreed to sell the materials at a price slightly lower than that paid by the Shazhou plant.

The director of the Jieshou firm is the wife of a government official who had served in the public security bureaus of several counties before he was transferred to Jieshou in 1979. The director had seen that elastic ribbons were in short supply on the market and had wanted to go into that field for a long time. The ownership of the enterprise is ambiguous. The two investing founders took back their principal quickly and now earn no dividends or interest. All after-tax profits are plowed back into the enterprise. Although the firm is officially listed as an individual/jointly operated enterprise, it has a relationship with the local neighborhood committee, which occasionally provides administrative help. In practice, the director makes all the key decisions.

CASE STUDY 3: A FRUIT-CANNING PLANT IN SHANGRAO. This example is exceptional in that an entrepreneur moves across provinces. The director came from Zhejiang Province, where he had run a private garment business that was initially profitable but later lost money and was shut down. Before that he had been in purchasing and marketing. Orange canning was an important activity in his home community, but profits were declining because of increasing production and competition. Shangrao, by contrast, had much cheaper labor, somewhat cheaper oranges, and, as a "backward" area, tax advantages for new enterprises. In June 1986 the entrepreneur went to Shangrao to look into the possibilities. He first contacted a township where he had a business relationship with a factory, but he found that the water supply, an essential element in fruit canning, was not good. Later, through an acquaintance in a county government bureau, he found the right spot, with abundant supplies of clean water and large numbers of orange trees that had been planted several years earlier.

Negotiations with township authorities went smoothly, and once they were completed the factory was put into operation within two and a half months. The Zhejiang entrepreneur invested Y80,000: Y50,000 in equipment and Y30,000 to renovate the factory building. (He reportedly borrowed Y20,000–Y30,000 from friends and relatives; the rest was his own money.) The building, valued at Y100,000, was provided rent-free by the township. In addition, with the help of county authorities the township arranged for a quota, or line of credit, of up to Y100,000 from the local bank. It also guaranteed the enterprise's supply of water and electricity and provided free housing for the director, his family, and some employees who were brought from Zhejiang. These employees included four master technical personnel, a cashier, two salesmen, and the director's two sons, who became middle-level managers. The enterprise now has 21 regular employees and will use up to 240 seasonal temporary workers. The primary benefits for the township are the employment generated and the 3.5 percent of gross output value that it receives. Another 1.5 percent goes into a pension fund, and 1.5 percent is for workers' bonuses. Given an anticipated gross profit rate of about 10 percent, this leaves about 3.5 percent of gross output value for the director, the residual claimant. As a new food-processing enterprise the firm can be exempted from both direct and indirect taxes for one to three years.

The plant's annual production capacity is Y2 million, but the limited supply of local oranges will hold down output in the first few years. (Some oranges will have to be imported from Fujian Province.) Once local orange trees have reached full maturity, there will be no supply constraints. The director anticipates recovering his investment costs in two years if the tax exemptions last that long. He plans to settle down and retire in Shangrao. The firm is officially registered as a jointly run collective firm contracted to individual management. The director is fully responsible for supply, production, and marketing, and the output is sold all over north China.

These case studies illustrate the main features of entrepreneurship in China's TVP sector: alertness to unexploited opportunities (a characteristic of entrepreneurship in general), the ability to bring together and organize the ingredients needed for successful production, personal commitment and willingness to take risks, and the use of personal connections [guanxi]. As in other developing countries, many services that are provided by markets in the industrialized countries have to be arranged by entrepreneurs themselves. Entrepreneurs' rootedness in their home communities is a common pattern. (Even the third case study sheds light on the community ties of TVP entrepreneurs. The person from Zhejiang made Shangrao his home, and the know-how and key personnel for his business came from his original community.)

Entrepreneurship under Different Forms of TVP Ownership

The shares of different forms of ownership in the value of TVP industrial output for China as a whole and for the four counties in 1985 are shown in table 9-1. TVCEs have a dominant share in Wuxi (95 percent), a considerably lower share in Nanhai (74 percent), and even lower shares in Jieshou (49 percent) and Shangrao (65 percent). Production team enterprises account for a significant share of the total only in Nanhai. Private enterprises are proportionately most important in Jieshou. The figure for private firms in Shangrao is also high, but it reflects handicraft production and the lack of development of community enterprises rather than dynamism in the private sector. In absolute terms the private sector is most important in Wuxi (more than twice as large as in Jieshou), although its percentage share is smallest there.

The locus of entrepreneurship varies for TVPs with different forms of ownership. Four main variants can be identified: entrepreneurship by the community government itself; managerial entrepreneurship in traditional community enterprises; community and cooperative entrepreneurship in some villages and production teams (a rare variant); and private entrepreneurship.

Community governments may become directly involved in entrepreneurial activities if there is no strong base of existing community enterprises (as, for example, in Shangrao) or if development of an entirely new product is undertaken and the idea did not emanate from and is not taken up by an existing

Table 9-1. *TVP Ownership Structure in China and in the Sample Counties, 1985*
(percentage of GVIO for TVPs)

Ownership	All China	Wuxi	Jieshou	Nanhai[a]	Shangrao
Township and town	45	48	36	43	43
Village	38	47	13	31	22
Production team	9	2	—	16	—
Private	8	3	51	10	35
Total value of output (millions of yuan)	175,008	3,705	127	1,421	31

— Not given.
Note: GVIO, gross value of industrial output.
a. Share of gross revenues of industrial TVPs.
Sources: Table 9-5 and 9-6 and information from fieldwork.

enterprise. Entrepreneurship in this case involves both setting up a new enterprise and making a (locally) new product.

Much more common in localities with a strong base of traditional community enterprise development is entrepreneurial activity by enterprise leaders, as illustrated by case study 1. The key entrepreneurial decision is to try out and develop a new product; the decision to establish a separate enterprise is administrative, although it does involve a large inflow of capital and hence financial risk-taking of a venture capital nature. Enterprises, as well as governments, may also decide to develop new products that are not closely related to existing ones. The ability of firms to develop and try out new products varies greatly with the industry concerned; innovation is particularly easy in the machinery industry, so important in Wuxi.

In some cases involving the establishment of village or production team enterprises, collective entrepreneurship by the members of the community seems to occur. Ideas emanate from the members and are discussed at village meetings, and in some cases the decision to go ahead is taken collectively. Collective entrepreneurship is most common at the production team level.

In the private sector decisions to establish firms or to develop new products are made by individuals or partnerships, who invariably also manage the firms. This is no different, at least in theory, from the pattern of small-scale entrepreneurship observed in market economies.

The number of important new products that enterprises in our sample reported putting into production between 1980 and 1985 (or between time of establishment and 1985) provides some indication of entrepreneurial activity. This information suffers from a number of deficiencies, the most obvious of which is its subjective nature—how main products are defined was left entirely to the firm. The ease of new product development also differs markedly for different industries and for enterprises of different sizes. Nevertheless, there appears to be significant, nonspurious variation among counties and ownership types.

Table 9-2 provides summary information on new product development. The raw data were weighted by the inverse of the number of years each enterprise was in existence (up to five). Five identical observations were then created for each enterprise set up in 1980 or earlier, four for firms established in 1981, three for those set up in 1982, and so on. The resulting data corrects for the smaller amount of information provided by enterprises set up after 1980 and the shorter time these firms had to develop new products.

The table indicates that private enterprises are much more likely to engage in extensive development of new products than are community enterprises at the township and especially at the village and production team levels. But TVCES in Wuxi are significantly more likely to engage in at least moderate new product development than are sample firms in the other three counties. This strongly suggests that the relationship between ownership and new product development is not spurious. Indeed, cross-tabulations for Jieshou show

Table 9-2. *Development of New Products by TVPs, 1980–85*
(percentage of total new product development in sample or subsample)

Ownership or location	None	Moderate	Extensive
Full sample	37	37	26
Township and town	35	40	25
Village and production team	57	24	19
Private	13	35	52
Wuxi	25	51	24
Nanhai	29	41	30
Shangrao	62	24	14
Jieshou	34	32	34
Township and town	34	36	30
Village and production team	67	0	33
Private	14	39	47

Note: None, no new product development; Moderate, one or two new products in a five-year period; Extensive, three or more new products in a five-year period.
Source: Enterprise Quantitative Questionnaire.

that private enterprises are significantly more likely to engage in moderate and especially extensive new product development than are community enterprises. Because of the data problems, these results should be interpreted with caution, but they are suggestive.

Data on the establishment of new firms are difficult to interpret, particularly since the available information invariably is for net new enterprise creation, after exits have been subtracted. Moreover, the ease with which new enterprises are created almost certainly varies systematically and inversely with size—most new firms start out small and grow big only later—and size is in turn related to ownership. Finally, decisions to create new community enterprises, especially township firms, are often merely administrative confirmations of the successful development of new products by existing firms. Nevertheless, the same pattern holds as for the development of new products; Wuxi among the four counties and private enterprises in general are more active in new enterprise creation. In Wuxi the number of TVCEs nearly doubled between 1982 and 1985 and increased by another 11 percent in 1986 despite a difficult market and credit situation.

Sources and Motivation of Entrepreneurs

In the past many managers of traditional community enterprises came from the ranks of rural cadres at the village or production team level. This often was not conducive to good management or to successful entrepreneurship. In places such as Wuxi managers of township enterprises now increasingly rise through the ranks of their enterprises or are transferred from other local firms. There appears to be little movement of community enterprise managers among townships, although movement among villages within a township does occur in Wuxi (see chapter 7). In other localities (for example, Nanhai) directors of village enterprises often serve concurrently as village leaders. This practice is nearly universal at the production team level, even in Wuxi. Many village and production team enterprises have been contracted to individual management or sold outright to private individuals. The backgrounds of entrepreneurs of this type do not appear to differ greatly from those of private entrepreneurs (see below).

The motivations and incentives of community enterprise entrepreneurs are complex. As is true of substantial non-owner-operated establishments in any country, direct pecuniary rewards are only part of the story. Promotion possibilities, the perquisites that come with managing larger firms, pride in one's accomplishments, recognition, and even the perception of helping the community all may play a role. Formal pay incentives for community enterprise managers are typically linked to enterprise performance (profits or output growth), to the average pay of enterprise workers, or to both. Nonpecuniary incentives are all the more important because there are still limits on how much the incomes of enterprise leaders can exceed the average level in the enterprise and the local community.

There are five main sources of private entrepreneurs: lower-level community government cadres and former cadres; supply and marketing personnel for TVPs; employees of community enterprises, particularly those with some technical skills; community residents who have worked in state enterprises; and farmers, usually with some business experience. All of these groups are likely to have useful personal networks.

Because TVP entrepreneurs are so immobile, the traditional base of entrepreneurship in a rural locality is crucial in determining their supply. Existing community enterprise development is also important. Wuxi has a machinery industry that dates to before the 1930s, and its supply of potential entrepreneurs was augmented when, during the early 1960s and the Cultural Revolution, large numbers of local people who had been working in big-city enterprises returned home. Similarly, urban workers originally from Nanhai were "sent down" to their home villages and there established private enterprises under the protection of county authorities. Prereform rural industrialization generated an important base of entrepreneurial talent in Nanhai and especially in Wuxi, and commercialized agriculture was highly developed in both counties before 1949. Jieshou was a commercial center of some importance before 1949, and its human resources from that period were never entirely dissipated. In Shangrao, by contrast, there was almost no traditional base of entrepreneurship before 1949, and TVP development during the prereform period was minimal. The large numbers of university and high school graduates generated by Shangrao's relatively good education system left the county instead of augmenting the entrepreneurial base. Thus Shangrao, alone among the four counties, may lack an adequate supply of indigenous entrepreneurs.

Making money is a motivation for private entrepreneurs, but it is never the only goal and is sometimes not the most important one. Nonpecuniary goals include providing employment and a secure future for family members and, to a lesser extent, other relatives; improving one's social and official status (for example, by becoming a second-class urban resident as many Jieshou entrepreneurs did); and even contributing to local community welfare and employment.

Since the right to private industrial property and to the full financial rewards of entrepreneurship are not secure, the incentives of private entrepreneurs are distorted. They may use a large part of their firms' profits for their own consumption and housing, or they may demonstrate that they are good corporate and community citizens by plowing all surplus back into the enterprise. For many, the possibility of changing their household registration status may make takeover of their firms by the community government palatable. The family motive is extremely strong for private entrepreneurs, especially since in many rural areas there is surplus labor and nonagricultural employment opportunities are limited. This motive alone suffices to explain a great deal of small-scale private entrepreneurial activity.

Capital Allocation and Financial Risk-Bearing

This section surveys the different sources of financial capital that TVPs draw on and examines how business risk is distributed in the TVP sector.

The Capital Allocation Mechanism

The sources of capital for TVPs can be divided into household capital, community capital, and enterprise capital, each with a corresponding mechanism for capital allocation. These sources cut across the traditional debt-equity bifurcation, which is reasonable since in China's TVP sector debt capital often bears a great deal of risk, bankruptcy is not well-established as a means of dealing with financial losses, the concept and role of equity capital are poorly understood, and the notion of individuals reaping large capital gains is not widely accepted.

Household capital consists of private funds invested directly in TVPs by households. It includes investment by partners or proprietors, informal loans to private entrepreneurs (usually by friends or relatives of the lenders), purchase of bonds issued by community enterprises, and provision of capital in return for jobs. The community government regulates the terms and conditions under which individuals can invest in community enterprises, but this is not as true of investment in private enterprises. Household capital is available to finance small firms in significant aggregate amounts, particularly after the sharp increases in rural personal incomes in recent years. Many workers in our samples indicated on the Worker Survey Questionnaire a willingness to invest in an enterprise or buy stock (see chapter 13). But the amount of household capital that can be tapped by any one private firm is limited. Township enterprises can gain access to larger amounts of household capital by issuing short-term bonds with the support of the community government.

Community capital consists of investment funds the allocation and use of which are determined or at least strongly influenced by community governments, particularly at the township level. This capital includes local government budgetary funds for TVP investment (typically minuscule), loans of fiscal revolving funds to TVPs, profits from community enterprises pooled by township or village industrial corporations, and bank and rural credit cooperative (RCC) loans. The use of retained profits of community enterprises may also be influenced by the community government.

The Agricultural Bank of China (ABC) is nominally a monolithic state institution with a well-defined headquarters-branch structure and an extensive system of top-down credit planning. The RCCs, although supposedly community-based cooperative institutions, have been subject to administrative supervision by the ABC. Thus the classification of ABC/RCC loans as community capital needs to be explained. An important reform of credit planning that began in 1979–80 links the total value of loans each ABC branch is allowed to make to the amount of deposits it generates. The difference between loans and deposits in a base year is calculated, and this gap determines the amount of lending in the following year. If deposits rise by a certain amount, loans outstanding can increase by the same absolute amount. The impact of this scheme has been somewhat diluted by bargaining, by the later imposition of separate redeposit requirements, and by the occasional imposition of tighter credit controls by the central government in the interests of macroeconomic stability. Nevertheless, increments in local community deposits for the most part translate into increments in loanable funds, and hence the level of lending to TVPs is to a large extent determined by the level of local deposits. The sharp rise in rural personal incomes and bank deposits has made the banking system an important source of community capital.

Township governments take the view that local bank funds form part of the community capital base, and they participate in important lending decisions. In the more advanced areas bank offices and township governments have a largely symbiotic relationship. According to one RCC official in Nanhai, "The RCC has good relations with township leaders. We go to them periodically, show them how much money we have, and ask them to think about how they want it lent out." Banks and RCCs do have the theoretical right to veto proposed loans that they find questionable. In Shangrao and Jieshou, where community governments frequently misused bank funds, this right is becoming more important in practice. In general, township ABC and RCC offices cannot lend money freely outside the township—a clear sign that their funds are still basically considered community capital.

Enterprise capital consists of the retained profits, depreciation allowances, and other funds of TVPs as well as funds provided by other enterprises. Capital from other firms is largely trade credit, of indefinite maturity and highly unstable. The allocation of part of the retained profits and other funds of community enterprises is influenced by the community government, but enterprises may have considerable autonomy in making smaller investments. The internally generated investment funds of private enterprises and the portion of community enterprise funds that can be used autonomously are the sources most easily tapped by factory directors to finance entrepreneurship.

Table 9-3 shows the liability side of the balance sheet for 200 large and

Table 9-3. *Sources of Funds for Large-Scale TVPs*
(percentage of total)

Source	At founding	End 1984	End 1985	End June 1986
State capital[a]	4.0	1.8	1.6	1.7
Community capital[b]	67.6	35.2	30.1	27.8
Bank loans	38.2	28.9	24.1	23.4
Contributions by community governments[c]	29.4	6.3	6.0	4.4
Enterprise capital[b]	13.0	55.8	59.8	63.0
Own funds[b]	0.0	41.0	40.7	43.2
Other firms[d]	13.0	14.8	19.1	19.8
Household capital	6.5	3.5	4.6	4.0
Enterprise's own workers[e]	5.4	2.8	3.6	3.1
Outside individuals	1.1	0.7	1.0	0.9
Unidentified[f]	8.9	3.7	3.9	3.5

Note: Figures for 1985 were adjusted to correct apparent arithmetic errors.

a. Includes grants and loans from state agencies.

b. The share of community capital for 1984–86 is understated and that of household capital is overstated somewhat because "own funds" includes nonrepayable capital provided by the township government as well as internally accumulated capital.

c. Includes fiscal revolving funds lent to TVPs, which may be to some extent controlled at the county rather than the township level. Grant funds from the community government for 1984–86 are not included.

d. May include some debts owed to government entities, since it includes payables as well as loans and capital investment provided by other enterprises. The bulk of this capital comes from outside the locality.

e. Wages payable to workers and investment contributed by them.

f. For time of founding, other funds; for 1984–86, other long-term debt.

Source: Zhou Qiren and Huang Zhuangjun (1987), from a sample of 200 relatively large and successful TVPs in ten provinces.

relatively successful community enterprises, primarily township enterprises, at four points in time. The state accounts for only a minuscule share of the capital requirements even of these larger TVPs run by higher levels of the administrative hierarchy. The critical importance of the community in providing seed capital for community enterprises at founding is obvious. The community's share diminishes as enterprises develop and generate investment funds internally. The role of household capital in financing community enterprises is relatively small.

Seed capital for new private enterprises comes in the first place from the founders, who themselves may borrow money from friends and relatives. They may also borrow on the informal credit market and require new workers to contribute some capital. The bulk of the relatively small capital requirements of private enterprises at time of founding is thus met by household capital. Successful private firms can rely heavily on reinvestment of internally accumulated funds, and many have generated sizable productive assets primarily through internal accumulation. But beyond a certain point self-accumulation may not be enough to finance rapid expansion, and the potential for tapping household capital is also quickly exhausted. Private enterprises then naturally turn to sources of community capital, particularly ABC or RCC loans. The balance sheets of relatively large and successful private enterprises are thus usually dominated by internal accumulation and bank loans. There is a potential inconsistency between ownership, which is in reality private (although this may be disguised and the enterprise may have virtually no equity capital on its books),[2] and capital allocation, which to a large extent involves community capital (exclusively debt finance). In traditional community enterprises, by contrast, ownership and the capital allocation mechanism are much more in harmony.

The role of prices (interest rates) in TVP capital allocation mechanisms is limited. In the case of household capital, interest rates on enterprise and community bond issues can be distorted upward or downward by community governments. Moreover, when the main benefit of providing capital is getting a job in a labor-surplus environment, the interest rate does not mean much, and in fact often no interest payment is involved. Community enterprises do not pay an explicit dividend on equity. Capital from other firms is often transferred involuntarily (as trade credits) or in return for rewards other than interest payments (for example, in some compensation trade arrangements). For community capital, interest rates on ABC and other bank loans are fixed by the central government at below-market equilibrium levels, and rates on RCC loans are only slightly more flexible. Capital from community governments is in the form of nonrepayable grants or low-interest loans.

In the more advanced areas such as Wuxi, capital seems to have been allocated relatively efficiently despite the lack of price signals. The main reason is probably that the community government has strong incentives for making the best possible use of its capital resources. In the first place, these resources are limited, and the community government faces a relatively hard budget constraint. Most of the risk in loan-financed investments is borne by community governments rather than by banks or enterprises. The community government is probably better acquainted with the enterprises and investment projects under its jurisdiction than a provincial or even municipal industrial bureau is with its subordinate enterprises. In any case, when discrete investment projects are large in relation to the total amount of funds available, the interest rate may not be a meaningful guide for the allocation of capital.

Financial Risk-Bearing

Closely related to the capital allocation mechanism is the mode of financial risk-bearing. Entrepreneurial activities inherently involve risk, most of which is typically not borne by the entrepreneur personally. In the case of community capital, both the community government and the financial system can absorb risk. When the government provides nonrepayable funds to community enterprises, this is a form of risk capital. In the traditional system the township government also explicitly or implicitly serves as a guarantor for bank borrowings by township enterprises under its jurisdiction, and the village government does the same for village firms. If an enterprise shuts down, outstanding debts become the responsibility of its community government owner and are usually transferred to another enterprise under the same government.

The community government's ability to absorb risk by varying its public expenditures may be limited, but it can spread risk across its enterprises to increase the flexibility and ability to absorb losses of any one firm. This risk-sharing is usually ad hoc and informal and is most effective when the community industrial structure is relatively diversified. Fluctuations and losses that are not life-threatening to the enterprise are absorbed by varying the flows of profits between the enterprise and the community government and, through delayed loan repayments, between the enterprise and the bank. Other measures are needed to deal with severe losses, but only rarely is the firm completely shut down, since bank debts need to be serviced anyway. Only if there is no cash flow at all is it rational from the viewpoint of the community government to shut down an enterprise.

The above description applies mainly to areas in which traditional community enterprise development has been relatively successful. Elsewhere much of the risk associated with TVP activities may be borne by banks or RCCs. The financial resources of community governments in the more backward areas are too limited to absorb much risk, and the financial performance of community enterprises may be so poor that they cannot credibly cover each other's losses and take over the burden of loan repayment. In Shangrao, for example, a large loan to a hydropower station was collectively guaranteed by all of the other local township enterprises. By the time the loan fell due, nearly all of these firms were running losses and could not even repay their own bank loans, and so the guarantee was meaningless. In this situation bank loans become highly risky, and banks in effect provide risk capital.

Banks and RCCs can absorb risk by writing off loans, possibly after selling off the assets of a defunct enterprise, and by allowing firms to delay repayments of principal and interest, sometimes indefinitely. The latter method is far more common, especially for community enterprises. Banks often have an incentive to prevent a community enterprise from failing because once it shuts down, there is no hope of recouping loans. In Shangrao ABC offices never call in an overdue loan of a community enterprise. Instead they allow indefinite delays in repayment and request only that the firm service a small part of its debt. Sometimes they even provide additional credit in the hope that the enterprise will be able to turn the situation around.

Risk absorption by the ABC in Shangrao is facilitated by the unusual practice of permitting enterprises to pay interest only on the portion of an overdue loan that is actually being repaid. This allows principal payments to be much larger than otherwise, and the total annual repayment of principal and interest may be less than the interest charges alone on the entire loan. With constant annual repayments, the amount of principal repaid decreases progressively, and in many cases a loan will never be entirely repaid. ABC profits may be severely affected. But stretching out repayments and not charging interest when it is due does at least leave open the possibility that a loan eventually will be repaid if the enterprise returns to profitability. Many loss-making TVPs in Shangrao, however, have such severe problems that they will never recover.

The risk-bearing and loss absorption functions taken on by the banking system in Shangrao severely undermine the banks' symbiotic relationship with the community government. Banks become very conservative in their lending, and as they gain independence through banking system reforms they tend not to lend all of the money absorbed locally in the form of household deposits. Thus some important linkages are broken, and the severe problems of these localities may be exacerbated. Forcing banks to lend to questionable projects and poorly managed firms, as was done in the past with disastrous results, obviously is not the answer. Bank conservatism is a symptom, not a cause, of the problems of backward areas.

The banking system in Jieshou has adopted a different strategy of more aggressive lending, especially to private enterprises, and strong actions to recover unrepaid loans by selling off the property of defunct firms. This is more feasible because the main asset of many smaller enterprises is their real estate (land and buildings) and because of the relatively lively real estate market in Jieshou. Banks' reluctance to lend to traditional community enterprises is evident, however.

Table 9-4, which pulls together available information on the share of over-

Table 9-4. *Share of Overdue Loans in Total Value of Loans Outstanding*
(percent)

Locality	Date	Share of overdue loans	Source of loans
Wuxi	End 1985	8	ABC system
	End 1986	17ᵃ	ABC system
Dongjiang township, Wuxi	End 1985	6	ABC/RCC
Jieshou	End 1985	8	ABC, loans to TVPs only
	End 1985	10	ICBC, total loans
Hebei township, Jieshou	End 1985	8	RCC only
Nanhai	April 1986	23	ABC system
	End 1986	8	ABC system
Pingzhou district, Nanhai	April 1986	15	ABC/RCC
	End 1986	7ᵇ	ABC/RCC
Shangrao	End 1986	46	ABC, loans to TVPs

Note: ABC, Agricultural Bank of China; ICBC, Industrial and Commercial Bank of China; RCC, rural credit cooperative.

a. Less than 4 percent consisted of bad debts considered unrepayable in the long run.

b. The share of late repayment loans would have been 17 percent if an unrepaid loan that had financed imports of fake calculators from Hong Kong had not been put in a special category.

Source: Information from fieldwork.

due loans in total loans outstanding in the four counties, indicates the importance of risk absorption through delayed repayments. The magnitude of overdue loans in Shangrao is striking. Wuxi and Nanhai also sometimes have relatively high shares of late loans, but this is a temporary phenomenon largely related to fluctuations in market conditions, central government monetary policy, and credit controls.

The willingness of the banking system to absorb risks of private enterprises is severely limited. After a period during which large loans to private enterprises were encouraged, ceilings have been sharply reduced, and in many cases the bank requires a guarantee from another enterprise or entity. Although some borrowers default, the overall repayment record of private enterprises is probably much better than that of community enterprises, as is suggested by the experience of Jieshou with its disproportionately high share of private enterprises.

For household capital provided to private enterprises, any losses are borne by the provider of the capital. For household capital raised by community enterprises, repayment of principal and even the return may be guaranteed by the enterprise or sometimes the community government. Even so, the risk of late repayment has reportedly made individuals in Wuxi less willing to provide capital directly to enterprises and more willing to deposit their money in banks, even at a lower rate of interest.

TVPs' internally accumulated funds have considerable risk-bearing capacity if they account for a substantial portion of total capital. In the more developed areas the return these funds earn is usually free to decline sharply in the face of market fluctuations. In poorer localities, however, community enterprises may be forced to turn over funds to community governments regardless of whether they are earning profits (see chapter 17). Capital—often involuntary payables—provided by other firms also absorbs some risk. But trade credit is a highly unstable, short-run device, and in any case the receivables of the sample of firms shown in table 9-3 exceeded their payables (although by only a small margin in 1986).

Risk-bearing mechanisms for TVPs have obvious imperfections, but they work reasonably well in the more advanced areas and for the most part function far better than risk-bearing mechanisms for state enterprises. The flexibility provided by the pooling and absorption of risk by community governments in the traditional community enterprise system may in part explain the success of places such as Wuxi. There are serious problems, however, in more backward areas.

Interrelationships and Implications

The interrelationships among the different elements discussed above can now be analyzed. Several combinations of entrepreneurship, capital provision, risk-bearing, and enterprise management have evolved in the TVP sector. (The concept of management, which has not yet been discussed, is used in this chapter as a catchall that includes the host of routine decisions and activities required to keep a firm running on an even keel. Its scope is broad and includes some "smaller" entrepreneurial activities.)

The Wuxi System

In the Wuxi model the main locus of entrepreneurship is the enterprise itself, and the leaders of existing firms are the entrepreneurs. The early stages of new product development are financed by enterprises' own capital, which is allocated in small amounts in a fairly autonomous way by enterprise leaders. The main source of funds for creation of new firms and for large investment projects is community capital. In some respects the community government's role is similar to that of a provider of venture capital or a diversified corporation or holding company in a market economy. The community government also bears some risk and covers financial shortfalls (generally only temporary) of specific firms. Finally, management is in the hands of the enterprise leadership. Some managerial decisions—for example, hiring labor—may be affected or even determined by the community government, but the day-to-day conduct of business is left to the director.

Many of these elements were already present in the prereform period, but some crucial ones have been added or reinforced since the late 1970s. One is the linkage between community bank deposits and lending. Greater autonomy for enterprise management and the selection of directors with technical and managerial backgrounds rather than former community government cadres have also helped to improve the efficiency of the Wuxi model and allowed Wuxi to remain in the forefront of TVP development. In addition, the fundamental change in the wage system from community work-points to enterprise-based wages with strong piece-rate and profit-sharing components appears to have brought about substantial improvements in incentives and efficiency.

For traditional community enterprises in developed areas, the different elements fit together consistently. Community ownership is consistent with the mechanism for allocating community capital and with risk-bearing by the community government, and relatively autonomous management (supported by appropriate worker incentives) promotes efficiency in operations. The hard budget constraint of community governments gives them a strong incentive to allocate community capital resources efficiently.

Unsuccessful Community Enterprise Systems

A somewhat different combination of these elements can lead to slow development and costly entrepreneurial failures in the community enterprise sector. In the more backward areas that lack an established base of community enterprises, entrepreneurial decisions are made by community officials themselves. The inherent difficulties of direct government involvement in entrepreneurship are worsened by the poor quality and lack of relevant experience of many community government cadres in these areas. Although the community government is forced to take a direct role in entrepreneurship, it is unable to take responsibility for the financial risks of such activities, which are effectively borne by the banking system. Severe conflicts between the interests of the banking system and the community government have arisen and have been exacerbated by the independence that banks gained in the reform period. Finally, in places such as Shangrao there are severe problems with excessive community government intervention in community enterprise management and with heavy financial burdens on enterprises (see chapter 17). The lack of a traditional entrepreneurial base and of experience with establishing and operating TVPs contributes to the difficulties in generating self-sustaining TVP development.

Private Enterprise Systems

There are a number of variants among private enterprises, but in all cases the initial entrepreneurial impulse comes from the owners or founders of the firm, who in the early stages have full management autonomy. Household capital is the primary source of funds for new private enterprises, and risk is borne by the founders and providers of capital. The relationship among the different elements is thus consistent, probably reasonably efficient, and not too different from the configuration for small new firms in other countries.

This changes when private enterprises reach a certain size and their capital needs exceed what can be supplied from internal accumulation and the limited household capital available. They then typically rely more on community capital from the banking system, which consequently bears some of the financial risks. This leads to a contradiction between private ownership and the mechanisms for allocating community capital and for risk-bearing. The insecurity of private ownership of substantial concerns exacerbates the problem. There may be strong pressure to convert large and successful private enterprises into community enterprises of one sort or another. This may not be opposed by the private owners because it offers a sounder political position, better access to community capital coffers, and improved social status for the owners and their families. Conversions are especially easy where, as in Jieshou, many private enterprises officially registered as collective firms in the early 1980s.

In Nanhai conversion takes the form of a joint venture by the private entrepreneur and the community government. The firm typically becomes a collective that is "contracted" to the owner-founder. The private partner often seems to retain some kind of claim on the assets he provides to the new enterprise, as well as management authority and status as residual claimant. He may be able to solidify his position and perhaps even to reap some of his successful firm's large capital gains. In one case the private partner "contributed" all of his enterprise's large debts as well as its assets to the joint venture. Moreover, the assets consisted largely of inventories of goods that were selling very slowly, such as electric fan motors. In another case there may have been side payments to relatives of the owner who worked in government offices.

Since the collectivization of private enterprises involves only rather large firms, quantitatively this trend is overwhelmed by the rapid growth of the private sector as a whole. But as more and more private enterprises grow to respectable size, the problem could become more serious. Incentives for large private enterprises are distorted, and there is great scope for corruption and other irregularities involving community government officials. Moreover, in the areas where large private enterprises have been allowed to develop, the traditional community enterprise sector was generally unsuccessful owing to the reasons mentioned above and to the predatory fiscal practices of local community governments (see chapter 17). There is no reason why these same problems will not arise in converted private enterprises. This seems to be occurring in Jieshou, where government agencies pad the payrolls of converted firms to relieve local employment problems. The director of a large (about ninety employees) food-processing factory asserted that the efficiency of his firm would decline if it became a collective because he would no longer have sufficient autonomy in relations with the local government. In another large private food-processing plant (150 employees), one-third of the workers were hired at the request of government cadres.

If outright conversion of private enterprises into community enterprises is avoided, a somewhat different pattern may emerge. Banking institutions already see well-established private enterprises as solid borrowers. If past experience leads banks to distrust traditional community enterprises, as is true in Shangrao and to a lesser extent in Jieshou, the banks may increasingly provide loans directly to private enterprises, with significant implications for the future role of community governments. This is only a potential long-term trend, since at present lending to large private enterprises is still heavily mediated by community governments.

Trends and Issues

This section first looks at trends in the ownership structure of China's TVP sector. It then briefly discusses the future evolution of the local banking system and how it might affect TVP capital allocation and risk-bearing mechanisms. Finally, the section focuses on how to promote TVP development in the backward areas where it has largely failed so far and how to deal with the increasing number of large and successful private enterprises.

Ownership Trends

Table 9-5 shows trends in the ownership structure of Chinese industry as a whole over the past fifteen years. The two most striking features are the steady decline in the share of the state sector in gross value of industrial output (GVIO) in the 1970s and 1980s and the rise in the share of the TVP sector, which began accelerating in 1984. The latter trend makes the changing structure of ownership within the TVP sector all the more important. Unfortunately there is no breakdown below the village level, but the sharp rise in the share of below-village industry in 1985 and 1986 suggests that the share of private enterprises has indeed grown considerably. (Before 1980 virtually all of the village-and-below portion of GVIO must have been produced by village and production team enterprises.) Hence the share of private enterprises is rising steadily at the expense of community enterprises, and within the community enterprise sector the share of the top tier (township enterprises)

Table 9-5. *The Ownership Structure of Chinese Industry, 1971–78*
(percentage of total GVIO)

Ownership	1971	1975	1978	1980	1981	1982	1983	1984[a]	1985	1986
State	85.9	81.2	77.6	75.1	74.3	73.8	72.6	67.6	64.9	62.2
Urban collective	10.9	13.7	13.7	14.4	14.1	14.3	14.4	15.9	15.6	14.8
Urban individual	. .	. .	. .	0.0	0.0	0.1	0.1	0.2	0.3[b]	0.2
Urban other	. .	. .	. .	0.5	0.6	0.7	0.8	1.1	1.2[b]	1.5
Rural nonstate	3.2	5.1	8.7	10.0	11.0	11.2	12.1	15.2	18.0	21.3
Township	1.6	2.6	4.8	5.4	5.9	6.0	6.3	7.7	8.1	9.3
Village								6.0	6.8	7.5
Below village	1.6	2.5	3.9	4.6	5.1	5.2	5.8	1.5	3.1[c]	4.5
Share of TVP GVIO										
Township	50.2	51.2	55.5	53.9	53.8	53.8	52.4	50.5	45.1	43.5
Village	49.8	48.8	44.5	46.1	46.2	46.2	47.6	39.6	37.9	35.2
Below village								9.9	17.0	21.3

. . . Zero or negligible.

Note: Percentages for 1971–80 were calculated from gross industrial output value figures in 1970 constant accounting prices, for 1981–83 in 1980 constant prices, and for 1984–86 in current prices.

a. Since data for current prices are not available for 1984, the shares of ownership forms other than rural nonstate industry (for which data in current prices are available) were calculated from their constant price shares.

b. Since nominal figures were not available, shares were calculated on the assumption that the relative shares of each in nominal individual and other industrial output value are the same as the real shares.

c. Of this, 1.6 percent consisted of output of partnerships and 1.5 percent was output of individual enterprises.

Sources: State Statistical Bureau (1983), p. 215; (1985a), pp. 20, 239; (1986a), pp. 130, 182, 224, 227; (1987b), p. 3; (1987c), p. 20; (1987d), p. 21.

is increasing or at least stable, whereas that of the lower tiers (village and especially production team enterprises) is declining. These trends mean that in addition to a shift from community to private enterprises, a "hollowing out" of the middle of the TVP sector may be occurring. There is a great deal of diversity among provinces, counties, and even local rural communities, however, and in some areas trends may be different.

Information from the four counties, which are at least to some degree representative of the rest of China, illustrates the trends. Table 9-6 shows output shares of different types of industrial TVPs in Nanhai during 1978–86. After an initial sharp decline the share of township enterprises has stabilized and even increased somewhat, reflecting the county's policy of developing large "backbone" enterprises in every township. The share of village firms first rose rapidly and then fluctuated at about 30 percent. The share of production team firms has fallen sharply since 1984.

The trend toward privatization of lower-level community enterprises in Nanhai is even more striking if the large number of such firms contracted to individuals is taken into account. Contracting gives the manager effective control over the enterprise and status as residual claimant and often serves as a prelude to outright sale of the firm to the individual concerned. Sometimes the very act of contracting seems to involve an implicit transfer of ownership rights. In one case a village enterprise was contracted to individuals who were required under the contract to turn over Y20,000 in profits to the village each year. The firm became highly profitable, and two years later the contractors bought it from the village, but they paid only Y10,000, the depreciated book value of the enterprise's assets. The price did not reflect the increased value of the firm (in income-generating capability) during the period of the contract. In effect, the right to capital gains from increased profitability was implicitly given to the contractors in the act of contracting. If this example is at all representative, a large part of the village and production team sector is already effectively under private management and control. In Xiqiao town, Nanhai County, nearly half of all industrial village enterprises

Table 9-6. *The Changing Ownership Structure of Industrial TVPs, Nanhai, 1978–86*
(percentage of gross income of industrial TVPs)

Ownership	1978	1980	1983	1984	1985	1986
Township and town	68	35	32	35	43	40
Village	11	39	36	37	31	35
Production team	} 21	26	32	{ 22	16	13
Private				6	10	12

Source: Information from fieldwork.

and more than 90 percent of production team firms have already been contracted to individual management. In Nanzhuang town, Nanhai County, there was a wholesale privatization of production team enterprises and a flowering of private enterprises in 1984 after the Central Committee's Document No. 1 clearly permitted the development of private enterprise.

In Shangrao, as can be seen from table 9-7, township enterprises, village enterprises, and production team firms have all seen their shares in the GVIO of the TVP sector decline precipitously. Community enterprises in Shangrao are in danger of being left behind if they cannot improve their efficiency. Private enterprises have the great advantage of being better able than community enterprises to escape predatory fiscal practices by community governments. Comparable data are not available for Jieshou, but they would show a similar "tipping" away from community enterprises and toward private enterprises. In Jieshou's rural areas wholesale privatization of village and production team enterprises through outright sale or contracting occurred when the PRS was implemented in 1979–80. In Zhuanji township all village and production team enterprises were contracted or sold to individuals at that time. In Jinzhai township about half of the registered industrial township enterprises are actually private firms that had received financial support from the township government.

Production team enterprises are dying out in most if not all of rural China. This is not surprising, since with the implementation of the PRS teams lost their main economic and administrative function, the exercise of control over agricultural land. Village enterprises are also generally declining, especially if contracting is taken into account. The private sector continues to boom, and township enterprises appear to be holding their own in many localities and even continue to be the leading sector of TVP growth in places such as Wuxi, where village enterprises are also in a strong position.

Table 9-7. *The Ownership Structure of Industrial TVPs, Shangrao, 1978–86*
(percentage of GVIO of TVPs)

Ownership	1983	1984	1985	1986
Township and town	43	47	43	32
Village	41	30	22	18
Production team	16	1	0	0
Private	0	22	35	50
Partnerships[a]	0	17	23	27
Individual	0	5	12	23

— Not applicable.

a. It is likely that a number of production team enterprises simply switched to the joint-household (cooperative) category in 1984 without greatly changing their organizational or management structure.

Source: Information from fieldwork.

Analysis of Trends

The analytical framework developed earlier can aid understanding of ownership trends. The communities to which village enterprises and especially production team firms belong appear suboptimal in size for their capital allocation and risk-bearing roles: they can neither raise sufficient capital for large-scale expansion nor absorb much risk. Production teams, in particular, do not have enough firms to spread the risk to any great extent. In addition, since RCCs are township-level organizations, village and production team authorities do not participate much in determining their lending. And when the PRS was implemented, many teams simply wiped out their collective industrial assets by selling or contracting their enterprises to individuals.

Township enterprises have the best access to community capital and are part of a high-level risk-sharing system in large communities. The richer, more industrialized rural areas generate more community funds than are needed for basic local public expenditures, and these funds are available for risky TVP investments. Since townships are now established as the lowest level of government, township enterprises also have superior administrative connections. Private enterprises, however, have greater flexibility and stronger incentives for proprietors, and the pressure of rural surplus labor stimulates the creation of small enterprises. Thus firms at both extremes of the TVP spectrum have strengths that may give them a competitive edge over the TVPs in the middle.

By this reasoning villages with more economic resources, more firms, greater diversification of product structure, and better administrative connections with the banking system should be able to survive and even thrive. Villages in Wuxi for the most part fit this description, which partly explains why the village enterprise sector has done so well there. The integration of village enterprises into industrial administration at the township level also is greater in Wuxi than in other localities (see chapter 7). Hence Wuxi's village enterprise sector should be viewed to a large extent as an integral part of the township enterprise sector. By contrast, townships that are too small and lack economic resources and risk-bearing capabilities may stagnate because they cannot put together the "critical mass" needed for successful development of community enterprises. Most of Shangrao's townships are in this category. Townships in Jieshou that are distant from the central town also are having great difficulties in developing community enterprises.

Thus three different patterns of local TVP development contribute to the overall trends: maintenance of a dominant township enterprise sector in a relatively few counties like Wuxi; a steady shift toward private development at the expense of all levels of community enterprises, as in Shangrao and Jieshou; and, where a more diversified pattern of ownership persists, as in Nanhai, a tendency for the top and bottom tiers (township enterprises and private enterprises) to expand at the expense of the middle tiers (village and production team enterprises). The tendencies toward polarization and privatization of the TVP sector will have interesting implications if they continue over a long period.

The Future of the Community Banking System

In the traditional community enterprise system local banks funnel community savings into investment projects and enterprises chosen by the community government. The banks are an integral part of the mechanism for allocating community capital, but at least in the advanced areas they bear almost no risk. Reforms in the banking system, changing ownership patterns for TVPs, and increasing factor mobility may drastically alter the role of local banks and RCCs, with consequences for investment financing and risk-bearing in the TVP sector that are important but hard to predict. As long as banks remain community financial institutions that do not freely lend funds outside, measures to increase their independence in decisions on specific loans are not likely to generate great changes in localities such as Wuxi where the traditional community enterprise system is working well. The reforms may even improve efficiency by providing a further check on inappropriate capital allocation decisions. The linkage of loans and deposits and the near inability to lend outside the locality mean that banks, in effect, will still function to a great extent as community financial institutions. Greater independence for the banking system in the more backward areas or where traditional community enterprise development is not working well has more serious consequences, since the banks are likely to become more conservative about lending to community enterprises. To the extent that this results in less total lending within the community, capital could flow out of the community through the hierarchical banking system itself if not as a result of deliberate decisions by branches. Within the community banks may prefer to lend to private enterprises, which would accelerate the decline in the share of the community enterprise sector. If local banks increasingly pull capital out of their communities and invest it elsewhere, deposit mobilization, hitherto aided by community government support and campaigns, might suffer. The community government might even establish its own captive financial institutions, which would siphon deposits away from the banks.

Making interest rates more important in capital allocation in the TVP sector would be difficult at present. Community governments strive to support TVP development regardless of interest rates, although higher rates do increase financial risks. Moreover, even rather high interest rates would probably not attract a great deal of community capital out of the localities where it is generated. This is certainly true of the more advanced areas, where returns to local investment are high. Any intercommunity credit flows elicited by higher interest rates would be primarily from poorer communities to more industrialized ones.

Decentralization of ownership of banks and RCCs to the township level or even below might have little effect on relationships between banks and community governments in such places as Wuxi. But it could easily promote continued or even greater misuse of community savings by community governments in backward areas. Hence decentralization of bank ownership to this level might be dangerous.

Decentralization of ownership in the banking system would be counterproductive unless there is competition. But it may be hard to introduce much competition into the banking system at the township level in the near future. Where RCCs have been made more independent from ABC township credit offices, as in Jieshou and Shangrao, there tends to be a strict division of labor and clients between the two institutions. Any competition in the system usually comes when the urban Industrial and Commercial Bank sets up branches in townships, as has occurred in Nanhai. Competition between community and noncommunity financial institutions would be unequal, since the community government would invariably favor the former,[3] but over time it might undermine the mechanism for allocating community capital.

The banking system as presently structured is not well suited to bear a great deal of risk from TVP activities. First, liabilities (deposits) are risk-free, which makes it difficult for banking institutions to hold risky assets such as TVP loans, and banks have no reserve cushions to absorb losses from bad loans. Second, since banks are not owners or formal residual claimants on the income flows from TVPs, it is not appropriate for them to absorb a great deal of risk. For community enterprises the primary risk-bearing institution should be their owners, the community governments.

Over the longer term the question of how community governments themselves should diversify their risks will become increasingly important. In developed areas such as Wuxi community governments diversify risks by setting up numerous enterprises in different industries. Even so, Wuxi is buffeted by the changing fortunes of the machinery industry, and Xiqiao town in Nanhai County is even more seriously affected by market changes in the textile industry. In backward areas community enterprise development is difficult and highly risky, and the limited financial and human resources of community governments leave little room for diversification. The introduction of financial instruments that could be bought and sold by community governments and that allow flows of capital among localities would help diversify risk. Moreover, such instruments would enhance capital mobility and help ease the capital constraints that limit firm size in the TVP sector.

Backward Areas

The misalignment of the different elements of the entrepreneurship-capital-ownership nexus contributes significantly to the problems of backward areas such as Shangrao. But perhaps even more fundamental is the problem of fiscal predation by community governments in those areas (see chapter 17).[4] If this problem is solved, the limited mobility of entrepreneurs among communities, localities, and regions could become a serious constraint. An area such as Shangrao has most of the ingredients needed for successful development of small-scale manufacturing industries: cheap, relatively well-educated labor, natural resources, and enough capital, including some aid from the central government, to get started at least. What it seriously lacks are entrepreneurs and their networks, as well as good, experienced managers. If these could be brought in from outside and if the problem of fiscal predation could be resolved, Shangrao would have good potential for TVP development.

Private Enterprises

The problems and distortions caused by ambiguous government policy toward sizable private enterprises are becoming more and more evident. The insecurity felt by successful private entrepreneurs may adversely affect their incentives once their firms grow to a certain size. Moreover, it leads to all sorts of distortions and to great leeway for corruption in the relationships between these enterprises and community government officials. None of the ways of dealing with large private enterprises practiced in the four counties is particularly effective or efficient. The central government has made an important first step toward rectifying the problem by formally legalizing large private enterprises and removing the previous (unenforced) ceilings on the number of employees individual proprietorships could hire. But it will take considerable time and effort to change ingrained patterns of status stratification and discrimination against private enterprises at the local level (see chapter 7).

Clarifying and strengthening the property rights of large private entrepreneurs is clearly necessary and would undoubtedly improve the situation in many respects, but it would exacerbate the inconsistency with the mechanism for allocating community capital. A possible solution would be to have community capital supplied to private enterprises, particularly risk capital, carry certain limited ownership rights—most important, the right to reap profits and capital gains from subsequent development of the enterprise. Bank loans to large private enterprises could be converted into a form of nonvoting equity held by the bank that provided the funds. Since the private enterprises concerned are large and successful, the increased risk to the banking system should be manageable.

Notes

1. The Wuxi plant's main competitor is a state-owned machinery workshop under Shengli Oilfield that produces several hundred units per year. But the state firm's production costs are much higher, and quality is poor.

2. The common practice of "repaying" the founders' seed capital as soon as the enterprise

is financially comfortable leaves it with no equity other than internal accumulation, and it is commonly thought in China that internally accumulated assets belong to "the enterprise itself" rather than to the founders or owners.

3. But the ability of community governments to influence local residents' choices of where to put their savings may be limited. Many rural people deposit their money in outside banks, sometimes because they feel that big-city banks offer greater security but more often because they do not want local bank or RCC personnel to know how much money they have.

4. Fiscal predation is related to the inability of community governments to absorb risk. Their largely fixed public expenditures are so great in relation to their normal revenues that they cannot tolerate much variation in the latter and hence cannot absorb much risk.

Part III

Performance

A careful evaluation of the performance of China's TVP sector and its components is a prerequisite for an overall assessment of the sector and of the reform and policy options for the future. The three papers in this part contain a preliminary analysis of different aspects of TVP performance.

In chapter 10 Wang Xiaolu focuses on capital formation and utilization and its impact on TVP efficiency and performance. He first looks at the external environment for capital formation. Originally TVPs depended on transfers of agricultural surplus (in several forms) to finance their development. Currently, however, there is considerable variation in sources of funding, as a survey of the four sample counties indicates. In all cases community accumulation (including retained profits), bank loans, and payables are the main sources of funds, but their relative importance varies by ownership as well as geographically. As a result of administrative pressures and distortions (rather than purely economic factors), community enterprises rely on bank loans much more than do private enterprises.

Wang then turns to internal mechanisms for capital formation. Community governments strongly press community goals on their enterprises, whereas enterprise managers tend to emphasize firm-level objectives. A large proportion of the profits of community enterprises is remitted to community governments, and the proportion of these profits reinvested in the enterprises is highly unstable. As a result, firms depend increasingly on credit financing. Excessive community government levies on TVP profits have interfered with the smooth development of enterprises, especially in Shangrao. The rapid run-up of workers' wages and managers' compensation in many community enterprises also saps firms' reinvestment capacities.

Wang next discusses capital productivity and the substantial differences among the four counties and among firms under different forms of ownership. Township enterprises generate fewer profits and tax payments per unit of capital than other types of TVPs in the same locality, a phenomenon for which Wang suggests several possible explanations. Capital productivity has declined in the township enterprises of Wuxi and Nanhai, but it has risen in Jieshou, from a much lower initial level. Wuxi and Nanhai have also seen substitution of capital for labor, a tendency that has not been significant in Jieshou. These different patterns are related to local labor market conditions—as soon as local surplus agricultural labor is absorbed, communities tend to increase capital intensity rather than hire additional workers from outside. Wang argues that capital intensification, although rational from the viewpoint of individual communities, is inefficient from a national perspective.

The chapter closes with a discussion of the continuing inability of TVPs to attain larger firm sizes and of the consequences—high costs, scattered location patterns, excessive competition, and other problems. The persistence of small firm size is traced to the community orientation of TVPs, which limits their expansion.

In chapter 11 Jan Svejnar looks at productive efficiency and employment in Chinese TVPs on the basis of theoretical models and econometric approaches developed for the study of cooperative firms in other countries. His analysis of productive efficiency is based on Cobb-Douglas and translog production functions, augmented by dummy variables that represent different counties, ownership forms, and worker compensation schemes. The analysis of labor utilization is based on an enterprise objective function equation, which is specified as a geometric average of three possible enterprise goals: maximizing profits, generating employment, and increasing average wages above local market-clearing levels.

The next section presents the main empirical results. An important finding is that, other things being equal, ownership appears to be unrelated to productive efficiency. The coefficients on county dummy variables indicate that the productivity of sample firms in Wuxi, Nanhai, and Jieshou counties is more or less the same but that firms in Shangrao lag significantly behind. The substantial technical progress over time confirms that intensive rather than merely extensive growth has been responsible for the TVP sector's observed successful performance. The coefficients on labor and capital suggest that TVPs operate in the zone of mildly increasing returns to scale. Finally, sample TVPs that use a fixed-wage-plus-bonus system or an internal workpoint system tend to be more productive than those that use pure piece rates, a combination of fixed wages and piece rates, or a fixed wage plus year-end dividend.

The analysis of labor utilization practices also yields some significant results. In general, TVPs appear to link employment closely to output levels and to economize on labor as wages rise. Thus they recognize the tradeoff between wages and employment, and featherbedding seems not to be a significant phenomenon overall. (This last result contrasts with qualitative evidence of overstaffing in some enterprises reported in chapter 14.) Significant associations between ownership forms and compensation schemes are lacking, except that private enterprises appear to have paid more attention to local alternative wage levels in their employment decisions in recent years.

The chapter closes with a reiteration of the most important findings: ownership does not appear to be systematically related to productive efficiency; group incentive schemes may be associated with higher productivity than individual incentive schemes; the behavior of local authorities may have a significant influence on TVP productivity, as is indicated by the relative inefficiency in Shangrao County; TVPs seem to operate under mildly increasing returns to scale and have on the whole experienced rapid increases in productivity over time; and there is some evidence that the employment practices of TVPs have been shifting away from the objective of employment generation as such and toward employment levels that reflect the marginal productivity of labor.

In chapter 12 Wang Tuoyu undertakes an empirical analysis of regional patterns of TVP development, assesses recent and current trends, and draws some policy implications. He first looks at indicators of TVP development and efficiency for three groups of provinces, classified according to whether their TVP sectors are developed, developing, or underdeveloped. Wang shows that the level of development of China's TVP sector declines progressively from east to west. Moreover, there are big differences in the internal structure of the TVP sector among the three regions. The share of industry is highest in the developed region, whereas construction plays an important role in the underdeveloped areas and commerce is relatively more important in the developing region. In general, the developed areas emphasize capital- and technology-intensive industrial activities, whereas in the underdeveloped region labor-intensive activities and industries based on natural resources are more important.

The chapter moves on to review recent growth performance in different regions. One of Wang's most important findings is that the gaps in TVCE development between more developed and less developed regions have been widening. In the TVP sector as a whole, however, this tendency was offset in 1984–85 by the rapid growth of private enterprises, which showed more regional balance.

Wang then looks at the prospects for reducing regional imbalances in future TVP development. After reviewing the sources of investment financing for TVPs, he concludes that the possibilities for redirecting resources to the underdeveloped region are limited and that there is a danger that regional imbalances will grow worse. A number of policy measures to ameliorate the situation are put forward: free interregional flows of labor and of other factors of production should be encouraged; private enterprises, which have already played a significant role in reducing regional imbalances, should be allowed to develop further; and the limited amount of state support available for the more backward areas should be targeted at sound investment projects and at areas with low per capita incomes and poorer agricultural resources.

10

Capital Formation
and Utilization
Wang Xiaolu

China's industrial TVP sector has developed rapidly over the past several years—much faster than state industry in number of enterprises, value of output, and profits. Community enterprises, especially those run by townships and villages (TVCEs), form the mainstay of the industrial TVP sector, whereas individual firms and partnerships comprise the private sector. Enterprises run by production teams share some of the characteristics of community enterprises but increasingly resemble private enterprises in many ways. This chapter analyzes capital formation and capital productivity in China's TVP sector and especially for TVCEs.

The External Environment for Capital Formation

The sources of funds for TVP industry vary considerably among counties. The capital structure of sample firms in 1985 is shown in table 10-1. After short-term funds such as payables are deducted, the principal and most stable sources of capital are community financial accumulation (including internal accumulation by the firms themselves) and bank loans. This section will look at external sources of capital. A subsequent section discusses internal accumulation, which TVPs also rely on heavily for expansion.

Agricultural Surplus and Initial Rural Industrial Development

In its early stages TVP industry depended greatly on capital from agriculture. Since Wuxi and Nanhai counties were agriculturally developed, TVP industry there got an early start and developed rapidly. In Shangrao and Jieshou counties agriculture was backward and TVP industry developed slowly.

Agricultural surplus is turned into investment for TVP industry in three ways.

- *Mandatory agricultural accumulation through communes and brigades.* This channel was important during the people's commune period but no longer exists.

- *Personal savings.* Most new private enterprises use this channel to get established. Community enterprises often raise funds by requiring new workers to invest in the firm.

- *Support from financial institutions.* The level of lending by banks and credit cooperatives is linked to local deposits. Earlier, the agricultural surplus had a decisive influence on the supply of credit funds, but in some developed regions bank savings now come mainly from industrial income.

The Significance of Credit Funds

The proportion of bank loans in total capital varies among counties and has changed over time (table 10-2). Wuxi and Nanhai counties are both economically developed but represent two different patterns. Wuxi's dependence on bank loans was extremely small in the early stages but has increased steadily over the past several years. To satisfy demand from TVPs, local banks are systematically borrowing from banks in other areas that have surplus funds and are lending this money to local enterprises. Nanhai TVPs relied heavily on bank loans from the very beginning, and their dependence has continued to grow. In general, bank loans have occupied a dominant place in enterprise capital. Of the two less developed counties, Jieshou relies heavily on bank loans, while Shangrao is the least dependent on bank loans, mainly because numerous investment failures there destroyed local TVPs' credibility and banks tightened controls to cut down on risk.

In general, the scale of credit is closely related to local bank deposits. The

Table 10-1. *Sources of Funds for Sample Firms, 1985*
(percentage of total capital)

Source	Wuxi	Jieshou	Nanhai	Shangrao[a]
Township and village government funds[b]	43.5	33.3	22.8	41.3
Bank loans[c]	16.4	24.1	49.7	4.2
Payables	19.4	13.3	12.0	17.9
Other[d]	20.7	29.3	15.5	36.6

a. Based on aggregate statistics for six townships in Shangrao rather than for sample firms.

b. Includes both grants from community governments and internal accumulation by TVPs from retained profits. In addition, sample firms tended to include in this category capital from "owners," even if they were private individuals.

c. Includes loans from rural credit cooperatives.

d. Includes wages payable, state support funds, loans from government departments, capital from individuals and groups, special funds, depreciation funds, and miscellaneous funds.

Sources: Enterprise Quantitative Questionnaire and information from fieldwork.

Table 10-2. Bank Loans as a Share of Total Capital of Sample TVPs, 1970–85
(percent)

Year	Wuxi	Jieshou	Nanhai	Shangrao[a]
1970	4.4	38.3	n.a.	n.a.
1975	0.5	44.0	n.a.	n.a.
1978	0.9	34.2	n.a.	n.a.
1980	8.8	20.7	32.2	7.2
1981	9.0	27.6	34.4	n.a.
1982	7.3	24.8	42.0	n.a.
1983	10.7	26.8	36.4	n.a.
1984	23.0	30.2	50.5	n.a.
1985	16.4	24.1	49.7	4.2

n.a. Not available.
a. Based on aggregate statistics for six townships.
Sources: Enterprise Quantitative Questionnaire and information from fieldwork.

banking system is highly regionalized. Local deposits constitute the basic source of funds for loans to support the growth of local TVP industry, and cross-regional financial exchanges are limited. This creates a feedback mechanism whereby wages, personal bank deposits, and loans to local TVPs ratchet upward. Once bank deposits exceed a certain level, they can have a snowball effect on the development of TVP industry. All of the sample counties except Shangrao have reached this stage.

This kind of capital circulation has some weaknesses. Lack of a competitive mechanism (the result of limited cross-regional capital mobility) affects the optimization of factor allocation and reduces the efficiency of capital utilization.

Soft Constraints on Credit Funds

TVPs' dependence on bank loans varies greatly with ownership. Community enterprises depend much more heavily on bank credit than do private enterprises. As the figures below, from the Enterprise Quantitative Questionnaire, show, the share of bank loans in total capital for the sample private enterprises in Jieshou was consistently lower than for the community enterprises.[1]

	Percentage of total capital			
Type of enterprise	1983	1984	1985	1986
TVCES	25.4	29.1	33.3	25.6
Private enterprises	21.0	13.5	14.5	17.7

The discrepancy is even greater in Nanhai, where township enterprises depend more heavily on bank loans than do village enterprises.[2] (Lending to private enterprises was minuscule during 1980–85.)

			Percentage of total capital			
Type of enterprise	*1981*	*1982*	*1983*	*1984*	*1985*	*1986*
Township enterprises	33.4	39.6	45.9	40.3	60.4	46.7
Village enterprises	9.6	7.2	8.3	4.3	13.7	16.6
Private and production team firms	0	0	0	0	3.5	0

Bank loans have become an essential source of funds for the normal business operations of township enterprises. This is not because township enterprises are less risky investments or have better credibility than other types of firms. Indeed, the profit rate on capital for township enterprises in the four counties is invariably lower than that of other types of TVPs, and the proportion of township enterprises in financial difficulties is higher. In 1985, 11 percent of industrial township enterprises in Wuxi suffered losses, and the loss rate (the ratio of total losses to aggregate profit) for all township enterprises was 3.2 percent, whereas that for village enterprises was only 0.6 percent. In Nanhai 18 percent of industrial township enterprises were operating in the red in 1985, and the loss rate was 9.1 percent. Only 1.5 percent of village enterprises suffered losses, and the loss rate was 0.7 percent. In 1986, 30 percent of industrial township enterprises in Nanhai had losses, and the loss rate rose to 61.3 percent, but only 3.1 percent of Nanhai's village enterprises had losses, and the loss rate was only 1.9 percent.[3]

Money-losing TVCEs typically stay in business, despite their inability to repay debts, for two reasons. First, the community government can shift the responsibility for repaying the debts of a specific firm to its other enterprises, which reduces the risk for both the community government and the bank. Second, in the absence of a capital market, the bank provides the only access to capital for enterprises, and banks keep investing in debt-ridden TVCEs because of pressures from community governments acting from nonprofit motives. Moreover, since the principle of a regional balance of loans and deposits has severed horizontal links among banks, local banks can hardly find any better lending channels on their own. Bank loans are obviously beneficial for the enterprises. Interest rates are low and rarely fluctuate with changes in supply and demand (although there has been some tendency for nominal rates to rise in recent years); part of the loans can be paid off from before-tax profits, which in fact transfers the burden of repayment to government finance; and if firms run into operational difficulties, they can postpone repayment.

The Agricultural Bank of China (ABC) branch in Jieshou reports that by the end of 1985 the county's TVPs had Y2.09 million in overdue loans. This figure included Y490,000 in bad debts owed by 124 firms that had closed. Overdue loans accounted for more than 20 percent of the Y9 million in outstanding loans to TVPs in the county, and bad debts exceeded 5 percent of the outstanding balance. In 1986 the bank took steps to press for repayment, deduct guarantors' money, and clear bankrupt firms' assets, but it got back only 26 percent of overdue payments and 18 percent of bad debts.

The lack of laws and regulations to protect the legal rights of creditors is another important reason for the worsening situation. In general, TVPS (mainly township enterprises) have little trouble obtaining credit, and this partly explains their heavy dependence on debt in their operations. This method of "debt management" (see Zhou Qiren and Huang Zhuangjun 1987) has enabled TVP industry to develop rapidly, but it has also meant that some firms have a shaky financial structure. Severe fluctuations occur because the growth of TVP industry is only too easily affected by changes in the supply of credit. Furthermore, the availability of abundant credit has masked poor management in some firms. Unprofitable or money-losing firms have been able to coexist with successful enterprises and have wasted large amounts of scarce capital funds.

The Internal Mechanism for Capital Formation

Capital formation within firms is influenced by the claims and priorities of community governments and by the enterprises' own capacity to make and reinvest profits. The similarities and differences between the goals of community governments and community enterprise managers as well as the influence that governments have on enterprises are important issues.

Township Goals and Enterprise Objectives

In the four sample counties township governments exercise supervision over subordinate firms directly or through organizations such as township industrial corporations (TICs). Township governments usually have authority to appoint factory directors, inspect factory performance, set annual targets for profits and value of output, allocate labor and manage wages, guarantee enterprises' bank loans, act as liaison agencies in expanding enterprises' business ties, and help enterprises sell part of their production. The relations between township governments and their enterprises resemble in some ways the ties between state institutions and state-owned enterprises and in other ways those between a general corporation and its branch companies or factories in a market economy. But unlike state institutions on the one hand, township governments face a competitive market that does not allow them to provide monopoly protection to township enterprises. They cannot implement mandatory production plans or determine prices. On the other hand, they differ from market-economy corporations in that they are not merely superior managers or parent corporations of township enterprises. As government institutions, they have multiple objectives, not just profit maximization or enterprise development, and they often try to push their noneconomic goals on firms.

According to responses to the Township Leader Questionnaire, township governments see TVP development as having three main objectives: providing employment opportunities for surplus rural labor in the township, raising local living standards, and increasing township governments' financial revenue. Communities that face a surplus labor problem give priority to increasing employment; otherwise, the emphasis is on the latter two objectives. The survey results show that township governments act as strong representatives of their communities. They expand their revenues through profit remittances from the firms, and they seek to increase employment and raise local living standards by requiring township enterprises to absorb more labor, by supporting unprofitable or money-losing firms, and by transferring part of enterprises' profits to local residents. There is a premise that income within the community should be relatively balanced, and local TVPs are asked to pursue steady increases in wages for their workers. Since the employment and welfare targets obviously run counter to profit maximization, township governments weigh the tradeoffs and often sacrifice the profit motive.

The industrial development targets set by village leaders are usually similar to those set by township governments. The difference is that villages may have less power to manage and control enterprises and have less money for public expenditures at the village level. But village leaders are often prompted by a stronger desire to maximize per capita income in the village.

Although TVCEs are subordinate to community governments, the objectives of TVCE directors differ sharply from those set by these governments. In response to a question about objectives, almost all directors of sample firms (the bulk of which were TVCEs) placed "pursuing long-term and stable development of the firm" first among nine choices. Other targets singled out by directors included "creating famous brand products and improving the enterprise's credibility," "pursuing maximum profits," "improving workers' per capita income level," and "improving the internal management of the enterprise." These choices are all related to the prosperity of the enterprise and its workers. Factory directors placed at the bottom of the list the objectives that are the main ones for township governments—increasing employment, promoting local prosperity, and increasing financial revenue.

The motives of enterprises fall into three main categories: long-term development, maximum profits, and maximum per capita income within the enterprise. Thus TVP managers have the same set of motivations and objectives as their counterparts in a typical market economy, although in their pursuit of maximum per capita income they exhibit the characteristics of cooperative firms to a certain degree.

The differences between the targets of community governments and those of their subordinate firms have affected enterprise operations and have led to some restraints on firms' behavior by community governments. For instance, community governments' pursuit of employment opportunities may lead to overstaffing of local community enterprises, which affects profits.

Table 10-3. *Shares and Uses of Profits Remitted to Township and Village Governments by Wuxi Industrial TVCEs, 1977–86*
(percent)

Item	1977	1978	1979	1980	1981	1982	1983	1984	1985	1986
Share of total profits remitted to community governments	82	86	85	66	47	51	58	54	35	40
Use of profits[a]										
Subsidies to agriculture	7	27	19	25	35	36	29	0	0	12
Agricultural investment	20	12	9	12	23	21	7	19	10	0
Subsidies for agricultural mechanization and water conservancy	21	5	3	9	12	8	6	7	6	7
Village and town construction	5	6	4	5	11	13	13	14	16	19
Culture, education, and public health	3	3	2	3	5	6	7	8	9	10
Industrial investment	38	40	52	44	0	0	16	24	27	21
Cadre salaries	0.1	0	3	3	8	9	9	13	11	12
Other	0	8	8	0.1	7	8	12	15	21	19

a. Includes profits retained by enterprises, as well as remitted profits. Numbers may not add to 100 percent because of rounding.
Source: Information from fieldwork.

228

Community governments' desire for higher financial revenue may lead them to draw off huge amounts of profits for government expenditures and so hamper the enterprises' long-term development. The community enterprises' pursuit of maximum per capita incomes may in its turn create sharp discrepancies between the incomes of enterprise workers and those of other members of the community. Community governments may respond by acting to keep workers' wages from growing too rapidly, transferring part of community enterprise profits to other members of the community, or forcing firms to increase their accumulation.

Distribution of Profits and Community Government Investment

The difference between the profit motive of township governments and that of the owners of capital in a capitalist system can be seen in the distribution of township enterprises' profits and the expenditures of township governments. The method of distribution, which obviously affects enterprises' reinvestment rate, is a key element of enterprise capital formation.

In the four counties surveyed, a large part of township enterprises' profits are usually turned over to township governments for general distribution, leaving only a small portion for reinvestment. Table 10-3 shows the share of profits remitted to township and village governments by TVCEs in Wuxi for 1978–86 and the use of these profits. The proportion of profits handed over has fluctuated between 35 and 86 percent but has been declining over the past several years. The amount of remitted profits that goes for subsidies to agricultural production and distribution to community members has fallen sharply. Meanwhile, the proportion spent on township construction, cultural and health projects, and cadres' salaries and bonuses has increased steadily, from 18 percent in 1977 to 41 percent in 1986. The proportion of other spending has also increased, to 20 percent. The share devoted to reinvestment in TVP industry has been unstable. It has fluctuated between 0 and 44 percent and has fallen since the late 1970s.

The situation in Wuxi suggests that in relatively developed areas public welfare and administrative expenditures are replacing support for farming as the main way in which TVCEs' profit remittances are utilized. The declining proportion of reinvestment in industry is making TVCEs increasingly dependent on credit financing. Surveys indicate that in the other three counties profits drawn by township governments from industrial TVCEs were seldom used for reinvestment. The proportion of profits handed over to township governments in Shangrao seems to be larger than that in the other counties.

Jieshou, like Wuxi, can be considered an exception. After several local TVCEs had failed, the county began to take a laissez-faire attitude toward the local TVP sector. As a result, private enterprises have developed rapidly, and TVCEs enjoy a more comfortable environment. According to statistics for thirty-six sample firms in the county, profits remitted to community governments amounted to only 2–5 percent of total net profits in the past several years. Even when management fees are taken into account, the figure is only about 20 percent of total net profits, which leaves large amounts for reinvestment.

Excessive levies on TVPs' profits have hindered their smooth development. The problem has been especially prominent in Shangrao, where enterprises are moving ahead at a snail's pace, since they must submit a large part, if not all, of their profits to community governments. (Some firms even handed over their depreciation funds when they failed to fulfill the profit target and had difficulty in obtaining bank credit.) The average annual growth rate of TVP industrial output between 1978 and 1985 in Shangrao was only about one-third the level in the other three counties. In developed regions such as Nanhai and Wuxi enterprises are able to obtain an ample and cheap supply of bank credit, which to a great extent helps make up for the shortfall caused by profit remittances, and community governments are willing to act as firms' guarantors to improve their access to credit funds. Guarantees of this kind, however, are more often than not pledged without any collateral.

Enterprises also acquire funds through tax reductions and exemptions. In 1985 industrial TVCEs in Wuxi were supposed to have paid Y143.4 million in indirect taxes and Y67.5 million in profit taxes. But in fact, reductions and exemptions of Y57.3 million on the former and Y19.6 million on the latter decreased the total tax paid by 27 percent. This is one of the ways in which community governments uphold local interests under the existing government finance system.

Distribution of Profits and Self-Accumulation in Enterprises

Statistics from sample firms show that a sizable portion of the profits remaining after remittances to the community government is used to invest in fixed assets and replenish floating capital and that only a small part is distributed to individuals. The reinvestment rate in Wuxi and Jieshou counties is higher than in the other two counties. Nanhai devotes more retained profits to bonuses than does Wuxi or Jieshou (see table 10-4).

Differences in mechanisms for determining wages caused huge gaps in county distribution patterns. From 1980 to 1985 the average annual growth rate of income per worker in Jieshou's sample enterprises was a mere 8.2 percent, as against an average annual growth of gross profits per worker of 41.6 percent. Average income per worker climbed by 21.0 percent in sample firms in Nanhai and by 16.8 percent in Wuxi, whereas the average annual growth of gross profits per worker was only 7.0 percent in Nanhai and 9.6 percent in Wuxi (see chapter 14).

There are many reasons for these differences. In addition to variations in labor demand and supply conditions and per capita incomes in agriculture,

Table 10-4. *Uses of Retained Profits by Sample TVPs, 1985*
(percentage of total retained profits)

Use of funds	Wuxi	Nanhai	Jieshou
Working capital	39.0	12.4	49.1
Modernization and development	53.2	63.3	34.0
Total	92.2	75.7	83.1
Collective welfare	1.7	1.9	8.5
Bonuses	7.7	22.3	5.9
Total	9.4	24.2	14.4

Note: Totals are not 100 percent owing to unclear uses of profits and inconsistencies in the reported figures.
Source: Enterprise Quantitative Questionnaire.

there are differences in operational behavior. In the Wuxi and Nanhai samples, community enterprises, which tend to pursue higher per capita income, greatly outnumber private enterprises. Moreover, township leaders, in striving to maximize average incomes in the entire community, permit community enterprises to raise wage levels rapidly provided that the growth of their incomes is well coordinated with income growth in the community as a whole. In Nanhai community governments regulate the salaries of enterprise directors on the basis of profits and thereby indirectly control workers' wage levels through factory leaders' interest in profits. This kind of control is relatively weak.

In Wuxi community governments set the per capita wage level target for firms in advance, in accordance with the principle of "appropriate progressive growth." Workers' wages are linked to firms' quotas for output and profits. Enterprises that overfulfill their targets are entitled to use a certain amount of profits for extra wages or bonuses, and those that fail to fulfill targets are subject to a reduction in the growth rate of wages. But even firms that are operating in the red can maintain their wages at the previous year's level or enjoy a small increase. Although this kind of control plays some role in restricting wage inflation, the speed of increase is still fairly fast. Wuxi witnessed a sharp growth of TVCE wage levels in 1984 when it relaxed controls over wages. Profits kept by local TVCEs rose by 129 percent, but bonuses increased by 280 percent and accounted for 18 percent of enterprise retained profits as against 12 percent in the previous year. Average wages increased 29 percent over the previous year. This wage expansion was not brought under control until 1985.

Rapid wage increases in community enterprises mean that employees in effect participate in the distribution of enterprise profits. This undoubtedly helps stimulate workers to care about their firms and work hard. But the rate of increase of wages has exceeded that of profits, and the consequent rapid rise in wage costs may eliminate the competitive advantage that TVPs have because of their low costs. Wage inflation also has some effect on the reinvestment rate and could be a factor in enterprises' heavier dependence on bank loans and credit.

In Jieshou private enterprises make up a larger proportion of the total number of TVPs throughout the county and in the sample. Of the thirty-six sample firms in the county, seven identify themselves as private enterprises, and another seven claim to be owned by township governments but actually belong to private owners. Most of the remaining sample township enterprises had no investment from township governments. The goals and motivations of these firms may be close to those of private enterprises.

In general, private enterprises' capital accumulation motive, especially for individually owned firms that hire wage labor, may be stronger than that of township enterprises, whereas their desire to increase workers' wages is relatively weak. This may be a reason for the slow growth of their wage levels. Impressions from interviews with some private enterprises indicate, however, that noneconomic considerations lead these firms to turn part of their profits into consumption or public welfare expenditures, usually when the firm's scale reaches a certain level. The low growth rate of wages in sample firms of Jieshou could therefore be attributable to other factors—for example, the firms' high dependence on bank loans. As there are many newly established firms in the sample, the pressure of loans falling due is heavy. In fact, a large percentage of the profits used for reinvestment actually go into repayment of bank loans for equipment and working capital. Stricter requirements for timely repayment of bank loans by private enterprises have forced the enterprises to increase their internal accumulation rate, in part by holding down wages.

Capital Productivity

Data from the four counties show sharp differences in the capital productivity of different types of enterprise. Table 10-5 and data for sample firms indicate that industrial township enterprises are markedly less efficient than other types of firm, as measured by profit and tax per unit of capital, despite their advantages in scale and equipment. Table 10-6, which shows average fixed assets and number of employees for different types of TVP in Nanhai and Wuxi, highlights the relative inefficiency of township enterprises.

Differences in the profit and tax rate on capital among different types of TVPs are not caused by differences in industrial composition. A comparison of profit and tax per unit of capital for township and village enterprises in the same industries in Nanhai still shows a great gap (see table 10-7). There are several reasons for the lower capital profitability in township enterprises.

- Township enterprises absorb large amounts of loans and credit funds be-

Table 10-5. *The Ratio of Profit and Tax to Total Capital for Industrial TVPs* (percent)

County	Township enterprises	Village enterprises	Production team firms	Partnerships	Individual enterprises
Wuxi (1985)	29.8[a]	39.8[a]	n.a.	n.a.	n.a.
Jieshou (1985)	32.4[a]	54.4[a]	n.a.	57.1	56.4
Nanhai (1986)	11.2	34.6	26.5[b]	31.2[b]	41.9[b]
Shangrao (1983)	22.0	55.8	n.a.	n.a.	n.a.

n.a. Not available.

Note: Profits and taxes are net of losses of loss-making firms. Unless otherwise indicated, the denominator is year-end net (depreciated) value of fixed assets plus physical circulating assets.

a. Net value of fixed assets at year-end, plus average value of physical circulating assets during the year.

b. Original (undepreciated) value of fixed assets plus value of physical circulating assets at year-end.

Source: Information from fieldwork.

Table 10-6. *Average Size of Industrial TVPs, Wuxi and Nanhai, 1986*

	Wuxi		Nanhai	
Type of enterprise	Average value of fixed assets[a] (yuan)	Average number of workers	Average value of fixed assets[a] (yuan)	Average number of workers
Township enterprises	492,000	111	977,000	155
Village enterprises	138,000	57	96,000	40
Production team firms	n.a.	n.a.	45,000	20
Partnerships	n.a.	n.a.	39,000	14
Individual enterprises	n.a.	n.a.	8,000	6

n.a. Not available.   a. Original value.

Source: Information from fieldwork.

Table 10-7. *Ratio of Profit and Tax to Total Capital in TVCEs in Nanhai, by Industry, 1986*

Industry	Township enterprises	Village enterprises
Textiles	−4.5	42.4
Garments	19.6	32.7
Leather and fur	23.0	42.9
Plastic products	4.2	74.1
Building materials and other nonmetallic mineral products	15.0	116.7
Metallurgical products	14.4	60.7
Machinery industry	16.3	48.9
Light industry	10.7	54.9
Heavy industry	16.6	76.3

Source: Information from fieldwork.

cause of their soft constraints in this sphere, and this decreases the efficiency of capital utilization. The textile industry in Nanhai is an example. In 1986 township enterprises suffered large losses, whereas other types of textile firm enjoyed considerable profits. The main reasons for the losses were that township enterprises had stockpiled raw materials and were faced with unsatisfactory market conditions. Excessive use of capital also leads to a reduction in profitability when business operations are normal.

- Since township enterprises tend to avoid hiring labor from other places, they are more likely than any other type of TVP to substitute capital for labor if there are no employment problems in the community. For instance, in 1986 the average value of fixed assets per employee for industrial township enterprises in Wuxi was Y4,200, but for village enterprises it was only Y2,100. In the same year the figure was Y6,390 for industrial township enterprises in Nanhai, Y2,400 for village enterprises, Y2,280 for partnerships, Y2,780 for cooperative enterprises, and Y1,450 for individual firms. Township enterprises use more fixed assets than other firms to produce the same level of output, and the cost of shifting their product lines is higher than in more labor-intensive enterprises.

- Township enterprises—plagued by noneconomic targets forced on them by township governments—often suffer from overstaffing. The proportion of surplus labor was as high as 20–30 percent in some firms. Other types of enterprise seldom had this kind of problem. This is an obvious reason for higher production costs in township enterprises. The reverse side is that township governments, bound by their community targets, are willing to support unprofitable or money-losing township enterprises.

- Unlike private enterprises, which have to shoulder their entire business risk, township enterprises sometimes do not have clear responsibilities for investment decisions. This adds to the possibility of investment failures.

- Requiring township enterprises to hand in their profits and the attempt to balance incomes among enterprises may to a certain degree reduce incentives for managers and workers and lead to poorer efficiency in township enterprises than in other types of firm.

The latter three factors affect township enterprises more conspicuously in underdeveloped areas, where poor management quality also restricts the development of these enterprises. We found many examples of management failures in Jieshou and Shangrao counties. Jieshou has adopted a policy that encourages the development of various kinds of private enterprise and has achieved some success in this regard. Shangrao, where industry is still mainly based on township enterprises, remains the least industrialized county of the four.

Trends in Capital Productivity

Although the proportion of private enterprises in the total number of TVPs has increased rapidly during the past several years, TVCEs still hold the dominant position, and township enterprises are at present more important than village enterprises. It is therefore important to analyze changes in the capital productivity of industrial township enterprises, with the help of historical materials available from several of the counties.

Figure 10-1 shows changes in the capital productivity of industrial township enterprises in Wuxi and Nanhai counties.[4] Capital productivity has tended to decline unsteadily in both counties but more sharply in Nanhai. Wuxi is greatly influenced by changes in national industrial structure and by economic fluctuations, and the result is abrupt rises and falls. Figure 10-2 shows changes in the ratio of profit and tax to total capital for collective industry (mainly township enterprises but including some firms run by the county government) in Wuxi, for industrial township enterprises in Nanhai,

Figure 10-1. *Capital Productivity of Industrial Township Enterprises, Wuxi and Nanhai, 1979–86*

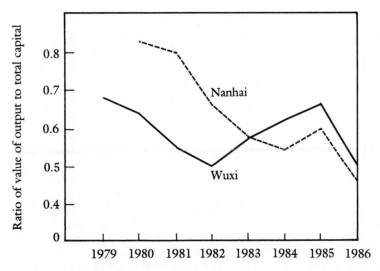

Note: Total capital is the sum of the net (depreciated) value of fixed assets and the physical ("quota") working capital.
Source: Information from fieldwork.

and for thirty-six sample TVPs in Jieshou. The curves for Wuxi and Nanhai
in figure 10-2 are similar to those in figure 10-1, but they decline more
sharply, indicating that the proportion of wage and other nonmaterial production costs in net value of output increased while the capital productivity
rate decreased. Although capital profitability in Jieshou had not yet reached
the level of that in Wuxi and Nanhai by 1985, it showed a consistent rising
trend which indicates a gradual improvement in financial performance.

The reasons for the decline in capital productivity and profitability in the
more developed counties are complicated. Aside from the causes mentioned
in the last section—heavier dependence on bank loans and the higher capital
intensity that has accompanied full employment—the restricted circulation
of factors of production under the township enterprise ownership pattern can
easily lead to relative saturation of investment opportunities at an early stage.
The rest of this chapter focuses on the analysis of these topics.

Changes in the Degree of Capital Intensity

In the two relatively developed counties, Wuxi and Nanhai, there has been
a clear trend toward substituting capital for labor in TVP industry. Between

Figure 10-2. *Ratio of Profit and Tax to Total Capital, Wuxi, Nanhai,
and Jieshou, 1979–86*

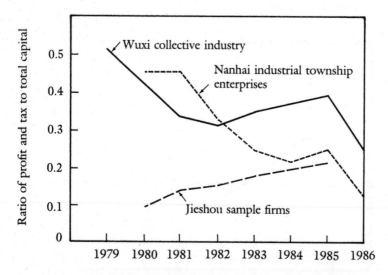

Note: Total capital is the sum of the net (depreciated) value of fixed assets and the physical
("quota") working capital. Collective industry includes industrial township enterprises and
"urban" collective industrial firms of various kinds. Village enterprises are excluded. In Wuxi
the bulk of the collective industrial sector consists of township enterprises.
Sources: Enterprise Quantitative Questionnaire and information from fieldwork.

1979 and 1986 the capital coefficient of industrial township enterprises in Wuxi climbed from 1.46 to 2.01 while the labor force coefficient dropped from 4.13 to 2.73.[5] In Nanhai between 1977 and 1986 the capital coefficient rose from 1.5 to 2.15 while the labor force coefficient declined from 6.60 to 2.03. Comparatively speaking, substitution of capital for labor has been greater in Nanhai. This can be seen clearly from the capital-labor ratios in table 10-8. That the capital and labor force coefficients rise and fall together in Wuxi means that short-term changes in efficiency are strongly influenced by macroeconomic fluctuations.

For the thirty-six sample firms in Jieshou the labor force coefficient declined sharply, from 9.66 in 1980 to 2.60 in 1985, but the capital coefficient did not increase accordingly. On the contrary, it decreased somewhat, from 1.66 to 1.04.[6] This strongly suggests that whereas overall productivity grew rapidly in Jieshou, the tendency to substitute capital for labor was not as strong. By 1985 the labor and capital coefficients in Jieshou were 100 percent and 40 percent higher than the corresponding figures in Wuxi, while capital per employee was only 70 percent of that in Wuxi (see table 10-8). That Jieshou's capital coefficient is still higher than Wuxi's is attributable to the difference in efficiency. The changing difference in the ratios of the two coefficients indicates that the degree of capital-labor substitution in Jieshou is lower than in Wuxi. The substitution of capital for labor in Wuxi and Nanhai counties occurred in tandem with the absorption of local surplus agricultural labor, but Jieshou still has a lot of surplus labor. (See chapter 14 for calculations on the magnitude of surplus labor in the four counties.)

These facts suggest that substitution of capital for labor is a phenomenon brought about by rural industrialization. But because of the influence of targets set by community governments, different development phases have different characteristics. When a community has a large amount of surplus labor, community enterprises are more inclined to use labor-intensive factor input mixes. After the community has reached full employment, the tendency not to use outside labor often persists because the admission of a large number of outsiders may reduce local per capita income. This leads to a more capital-intensive factor mix, and a decline in the capital productivity rate is hardly avoidable.

The behavior outlined above is rational from the perspective of community interests, but in aggregate terms it makes inefficiency in the allocation of capital hard to avoid. National surplus labor cannot be fully utilized in regions that already hold too much of the scarce factor, capital. It is possible to conclude that the marginal profitability and productivity of capital in developed areas such as Wuxi and Nanhai are now lower than in backward localities such as Jieshou.

Table 10-8. *Capital-Labor Ratios, 1977–86*
(yuan per employee)

County	1977	1978	1979	1980	1981	1982	1983	1984	1985	1986
Wuxi[a]	n.a.	n.a.	3,538	3,907	4,825	4,961	4,926	5,442	6,466	7,358
Wuxi[b]	n.a.	5,100	n.a.	7,200	9,700	10,900	10,900	13,100	15,500	n.a.
Nanhai[a]	1,898	n.a.	n.a.	2,924	3,551	3,934	5,108	5,927	8,193	9,326
Jieshou[b]	n.a.	6,800	n.a.	4,000	4,400	4,800	5,900	7,300	10,800	n.a.

n.a.: Not available.

a. Average for all industrial township enterprises.

b. Sample firms. These figures may be distorted owing to changes in the size of the sample over time.

Sources: Enterprise Quantitative Questionnaire and information from fieldwork.

Economies of Scale and Factor Mobility

With the rise of capital intensity in TVPs (especially in township enterprises), the production scale and location pattern of enterprises have an increasing effect on economic benefits, since scale economies are much greater for capital-intensive than for labor-intensive production. Until now, most rural industrialization in China has followed the principle of "leaving the farm but not the community." Undoubtedly this helped with the absorption of rural surplus labor, but it may encourage small production scales and dispersed location patterns that will affect economic efficiency when capital intensity develops to a certain degree. Since factors of production have difficulty in moving across regions and localities, TVCEs may experience problems in expanding their production scales and concentrating their locations geographically.

The sample firms in Wuxi provide an example. No firms have set up factories outside their own communities. Three firms are in towns, but all the rest are located in the countryside. In 1985 investment from other regions made up only 0.5 percent of the total capital of Wuxi sample firms, and investment by these enterprises in other units accounted for only 0.1 percent of their total fixed investment. Cross-regional investment in Nanhai is a little higher than in Wuxi owing to Nanhai's diversified ownership structure and the stronger functioning of markets.

Although the average size of TVCEs is still much larger than that of private enterprises, there is a tendency toward slower expansion of firm size. From 1975 to 1986 total employment in industrial township enterprises in Wuxi rose by 502 percent, but the average number of employees per enterprise increased by only 23 percent (table 10-9). The original value of fixed assets increased by 2,160 percent, but the average value per enterprise rose by only 360 percent. The same pattern holds for village enterprises. Obviously this kind of industrial development consists mainly of the birth of large numbers of new firms. Especially since 1984 the average size of enterprises, measured by employment, has begun to shrink. In 1986 there were 1,247 industrial township enterprises in the county, an average of 36 per township or town. The number of industrial village enterprises reached 3,486, about 6 per village. On average, there were 46 industrial TVCEs for every 10,000 members of the population in the county, and there were 445 enterprises per 100 square kilometers.

The constant birth of small firms leads to sharp competition. Among the 185 relatively large "backbone" township enterprises in Wuxi there are about 40 machinery and equipment plants, of which 7 make cranes and construction machinery, 4 make dyeing equipment, and 3 are general equipment works. In addition, there are 7 steel-rolling plants, 4 metal pipe works, 6 woolen textile factories, and 4 printing and dyeing plants. It is difficult to calculate how many small plants there are in each industry or how many pro-

Table 10-9. *Average Size of Industrial TVPs, 1970–86*

County and type of enterprise	1970	1975	1978	1980	1981	1982	1983	1984	1985	1986
Wuxi township enterprises										
Number of firms	155	254	353	458	478	509	524	821	1,017	1,247
Average employment	59	99	122	130	134	136	153	116	131[a]	114[a]
Average fixed assets (thousands of yuan)	n.a.	107	220	292	360	382	442	342	451	492
Wuxi village enterprises										
Number of firms	859	1,380	1,629	1,848	1,749	1,695	2,034	2,656	3,232	3,486
Average employment	30	28	35	39	44	49	49	47	44[a]	43[a]
Average fixed assets (thousands of yuan)	n.a.	15	32	46	61	76	79	72	108	138
Nanhai township enterprises										
Number of firms	n.a.	n.a.	195	246	276	280	287	291	311	332
Average employment	n.a.	n.a.	105	89	90	97	98	112	129	155
Average fixed assets (thousands of yuan)	n.a.	n.a.	n.a.	178	214	226	359	454	695	977
Jieshou township enterprises[b]										
Number of firms	n.a.	n.a.	n.a.	160	120	160	151	375	261	n.a.
Average employment	n.a.	n.a.	n.a.	29	33	27	26	26	35	n.a.

n.a. Not available.

a. 1985–86 employment figures were adjusted to offset false reporting by firms that were trying to evade wage controls.

b. Includes all township enterprises, but industrial firms account for the bulk of the total number and employment.

Source: Information from fieldwork.

duce the same products. Since enterprises in the same industry generally belong to different township governments, they can produce and sell independently, and they compete with each other. It is almost impossible to combine them because of their differing ownership and the influence of targets set by different township governments. This has blocked the expansion of enterprise scale and led to much waste of resources. For example, Wuxi has set up sixteen aluminum extrusion and processing plants in the past several years. Most of them cannot operate at full capacity, and some face bankruptcy because of deteriorating market conditions.

The situation in Nanhai is a little different. The average employment scale of township enterprises was stable at about 100 workers before 1983, whereas the capital scale increased continually. But since 1984 both factors have grown rapidly even as creation of new enterprises has increased. There is reason to believe that, as private enterprises developed rapidly over the past several years, the opening of markets and increased factor mobility had some effect on the actions of community governments and their enterprises.

There was no obvious expansion of the scale of township enterprises in Jieshou between 1979 and 1985. Both township enterprises and the number of employees were unstable and changing, as the sector had not yet entered a steady expansion phase. This is different from the trend in developed areas toward a constant increase in the number of enterprises and stagnation in their average scale.

The dispersed distribution of firms and scattered infrastructure facilities create other problems. Each community or enterprise has to deal independently with such problems as obtaining supplies of electricity, water, and heat; gaining access to roads, transport, and communications; and maintaining equipment. The inevitable results are higher investment costs, loss of efficiency, and difficulties in gaining access to market information and technology.

For example, to cope with shortages of electricity in Wuxi, almost every TVCE has installed diesel generators to meet its own needs. The unit cost of electricity from diesel generators is as high as Y0.3–Y0.5 per kilowatt-hour, several times more than that of power transmitted through the electric power network. In 1986 industrial self-generation of electricity with diesel generators reached 225.883 million kilowatt-hours, which is equivalent to the capacity of a middle-size power plant. If all township government decisionmakers regarded economic benefits as the most important objective, it would not be difficult to raise funds to build a relatively large power plant, and more than Y10 million could be saved every year. Moreover, if the distribution of enterprises were relatively concentrated, considerable savings might be realized on transmission equipment and from reduced losses in transmission.

Responses to the Enterprise Director Questionnaire show an awareness of the difficulties caused by the dispersion of TVPs. But since the many ties that link firms with community governments can hardly be severed, the possibilities for moving and combining enterprises are small. The survey found that private enterprises have a stronger desire to concentrate their location in urban areas.

At present, owing to the effect of community objectives on firms, community enterprises are facing problems in factor mix, scale, and location patterns that may pose serious obstacles to further rural industrialization. It seems that the only way out lies in rationalizing the actions of both owners and managers of community enterprises while taking community targets into consideration. Objectives set by enterprises themselves can be achieved through activities conducted in accordance with market principles. A diversified ownership system might be a prerequisite.

Notes

1. There were twenty-two sample TVCEs. Sample private enterprises—including firms officially registered as community enterprises but deemed by field researchers and county officials to be actually private in nature—numbered five in 1982, seven in 1983, ten in 1984, and fourteen in 1985.

2. Our sample for Nanhai contained no private enterprises or production team firms for 1981 and 1982.

3. These figures are from information gathered during fieldwork. Since the introduction of higher tax rates for TVPs, hiding profits and reporting nonexistent losses have reportedly become widespread practices, but there is no way to measure to what extent this distorts the data.

4. The index of capital productivity is the ratio of net industrial output value to total capital (the sum of net depreciated value of fixed assets and physical circulating assets). This index avoids distortions caused by differing net-gross ratios of industrial output value.

5. The capital coefficient equals total capital divided by net value of output, or the sum of the net value of fixed assets and annual average outstanding floating capital divided by the net value of output. The labor coefficient equals the annual average number of workers divided by the net value of output (in millions of yuan).

6. The capital coefficients for sample firms were calculated by dividing the original value of fixed assets by the net value of output. They are not comparable with the corresponding indexes reported for Wuxi and Nanhai counties.

11

Productive Efficiency and Employment

Jan Svejnar

This chapter tests several hypotheses about the economic performance of Chinese TVPs. It provides econometric evidence on the effects that different enterprise ownership and control systems, worker compensation schemes, and geographic locations (levels of economic development) have on productive efficiency and labor utilization in TVPs.

As chapters 4 and 7 indicate, the four counties covered in the survey vary substantially in the ownership makeup of their TVPs. Wuxi, for instance, exemplifies the model of township and village firms with emphasis on community government ownership, whereas Jieshou has supported the development of private firms. A question naturally arises about the relationship between TVP ownership and efficiency. As table 11-1 shows, the data in our sample vary significantly as to ownership and hence lend themselves to an analysis of this issue.

The TVPs in our sample also display considerable variation in the form of worker compensation (see table 11-1). In particular, although a majority of the 122 sample firms use piece rates as the principal form of compensation, some rely on fixed wages supplemented with bonuses, dividends, or piece rates, and others use an internal work-point system. One firm still has a community work-point system; workers accumulate work-points in the factory, but their income depends on that of the entire community because enterprise income is pooled with other community income. Since different compensation schemes provide different incentives for worker effort, discipline, and motivation in general, it is of interest to explore whether differences in compensation schemes affect enterprise efficiency.

Finally, the statistics in table 11-1 confirm that our data reflect enterprise behavior in both the more developed (Wuxi and Nanhai) and the less developed (Jieshou and Shangrao) counties of China.

The chapter focuses on two measures of enterprise performance: productive efficiency and labor utilization. The former is of primary interest for two reasons. First, Chinese state enterprises are generally regarded as inefficient, and

Table 11-1. *Summary Statistics of Variables Used*

Variable	Mean	Standard deviation
Enterprise ownership[a]		
Township and town	0.64	0.48
Village and production team	0.17	0.38
Partnership, family, or individual	0.11	0.32
Joint venture	0.07	0.26
Enterprise location[a]		
Wuxi	0.26	0.44
Jieshou	0.30	0.46
Nanhai	0.19	0.39
Shangrao	0.25	0.43
Principal form of worker compensation[a]		
Fixed time wage and auxiliary piece-rate wage	0.03	0.18
Fixed time wage and bonus	0.10	0.30
Fixed time wage and year-end dividend	0.03	0.13
Piece-rate wage	0.56	0.50
Internal work-point system	0.07	0.25
Community work-point system[b]	0.01	0.09
ln Q	13.35	1.76
ln L	4.77	0.98
ln K	12.38	1.57
ln W	4.12	0.53
ln W_a	3.35	0.73
Time[c]	5.50	4.68

Note: The variable W_a is the average agricultural wage in the county.

a. These variables are binary (dummy) variables that are coded 1.0 in the presence of the given phenomenon and 0.0 in its absence. The mean of this variable reflects the percentage of observations falling into the particular category.

b. In this system workers accumulate work-points in the enterprise, but their income depends on the income of the entire community (enterprise revenues are pooled with other community income).

c. Time has values of 1 in 1975, . . . , 11 in 1986.

Sources: Enterprise Quantitative Questionnaire and Enterprise Survey Questionnaire.

TVPs are frequently mentioned as examples of more (productively) efficient firms. Second, as in other centrally planned and developing economies, economic growth has been regarded in China as an important performance indicator—one that is closely linked to productive efficiency at the firm level.

Labor utilization is of interest because employment generation was the principal goal of most TVPs at time of founding. Moreover, although Wuxi and Nanhai have largely exhausted their surplus labor and now emphasize income maximization more, in Jieshou and Shangrao the employment objective remains predominant. Hence it is of interest to see whether TVPs' criteria for labor utilization differ among counties and whether they are linked to the ownership structure of the firm.

Methodology

In this section a method of testing for differences in productive efficiency with the use of a production function estimation approach is developed. An employment equation is also derived that can be used to test hypotheses about the goals TVPs pursue.

Productive Efficiency

The analysis of productive efficiency is based on Cobb-Douglas (CD) and translog production functions, augmented by relevant ownership, county, and compensation scheme variables. If Q = output, L = labor, K = capital, Z = a vector of ownership and compensation scheme variables, C = a vector of location (county) dummy variables, and T = a vector of annual dummy variables, the basic specification of the CD function can be written

$$(11\text{-}1) \quad \ln Q = \alpha_0 + \overline{\beta}Z + \widetilde{\beta}C + \widehat{\beta}T + \alpha_1 \ln L + \alpha_2 \ln K + \epsilon$$

where ϵ is the error term, $\overline{\beta}$, $\widetilde{\beta}$, and $\widehat{\beta}$ are (row) vectors of parameters corresponding to the Z, C, and T vectors of variables respectively, and the αs are the parameters corresponding to the other variables. In this framework, Z, C, and T are dummy variables that take on a value of 1 when an observation falls into the particular ownership or compensation system, county, or time period respectively and 0 otherwise. For small values of $\overline{\beta}$, $\widetilde{\beta}$, and $\widehat{\beta}$ the estimated coefficients hence approximate percentage differentials in productive efficiency (total factor productivity) among firms with different ownership forms, compensation systems, locations, or time periods. For large parameter values, however—for example $\overline{\beta} > 0.3$— it is preferable to calculate the percentage differential as $100 \cdot [\exp(\overline{\beta}) - 1]$. (See Halvorsen and Palmquist 1980.)

The translog equation was specified similarly as

$$(11\text{-}2) \quad \ln Q = \alpha_0 + \overline{\beta}Z + \widetilde{\beta}C + \widehat{\beta}T + \alpha_1 \ln L + \alpha_2 \ln K$$
$$+ \alpha_3 (\ln L)^2 + \alpha_4 (\ln K)^2 + \alpha_5 (\ln L)(\ln K) + \epsilon$$

Employment

In addition to examining how much output different TVPs can produce from a given set of inputs (productive efficiency), this chapter analyzes patterns of labor utilization. Most TVPs have three important goals: maximizing profits, generating employment, and increasing wages above the competitive (market-clearing) level in the economy. The relative weight of these goals in the enterprise objective function varies among counties and among types of TVPs.

A convenient way to capture these behavioral features analytically is to specify the objective function of a TVP as a weighted geometric average of these three goals (see Kalai 1977, Roth 1979, and Svejnar 1986). If W = the actual wage (labor income), W_a = the reservation or best alternative wage of TVP workers,[1] and Π = profit, the objective function U of the TVP can be written

(11-3) $$U = L^{\partial_L} (W - W_a)^{\partial_W} \Pi^{(1-\partial_L-\partial_W)}$$

where ∂_L, ∂_W, and $1 - \partial_L - \partial_W$ are the relative weights given to employment, wages, and profitability respectively. Note, for example, that if a TVP maximized only profit, $U = \Pi$ as $\partial_L = \partial_W = 0$, and the firm would behave like a traditional "capitalist" firm. In contrast, if the firm only maximized income per worker, then $U = (W - W_a)$ as $\partial_L = 0$ and $\partial_W = 1$, and the firm would behave according to the traditional labor-management model (see, for example, Domar 1966, Vanek 1970, and Ward 1958). The advantage of equation 11-3 is that it nests various forms of enterprise behavior as special cases, which can be identified if one can estimate relatively precisely the values of ∂_L and ∂_W. The empirical work here follows earlier studies by Brown and Ashenfelter (1986) and Svejnar (1986). It exploits the fact that if equation 11-3 is maximized subject to a constant elasticity of substitution (CES) production function, one can in principle identify enterprise employment behavior from the linear estimating equation

(11-4) $$\ln L = Y_0 + \overline{\Theta}Z + \tilde{\Theta}C + \hat{\Theta}T + \frac{1 + v\sigma - \sigma}{v} \ln Q - \sigma(1 - \partial) \ln W - \sigma\partial \ln W_a$$

where $\partial = \partial_L/\partial_W$, σ = the elasticity of substitution, v = a return to scale parameter, and Y_0, $\overline{\Theta}$, $\tilde{\Theta}$, and $\hat{\Theta}$ are undetermined parameters. From equation 11-4 it is clear that $\partial = 0$ implies $\partial_L = 0$, and, in terms of equation 11-3, the firm does not expand employment beyond the profit-maximizing level given by the equality of marginal product of labor and the actual wage W. In contrast, if $\partial = 1$, the enterprise gives identical importance to increasing wages and generating new employment ($\partial_L = \partial_W$). In this case the coefficient on $\ln W$ is zero in equation 11-4, and the employment behavior of the TVP depends on the alternative wage W_a but not on own wage W. In fact, it can be shown that in this case the firm equates the marginal product of labor to W_a. An important problem in the empirical implementation of equation 11-4 is then, of course, one's ability to approximate closely the concept of the reservation (alternative) wage W_a.

In estimating equation 11-4 it is useful to interact ∂ with the variables in vectors **Z** and **C** to establish whether ∂ varies systematically with ownership and the level of economic development (proxied by county dummies).

Data and Empirical Results

As the summary statistics in table 11-1 indicate, the sample displays considerable variation in the values of most of the variables used in this study. Town and township enterprises account for 64 percent of the observations, village and production team firms for 17 percent. Private firms (partnerships and household, family, and individually owned enterprises) represent 11 percent of observations, and joint ventures of all types make up 7 percent. It should be noted that these figures refer to observations that are usable for the purposes of this study. Since different firms had data panels of different lengths, the figures do not necessarily reflect the number of firms of a given type that were sampled. An important point, which is not discernible from table 11-1, is that the data include no observations of private firms in Wuxi or of joint ventures in Shangrao.

Estimates of Productive Efficiency

Since the CD and translog estimates are very similar, we report the CD results, which are easier to interpret. Table 11-2 presents the CD estimates obtained from three panels of data. The results in column 1 are based on all available data for the entire 1970–86 period. But since the data were collected retrospectively and many enterprises were reorganized or established after 1970, the estimates may be biased by data errors, which are likely to be more serious in the early period. To assess the severity of this problem, columns 2 and 3 present results based on data from more recent periods. Cross-sectional estimates were also generated for several years. Since they turned out to be similar to those in column 3, they are not presented here.

The two main competing views about the relationship between efficiency and ownership are (a) that TVCEs are more efficient than private enterprises because they have better access to new technologies or can take better advantage of economies of scale, and (b) that private firms are likely to be more efficient than community-owned firms because the owner-manager has stronger incentives. The results in table 11-2 indicate that when differences in inputs and other variables are controlled, productive efficiency is not related to ownership.

Table 11-2 also suggests that enterprises that offer their workers a fixed time wage with a bonus and those that use the internal work-point system tend to be more productive than those operating under piece rates, a combination of a fixed wage and piece rates, or a combination of a fixed wage and a year-end dividend. The one enterprise that uses a community work-point system,

Table 11-2. *The Impact of Ownership, Worker Compensation Schemes, and Location on Productive Efficiency in a Cobb-Douglas Framework*

Variable	1970–86	1981–86	1983–86
Intercept[a]	5.686*	6.769*	7.468*
	(0.508)	(0.450)	(0.547)
Ownership dummy variables			
Village and production team	−0.020	0.028	0.063
	(0.110)	(0.120)	(0.140)
Joint household, family, and	0.089	0.008	−0.232
individual	(0.151)	(0.158)	(0.176)
Joint venture	0.087	0.130	0.078
	(0.141)	(0.159)	(0.186)
Compensation scheme dummy variables			
Fixed time wage and bonus system	0.276**	0.308**	0.388*
	(0.162)	(0.167)	(0.181)
Fixed time wage and year-end	0.018	0.047	0.044
dividend system	(0.468)	(0.473)	(0.473)
Piece-rate system	−0.030	0.005	0.088
	(0.103)	(0.109)	(0.126)
Internal work-point system	0.247**	0.302**	0.304
	(0.157)	(0.173)	(0.208)
Community work-point system	−1.284*	−1.333*	−1.426*
	(0.372)	(0.382)	(0.443)
Location dummy variables			
Jieshou	−0.126	−0.139	−0.111
	(0.110)	(0.121)	(0.147)
Nanhai	−0.165	−0.068	−0.017
	(0.117)	(0.128)	(0.149)
Shangrao	−1.260*	−1.369*	−1.507*
	(0.121)	(0.137)	(0.171)
Inputs			
ln L	0.987*	0.966*	0.923*
	(0.064)	(0.071)	(0.092)
ln K	0.164*	0.158*	0.140*
	(0.040)	(0.045)	(0.057)
Industries			
Mechanics and electronics	0.413*	0.365*	0.363*
	(0.114)	(0.126)	(0.148)
Wood processing and furniture	−0.108	−0.127	−0.204
	(0.166)	(0.178)	(0.205)
Chemicals	0.247*	0.190	0.105
	(0.128)	(0.140)	(0.167)
Metallurgy	0.795*	0.754*	0.639*
	(0.153)	(0.166)	(0.199)
Paper processing	0.040	−0.082	−0.291
	(0.150)	(0.167)	(0.196)
Food processing	−0.046	−0.090	−0.105
	(0.165)	(0.173)	(0.191)

Variable	1970–86	1981–86	1983–86
Time			
1975	0.184	—	—
	(0.427)		
1978	0.489	—	—
	(0.418)		
1980	0.759*	—	—
	(0.385)		
1981	0.890*	—	—
	(0.385)		
1982	0.987*	0.095	—
	(0.383)	(0.124)	
1983	1.118	0.231**	—
	(0.384)	(0.121)	
1984	1.161*	0.276*	0.056
	(0.384)	(0.118)	(0.107)
1985	1.540*	0.659*	0.454*
	(0.385)	(0.118)	(0.107)
1986	1.554*	0.645*	0.451**
	(0.437)	(0.244)	(0.243)
R^2	0.88	0.88	0.89
N	415	347	240

— Not applicable.

*Significant at 5 percent statistical test level or better.

**Significant at 10 percent statistical test level or better.

Note: The dependent variable is the logarithm of the gross value of output. The values in parentheses are standard errors.

a. The intercept represents township enterprises in the textile and clothing industry of Wuxi that use a fixed time wage and auxiliary piece-rate system; it also corresponds to the base year of the particular regression.

Source: Enterprise Quantitative Questionnaire.

which dilutes worker incentives, is found to be greatly inferior in productive efficiency. Other things being equal, group incentive schemes seem to be associated with higher productivity than individual incentive schemes. Group coordination and team spirit may thus be important for efficiency.

The coefficients on the county dummy variables indicate that TVPs in Wuxi, Jieshou, and Nanhai are more or less equally productive but that firms in Shangrao lag significantly behind. Shangrao is, of course, the least developed of the four counties but, perhaps more important, Shangrao TVPs suffer from neglect and even exploitation by local authorities (see chapter 17). Since Jieshou is also a less developed county, it may be that different attitudes and policies of local authorities toward TVP development account for the strikingly different productive performances (see also chapter 4).

The time dummies indicate that TVPs have achieved a significant rate of technical progress over time, with the most rapid gains occurring in 1985. The estimates confirm that the rapid development of the TVP sector has not been brought about merely by extensive growth; intensive growth has contributed significantly to the observed success.

The coefficients on labor and capital are both significant, and they suggest that TVPs operate in the zone of mildly increasing returns to scale. This result is not improbable in view of the small scale of many TVPs. The two input coefficients also suggest that the output elasticity of labor is much greater than that of capital. Finally, there appear to be significant technological differences among industries.

The results in table 11-2 are based on the ordinary least squares (OLS) estimating technique, which is a traditional method that is more robust against specification errors than simultaneous equations methods. But since variables K and L are at least to some extent endogenous (that is, subject to enterprise decisionmaking), the OLS regressions of table 11-2 were also reestimated by instrumental variables. The instruments used were price indexes, interest rates, time trends, alternative wages, and firm-specific intercepts. The main results remain unaltered under this estimating technique.

Labor Utilization

In estimating equation 11-4, one must select a suitable reservation (alternative) wage, W_a. After considerable search, the average monthly income of an agricultural worker in each county in a given year was adopted as the best measure of the reservation wage. The motivation for using W_a as a proxy for the true (unobserved) reservation wage W_a^* was that it is close to and very likely proportional to W_a^*. In particular, if

$$(11\text{-}5) \qquad W_a^* = \eta W_a \,,$$

then

$$(11\text{-}6) \qquad \ln W_a^* = \ln \eta + \ln W_a$$

and using $\ln W_a$ will produce an unbiased estimate of the coefficient on $\ln W_a^*$, since $\ln \eta$ will be captured in the regression intercept.

As the results in table 11-3 show, the available data do permit one to draw conclusions about the employment behavior of Chinese TVPs within the framework of equation 11-4. The coefficients on $\ln W$ and $\ln W_a$ reflect the situation in Wuxi (the base county) and suggest that, although it is impossible to identify ∂ from the 1980–86 data set, the value of ∂ appears to be zero in the more recent (1983–86) period. That is, in recent years TVPs in Wuxi seem to place no extra emphasis on employment and to operate along the marginal product curve of labor. This implies that they have reduced their labor input in response to actual wage increases, rather than being guided by the alternative wage.

Table 11-3. *The Impact of Ownership and Location on Enterprise Employment Policy*

Variable	1980–86	1983–86
Intercept[a]	$-2.038^{\bullet\bullet}$	-1.930
	(1.604)	(1.776)
$\ln Q$	$0.523^{\bullet}$	$0.523^{\bullet}$
	(0.025)	(0.035)
$\ln W$	$-0.531^{\bullet}$	$-0.745^{\bullet}$
	(0.148)	(0.219)
$\ln W_a$	$0.643^{\bullet}$	0.779
	(0.321)	(0.503)
Ownership		
Village and production team (VTO)	-0.235	0.144
	(0.604)	(0.875)
Joint household, family, and	$1.805^{\bullet}$	$2.842^{\bullet}$
individual (HFIO)	(0.766)	(1.001)
Joint venture (JV)	0.555	-0.061
	(0.965)	(1.444)
VTO $\ln W$	-0.012	0.236
	(0.197)	(0.377)
HFIO $\ln W$	$-0.570^{\bullet}$	0.073
	(0.225)	(0.373)
JV $\ln W$	-0.022	0.483
	(0.282)	(0.441)
VTO $\ln W_a$	0.026	-0.368
	(0.144)	(0.367)
HFIO $\ln W_a$	0.109	$-0.975^{\bullet}$
	(0.153)	(0.451)
JV $\ln W_a$	-0.144	-0.566
	(0.174)	(0.370)
Location		
Jieshou	0.076	1.828
	(1.131)	(2.526)
Nanhai	1.623	-1.266
	(0.932)	(3.115)
Shangrao	-0.728	2.363
	(1.148)	(4.706)
Jieshou $\ln W$	$0.560^{\bullet}$	0.108
	(0.268)	(0.360)
Nanhai $\ln W$	$0.504^{\bullet}$	$0.703^{\bullet}$
	(0.236)	(0.321)
Shangrao $\ln W$	$0.669^{\bullet}$	$0.844^{\bullet}$
	(0.180)	(0.244)
Jieshou $\ln W_a$	$-0.736^{\bullet}$	-0.721
	(0.245)	(0.739)
Nanhai $\ln W_a$	$-0.982^{\bullet}$	-0.523
	(0.293)	(0.773)
Shangrao $\ln W_a$	-0.451	-1.628
	(0.399)	(1.499)

(*Table continues on the following page*)

Table 11-3 (*continued*)

Variable	1980–86	1983–86
Compensation scheme		
Fixed time wage and bonus system	−0.148	−0.174
	(0.123)	(0.141)
Fixed time wage and year-end	−0.188	−0.229
dividend system	(0.316)	(0.326)
Piece-rate system	0.029	−0.018
	(0.078)	(0.095)
Internal work-point system	0.077	0.104
	(0.117)	(0.149)
Community work-point system	0.548*	0.796*
	(0.253)	(0.304)
Time		
1981	−0.095	—
	(0.119)	
1982	−0.070	—
	(0.128)	
1983	−0.094	—
	(0.181)	
1984	−0.074	0.078
	(0.237)	(0.155)
1985	−0.219	−0.063
	(0.244)	(0.156)
1986	−0.242	−0.135
	(0.365)	(0.374)
Industry intercepts	Yes	Yes
R^2	0.84	0.84
N	355	232

— Not applicable.

*Significant at 5 percent statistical test level or better.

**Significant at 10 percent statistical test level or better.

Note: The dependent variable is the logarithm of employment. The values in parentheses are standard errors.

a. The intercept represents township enterprises in the textile and clothing industry of Wuxi that use a fixed-time wage and auxiliary piece-rate system; it also corresponds to the base year of the particular regression.

Source: Enterprise Quantitative Questionnaire.

The interaction of ln W and ln W_a with the three county dummies identifies TVP behavior in Jieshou, Nanhai, and Shangrao. The estimated parameters imply that Jieshou TVPs placed more emphasis on W_a than on W in 1980–86 but that their behavior approximated that found in Wuxi in 1983–86. This suggests that Jieshou TVPs used to operate to the right of the marginal product curve of labor but switched to a more labor productivity–oriented employment policy in recent years. "Labor hoarding" is also observed in Nanhai in the 1980–86 data set, but no significant relationship between employment and either W or W_a is observed in recent years. The data from Shangrao display no significant relationship between employment and own or alternative wages. The results suggest that TVPs in Wuxi and Jieshou have changed their employment policies in the 1980s and place less emphasis on employment generation than they did before.

The interaction of ownership variables with ln W and ln W_a permits an assessment of whether employment behavior varies with ownership. Private ownership is the only variable with a significant interaction. The parameter estimates suggest that in 1983–86 private firms paid more attention to alternative opportunities of workers than did the other types of firms. Different compensation schemes do not appear to have wage-related interactive effects on employment of TVPs. The regressions with these insignificant coefficients are not reported.

Turning to the basic (noninteractive) effects of different variables, one can see from table 11-3 that private firms tend to be more labor-intensive and that after industry, output, wages, and the like are controlled, labor intensity does not vary among counties, among forms of compensation (except for the one community work-point firm), or over time within each sample. The one variable that is most strongly correlated with employment is the level of output.

The general picture that emerges from table 11-3 is that TVPs link their employment closely to output and, especially in the case of Wuxi and Jieshou, economize on labor as wages rise. To examine the overall validity of the latter statement, equation 11-4 was also estimated without any interactions of ln W and ln W_a with other variables. The exercise yields a significant negative coefficient of -0.18 (0.07) on ln W and an insignificant negative coefficient of -0.15 (0.12) on ln W_a. These results suggest that TVPs recognize the tradeoff between wages and employment and that, on average, featherbedding is not a significant phenomenon in these firms.

Finally, as in the production function analysis, we reestimated the employment equation by instrumental variables. The results were similar to those obtained in the OLS regressions.

Summary and Concluding Observations

Our analysis indicates that, after differences in inputs and other variables are controlled, productive efficiency does not vary systematically with the four types of ownership examined. In particular, private ownership and community ownership appear to have similar effects on productivity. Another finding is that group incentive schemes, such as a fixed wage with bonus or an internal work-point system, are associated with higher efficiency than individual incentive schemes such as piece rates or piece rates with fixed wages. This could signal the importance of teamwork for productive efficiency. TVPs have experienced rapid technical progress (productive efficiency has risen rapidly over time), and they seem to operate under mildly increasing returns to scale.

A comparison of the four counties suggests that there is no significant difference in the productive efficiency of TVPs in the more developed counties of Wuxi and Nanhai and the less developed county of Jieshou. But in Shangrao, where community authorities have sometimes neglected and even exploited TVPs, the level of efficiency is considerably lower. These findings suggest that the behavior of local authorities may significantly influence TVP performance.

The employment policies of TVPs, to the extent that they can be identified under our methodology, appear to have shifted away from employment generation as such toward employment levels that reflect the marginal productivity of labor. The findings suggest that TVPs operate with much less featherbedding than their state-owned counterparts. TVPs also display a very tight link (almost fixed proportions) between employment and output.

Note

1. The reservation wage concept refers to the minimum wage that a worker would be willing to accept in present employment rather than quit. It can also be thought of as the best wage that a worker can obtain in alternative employment.

12

Regional Imbalances

Wang Tuoyu

The development of China's rural enterprises, like the development of the national economy as a whole, is characterized by great regional imbalances. This chapter surveys the imbalances in China's TVP sector and their influence on the economic development of the country's inland and remote areas. Because the TVP sector has developed rapidly in recent years and because better statistical data are available after 1978, we concentrate on the years 1979–85.[1]

China is a large country, and its regions vary greatly in geography, natural resources, human resources, and material capital. Moreover, regional differences in economic history have created big gaps in current levels of development, especially in rural areas. Table 12-1 shows the regional distribution of employment, output value, tax payments, and year-end value of fixed assets for industrial and other TVPs in 1985. (The data on fixed asset values include only TVCEs.) The following areas account for only about 10 percent of the national totals of these four items: Qinghai and Gansu provinces and the Ningxia Hui and Xinjiang Uygur autonomous regions in northwest China, Guizhou and Yunnan provinces and the Guangxi Zhuang and Xizang (Tibet) autonomous regions in southwest China, Nei Monggol (Inner Mongolia) in north China, and Heilongjiang and Jilin provinces in northeast China. Jiangsu, Zhejiang, Shandong, Guangdong, Hebei, Sichuan, Henan, Liaoning, and Hubei provinces make up more than 60 percent of the national totals. China's existing TVPs are mainly located in economically developed provinces and in the heartland area made up of Henan, Hubei, and Sichuan provinces; only a few are in remote areas.

Tables 12-2 through 12-4 provide further evidence of the imbalances in the TVP sector. Table 12-2 displays value of output, profits, taxes, and year-end value of fixed assets for TVPs in each province and autonomous region, per thousand rural population. As a basis for classification by level of TVP development, table 12-3 compares these indicators with national averages. Table 12-4 shows the proportion of value of rural nonagricultural output in

Table 12-1. *China's TVP Sector, by Province, 1985*
(percentage of national total)

Province[a]	Employment	Gross value of output	Tax payments	Original value of fixed assets[b]
Anhui	5.0	3.1	2.0	2.4
Fujian	2.9	2.6	2.2	2.4
Gansu	1.0	0.6	0.4	0.7
Guangdong	6.0	7.0	6.2	7.1
Guangxi	2.0	1.1	1.0	1.0
Guizhou	1.4	0.7	0.7	0.5
Hebei	9.8	10.4	11.6	9.1
Heilongjiang	1.6	1.7	1.2	2.2
Henan	8.0	6.1	3.9	5.0
Hubei	5.1	4.1	3.1	5.0
Hunan	4.7	3.5	3.4	4.1
Jiangsu	12.7	20.1	26.5	19.2
Jiangxi	2.7	1.7	1.6	1.9
Jilin	1.4	1.4	1.3	1.4
Liaoning	3.4	5.0	6.6	4.9
Nei Monggol	1.0	0.6	0.4	0.7
Ningxia	0.3	0.2	0.2	0.2
Qinghai	0.2	0.1	0.1	0.1
Shaanxi	2.6	1.8	1.6	1.9
Shandong	9.4	9.0	8.0	11.5
Shanxi	3.1	3.1	3.1	3.4
Sichuan	6.7	5.3	4.4	5.8
Xinjiang	0.5	0.4	0.4	0.5
Xizang	0.0	0.0	0.0	0.0
Yunnan	1.6	1.0	0.7	1.3
Zhejiang	6.7	9.4	9.4	7.7
Selected municipalities[c]				
Beijing	1.2	2.0	3.3	2.7
Shanghai	2.0	3.5	7.8	5.6
Tianjin	1.0	1.7	2.6	1.7

a. For simplicity, throughout this chapter the term "province" covers all province-level political divisions, including autonomous regions.

b. Data are for TVCEs only.

c. Beijing and Tianjin are also included in the figures for Hebei, and Shanghai is included in those for Jiangsu.

Source: Information from fieldwork.

Table 12-2. *Per Capita Indexes of TVP Development, by Province, 1985*
(yuan per thousand rural population)

Province or municipality	Gross value of output	Profits	Tax payments	Original value of fixed assets[a]
All China	32.3	3.4	1.6	8.9
Anhui	19.1	2.2	0.6	4.0
Beijing[b]	139.2	19.4	11.6	52.0
Fujian	30.5	2.9	1.1	9.6
Gansu	9.8	0.9	0.3	3.2
Guangdong	37.0	4.0	1.6	10.3
Guangxi	8.5	0.7	0.4	2.1
Guizhou	7.1	0.9	0.3	1.5
Hebei	38.0	6.0	1.6	7.4
Heilongjiang	24.7	2.1	0.9	8.8
Henan	24.2	3.6	0.8	5.6
Hubei	28.7	2.9	1.1	9.6
Hunan	19.6	1.9	0.9	6.4
Jiangsu	86.8	5.9	4.9	19.7
Jiangxi	16.3	1.8	0.8	5.2
Jilin	26.8	2.9	1.2	7.3
Liaoning	62.1	7.9	4.1	16.7
Nei Monggol	12.1	1.8	0.4	3.7
Ningxia	18.9	2.5	0.9	3.1
Qinghai	10.1	1.0	0.7	3.5
Shaanxi	19.9	2.3	0.9	5.8
Shandong	36.9	4.1	1.6	12.7
Shanghai[b]	220.4	24.7	24.9	98.2
Shanxi	40.9	6.6	2.0	12.1
Sichuan	16.2	0.9	0.7	4.9
Tianjin[b]	126.8	10.9	9.6	34.3
Xinjiang	14.6	7.6	0.7	5.1
Xizang	1.7	1.2	0.0	n.a.
Yunnan	9.0	0.7	0.3	3.3
Zhejiang	75.3	6.6	2.0	12.1

n.a. Not available.

Note: Hebei does not include Beijing and Tianjin municipalities, and Jiangsu does not include Shanghai municipality.

a. Data are for TVCEs only.

b. Municipality.

Source: Information from fieldwork.

Table 12-3. *Provincial Per Capita Indicators for TVPs in Comparison with National Averages, 1985*

Index against national averages	Value of output	Profits	Tax payments	Original value of fixed assets[a]
Greater than 50 percent	Shanghai Beijing Tianjin Jiangsu Zhejiang Liaoning	Shanghai Beijing Tianjin Jiangsu Zhejiang Liaoning Shanxi Hebei Xinjiang	Shanghai Beijing Tianjin Jiangsu Zhejiang Liaoning	Shanghai Beijing Tianjin Jiangsu Zhejiang Liaoning
0 to 49 percent	Shanxi Hebei Shandong Guangdong	Guangdong Shandong Henan Liaoning	Shanxi Hebei Shandong Guangdong	Shanxi Hubei Fujian Guangdong Shandong
−30 to 0 percent	Fujian Hubei Jilin Heilongjiang Henan	Jilin Fujian Hubei	Fujian Hubei Jilin	Jilin Hebei Heilongjiang Hunan
−50 to −31 percent	Shaanxi Hunan Anhui Ningxia Jiangxi Sichuan Xinjiang	Shaanxi Heilongjiang Anhui Hunan Jiangxi Nei Monggol	Heilongjiang Hunan Henan Ningxia Jiangxi Shaanxi	Henan Shaanxi Jiangxi Sichuan Xinjiang
Less than −50 percent	Nei Monggol Qinghai Xinjiang Gansu Yunnan Guangxi Guizhou Xizang	Sichuan Qinghai Gansu Yunnan Guangxi Guizhou Xizang	Anhui Sichuan Xinjiang Nei Monggol Qinghai Gansu Yunnan Guangxi Guizhou Xizang	Ningxia Anhui Nei Monggol Qinghai Gansu Yunnan Guangxi Guizhou Xizang

a. Data are for TVCEs only.
Source: Table 12-2.

Table 12-4. *The Value of Nonagricultural Output as a Share of Total Value of Rural Social Output, 1980–85*

Province	1980	1984	1985
All China	31.1	36.6	42.9
Anhui	23.2	28.0	30.7
Fujian	29.0	34.7	37.5
Gansu	17.2	16.4	17.9
Guangdong	34.1	36.1	41.6
Guangxi	20.0	18.8	22.9
Guizhou	16.4	24.2	25.6
Hebei	40.7	48.3	54.8
Heilongjiang	15.5	20.0	30.3
Henan	30.7	30.6	34.2
Hubei	25.3	33.6	37.8
Hunan	21.5	28.8	31.2
Jiangsu	52.1	57.4	65.1
Jiangxi	26.6	27.9	30.5
Jilin	24.6	25.7	31.1
Liaoning	35.0	42.3	52.9
Nei Monggol	23.5	19.2	20.1
Ningxia	20.2	23.0	24.9
Qinghai	22.4	24.1	25.9
Shaanxi	25.0	27.5	36.4
Shandong	32.7	37.5	41.8
Shanxi	41.9	47.5	56.2
Sichuan	19.8	25.2	30.2
Xinjiang	13.6	14.4	15.9
Xizang	0.9	4.2	9.3
Yunnan	23.0	20.3	23.6
Zhejiang	40.1	52.7	60.8

Note: Beijing and Tianjin municipalities are included under Hebei, and Shanghai municipality is included under Jiangsu.
Source: State Statistical Bureau (1987c), p. 24.

the total value of rural social output for each province and autonomous region. The following table compares this figure for each province with the national average.

In relation to national average

Higher	Hebei, Shanxi, Liaoning, Jiangsu, Zhejiang
Same	Shandong, Guangdong
Lower, by less than 30 percent	Jilin, Heilongjiang, Anhui, Fujian, Jiangxi, Henan, Hubei, Hunan, Sichuan, Shaanxi
Lower, by more than 30 percent	Nei Monggol, Guangxi, Guizhou, Yunnan, Xizang, Gansu, Qinghai, Ningxia, Xinjiang

Table 12-3 and the above breakdown show that the level of TVP development ebbs progressively from east to west—that is, from the economically developed coastal areas, such as the Liaodong Peninsula, the Beijing-Tianjin-Tangshan area, the Eastern Shandong Peninsula, the Yangtse River Delta, and the Pearl River Delta, to the hinterland and western frontier areas. China can be divided into three regions according to level of development of rural enterprises (see map 12-1).[2]

- Region A, with a developed TVP sector, consists of Liaoning, Hebei (including Beijing and Tianjin), Shandong, Jiangsu (including Shanghai), Zhejiang, Guangdong, and Shanxi
- Region B, with developing TVPs, consists of Henan, Hubei, Fujian, Jiangxi, Hunan, Anhui, Shaanxi, Heilongjiang, Jilin, and Sichuan
- Region C, with an underdeveloped TVP sector, consists of Nei Monggol, Ningxia, Gansu, Qinghai, Xinjiang, Guangxi, Yunnan, Guizhou, and Xizang

Table 12-5 shows the distribution of TVPs among the three regions according to various indicators.

Great regional differences also exist in the internal structure of the TVP sector. In the country as a whole, industry ranks first among nonagricultural production sectors in rural areas, followed by construction, miscellaneous trades (commerce, catering, and services), and transport. But this is not true of all regions.

- In the areas with developed TVP sectors (region A) industrial TVCES account for a large share of TVCES' total number of employees and total sales revenues. The share of industrial TVCES is comparatively smaller where the TVP sector is underdeveloped (region C). The comprehensive proportion of industrial TVCES (the simple average of their shares in total TVCE employment and in total sales revenue) was more than 70 percent in 1985 in Tianjin, Shanghai, Jiangsu, Zhejiang, Beijing,

Table 12-5. *The Regional Distribution of China's TVP Sector*
(percentage of national totals)

Region	Rural labor force	TVPs				
		Employment	Value of output	Tax payments	Profits	Original value of fixed assets[a]
A	37.7	51.3	63.9	71.4	64.2	62.9
B	46.1	40.7	31.4	24.7	29.5	32.1
C	16.2	8.0	4.7	3.9	6.3	5.0

a. Data are for TVCES only.
Source: Information from fieldwork.

Hebei, and Shanxi. The comprehensive proportion was less than 55 percent in Xinjiang, Ningxia, Qinghai, Gansu, Xizang, Yunnan, Guangxi, and Hunan.

• In region C the construction industry is more important than elsewhere. In 1985, for example, the comprehensive proportion of the construction sector in the total for TVCEs surpassed the proportion of industry itself in Gansu, Qinghai, Ningxia, Xinjiang, and Yunnan. This proportion exceeded 20 percent in nine other provinces and autonomous regions—Nei Monggol, Anhui, Fujian, Henan, Hunan, Guangxi, Sichuan, Xizang, and Shaanxi.

• The region with developing rural enterprises (region B) has comparatively large proportions of commerce, catering, and services. In 1985 the comprehensive proportion of these subsectors in the total for TVCEs surpassed 10 percent in eleven provinces and autonomous regions—Nei Monggol, Jilin, Heilongjiang, Jiangxi, Shandong, Hubei, Hunan, Guangdong, Guangxi, Xizang, and Shaanxi. Of the eleven, only Guangdong, Shandong, and Hubei are in Region A.

There are large regional differences in industrial production structure (see table 12-6). First, the subsectoral composition of industrial TVCEs grows progressively "heavier" from the coastal areas in the southeast of the country to the northwest.

Comprehensive proportion of heavy industry in total for industrial TVCEs

More than 70 percent	Shanxi, Guizhou, Yunnan, Qinghai, Ningxia, Xinjiang
60–70 percent	Nei Monggol, Liaoning, Jilin, Heilongjiang, Anhui, Henan Shaanxi, Gansu
50–60 percent	Hebei, Jiangxi, Shandong, Hubei, Hunan, Sichuan
40–50 percent	Beijing, Tianjin, Shanghai, Jiangsu, Fujian, Guangxi
Less than 40 percent	Zhejiang, Guangdong

Regional differences in the composition of heavy and light industries in China's TVCEs are largely determined by the factors of production. China's natural resources are mainly located in the west and north, whereas its agricultural resources and population are mainly in the coastal areas of the south and east.

Second, although in the country as a whole the leading subsectors in the industrial TVCE sector are, in order of importance, machine building, building materials, chemicals, textiles, and food processing, there are substantial

Map 12-1. The Level of Development of the TVP Sector

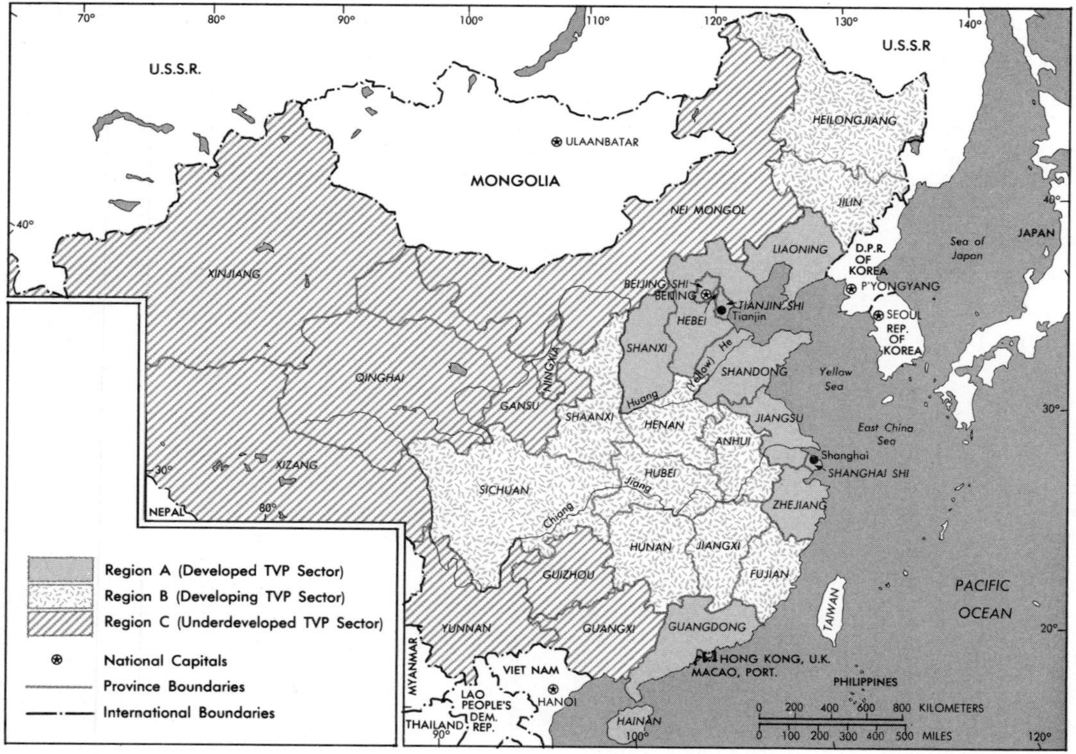

Region A (Developed TVP Sector)
Region B (Developing TVP Sector)
Region C (Underdeveloped TVP Sector)
⊗ National Capitals
Province Boundaries
—··— International Boundaries

Table 12-6. *Leading Industrial Subsectors in TVCEs, by Province, 1984*
(rank as measured by share of GVIO of TVCEs in province)

Province	First	Second	Third	Fourth	Fifth
All China	MACH	BLDG	TEXT	CHEM	FOOD
Anhui	BLDG	FOOD	MACH	OTH	CHEM
Fujian	BLDG	MACH	FOR	FOOD	OTH
Gansu	BLDG	MACH	CHEM	COAL	FOOD
Guangdong	MACH	BLDG	OTH	TEXT	CHEM
Guangxi	BLDG	OTH	FOOD	MACH	CULT
Guizhou Zhuang	COAL	BLDG	MET	CHEM	FOOD
Hebei	MACH	BLDG	CHEM	OTH	TEXT
Heilongjiang	BLDG	FOOD	MACH	COAL	OTH
Henan	BLDG	MACH	OTH	FOOD	CHEM
Hubei	BLDG	MACH	OTH	FOOD	TEXT
Hunan	BLDG	FOOD	OTH	MACH	COAL
Jiangsu	MACH	TEXT	BLDG	CHEM	OTH
Jiangxi	BLDG	CULT	COAL	MACH	FOOD
Jilin	BLDG	MACH	FOOD	OTH	COAL
Liaoning	MACH	BLDG	OTH	FOOD	CHEM
Nei Monggol	BLDG	COAL	MACH	FOOD	OTH
Ningxia	BLDG	MACH	FOOD	COAL	OTH
Qinghai	BLDG	MACH	COAL	FOOD	OTH
Shaanxi	BLDG	MACH	COAL	FOOD	OTH
Shandong	BLDG	MACH	FOOD	OTH	TEXT
Shanxi	COAL	BLDG	MACH	FOOD	CHEM
Sichuan	FOOD	BLDG	MACH	COAL	OTH
Xinjiang	BLDG	COAL	FOOD	MACH	CHEM
Xizang	n.a.	n.a.	n.a.	n.a.	n.a.
Yunnan	COAL	BLDG	FOOD	CHEM	MACH
Zhejiang	MACH	TEXT	BLDG	CHEM	OTH
Selected municipalities					
Beijing	MACH	BLDG	MET	GARM	CHEM
Shanghai	MACH	TEXT	CHEM	GARM	BLDG
Tianjin	MACH	GARM	CHEM	BLDG	MET

n.a. Not available.

Note: Based on GVIO in 1980 constant prices. BLDG, building materials; CHEM, chemicals; COAL, coal and coking; CULT, cultural/educational activities; FOOD, food processing; FOR, forestry; GARM, garments; MACH, machinery; MET, metallurgy; TEXT, textiles; OTH, other industry.

Source: Information from fieldwork.

regional differences (see table 12-6). Machine building and textiles dominate in Jiangsu, Zhejiang, Shanghai, and Tianjin; machine building and building materials in Hebei, Liaoning, Guangdong, and Beijing; building materials and (in second place) machine building in Jilin, Fujian, Shandong, Henan,

Hubei, Shaanxi, Gansu, Qinghai, and Ningxia; coal and building materials in Shanxi, Nei Monggol, Guizhou, Yunnan, and Xinjiang; and building materials and food processing in Heilongjiang, Anhui, Hunan, and Sichuan. These patterns demonstrate that rural industrial structure is mainly determined by natural resource endowments and the level of economic development. In general, given a roughly similar environment, the industrial structure in developed areas tends toward comparatively capital-intensive and technology-intensive undertakings and that in underdeveloped areas toward activities that use natural resources and labor more intensively. This does not contradict the common sense of economics.

The Evolution of Regional Imbalances in Recent Years

Economic growth is inherently a dynamic process that is necessarily accompanied by imbalances of various kinds, including regional imbalances. The problem is not that imbalances have emerged in TVP development but whether such imbalances will deteriorate in the future, how long the deterioration will continue, and what impact this will have on regional economic development, especially on per capita income gaps among regions.

Table 12-7 demonstrates that between 1979 and 1985 TVCEs in the three regions developed at different speeds. In region A the share of TVCE employees rose by 6.0 percentage points and the share of sales revenues by 6.7. In region B, however, the share of employees decreased by 4.0 percentage points and that of sales by 4.6, and in region C the share of employees dropped by 2.0 percentage points and that of sales by 2.1. If we looked only at the development of TVCEs, we might conclude that the gap between the developed region and the other two has been widening and the gap between the developing and underdeveloped regions has narrowed. But during this period private enterprise grew rapidly in China's rural areas. If we include private enterprises, between 1984 and 1985 the share of TVP employment in region A dropped by 6.5 percentage points and that of sales by 3.0. In region B the share of employment rose by 4.3 percentage points and that of sales by 2.6, and in region C the share of employment rose by 1.7 percentage points and that of sales by 0.4 (see table 12-8). Although the proportions of TVCE employment and gross revenues in regions B and C dwindled, those of all TVPs expanded.[3] Thus the mushrooming of private enterprises in rural areas since 1984 has had a positive impact on the regional structure of China's TVP sector and has begun to contribute toward reducing regional imbalances in the development of TVPs.

The fundamental purpose of encouraging rural nonagricultural production is to promote rural development and raise per capita incomes. It is therefore the evolution of the gap in rural average per capita income among regions that warrants our attention. The figures in table 12-9 show that the gap widened between 1981 and 1985. Per capita income in region B was 86.9 percent

Table 12-7. *Changes in the Regional Distribution of TVCEs, 1979–85*
(percentage of national total)

Item	Region A	Region B	Region C
1979			
Employees	53.7	38.6	7.7
Revenue	63.0	31.1	5.9
1980			
Employees	56.0	36.4	6.6
Revenue	65.2	29.7	5.1
1981			
Employees	58.6	35.6	5.8
Revenue	66.8	28.8	4.4
1982			
Employees	59.0	35.1	5.9
Revenue	66.4	29.0	4.6
1983			
Employees	59.4	34.7	5.9
Revenue	67.5	28.1	4.4
1984			
Employees	60.2	34.3	5.5
Revenue	68.0	27.9	4.1
1985			
Employees	59.7	34.6	5.7
Revenue	69.7	26.5	3.8

Source: Information from fieldwork.

of that in region A in 1981 but dropped to 76.4 percent by 1985, an average annual decline of 2.0 percentage points. Per capita income in region C in 1981 was 74.5 percent of that in region A; by 1985 it had dropped to 67.0 percent, an annual decline of 1.5 percentage points. But since 1983 the gap has grown more slowly. The relative index in region B dropped by 7.7 percentage points between 1981 and 1983 but by only 3.0 between 1983 and 1985. The relative index in region C dropped by 4.7 percentage points between 1981 and 1983 but by 2.8 between 1983 and 1985. The slower growth of the income gap is consistent with the better balance in TVP development brought about by the growth of private enterprises. The role of private enterprises in ameliorating regional income gaps should be recognized and policies adjusted accordingly.

Prospects for Promoting Rural Nonagricultural Production in Different Regions

This section discusses the prospects for nonagricultural development in rural

Table 12-8. *Regional Distribution of Employees and Gross Revenues in China's TVPs, 1984 and 1985*

Item	Region A	Region B	Region C
Percentage of TVP employment in national total			
1984	57.8	35.9	6.3
1985	51.3	40.7	8.0
Percentage of TVP revenues in national total			
1984	66.3	29.3	4.4
1985	63.3	31.9	4.8

Source: Information from fieldwork.

Table 12-9. *Changes in Relative Per Capita Incomes in Rural Areas, 1981–85*

Item	Region A	Region B	Region C	National average
1981				
Per capita income (yuan)	259.95	225.89	193.72	223.44
Compared with region A (percent)	100.0	86.9	74.5	86.0
1983				
Per capita income (yuan)	365.86	289.63	255.54	309.77
Compared with region A (percent)	100.0	79.2	69.8	84.7
1985				
Per capita income (yuan)	468.08	356.47	313.64	397.60
Compared with region A (percent)	100.0	76.2	67.0	84.9

Note: The per capita income figures are weighted averages of the income per rural resident in all the provinces and autonomous regions in each region. The 1981 weights are calculated according to the number of commune members, and those of 1983 and 1985 are worked out according to the size of the rural work force.

Source: State Statistical Bureau (1982, 1986a).

areas in light of the influence of the current Chinese system on the interregional flow and organization of the factors of production. The discussion focuses on sources for the funds needed for nonagricultural production in rural areas, since for some time to come capital requirements will be more of a problem than supplies of labor and land.

Prospects for Resource Mobilization

Capital comes from three sources: funds accumulated from local agricultural production, funds accumulated from local nonagricultural production, and loans and outside investments. These are here termed, with consideration

Table 12-10. *Distribution of Rural Net Income*
(percentage of net income)

Item	Taxes	Collective reserves	Individual incomes
1979	4.9	14.5	80.6
1985	5.4	8.1	86.5
Change	0.5	−6.4	5.9

Source: State Statistical Bureau (1982, 1986a).

for the kinds of statistics available, private bank savings, funds accumulated by TVCEs, and outside investments.

PRIVATE SAVINGS. Great changes in the distribution of net incomes have taken place since the introduction of the production responsibility system (PRS) (see table 12-10), and private savings in rural areas now play a much greater role in the development of nonagricultural production. Two factors determine whether private savings can be effectively channeled into nonagricultural production.

- *Government policies on private economic activities and investments.* If farmers have doubts about the consistency of government policies on the private economy, they will be reluctant to invest their savings in nonagricultural undertakings with slow economic returns and will prefer to invest in nonproductive assets such as houses or in nonagricultural activities that offer quick economic returns.
- *The degree of development and functioning of local capital markets.* Since China's state financial institutions are not yet providing large-scale loans for private investment, the accumulation of funds for private nonagricultural activities depends to a great degree on the development of nongovernment capital markets. In most underdeveloped and developing areas per capita incomes are low, and people have spent the greater part of the recent increases in income on consumption. Because of the underdevelopment of nongovernment capital markets and the poor industrial environment, there is an apparent tendency toward short-term investments, as reflected in the large proportions of private investment in construction, commerce, catering, services, and other trades. In a word, the conditions for turning private savings into nonagricultural investment funds are much poorer in region C than in regions A and B.

FUNDS ACCUMULATED BY TVCEs. The level of development of TVCEs differs from one region to another, as does the role of funds accumulated by these enterprises in the promotion of nonagricultural activities. In 1985 the net profits of TVCEs in region C were Y549.9 million, of which Y293.5 million were used for industrial investment. On the assumption that the net value of fixed assets of each TVCE plus its circulating funds totaled Y75,200 in 1985,[4] the net profits for the year could be used to set up 3,903 such firms, or fewer than seven in each county. If the per capita net value of fixed assets plus circulating funds of TVCEs was Y2,842 in 1985, the profits could be used to employ 103,283 workers, or only 169 per county.[5] This figure is less than 0.2 percent of region C's current rural labor force. The number of jobs created in 1985 by reinvestment by TVCEs in region B accounted for 0.2 percent of the total rural labor force in the region. In the same year TVCEs in region A generated Y12.54 billion in profits, of which Y5.58 billion (44.5 percent) were accumulated as production funds. This amount of money could be used to create 1.062 million jobs, or 1.9 percent of the rural labor force in region A. These calculations show that the funds accumulated by TVCEs will have only a limited influence on nonagricultural development in regions B and C.

OUTSIDE INVESTMENT AND PREFERENTIAL LOANS FROM THE GOVERNMENT. As China's economic reforms proceed and economic actors become more aware of their own interests, outside investment will increasingly be made only with an eye to profits. Whether a region can attract outside investment depends on its raw materials and transport facilities, its market prospects, and its supply of qualified labor. The first factor is decisive in region C's ability to absorb outside investment.

As for government support, two factors have to be taken into consideration: the level of support and its influence on nonagricultural development prospects. The central government will surely give priority consideration to economic efficiency in the future, and its supply of funds to underdeveloped areas will therefore not be large, since the efficiency of capital utilization in these areas is much lower than in more developed regions. Statistics for 1985 indicate that region A could generate a net output value of Y550 by turning one farmer into a worker, as against output figures of only Y213 in region B and Y383 in region C.[6] Moreover, every Y100 of investment can generate Y26.1 in taxes and profits in TVCEs in region A but only Y18.7 in region B and Y19.9 in region C. Under the current system, funds channeled into the developed region generate greater economic returns.

Another issue is the influence of the interregional flow of funds on TVP development. At present China's rural funds flow from one region to another through such channels as direct private investment, investment by TVCEs outside their localities, and interbank borrowing. Private funds cannot flow from one region to another on a large scale at present because of the underdevelopment of interregional transport and communications, the lack of transregional nongovernmental credit institutions, and the comparative isolation of private bank savings. Moreover, the tendency of TVPs to strive for maximum profits within the locality and the obstacles to horizontal invest-

ments have rendered it difficult for firms to make large transregional investments. Consequently the role of government financial organizations and of
the rural credit cooperatives under their control is extremely important.

The current management system of Chinese banks emphasizes "unified
planning, differentiating funds, extending loans according to absorption of
savings deposits, and mutual assistance." This system has restricted the interregional flow of funds. In particular, the principle of mutual assistance does
not permit a bank to reap any economic returns from financial assistance to
another region. This situation will inevitably have cumulative effects on regional imbalances, since the more funds a region has, the more bank loans
it will receive. Of the total bank loans received by China's TVCEs in 1985,
for example, 18.1 percent went to Jiangsu Province (including Shanghai),
10.6 percent to Shandong Province, 12.0 percent to Guangdong Province,
9.9 percent to Zhejiang Province, and 7.3 percent to Hebei Province (including Beijing and Tianjin). These five provinces got 57.8 percent of total
bank loans to TVCEs in that year. Region A received 65.2 percent of total
bank loans, region B 31.0 percent, and region C 3.9 percent. Thus the current bank management system intensifies imbalances in the distribution of
China's rural investment funds.

As banks have become increasingly aware of credit risk factors, a new situation has arisen in the underdeveloped region. Despite a great demand for
funds to develop rural nonagricultural production, banks in these areas have
large overstocks of lendable funds. The Guangxi Zhuang Autonomous Region provides an example. In 1985 the regional agricultural bank promulgated new regulations governing the extension of loans to TVPs. To borrow
money for a project, a TVP had to be able to supply 30 percent of the project's
total investment and it had to have an economic entity as guarantor. In 1986
the bank allotted Y13 million for equipment loans to TVPs in Yuling Prefecture. Since Y2.44 million in funds for special loans were left over from 1985,
the prefectural branch had Y15.44 million in funds available for equipment
loans, which would be accompanied by Y100 million in circulating capital
loans. By April 1986 the bank's equipment loans to TVPs accounted for only
8 percent of its total lendable funds for this purpose, and only 15 percent
of its total lendable funds for circulating capital had been extended. Under
pressure from the local government the bank lowered its requirements for
loans in the second half of the year: a TVP needed to have only 10 percent
of the project investment, and its guarantor could be a TVP bureau at the
county level.

How well banks can support local governments' development strategies depends to a considerable extent on the degree of local prosperity. In a more
developed area bank employees can reap more personal benefits from the
local economy, and the bank as a result tends to be more cooperative toward
the local government. In a less developed area bank employees can gain little
from the local economy, and bank branches are more willing to stay within

the confines imposed by the vertical management system of the nation's financial system. Once private savings are deposited in the agricultural bank in region C, they are less likely to be returned to circulation in the local economy, and the difficulties that stem from the limited amount of private savings in region C are exacerbated.

It is apparent that under China's current system there are no signs of improvement in the environment for capital supply in the country's vast underdeveloped rural areas. The existing market, technical, and labor force conditions for developing nonagricultural production in rural areas give cause for worry about a further intensification of regional imbalances. Although the imbalances may be improving somewhat, progress will not be sustained without further efforts to restructure the current system.

Measures to Ameliorate Regional Imbalances

All measures to solve the problem of regional development must start from two supporting bases: human development and income equalization. The following are areas in which actions grounded on these bases may be considered.

FACILITATING INTERREGIONAL FLOWS OF LABOR. The prerequisite for raising the overall efficiency of an economic system and achieving interregional equality in per capita incomes is a free flow of the factors of production. An important objective of China's economic reforms in recent years has been to break down the barriers of administrative jurisdictions and expand market mechanisms. Spatial flows of the factors of production have indeed increased in recent years—undoubtedly a good beginning. In light of practical conditions in China, priority should be given to interregional flows of labor, since without such flows interregional movements of other factors of production will only intensify regional imbalances in TVP development and, what is worse, widen regional gaps in per capita incomes and encourage the formation of independent communities on the basis of regional interests. The unified national market for other factors of production will inevitably disintegrate, bringing flows to a stop.

Legal and social restrictions hinder both rural-urban and rural-rural flows of labor. The restrictions on rural-urban movement are the inevitable outcome of an industrialization process based on public ownership of property, state monopoly, and exploitation of agriculture. Lack of inputs reduced agriculture's productivity and ability to accumulate funds, and industry also found it difficult to expand and to increase its financial surplus. Rapid population growth and low agricultural productivity left little surplus grain to support the shift of agricultural workers to the nonagricultural sector. Moreover, when all private businesses were banned, the state became the only employer and purveyor for urban residents and had to control the size of the urban population according to how much grain was available. Since the government decided who would have access to urban employment, it in effect recognized urban residents as holders of vested interests.

A principal reason for the government's slowness in opening up urban and rural areas to each other was its concern about the adverse effects of change on the interests of urban residents. Efficiency and equity were not considered when the current policy of separating the urban and rural populations was formulated. This policy should be gradually abandoned. The development of the private economy in urban areas and the increasing exchanges between urban and rural areas in recent years have already created the preliminary conditions for a reorientation of policy. As the country's grain production increases and more grain markets emerge, urban employers should gradually cease discriminating against rural residents when hiring workers. This will not only help narrow the income gap between urban and rural residents but will also lower the costs of industrial production and improve the efficiency of the national economy. As a first step, the Chinese government should relax controls over household registration in small cities and towns and reform the grain supply system accordingly.

Obstructions to the free flow of labor among rural areas are rooted in farmers' dependence on land. Under China's traditional system peasants could not engage in nonagricultural activities and were confined to agricultural production. Thus there was little reason for interregional labor flows. Under the rural economic reforms interregional flows of rural labor have greatly increased in recent years. But because the overall environment for nonagricultural activities in rural areas is not yet stable, most farmers cannot yet withdraw from their dependence on the land, and many rural households pursue nonagricultural activities only as a sideline. Rural movement of labor is mainly individual instead of by households (see Lu Mai and Dai Xiaojing 1987).

Because the income gap among regions is large, people in low-income areas have a strong desire to move once they have abandoned the traditional conception of "never leaving one's native land unless it is absolutely necessary." The main issue is the ability and willingness of people in high-income areas to accept them. Rural areas in economically developed coastal regions, especially near big and medium-size cities, have already handed over many of their traditional economic activities to outsiders in recent years because of the emergence of new opportunities for developing nonagricultural production (see chapter 14). The ownership structure of TVPs also influences the degree of acceptance of outside workers by people in developed areas. Generally speaking, townships and villages launch TVCEs with the interests of the locality in mind, and they would rather pay more to local workers than pay less to outsiders. Private enterprises may be more willing to hire outside labor at lower wages.

The increased flow of labor in China's rural areas in recent years has promoted the development of nonagricultural activities and helped achieve more balanced incomes among regions. Such flows should be encouraged by the Chinese government. To turn the interregional flow of labor into a reality, efforts should be made to institute land reform (see chapter 6) and retrain rural laborers.

REFORMING THE MICROECONOMIC BASIS FOR DEVELOPING RURAL NONAGRICULTURAL PRODUCTION. The development of nonagricultural activities in China's rural areas started with community governments' initiatives in setting up enterprises. This phenomenon, an inevitable result of China's traditional system, helped to promote the rural economy and increase farmers' incomes. It has great limitations, however. The ultimate objective of community enterprises is to reap maximum benefits for the community. This objective impedes the free spatial flow of factors of production and further splits up domestic markets that were already isolated from each other. Furthermore, by reproducing or intensifying China's traditional system it creates a new obstacle to economic reform, which is already beset with difficulties. The introduction of the PRS, the development of nonagricultural production in rural areas, and the elimination of the state monopoly in purchasing and marketing have created excellent opportunities for seeking a new road to rural industrialization through launching private enterprises. Our sample surveys show that the basic purpose of private enterprises is to maximize profits on capital. This goal in itself requires a breaking down of spatial barriers, which will provide a microeconomic basis for the free spatial flow of factors of production.

The Chinese government already has a basis for implementing a policy of promoting private enterprise. The changes in people's ideas and the improvement in their basic living standards have provided a good opportunity for altering the practice under which grass-roots rural governments are responsible for everything. Where TVCES are highly developed and local governments have been able to guarantee the basic income levels of their residents, authorities should try to solve the contradiction of "big governments with small treasuries" by encouraging the development of private enterprise. From a macroeconomic point of view, the development of private enterprise can help to weaken the economic functions of community governments. Where TVCES account for a comparatively small share of nonagricultural production, changes in their orientation should occur, away from a sole focus on maximizing benefits to the community. The contribution of private enterprises to ameliorating imbalances in the development of nonagricultural activities in China's rural areas in recent years and equalizing per capita incomes interregionally shows that this kind of policy is beneficial.

RATIONALIZING STATE SUPPORT FOR DEVELOPING AND UNDERDEVELOPED REGIONS. Since under the conditions prevailing in China it is difficult to achieve free interregional flows of labor, the government should provide some help to developing and underdeveloped areas. Such assistance should be given in proper forms and with due consideration for the advantages and disadvantages in each case. It should go mainly to areas with low per capita incomes, large populations, few agricultural resources, and great market potential, such as Yunnan, Guangxi, Guizhou, and Gansu in region C and Shaanxi in region B. Attention should be paid to selecting projects according to conditions in each area to promote a regional division of labor. The central government may also help local governments with agricultural production and investment to improve the local environment for nonagricultural development.

If the Chinese government adopts the policies outlined above, regional imbalances in the development of nonagricultural activities in rural areas will persist in the future, but with differences. Such imbalances, unlike the existing ones, will be accompanied by an intensification of regional specialization and an equalization of per capita incomes and will be widely accepted as part of a rational development process.

Notes

1. Some Chinese TVPs engage in agricultural production. Because they are small in number, these firms are included in our use of the term TVPs. In 1985, for example, the number of employees in agricultural enterprises accounted for only 6.1 percent of the total for all TVCEs, and their total revenues were 3.1 percent of those for all TVCEs. The percentages would be even smaller if private enterprises were included.

2. Because first-grade (provincial-level) administrative areas are used as our basic regional demarcation, differences within each province cannot be taken into account.

3. Statistical materials for 1986 show that for all types of TVPs (including private enterprises) the share of region A continued to decline while the shares of regions B and C continued to rise.

4. This figure is calculated by dividing the total year-end net value of fixed assets and circulating funds of the country's TVCEs in 1985 by the total number of these enterprises.

5. Based on the total of the net (depreciated) value of fixed assets plus quota circulating assets of TVCEs and their total employment in 1985.

6. These are arithmetic averages of the indexes of all the provinces in each region. The index in each province is the average net value of output created by each TVP employee minus the average net value of agricultural output created by each member of the agricultural labor force.

Part IV

Labor

Labor and wages in the TVP sector are of great interest and critical importance. Lower overall labor costs and apparently superior labor motivation and effort have been principal sources of TVPs' competitive advantages in relation to state enterprises. Wages of TVP employees are much more closely tied to individual and enterprise performance than are those of most state workers. Various types of piece rates are extremely common, and many firms pay a year-end bonus related to growth of enterprise profits or output. Most TVP workers probably work considerably harder and for longer hours than their counterparts in state enterprises. Labor relations in TVPs seem surprisingly good, particularly considering the hard work, long hours, difficult working conditions, and relatively low wages. Possibly this is because TVP employees are first-generation industrial workers accustomed to the rigors of farm life.

Rural labor markets are highly fragmented territorially and are not functioning smoothly in most areas. Labor is still rather immobile among provinces, localities, and communities, except for temporary migrant labor, mostly in low-skill activities. In such places as Wuxi labor is still allocated to community enterprises by township authorities, and inflows of workers from outside have been discouraged. In other areas there is much less administrative control, but various frictions impede the free flow of labor. The community-based rural institutional structure, the household registration system, and continuing restrictions against permanent migration to larger cities by rural people all adversely affect labor mobility among rural areas. The three chapters dealing with labor issues shed light on this vast topic from different angles.

In chapter 13 Alan Gelb surveys workers' attitudes, wage systems and incentives, and labor relations in the TVP sector on the basis of data from the Worker Survey Questionnaire. He first describes four models of labor relations that might apply to the TVP sector—the public enterprise and communal models for community enterprises and the Taylorist and Z-firm archetypes for private firms. Gelb argues that community enterprises fit the communal better than the public enterprise model and that private enterprises resemble Z-firms more than they do the Taylorist stereotype of labor relations in capitalist enterprises. The implication is that pay in all TVPs generally is related to firm (and community) economic performance. Moreover, differences between "communal" community enterprises and "Z-firm" private enterprises are relatively small.

The chapter contains interesting findings concerning the characteristics, attitudes, and pay of the TVP employees surveyed. Regardless of the pay system actually in use, workers perceive a close relationship between their incomes and firm profitability. In general, they seem to be fairly content and to regard labor relations in their firms as relatively good. Dispersion in average pay levels is substantial, but it is mainly among rather than within firms.

The striking differences among counties for the most part dominate any effects that different forms of firm ownership may have. Local labor markets appear to be more open in Nanhai and Jieshou, where a larger proportion of sample workers came to their present employment through "voluntary" routes, than in Wuxi and Shangrao. The proportions of female workers and young workers are highest in Nanhai, and Nanhai workers indicate significantly greater willingness to change firms than do those in the other three counties. Dispersion of pay is greatest in Nanhai, which has greater competition among different types of firms and fewer communal constraints; it is rather narrow in Wuxi. Shangrao workers show signs of dissatisfaction with poor management in their firms and—perhaps as a consequence—less concern about their enterprises and about their fellow workers' performance.

Gelb analyzes wage determination in some detail, estimating several wage equations. He finds that individual worker characteristics, occupation, and firm ownership fail to explain a large proportion of the overall variation in pay levels for sample workers. Simple firm dummies, however, do quite well; together with occupation, age, sex, and number of days worked in the year they explain 70 percent of the variation in pay. This may be because community income levels are an important determinant of wage levels. Not only is education insignificant in determining wages, but when the effects are (marginally) significant, they go the "wrong" way; that is, higher education is not necessarily associated with higher pay. This result is highly unusual in comparison with findings from similar analyses in other countries. Interfirm wage differentials reflect the impact of different growth rates of labor productivity.

Gelb concludes by suggesting that the community orientation of TVPs, regardless of form of ownership, may be the main reason why they follow the communal or Z-firm model rather than the public enterprise or Taylorist archetype. Another important finding is that because of the prevailing communal orientation and pay systems, TVP workers behave as though they have substantial de facto equity stakes in their firms.

In chapter 14 Meng Xin describes and analyzes the rural labor markets faced by TVPs. Her theoretical foundation is the model of economic development with unlimited labor supply developed by W. A. Lewis in the 1950s. In this model the unlimited supply of low-wage surplus laborers from the agricultural sector permits high accumulation rates and rapid industrialization over a relatively long period until the surplus labor is exhausted. But Meng points out that an unstated precondition for the model to work is a well-functioning rural labor market, and she demonstrates that this precondition is not met in China.

The chapter first looks at interregional, intercommunity, and inter-enterprise mobility of labor in the four counties. Flows of labor among counties and provinces are limited except in Nanhai, and flows among communities and enterprises are much more important in Nanhai and Jieshou than in Wuxi and Shangrao. The limited labor mobility in Wuxi is especially striking because of the high level of industrialization and TVP development and the emerging labor shortages in the county. (In Nanhai shortages have stimulated a substantial inflow of labor from outside.) Meng argues that the lack of labor mobility in Wuxi is attributable to the domination of TVCEs in the TVP ownership system. This contrasts with Nanhai, where the share of TVCEs is lower and a large proportion of TVCE employees are temporary laborers not under the supervision of community governments.

The author goes on to look at wage determination in the four counties. Not surprisingly, TVP wage levels in the two highly industrialized counties, Wuxi and Nanhai, are much higher than in the less developed ones, Jieshou and Shangrao, but wages in Nanhai exceed those in Wuxi by more than 70 percent. Wages have risen at a much more rapid rate in Nanhai and Wuxi than in Jieshou and Shangrao. Wage differentials at the intercommunity and interenterprise levels are large in Nanhai but small in Wuxi and Jieshou.

Meng argues that TVP wages are much more responsive to labor supply and demand conditions in Jieshou and Nanhai than in Shangrao and Wuxi. In Wuxi, despite the growing shortage of labor in the TVP sector, agricultural incomes caught up with and even surpassed those of TVP workers, partly because of strict administrative controls over wages in TVCEs. An apparent paradox is that despite greater labor mobility in Nanhai than in Wuxi, intercommunity and interenterprise differentials are much greater in the former than in the latter. Meng suggests that this is because of administrative controls in Wuxi and the greater degree of community specialization in particular industries in Nanhai. In Jieshou, where the industrial structure is less diversified and skill requirements are more uniform, differentials are relatively small. The higher differentials in Shangrao are attributed to immobility of labor and uneven distribution of natural resources, some of the rents from which accrue to labor.

In Wuxi community governments have succeeded in balancing income levels between agriculture and (TVP) industry. The egalitarian distribution system does not appear to harm efficiency, perhaps because TVP workers' employment and income prospects are uncertain and their wages are strongly linked with performance through various piece-rate systems. In Nanhai community governments are unable to control wages in TVCES because of well-functioning labor markets and the ability of private firms to attract employees away from community enterprises by offering high wages. This partly explains the rapid increase in TVP wages there.

The overall picture that emerges is that China at present does not have a unitary labor market for rural-urban flows or interregional flows. Even though the national situation may approximate the "unlimited supply of labor" of the Lewis model, labor costs in particular rural localities have sky-rocketed owing to localized labor shortages. As a result, the advantages of being able to draw on an unlimited supply of labor at a subsistence wage are lost; in the rapidly developing areas with local labor shortages, rising wages cut industrial accumulation and may also lead to greater capital intensity than is economically appropriate for the nation as a whole.

The impact of local labor markets differs according to the level of TVP development. In the early stages, when there is still surplus local labor to be absorbed from agriculture, a local labor market can be helpful in giving enterprises appropriate signals on factor mix and in holding down wage increases. Interference in wage determination by community governments can lead to excessively high wages and bloated payrolls. Once TVP development is relatively advanced and local labor shortages have emerged, a functioning local labor market facilitates excessively rapid increases in wages (as occurred in Nanhai before it was opened up to interregional labor flows in 1986). Paradoxically, community governments' involvement in wage determination can help limit wage increases in this situation.

In chapter 15 Wu Quhui, Wang Hansheng, and Xu Xinxin look at the influence of the structure of alternative labor opportunities on wage determination in three of the four counties—Wuxi, Nanhai, and Jieshou. Their main conclusion is that alternative opportunities play a great role in determining wage levels in different localities and can lead to significant differences in income levels even among localities with similar levels of economic development.

The authors assert that the structure of alternative labor opportunities is closely related to the ownership pattern and the degree of labor mobility. When the bulk of the TVP labor force is in TVCES (as in Wuxi), community governments can control wages effectively. If there is a substantial number of private enterprises (as in Nanhai), community governments cannot set TVCE wages below market-clearing levels because their employees would move to the private sector en masse. If, however, there is both surplus labor and a substantial private sector (the situation in Jieshou), TVCE wages will be held down by local labor market conditions. A high degree of interfirm labor mobility (associated with the existence of a significant private sector) weakens the ability of community governments to control wages.

The authors go on to describe how community governments try to balance the incomes of community members. This is easier if TVCEs account for the bulk of local employment and if alternative employment opportunities are limited. In Wuxi TVP profits are used to support agricultural incomes.

The structure of alternative employment opportunities also affects wage differentiation within firms, in particular managerial compensation. In Wuxi increases in managerial compensation are tied to increases in workers' pay, and the gap between the enterprise director's pay and the average wage cannot become too wide. In Nanhai, however, TVCE directors' pay is usually linked to enterprise profits, which puts directors in a more favorable position and gives them incentives to hold down wage increases. One reason for these different methods and the lower differentials in Wuxi is that in Nanhai compensation for TVCE managers has to be competitive with pay in private enterprises, whereas in Wuxi the monolithic ownership system allows community governments to exert effective control over management pay differentials both within and among firms. In Jieshou differentials within firms are small because of labor market conditions and the generally simple skill requirements. In actuality, many TVCEs are basically private enterprises, and their managers give themselves low nominal wages to show a narrow differential to the outside world and to facilitate holding down workers' wages; they can appropriate the returns from "their" enterprises in other forms.

The authors describe different modes of wage determination in the three counties for both workers and managers. In Wuxi wages are to a large extent under the discretionary control of community governments, whereas in Nanhai and Jieshou there is a strong linkage with profits (for managers) or output (for workers), and once the basic linkage is set there is little if any interference by community governments.

The chapter concludes with some additional implications. One is that TVP employees have more community consciousness in Wuxi, where pay is to a large extent controlled and balanced by community government authorities and differentials within communities are small. In Nanhai and Jieshou community governments do not play an important role in income distribution, and workers tend to demonstrate strong individualism (Nanhai) or to identify with their firms (Jieshou). As a result of these differences, the three counties will face different labor problems in the future. Community governments in Wuxi will have to concentrate more on efficient performance in the TVP sector and less on income distribution, whereas the opposite is true for Nanhai.

13

TVP Workers' Incomes, Incentives, and Attitudes

Alan Gelb

This chapter provides a perspective on workers in TVPs—on their working relationships within their firms, their income levels, and their occupational characteristics. The term "TVP workers" is used here in a broad sense to include technicians, managers, and other employees, except where it specifically denotes an occupational category.

The analysis is based on the Worker Survey Questionnaire, which contains fifty-nine subjective and objective questions. The subjective questions cover workers' views on such topics as industrial relations, attitudes toward work, and reward systems. The objective questions deal with pay and with demographic and similar variables. Since some questions have multiple parts, there are 107 responses, in all, to each questionnaire. Selection of workers within firms was done on a stratified random basis. Proportionately more workers were sampled for smaller firms, and technical and management personnel were somewhat oversampled to ensure sufficient diversity for statistical analysis. Researchers helped workers to complete the questionnaire. In the four sample counties 1,174 usable questionnaires were obtained, but 2 were dropped because their firm classifications were probably incorrect.

To facilitate analysis, thirty-six questions were selected to yield a clean, compact data set. In addition, certain response options offered in the survey were consolidated and simplified to render them more mutually exclusive and to weight responses according to frequency or intensity. The worker data were then linked up with selected firm variables from other questionnaires, including firm ownership type, work force, sales, and profitability, all for 1985 when possible.

The distribution of sample workers and their firms by county and firm type is shown in table 13-1; the 1,172 workers are distributed in 49 firms, with an average of 24 workers per firm. Although there is a wide spread of firms by type and county, township firms dominate, and there are no private firms in Wuxi and Shangrao. Thirty-two enterprises are owned by communal governments, nine are private, and eight are other types, mostly mixed ownership. Some minor adjustments were made to the data, but only where there were clear indications of unreasonable responses.[1]

This chapter reports on a first analysis of the survey data. Because only the TVP sector was sampled and there was no control group, the survey cannot be used directly to assess differences between TVPs and state enterprises. The responses can, however, shed light on the nature of the TVP sector itself in relation to various possible archetypes or models, and they can be used to test hypotheses on differences between the characteristics of the TVP sector in the four sample counties. Since the TVP sector has evolved in a wide variety of situations, different types and stages of development can be distinguished within the sector.

These differences and their systematic association with certain counties pose considerable difficulties for the interpretation of tests of hypotheses. For example, the hypothesis that pay is higher in larger firms might be preferred over the proposition that firm size is not correlated with pay. But the first hypothesis might look better only because firms tend to be larger in the more advanced areas where incomes are generally higher. Similarly, one might conclude that private enterprises pay less than community enterprises or employ fewer women, but it might simply be that private enterprises are concentrated in poorer, less advanced areas. Multivariate estimation techniques are generally preferable to bivariate ones in this situation, but owing to the preliminary nature of this analysis, bivariate relationships are frequently reported.

Another point, as will be seen below, is that the tails of the distributions of some variables are heavily influenced by the inclusion of a few firms that may not be representative of the TVP sector as a whole, although they are interesting. Care should therefore be taken in extrapolating the survey results to the whole TVP sector.

Some Broad Hypotheses and Models for TVPs

TVPs constitute an "in-between" sector. They are part public, part communal, and part private. They operate partly in free markets for factors, inputs, and products and partly in planned ones.

As a framework for the analysis, we develop four archetypes, each with its distinctive set of explicit or implicit labor contracts. First, we look at two models for community enterprises.

- *The public enterprise model.* Ownership is by a large community such as the nation-state. Pay levels are set administratively with little reference to individual or firm performance. Pay is compressed within firms and is similar among firms. Labor is allocated to firms rather than hired on the market, and workers have great job security.
- *The communal model.* Firms are owned and controlled by a small com-

Table 13-1. Distribution of Sample Workers and Firms (number)

Type of firm	Wuxi		Jieshou		Nanhai		Shangrao		Four counties	
	Workers	Firms	Workers	Firms	Workers	Firms	Workers	Firms	Workers	Firms
Township	361	11	57	3	121	4	110	7	649	25
Village	37	2	26	2	60	2	21	1	144	7
Private	0	0	128	7	17	2	0	0	145	9
Other	75	2	86	3	60	2	13	1	234	8
All firms	473	15	297	15	258	10	144	9	1,172	49

282

munity, in the sense that the employees form a significant part of the community. Workers have job security by virtue of being community members. They tend to be hired through a mixture of voluntary application and informal communal ties. Within a firm relative pay levels may be determined by a range of systems, such as piece rates, time rates, or work-points, but the average level reflects, to a large extent, the income of the community and is therefore tied to the performance of the firm if the latter is important to the community. In the extreme case the work force itself is the community, and the firm becomes a kind of cooperative. The stronger are the small communities (say, production teams, villages, or the firms themselves) in relation to the larger ones (say, townships or counties), the wider are the likely pay differentials among firms. If labor mobility is low, substantial pay differentials can arise among communities.

Two models can also be outlined for private enterprises.

- *The Taylorist model.* This model is usually considered to be the dominant type in Western economies. Labor is a variable factor of production, and turnover is high. Work patterns are systematically simplified to enable one worker to be easily replaced by another. Except for managers, pay is not tied to firm performance.

- *The Japanese, or Z-firm model.* In contrast to the Taylorist model, this pattern emphasizes strong identification of workers with their firms, low turnover, and close ties between the firm's profitability and payments to labor. This "paternalist–lifetime commitment" model is more plausible where labor mobility is naturally low and family members and partners make up a substantial part of the work force. (The term Z-firm was introduced by Ouchi to denote U.S. firms that were following the Japanese model; see Ouchi 1982. It is used here to avoid exclusive identification of this system of labor relations with Japan; many firms in many countries have larger or smaller degrees of "Z-ness." See also chapter 19.)

Most firms would be expected to be some combination of the above four models. Moreover, it may not be easy to distinguish a Z-firm from a communal firm except by ownership (private or public). A number of hypotheses about how TVPs fit into these categories can be proposed.

- *Hypothesis 1.* In the TVP sector as a whole, community enterprises tend to follow a communal rather than a public enterprise model, and private enterprises follow the Z-firm rather than the Taylorist model. This implies that pay is generally related to enterprise performance and that differences between private and community enterprises are minimal.

- *Hypothesis 2.* There are significant differences among the four counties. Small communities and firms are stronger in Nanhai than in Wuxi, so that the former is more "communal" and varied, whereas the latter displays more of the characteristics of the public enterprise model. Jieshou is more market oriented than Shangrao, which displays signs of a more traditional attitude toward TVPs.

- *Hypothesis 3*. There are also significant vintage effects that stem from the timing of the establishment of the TVP sector in relation to the phase of reform.
- *Hypothesis 4*. Because of the communal nature of both community and private enterprises and low labor mobility in China, pay is still largely determined by firm and community. Personal characteristics such as type of work and educational level have only a secondary impact. Inequality generated by the growth of the TVP sector therefore largely reflects the fortunes and dynamism of different firms and communities, not the emergence of wide differentials within firms.

These four hypotheses, together with the characteristics of the models outlined above, imply some specific propositions that can be tested against the survey data. For example, hypothesis 1 suggests that there should be few significant differences between private and community enterprises once regional effects are allowed for. Hypothesis 2 suggests that income levels in Nanhai should be more dispersed than in Wuxi and that the reason is greater between-firm variability rather than especially wide differentials within firms. Labor markets should operate in significantly different ways in the four counties and for workers of different vintages. Such propositions are tested in the following sections.

General Features of the Sample

The sample respondents are generally young; 13 percent are under 20 years of age and only 14 percent are over 39 years of age. Males constitute 53 percent of the total and females 47 percent. Most workers have gone through junior middle school, but only 2 percent have attended any type of college. Sixty-three percent classify themselves as workers (in the narrow sense), and the rest are more or less equally distributed among shift leaders, operations personnel, technicians, ordinary staff, and middle-level staff, with a few apprentices. The factory is their main source of income. Sixty-one percent work in their firms for twelve months a year and for six or (mostly in Wuxi) seven days a week. Few work less than ten months in the firm or less than five days a week.

Satisfaction Levels

Overall, sample workers seem fairly content—80 percent consider themselves to be basically or very satisfied and only 8.5 percent express a desire to leave their firms. Seventy-five percent plan to stay with their firms for at least five years, and only 9 percent consider it possible that they might lose their jobs. Many thought that a decision to leave their firms would be "difficult" to carry out. Only 22 percent agree with the statement that TVP workers' status is lower than that of workers in state enterprises, even though most of the respondents are rural residents and state enterprise workers enjoy the advantages of urban registration.

Labor Relations

Only 9 percent of sample workers consider that labor relations in their firms involve serious or frequent conflicts, and only 14 percent rate the management of their firms as poor. (This proportion was significantly higher in Shangrao, confirming impressions from interviews that many Shangrao firms are poorly managed.) Fully 83 percent of the workers see a substantial need for some type of trade union to protect their interests.

Labor Allocation

At least in a local sense, much of the TVP sector seems to operate in a fairly free labor market. Fifty-four percent of respondents came to their firms through modes that can be considered voluntary: their own initiative, introductions by friends and relatives, or competitive examinations.[2] The remaining 46 percent arrived through labor allocation, resource pooling, or other arrangements by the local government. This is one of the areas of large differences among counties. In Wuxi and Shangrao 57 percent of the workers were allocated, whereas in Nanhai and Jieshou only 33 percent were. There is also a strong vintage effect; only 26 percent of the workers under 20 years of age were allocated, compared with almost 60 percent for the oldest cohorts. This reflects the evolution of policies relating to the TVP sector.

Pay, Profits, and Attitudes toward Work and Investment

Pay systems differ considerably among TVPs, and there is a tendency for those in the more advanced counties to be more complex and have a wider range of benefits than those in the less advanced areas. Few of the workers report that time rates are the main method of payment; piece rates and floating wages are more common. Only 19 percent of the workers indicate that bonuses are unimportant or unavailable. Other pay components often mentioned as important include medical subsidies, pensions, and factory subsidies. Guaranteed employment for children in the same firm seems to be a less important benefit.

Whatever the specific method of payment, workers clearly perceive a close relationship between their incomes and the profitability of their firms. Only

10 percent see no relationship, whereas 71 percent consider the link to be strong or very strong. The relationship is powerful for all counties and types of firms; regressions to predict it have little explanatory power, although it is somewhat stronger in larger than in smaller firms.[3]

Correspondingly, it appears that a large majority of respondents are prepared to assume some responsibility for the quality of their fellow employees' work. Only 14 percent are indifferent to poor performance or consider that it is a matter for managers alone; 32 percent would like to speak to the shirkers in their firm but feel inhibited; and 54 percent indicate that they would speak out. Again, this response appears to be widespread across counties, types of ownership, and occupations.[4] In particular, it is not significantly lower in Wuxi than in the other counties.

About half of the sample workers regard pay differentials between workers and managers in their firms or among workers as "substantial." Workers are divided on whether differentials should be allowed to widen (17 percent), should stay the same (41 percent), or should be narrower (42 percent). Most workers would deposit surplus income in a bank, use it to purchase consumer goods, or (especially in Wuxi) invest in housing. A smaller but appreciable number would prefer to use funds to purchase producer goods (including farming equipment) or to buy stock in their own or other firms. Although only 7 percent want to set up their own firms, alone or with others, 15 percent would buy a "large number" of stocks in their firms if these were offered, 71 percent would buy a "small" number, and 12 percent would not buy stocks. There is thus evidence of considerable willingness to help with their firms' financing.[5]

Communal Variables

Only 27 percent of sample workers say that the best use of factory profits is direct distribution to workers; 65 percent favor substantial reinvestment of profits in the firm. This response is probably related to the low mobility of labor and the consequent importance of firms in the future income streams of workers and their families. In response to a hypothetical question, 65 percent indicate they would accept a 50 percent pay cut and remain to help their firm through difficulties rather than actively look for another job. More than half of the respondents indicate that if they were faced with personal problems, they would first approach other workers or managers in their firms rather than family members or communal leaders.

Sample workers consider their income levels to be average or slightly above the levels in their communities; only 2 percent describe their incomes as very high and only 9 percent as low. Interestingly, there is not a systematic relationship between income level and perception of income level in relation to the community, despite the wide range of incomes reported in the sample. This suggests that pay tends to be set largely with reference to the income levels prevailing in the community of which the firm is a part.[6]

The general picture is consistent with the hypothesis that the TVP sector follows a communal model and that in some cases the firm itself is a considerable part of the community. It also confirms the propositions that workers perceive a strong link between pay and profits and that many view their relationship with their firm as long term rather than transient. This is no doubt because of the limited mobility of labor. In this sense TVP workers have de facto equity in their firms even if they do not formally own shares. Many, it seems, would consider a degree of formal shareholding in their firms as well.

It is also clear, however, that TVPs are not worker cooperatives, if the term is taken to mean that workers exert a large degree of control. Responses indicate that recruitment and dismissal, pay, work assignments, product development, investments, and use of retained profits are overwhelmingly decided on by enterprise leaders and that the leaders are appointed by the government or chosen by other leaders rather than elected. On average, only 6 percent of respondents felt that the views of factory workers had any weight in such decisions. Surprisingly, Shangrao workers indicate a somewhat higher degree of participation, including election of leaders by workers.[7] There is some sentiment for more decisionmaking power for workers, but the desire is not overwhelming. Only 14.2 percent of respondents indicated that they would like workers to have total or partial decisionmaking power in the areas listed above.

Differences among Counties and Firm Types

Because the TVP sector differs among counties in so many ways, many if not most relationships between survey variables and location by county differ significantly from randomness. This section discusses certain systematic patterns and their implications rather than trying to identify all points of difference.

The Labor Market

As table 13-2 shows, Nanhai and Jieshou appear to have freer labor markets than Wuxi and Shangrao, and younger workers there are less likely to have been allocated to their firms. Private enterprises also operate in a freer labor market. These differences are an aspect of county patterns of labor use. Nanhai employs more women workers (57 percent) and the most young workers (22 percent of Nanhai workers are under 20 years of age). Wuxi and Shangrao have the largest proportions of old workers. Many of Wuxi's TVPs are long established, and Shangrao's firms are less dynamic than elsewhere, so the proportion of young workers is lower.

Nanhai workers are more mobile than those in Wuxi; 27 percent plan to leave their firms within one to three years.[8] Faced with the option of taking a 50 percent pay cut or leaving, 53 percent of Nanhai workers, by far the

Table 13-2. *Recruitment of Sample Workers*
(number of workers)

Item	Allocation	Voluntary	Total
By county			
Wuxi	270	191	461
Jieshou	84	209	293
Nanhai	99	154	253
Shangrao	78	66	144
Total	531	620	1,151
By age			
Under 20	40	114	153
20–29	233	320	554
30–39	168	117	285
40–49	71	57	128
50+	19	12	31
Total	531	620	1,151
By ownership			
Public	398	380	778
Private	33	111	144
Total	431	491	922
Pay (yuan per year)			
Less than 625	82	180	262
625–1,249	212	263	475
1,250–2,499	173	142	315
2,500–4,999	44	31	75
5,000+	20	4	24
Total	531	620	1,151

Note: For counties, $\chi^2 = 73.4$; for age, $\chi^2 = 54.9$; for ownership, $\chi^2 = 38.9$; for pay, $\chi^2 = 51.5$. In all cases in tables 13-2 through 13-5, the probability that the distributions are random is less than 0.1 percent.

highest proportion in the sample, opted for the latter. Probably because many Nanhai workers are not tied to their firms, there are far stronger pressures to distribute profits to the work force. Fifty-seven percent considered this to be the best use of profits, compared with only 27 percent in the entire sample.

Young female workers are usually the lowest paid. This contributes to a pattern whereby the lowest-income workers are freely recruited whereas the highest-income workers tend to be allocated to their firms (table 13-2). In fact, the few college graduates in the sample are the workers most likely to want to leave their firms; 44 percent indicate a desire to leave compared with only 8 percent for the sample as a whole. The other category of workers who wish to leave are the low-paid or those who consider their pay low in relation to the local average. The desire to leave is also related to perceptions of management (table 13-3), especially in Shangrao, where 33 percent consider the management to be poor and 22 percent desire to leave their firms.

Table 13-3. *Management and Desire to Leave the Firm*
(number of workers)

Workers' opinion of management	Desire to leave?		
	Yes	No	Total
Very good	8	167	175
Relatively good	45	761	806
Not very good	31	108	139
Very poor	12	11	23
Total	96	1,047	1,143

Note: $\chi^2 = 103.8$.

Income Distribution

The size distribution of annual pay is shown in table 13-4, by county and by type of firm ownership. In the analysis, ownership variables were repre-sented in three ways: on a 2-point scale (public and private), on a 4-point scale (township and town; village and production team; joint, family, and individual; and joint venture with government or foreign entities), and on an 8-point scale in which all the above segments are separate items. The 4-point scale is used in table 13-4. It is apparent that Nanhai has the widest range of pay dispersion and that incomes in Wuxi are more tightly concen-trated, with smaller lower and upper tails. Incomes in Jieshou and Shangrao cluster at the lower ends of the distributions.[9] The table suggests that the widest dispersion of income levels is in the firms owned by "small" (village and production team) community governments.[10] This is not mainly be-cause of wider differentials within such firms but rather because differences in the fortunes of smaller communities permit a greater range of variation in pay levels among firms.

The apparently concentrated income distribution of private enterprises may reflect inaccurate reporting of incomes at the upper end or noninclusion of proprietors in the sample. Workers in private enterprises seem not to be unduly concerned over wide differentials, and the proportion of workers who believe that differentials should be wider is the highest in the sample, at 26 percent. (Most workers in private firms believe that differentials are about right.) Only 8 percent of Shangrao workers favor wider differentials, despite the absence of a marked upper tail in that county.

Workers' Attitudes

Workers in private enterprises and, among the counties, in Jieshou seem to be content—to an almost suspicious extent. Only 11 percent of Jieshou workers agree with the proposition that TVP workers have lower status than those in state enterprises, as against 41 percent in Shangrao, 21 percent in

Table 13-4. *Dispersion of Income in Sample Firms*
(number of workers)

	Annual income (yuan)					
Item	Less than 625	625– 1,249	1,250– 2,499	2,500– 4,999	5,000+	Total
By county						
Wuxi	47	178	210	36	2	473
Jieshou	90	176	28	3	0	297
Nanhai	43	77	81	36	21	258
Shangrao	84	55	4	0	1	144
Total	264	486	323	75	24	1,172
By ownership						
Township and town	126	241	234	47	1	649
Village and production team	33	51	22	17	21	144
Private	42	86	14	3	0	145
Other	63	108	53	8	2	234
Total	264	486	323	75	24	1,172

Note: For counties, $\chi^2 = 379.2$; for ownership, $\chi^2 = 209.1$.

Wuxi, and 25 percent in Nanhai. Only 3 percent of Jieshou workers are not satisfied, compared with 20 percent in the whole sample, and only 3 percent would like to leave their firms. If anything, Jieshou workers see a lower probability of losing their jobs than other workers. They are more inclined to buy shares in their firms; 23 percent would buy "a lot," whereas 47 percent of Shangrao workers would not buy any stocks. (Given the problematic situation of many of Shangrao's TVPs, this may reflect simple prudence.) Jieshou workers are also far more likely to use surplus funds to buy producer goods and to set up their own firms; since there is a high proportion of private enterprises in Jieshou, the same finding probably holds for workers in private enterprises. There is therefore some evidence that private entrepreneurship is ready to flourish in areas where it is encouraged.

Finally, it is interesting to note the absence of a marked generation gap in workers' responses. Substantial age-related differences in attitudinal variables might be expected in a similar survey carried out in a Western country. The reason for the absence of a gap and also for the favorable labor relations climate may be that virtually all of the TVP sector's work force consists of first-generation industrial workers.

Private versus Public Firms

Some of the most important differences between private and community enterprises have already been noted. Not all go in the directions one might expect. Although there are many statistically significant differences between the responses of workers in public and in private firms, the degree of difference is usually small, so the explanatory power of the public-private distinction is limited. Private enterprises are smaller and less advanced, as is shown, for example, in their narrower range of occupational groups; 72 percent of respondents in private firms, but only 58 percent in community enterprises, are workers rather than technical and managerial personnel. Private enterprises employ a higher percentage of women and pay less than community enterprises (although this is a "county," or locational, effect; see below). They also operate in freer labor markets.

Private enterprises do not diverge from community enterprises in the ways suggested by the Taylorist model, however. Pay distribution does not seem to be less equal than in community enterprises, and responses by workers in private enterprises suggest at least similar, if not greater, enthusiasm for their firms. There are no significant differences between community and private enterprises regarding the degree to which workers have decisionmaking power in the areas mentioned earlier.

There is also no significant difference in average profitability between the community and private enterprises in the workers' survey. The dispersion of profitability is larger for community enterprises; table 13-5 shows that no workers were in private enterprises that were extremely profitable or declared losses. The reason may simply be that there are fewer private firms or that they underreport their profits. But it is also true that private firms, unlike community enterprises, cannot turn to local governments for help when they make losses and that the tighter technical and financial constraints placed on them limit their chances of making especially high profits. Workers in private enterprises feel somewhat less well-off in relation to their communities than do those in community enterprises.

Wage Equations

The variables that determine the pay of TVP workers may be grouped into several classes. *County variables* represent the stage of development of the locality; counties are represented by dummies with Wuxi as the base. *Ownership*

Table 13-5. *Distribution of Workers by Firm Ownership and Profitability*
(number of workers)

Ownership	Profitability (profits ÷ sales) (percent)					
	<0	<10	<20	<30	>30	Total
Government	37	259	310	164	90	860
Private	0	20	62	19	0	101
Total	37	279	372	183	90	961

Note: $\chi^2 = 54.9$

variables are measured, as described above, on a 2-point, 4-point, or 8-point scale. *Firm dummies*, forty-eight in number, distinguish among workers in different enterprises and are intended to pick up systematic effects not captured by the intersection of county and ownership type—for example, a large village firm in a prosperous community. They are a proxy for communal variables, since most firms are identified with smaller or larger communities. The *characteristics of the firm* are its size (as measured by number of workers) and its profitability (the profit-sales ratio).[11]

Individual variables are age, sex, number of days worked (from data on days per week and months per year), occupation, and education. Occupation is represented by seven dummies—shift or group leader, operations personnel, technical personnel, ordinary staff, middle-level staff, apprentice, and driver—with worker as the base. Education is represented by six dummies— no school, four-year primary school, six-year primary school, senior middle school, college, and technical and vocational school or vocational college— with the most common category, junior middle school, as the base. An experience variable (age − 15) and its square were substituted for age in some regressions to permit the familiar inverted-U pattern to emerge.

The dependent variable, annual income, was specified in three ways: in five ranges, in nominal value, and in logarithmic form. The results are broadly similar for all specifications. To help interpretation, results are reported for log income so that coefficients of unit dummies may be interpreted as percentage shifts in income.

Five statistical models are shown in table 13-6.[12] Model 1 uses only county dummies. The correlation coefficient ($\bar{R}^2$), adjusted for degrees of freedom, is only 0.30. Incomes are higher in Nanhai than in Wuxi by 29 percent, but they are lower in Jieshou by 55 percent and in Shangrao by 70 percent.

Model 2 adds occupational dummies. These all have sensible signs. They suggest that more skilled staff are paid 20–45 percent more than a worker and that apprentices get 32 percent less. Although these variables are mostly significant, the explanatory power of occupation is small.

Adding the simple private ownership–community ownership distinction to the county dummies makes little difference. Although workers in private enterprises do earn less than those in community enterprises, this is mainly a county effect. Adding the 4-point ownership distinction is not much better. Model 3 combines the county dummies, the most detailed (8-point) ownership specification, firm size and profitability, occupation, age, sex, and number of days worked. The explanatory power rises to 0.52, and pay relates positively to firm size, age, days worked, and the profitability of the firm (confirming the link asserted by sample workers). An increase of 10 percentage points in the ratio of profits to sales is associated with a 5 percent increase in the level of TVP pay. Women's pay is 14 percent lower when other variables are held constant. The sizes of the county and occupational dummy coeffi-

Table 13-6. *Wage Equations*

	Model				
Dummy	1	2	3	4	5
County					
Jieshou	−0.55	−0.47	−0.23		
	(11.9)	(−12.4)	(−4.3)		
Nanhai	0.29	0.14	0.22		
	(5.8)	(3.2)	(5.8)		
Shangrao	−0.70	−0.71	−0.37		
	(−12.1)	(−13.8)	(−5.6)		
Ownership					
D1			−0.03		
			(−0.8)		
D2			0.15		
			(3.3)		
D3			0.04		
			(0.5)		
D4			0.18		
			(2.5)		
D5			0.23		
			(3.3)		
D6			−0.19		
			(−1.4)		
D7			(0.29)		
			(2.8)		
Firm					
Work force			0.06		
			(2.1)		
Profitability			0.05		
			(3.5)		
Occupation					
Shift or group leader		0.19	0.08		0.11
		(3.5)	(1.7)		(2.7)
Operations personnel		0.25	0.10		0.20
		(3.8)	(1.7)		(4.1)
Technical personnel		0.33	0.16		0.18
		(5.6)	(3.1)		(4.0)
Ordinary staff		0.26	0.10		0.10
		(4.1)	(1.7)		(2.2)
Middle-level staff		0.45	0.28		0.30
		(7.1)	(5.1)		(6.3)
Apprentice		−0.32	−0.10		−0.26
		(−2.4)	(−0.9)		(−2.9)
Driver		0.74	0.42		0.49
		(1.5)	(1.0)		(1.3)

(*Table continues on the following page*)

Table 13-6 (continued)

| Dummy | Model | | | | |
	1	2	3	4	5
Age			0.01		0.01
			(7.0)		(4.8)
Sex			−0.14		−0.14
			(−5.0)		(−5.7)
Days worked			0.02		0.01
			(14.2)		(13.0)
R^2	0.30	0.34	0.52	0.57	0.70

Note: Figures in parentheses are t-statistics. Blanks are not applicable. The 8-point scale described in the text is used for the ownership dummies; joint venture is the base. The base for occupation is worker.

cients are considerably reduced, which suggests that the earlier estimates were correcting for other variables.

Data on incomes in the communities of which these firms are part are not available, but it was argued above that TVPs might be considered broadly representative of their communities and that in some cases the firm itself has some status as a community. Model 4 simply consists of the forty-eight firm dummies, which alone have higher explanatory power than model 3. Model 5 adds to the firm dummies the individual variables of model 3. By the standards of cross-section regressions, explanatory power is high, with a correlation coefficient, adjusted for degrees of freedom, of 0.70. The pattern of individual coefficients is fairly stable, with somewhat higher occupational coefficients than in model 3.

The substitution of experience and its square for age produced the familiar inverted-U relationship whereby the rate at which income rises with age declines as age increases. The effect of adding the education dummy coefficients was more surprising. Most of the dummies are small and not significant, but those that are significant suggest that people with some college receive lower pay than would be expected on the basis of firm, sex, age, and occupation. This pattern is most unusual. [13]

These results suggest that a large part of the dispersion of earnings in the TVP sector can be explained on the basis of communal and personal characteristics. But they also indicate that communal characteristics are more powerful, especially near the tails of the income distribution. The reason seems to be that the community is a powerful reference point for the acceptable level of pay in the firm, and so the association between pay and relative income status in the community is weak, as noted earlier.

Consider, for example, the highest-paying firm in the sample, a large and successful ceramics factory owned by a small village in Nanhai. Workers in this factory receive about Y5,000 a year; pay of the manager (and of village leaders) is believed to be about Y15,000. Such pay levels are acceptable only because the factory, in effect, is the community; it employs most of the working population, and it distributes 40 percent of its net income to the village for communal projects, subsidies, pensions, and education. Moreover, the survey data suggest that this firm has an unusually small dispersion of pay.

It might be expected that dispersion within firms would relate systematically to pay levels or would differ among counties. Measures of pay dispersion within firms, however, have no significant association with average pay in firms, and there is no significant relationship among counties. Any differences in income dispersion among counties probably have more to do with the power of small as against large government units and with the degree of homogeneity of the area. Regressions were also run with a dummy that separated community insiders and outsiders. This showed only an insignificant effect on pay when firm and other personal variables were included.

Finally, we are left with the question of what determines the degree of dispersion of average pay among firms. The regressions indicate that county, size, and profitability make some contribution. These are static variables, however, whereas sizable pay dispersion plausibly reflects dynamic features, notably slow adjustment of the labor market in relation to different speeds of economic development. In a broad sense, such a relationship is observable in the higher incomes in Wuxi and Nanhai, which have developed more rapidly in comparison with Jieshou and Shangrao. But does it hold on a firm-by-firm basis? Or do the highest-paying firms seem to be stagnating owing to their need to pay high wages?

Investigation of this question is not straightforward because data for many firms are not sufficiently complete to allow dynamic comparisons over a number of years. Therefore, to ensure maximum dispersion, firms were ranked in order of decreasing average pay. Those for which there was enough data to calculate growth rates for labor force and current-price industrial output at least for 1981–85 and preferably for 1980–85 were identified, and the highest five and lowest five of these were chosen. In the top five firms the average growth rates were 27 percent for labor force and 77 percent for output; for the lowest five the rates were 21 percent for labor force and 44 percent for output. This supports the proposition that the higher-paying firms are more dynamic and are characterized by a higher rate of growth of output per worker than the lower-paying ones.

These averages, however, are strongly influenced by two firms, one in the lowest five and one in the top five, which began from small bases and therefore have very high average growth rates. Regressions were also carried out between the rankings of the ten firms by pay and their rankings by labor growth, output growth, and growth of output per worker. Coefficients and *t*-values were as follows.

Regression	Coefficient	t-value	$\bar{R}^2$
Pay rank with:			
Labor force growth	0.54	1.80	0.29
Industrial output value	0.60	2.14	0.36
Output value per worker	0.50	2.03	0.35

These results provide considerable support for the proposition that large pay differentials among firms arise from the "pull" effect of labor productivity gains (or favorable price trends) in the more dynamic firms that also have increased their labor forces somewhat more rapidly.

Conclusions

This chapter has set forth a number of hypotheses on the nature of ownership and labor relations in the Chinese TVP sector. Although it is only a first look at the data, it does suggest a number of interesting points. In broad terms TVPs appear far closer to the communal or Z-firm model than to the other models. This implies that there are few really outstanding differences between community and private enterprises once account is taken of the different levels of development of the counties where the respective types dominate.

Why should this be so? The reason is probably the close relationship with local communities needed if private enterprises are to obtain permission to go into business and to secure land, bank loans, and so on, as well as the still fragile nature of private property rights. Interviews confirm that private proprietors do not really act as though they had exclusive claim to their firms' equity. Some seek to recover their investments rapidly, leaving the firm in a fuzzy ownership position. Some may see advantages in then changing the firm's registration from private to community enterprise or may be powerless in the face of a decision by the local government to change its ownership.

The work force seems to be relatively content, although workers have little say in running their firms. Workers perceive a strong link between pay and performance, both of the individual (piece rates are more common than time rates) and of the firm. This helps to induce a positive attitude toward the firm and some concern for its profitability. The link between profitability and pay has a short-run dimension, through bonuses and other benefits. But the long-run dimension may be more important because the average pay of a firm relates to its dynamism and to growth of output per worker, and where there is little intercommunity mobility workers can expect long-term employment in their firms. TVP workers therefore have substantial de facto equity stakes in their firms. This, together with the limited alternative investment options available, may explain their stated preference that profits be reinvested. An issue for policymakers is how and to what extent such an implicit equity stake should be formalized. Workers' attitudes may be influenced by the newness of the TVP sector and the fact that almost all workers were previously farmers.

How attitudes and labor relations will evolve as the TVP sector matures is an important question.

Wage equations confirm the explanatory power of firm variables as against individual variables, although the patterns of most of the latter are as expected. The relationship of pay to age is progressive and of the inverted-U shape. Females earn 14 percent less than males. Technical and management personnel earn 10–30 percent more than workers, and apprentices earn 26 percent less. Educational level does not seem to be a significant factor in earnings, and when it is significant, its direction is the opposite of that expected. Zero or even negative differentials at higher educational levels may be common in China, but they are unusual elsewhere. This is a subject for further research.

These patterns are of course not uniform, and the survey reveals too many cross-county differences to be easily summarized here. One notable difference is the much freer labor market in Nanhai than in Wuxi, which leads to a larger proportion of workers with short time horizons, to more pressures for the distribution of surplus to the work force, and perhaps to a two-tier labor force structure. The survey results should be further analyzed to extract the implications for China of different TVP development patterns.

Notes

1. In four cases responses on pay were unrealistic; annual incomes far higher than twelve times the greatest monthly income were declared, or income was stated as zero. These cases were modified in line with information on the highest and lowest monthly incomes and months worked.

2. In Wuxi the examination method is based on work force allocations to enterprises by community governments; only the choice of which specific workers to take is left to the examinations. "Voluntary" choice of firms by workers hence does not necessarily mean that firms can choose the number of workers.

3. The explanatory variables tried include county dummies, firm dummies by eight ownership types, firm size, and occupational dummies. In comparison with Wuxi, the perceived link between profits and pay is stronger in Jieshou and weaker in the other two counties. It is stronger in larger firms and greater for the other occupational categories than for workers, except in the case of apprentices. But although many of these variables are significant, the $\bar{R}^2$ (adjusted for degrees of freedom) is only 0.10.

4. Regressions suggest a significantly stronger reaction in Jieshou and from supervisory personnel. But the $\bar{R}^2$ is only 0.12.

5. TVP workers do, in fact, frequently participate in financing their firms, through purchasing bonds with a term of one to two years or through the withholding of part of their pay until year's end for use as working capital. The extent to which these contributions represent equity rather than debt (in the sense that bank debts have a preferred claim on firm assets) is not clear; it probably varies with each case and is often ill-defined.

6. A chi-squared test indicates departure from nonrandomness at the 2 percent level in the relationship between pay and relative income, but this does not seem to reflect a systematic progression with pay. Workers were also divided into two groups: those belonging to the five top-paying firms (as measured by the mean pay of the workers in the firm) and others. Those in the top-paying firms did not consider themselves much better-off, in comparison with their communities, than other workers.

7. In all but one of the decisionmaking areas, responses in Shangrao indicate greater worker involvement than in the other counties. In some Shangrao firms election of leaders by workers seems to have been introduced to counter the tendency of local government to make poor appointments out of political considerations (see chapter 17). Interviews with local officials indicated that they considered such elected leaders to have greater legitimacy in their firms than appointed leaders.

8. Thirty percent of Nanhai workers indicate that they were in another township, county, or province before joining their present firms. The prominence of workers from outside the community raises the question of whether there is a two-tier labor market, especially in the richer areas. In such a market, "outsiders" would be paid their reservation wage, and "insiders" would share in the surplus generated within the community. This question will be considered in the regressions below.

9. The coefficient of variation (ratio of standard deviation to mean) of pay is 0.49 in Wuxi and 0.70 in Nanhai. Workers in Wuxi and Nanhai usually work full time, whereas those in Jieshou and Shangrao are more likely to have worked for less than twelve months. This could increase the dispersion in the latter two counties at the lower end.

10. For township firms the coefficient of variation of income is 0.55, for village firms it is 0.80, and for private enterprises it is 0.55.

11. The preferred measure of profits to assets was not used because of concern about the quality of capital stock information.

12. Regressions are all by ordinary least squares, which is not appropriate unless explanatory variables are exogenous. This could be questioned for some variables. In particular, since payments to labor affect profitability, the coefficient of this variable may be biased and is probably less significant than it should be. Occupation might also be considered endogenous, as is the choice of firm for at least some workers.

13. The reason may be interaction effects between education and other variables, but the pattern of coefficients seems to be fairly stable. In most developing countries, education relates strongly to pay (see Knight and Sabot forthcoming). Human capital has been estimated to account for half of the difference in income between high- and low-income countries (Krueger 1968). Only four of the sampled workers had no formal education.

14

The Rural Labor Market

Meng Xin

China is known for its large labor force. According to the theoretical model of Lewis (1954) on economic development under a dual-structure economy, an inexhaustible supply of labor is a resource advantage that can check the rise of the wage level and boost accumulation in the process of national economic development. The validity of the theory, however, depends on the precondition that a labor market already exists. For a long time China restrained the development of the commodity economy and the formation of a labor market, which meant that there was virtually no flow of labor between urban and rural areas and between the industrial and agricultural sectors. The Lewis theory naturally cannot be applied under such circumstances.

After the introduction of the production responsibility system (PRS) in agriculture and of price reforms, and in reaction to the separation between urban and rural areas, rural industrialization got fully under way. As a result, industrial and agricultural sectors have come into being within China's rural economy. Has a labor market emerged in the course of rural industrialization? To what extent has the market developed? And what effects does it have on rural industrialization? This chapter will describe, compare, and analyze the formation and development of the labor market in the process of the development of the TVP sector, as well as the effects of the newly formed labor market on TVPs.

Reynolds (1982) defines the purely competitive labor market as follows.

- There is full freedom of occupational choice. This implies, among other things, that a young person choosing an occupation that requires training can always obtain the necessary funds.
- There is full freedom of exchange. Any employer may hire any worker, and any worker may work for any employer.
- There are many employers and many workers in the market, so that no one actor can influence the market price.
- There is no collusion on either side of the market. Employers do not

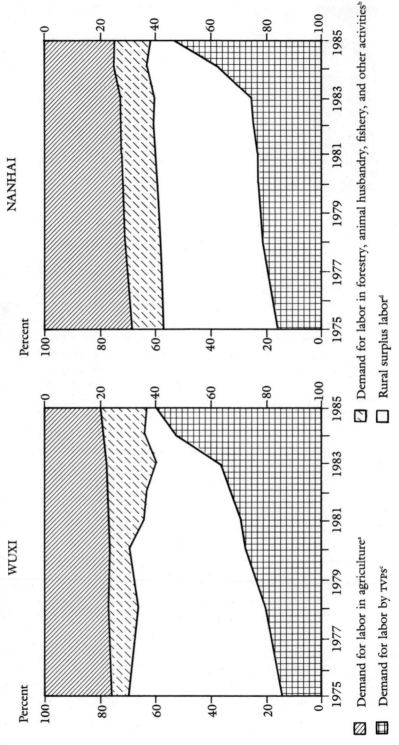

Figure 14-1. *Changes in Labor Supply and Demand for TVPs in the Four Sample Counties, 1975–85*

WUXI

NANHAI

Percent

Percent

☒ Demand for labor in agriculture[a]

▨ Demand for labor in forestry, animal husbandry, fishery, and other activities[b]

▦ Demand for labor by TVPs[c]

☐ Rural surplus labor[d]

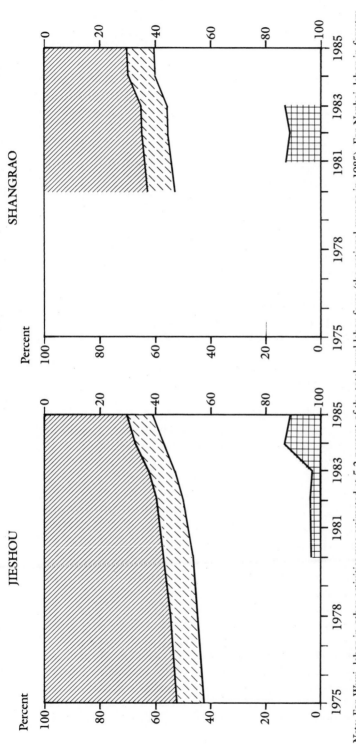

Note: For Wuxi, labor in other activities was estimated at 5.2 percent of the total rural labor force (the national average in 1985). For Nanhai, labor in forestry, animal husbandry, and fishery was estimated at 7 percent of the total rural labor force and labor in other activities at 5.2 percent. For Jieshou, labor in forestry, animal husbandry, and fishery was estimated at 5.0 percent of the total rural labor force and labor in other activities at 5.2 percent. For Shangrao, labor in forestry, animal husbandry, and fishery was estimated at 5.0 percent of the total rural labor force and labor in other activities at 5.2 percent.

a. See Appendix for method of calculation.   b. Actual use of labor.   Other activities include science, education, culture, public health, and government.

c. Actual employment.   d. Difference between total rural labor force and the three sources of labor demand.

Sources: Appendix and information from fieldwork.

301

unite to drive down the wage level, nor do workers unionize to drive up wages.

This definition is taken as the "perfect state" of the labor market as we examine the development of labor markets in the four counties. This means not that the purely competitive labor market is an ideal state but rather that it is the standard for analysis.

Most TVP workers come from rural areas. China's agricultural sector has large potential surplus labor, which determines the supply of labor to TVPs. The actual number of workers absorbed by TVPs indicates the demand in the labor market. Thus the labor market is viewed as being in varying degrees of disequilibrium, with the short side of the market (labor demand) determining the actual amount of labor in the TVP sector.

Figure 14-1 shows changes in the labor supply and demand in the TVP sectors of the four counties in 1975–85 under the assumption that there is local segmentation in labor markets (see the appendix to this chapter for details on the method of calculation of labor supply to TVPs). From the figure it is clear that in Nanhai and Wuxi labor supply can hardly meet the demand of TVPs, whereas in Shangrao and Jieshou labor supply still greatly exceeds the demand. This should always be kept in mind during the following discussion.

Labor Flows among TVPs

There are three types of rural labor flows: interregional, among provinces and counties; intercommunity, among villages and townships in the same county; and intracommunity, among firms in the same community.

Actual Labor Flows

Actual labor flows can be examined from three points of view: the origins of an enterprise's employees and the relative shares of permanent, casual, and seasonal laborers; a firm's ways of employing and dismissing laborers; and redundancy of personnel in an enterprise. Table 14-1 shows the family homes of employees in sample enterprises in the four counties and table 14-2 the proportions of permanent, casual, and seasonal laborers. There is a big difference between sample firms in Nanhai and in the other three counties. In Nanhai 51 percent of employees come from local communities, 85 percent from within the county, and 15 percent from other counties and provinces. In the other three counties the bulk of employees come from local communities, more than 90 percent come from within the county, and only a handful are from other counties or provinces. These figures indicate that at present the bulk of labor in China's TVPs comes from farmers in local communities. Except in Nanhai, intercommunity and interregional flows of labor are weak.

Table 14-1. *Original Homes of Employees in Sample Enterprises*
(percent)

County and type of worker	Same township (village)	Other townships (villages) in county	Other counties in province	Other provinces
Wuxi				
All employees	94.0	3.0	1.6	1.4
Workers	94.2	3.5	1.7	0.7
Technicians	78.6	1.4	5.3	14.6
Managerial staff	93.1	0.6	0.5	5.9
Jieshou				
All employees	79.7	12.7	4.8	2.8
Workers	80.6	12.1	5.2	2.7
Technicians	65.9	18.3	2.4	13.4
Managerial staff	78.1	16.5	2.3	3.2
Nanhai				
All employees	50.9	33.8	14.2	1.1
Workers	47.7	35.0	16.0	1.3
Technicians	85.1	3.0	10.9	1.0
Managerial staff	53.5	39.7	5.6	1.2
Shangrao				
All employees	80.9	14.8	2.1	2.2
Workers	83.6	11.4	1.9	2.7
Technicians	68.5	5.6	5.6	20.3
Managerial staff	73.9	18.5	1.7	5.9

Source: Enterprise Quantitative Questionnaire.

The proportions of permanent and casual laborers can shed further light on the volume of labor flows. These figures also show much greater mobility in Nanhai than in the other three counties. The data below, however, show that great shifts have taken place in recent years in the relative shares of permanent and casual laborers in Nanhai, indicating that the employment system in that county has undergone remarkable changes.

	1980	1981	1982	1983	1984	1985
Percentage of						
Permanent workers	91.8	87.9	86.3	76.1	48.3	40.2
Casual workers	8.2	12.1	13.7	23.9	51.2	59.8

The methods of recruiting and dismissing workers in sample firms are illuminated by responses to the Enterprise Survey Questionnaire and the Worker Survey Questionnaire. The latter asked workers how they came into their present employment (see table 14-3). Job assignment by township or village government was cited by 57 percent of sample employees in Wuxi, 44 percent in Shangrao, 38 percent in Nanhai, and 16 percent in Jieshou. Responses to the Enterprise Survey Questionnaire point to a similar conclusion: com-

Table 14-2. *Permanent, Casual, and Seasonal Workers in Sample Enterprises*
(percent)

County	Permanent workers	Casual workers	Seasonal workers
Wuxi	91.2	8.5	0.3
Jieshou	75.8	18.1	6.2
Nanhai	40.2	59.8	0.0
Shangrao	78.7	19.1	2.2

Source: Enterprise Quantitative Questionnaire.

munity government assignment constitutes the most important form of recruitment in Wuxi, whereas enterprises in the other three counties rely mainly on direct recruitment.

The Enterprise Director Questionnaire contains two relevant questions: "As the director of the factory, do you have the right to dismiss your employees?" and "In the past year, how many workers have you fired? For what reasons?" Enterprises whose directors have the power to dismiss employees accounted for 97 percent of the sample in Jieshou, 82 percent in Wuxi, 73 percent in Nanhai, and 68 percent in Shangrao. The average number of workers dismissed by each sample firm in the previous year stood at 0.87 in Nanhai, 0.75 in Jieshou, 0.67 in Wuxi, and 0.15 in Shangrao. Although nearly all directors in Wuxi thought that they had the power to dismiss workers, the actual number of workers fired was relatively small. Some community governments in Wuxi have issued regulations that ban enterprises from dismissing employees until they find new jobs and require that each dismissal be approved by the community government. The primary reason for dismissal given in all four counties was violation of labor regulations. Overall, sample enterprises in Jieshou and Nanhai seem to have relatively more freedom and those in Wuxi and Shangrao less freedom in employing and dismissing workers.

The presence of redundant personnel means that the enterprise has little decisionmaking power over its employment level. In addition, it is evidence from another angle of the absence of a free flow of labor. During fieldwork we saw obvious examples of redundancy in Wuxi and Shangrao. The director of the Xuelang Township Special-Shaped Steel Rolling Mill in Wuxi told us that in 1983 the mill set up a meter production workshop and employed seventy-eight workers (mostly women) under a land requisition contract. Later the workshop was closed because its products did not sell very well on the market, but the mill had to keep the workers who had been recruited for the workshop, since their employment was included in the land contract. The director told us that his mill could sack at least fifty workers, or 10 percent of the total, without affecting normal production. The director of the Luqu Township Food Products Factory, also in Wuxi, said that his factory

Table 14-3. How Employees Got Their Jobs in Sample Enterprises
(percent)

Method	Wuxi	Jieshou	Nanhai	Shangrao
Assigned by township or village government	56.8	15.5	38.0	44.4
Examination	15.8	30.7	3.9	2.8
Application	9.2	12.5	15.7	20.8
Contribution of funds	0.9	12.8	1.2	9.7
Recommendation	16.0	28.0	41.2	22.2
Other	0.6	0.3	0.0	0.0

Source: Worker Survey Questionnaire.

could cut employment by fifty to sixty workers (25–30 percent of the total) without affecting total value of output, but township government regulations barred it from dismissing any employees. The director of the Dongjiang Township Oil Production Equipment Factory in Wuxi told us that in 1985 the number of employees in his factory doubled from the previous year, not to meet production needs but because of pressures from the township government to increase employment and obligations resulting from land acquisition contracts. The Lingxi Township Hydropower Station in Shangrao reported that its redundant personnel accounted for about 60 percent of total employment. And the director of the Lingxi Township Fiberglass Plant believed that about half of the plant's employees were redundant. Personnel redundancy in Wuxi and Shangrao is related to township governments' interference in worker recruitment and dismissal. The problem was almost unheard of in Nanhai and Jieshou.

The above discussion has given us a picture of labor flows at three different levels in the four counties. The general impression is that whether labor is in short supply (as in Wuxi and Nanhai) or in surplus (as in Shangrao and Jieshou), interregional flows are weak but that the situation in Nanhai is better than in the other counties. Nanhai has much greater intercommunity and intracommunity labor flows than does Wuxi, and Jieshou has more than Shangrao.

Factors That Affect Labor Flows

In a commodity economy the supply and demand situation for labor strongly affects labor flows. In general, when the supply of labor is greater than the demand, the mobility of the labor force is small, but the contrary is true when demand is greater than supply. When labor is plentiful, the availability of cheap local labor makes it unnecessary for enterprises to recruit workers from other regions, and low wages and limited employment opportunities discourage laborers in other regions from coming to seek jobs. But when labor is in short supply, enterprises vie for workers by paying higher wages, and this attracts labor from elsewhere as well. It should be stressed that when there is a labor surplus, the diminished actual flow of labor does not mean a reduction in workers' freedom to choose their professions or in enterprises' freedom to choose laborers.

An analysis of labor flows in the four counties in accordance with the above-mentioned logic revealed various distortions. For instance, in Wuxi, where labor is in short supply, labor flows at the three levels are not only much smaller than in Nanhai, where the supply and demand situation is similar, but also smaller than in the other two counties, which have large numbers of surplus laborers. In fact, there was little tangible labor flow in Wuxi. Also, although the makeup of the places of origin of employees was basically the same in Jieshou and Shangrao, workers and firms in Shangrao had much less freedom in choosing each other than in Jieshou. How could such irrational situations arise? Supply and demand are clearly not the only factors that affect the flow of labor. To provide an explanation, we must introduce systemic variables.

Lower labor mobility in Wuxi than in Nanhai is directly related to differences in the ownership structure of TVPs. In Wuxi TVPs are dominated by TVCEs, whereas in Nanhai TVCEs account for only 30 percent of the total. Moreover, since TVCEs employ only about 60 percent of the total number of workers in Nanhai's TVP sector and 50 percent of these are casual workers, only 30 percent of the labor force is directly controlled by community governments. As community governments are inclined to restrain the flow of labor, the difference in ownership structure leads to differences in labor mobility. We will now discuss why community governments would want to restrain the inflow and outflow of labor.

RESTRAINING INFLOWS OF LABOR FROM OTHER AREAS. Since a community government is both the owner of local TVCEs and the community administrator, its goals are not only to develop its firms but also to increase local employment, local residents' income levels, and community revenues. The development of TVCEs is expected to serve these multiple social and economic goals, and the fundamental reason that communities restrain inflows of labor is that these inflows clash with their employment and income objectives.

At different stages of economic development the community government has different purposes in promoting TVPs. When there is a large labor surplus in the community, the goal is to expand community employment to its maximum; when all local surplus labor has been absorbed, the purpose becomes mainly to increase per capita incomes. (The revenue objective is always present.) Under both circumstances the community government tries to restrain the inflow of labor from other regions: in the former case labor inflows would reduce employment opportunities for local community members, and in the latter they would reduce the community's average per capita income.

RESTRAINING OUTFLOWS AND INTRACOMMUNITY FLOWS OF LABOR. Community governments in both Wuxi and Nanhai have issued regulations to restrain outflows and intracommunity flows of labor. For example, the flow of labor between enterprises must be approved by the township government; a fine of Y500–Y2,000 is imposed on anyone who goes to seek a job outside the community; and those who leave the community to find jobs outside face noneconomic punitive measures, such as denial of family members' right to a job assignment from the community government and higher tuitions for schoolchildren. Where there are labor shortages, these restraints help ensure the stable development of local firms.

The forces that restrict labor flows are basically the same in both Wuxi and Nanhai, but in Wuxi more than 90 percent of TVPs and their employees are controlled by community governments, whereas the figure for Nanhai is only about 30 percent. Thus in Nanhai community governments are unable to control the inflow of labor from other regions, and they can hardly stop the intracommunity flow because gaps among enterprises' wage levels are large and the benefits from taking another job can easily offset losses from punitive measures, such as fines, imposed by community governments.

The greater freedom of choice for both workers and firms in Jieshou than in Shangrao is also related to the difference in the two counties' ownership structures. TVCEs account for 64 percent of total sample enterprises in Jieshou and for 97 percent in Shangrao. As the TVCEs' owner, the community government has indisputable control over their labor forces, so where there are more TVCEs, laborers have less freedom to choose their professions and firms have less freedom to choose their employees.

Of course, the mobility of labor is not determined only by the supply and demand situation and the structure of ownership. To a certain extent it is also related to the dissemination of information and to social and cultural traditions.

Nanhai's local labor shortage and high wage levels, among other factors, make it highly attractive to laborers from other rural areas, and communities in Nanhai are unable to check the inflow of labor from other regions. Nevertheless, workers from other provinces and counties account for only 15.3 percent of total sample employees. The only reasonable explanations for this phenomenon are that many farmers in backward areas cannot get information about the labor market, that farmers are still under the traditional psychological influence of strong links to their hometown and land, and that the current household registration system hampers interregional flows of labor.

Wage Determination for TVP Employees

This section describes wage levels and differences in the four counties, the effect on wages of labor supply and demand in general and of supply and demand conditions for labor of different qualities, the effect of systemic variables on wages in Wuxi, and the reasons behind wage increases in Nanhai.

Wage Levels and Differences

Figure 14-2 shows average wage incomes in sample enterprises in the four counties during 1975–85. There is an evident gap between wage levels in Nanhai and Wuxi and in Shangrao and Jieshou, and there is a tendency for the gap to become wider. In 1985 the average monthly income in sample firms in Nanhai reached Y182, 73 percent higher than Wuxi's figure of Y105, which in turn was 67 percent more than the average in Jieshou, Y63. The average for Shangrao was Y59, about the same as for Jieshou. During 1980–

Figure 14-2. *Average Per Capita Monthly Incomes in Sample Firms, 1975–85*

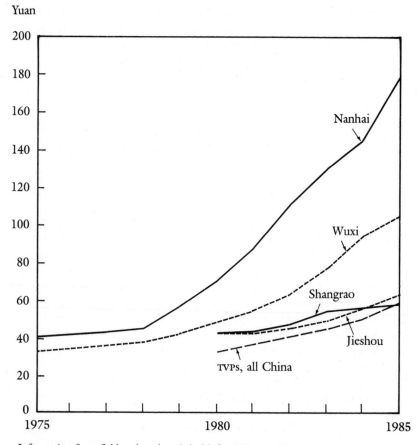

Yuan

Sources: Information from fieldwork and statistical information on China's TVPs.

85 the annual growth rate of average income in sample firms was 21 percent in Nanhai, 17 percent in Wuxi, 8 percent in Jieshou, and 6 percent in Shangrao.

Although wages in areas suffering from labor shortages are much higher than in areas with labor surpluses, absolute wages and the growth rate of wages are far higher in Nanhai than in Wuxi despite similarities in the two counties' labor supply and demand and the greater mobility of labor in Nanhai. We explain this phenomenon in a later section.

WAGE DIFFERENCES AMONG COMMUNITIES. Since the samples in each county are too limited to explain differences among townships, we base our analysis on statistics on TVPs provided by each county.[1] The data indicate that in 1985 the variance of average per capita pay (as a ratio to the mean) was 0.03 in Wuxi, 0.14 in Nanhai, 1.61 in Shangrao, and 0.005 in Jieshou.

WAGE DIFFERENCES AMONG ENTERPRISES WITHIN COMMUNITIES. We selected for analysis TVCEs in Wuxi's Dongjiang township, various types of enterprises in Jieshou town, and township enterprises in Nanhai's Yanbu district.[2] The variance of average pay in different enterprises was 0.12 in Dongjiang township, 0.12 in Jieshou town, and 0.27 in Yanbu district. Thus wage differences both among and within communities are large in Nanhai; wage differences at the intercommunity level are rather large in Shangrao; and wage differences at both levels are small in Wuxi and Jieshou.

The Effect of Labor Supply and Demand

In a competitive labor market the wage level is determined by supply and demand, and the price of labor equals the marginal product of labor. According to Lewis, when there is an inexhaustible supply of labor, the wage level of workers in the industrial sector should be a little higher than that of rural laborers so that the industrial sector can attract labor from the agricultural sector, but the differential does not need to be large. When labor is in short supply, the industrial sector has to pay much higher wages than the agricultural sector to gain the upper hand in competition for labor. The history of economic development in developed countries (and particularly in the United States) has demonstrated that with abundant funds and preferential conditions the industrial sector can constantly attract labor from agriculture. Therefore the relationship between the wages of industrial workers and the income of rural laborers can shed some light on the effect of labor supply and demand on wage determination.

Figures 14-3 through 14-6 show average monthly wage income in sample enterprises, in agriculture and rural industry, and in state enterprises in each county. These indicate that when there are plenty of surplus laborers the income of workers in sample firms remains at a higher level than that of local

Figure 14-3. *Average Monthly Incomes in Agriculture, Industry, and State Enterprises, Wuxi*

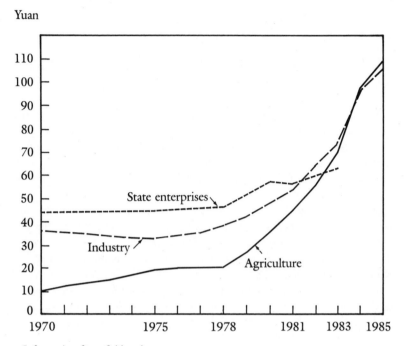

Yuan

Source: Information from fieldwork.

farmers, as in Jieshou and Shangrao. But in Jieshou the income curves for sample firms and for local farmers climb smoothly the same distance apart, whereas in Shangrao the two curves fluctuate irregularly. The correlation between the two curves is higher in Jieshou (0.99) than in Shangrao (0.92), which suggests that the impact of labor supply and demand on pay is greater in the former than in the latter.

When labor is in relatively short supply, the correlation between the average monthly income of workers in sample enterprises and that of local rural laborers is extremely high, as is the case in Wuxi (1.00) and Nanhai (0.99). But the income of employees in sample firms in Nanhai remained higher than that of local farmers during the survey period, whereas in Wuxi the income of local farmers caught up with and even surpassed that of employees in sample firms in 1984–85. Obviously the situation in Wuxi was irrational, since labor was in short supply. Therefore we may conclude that wage levels in Wuxi have little to do with local labor supply and demand.

Responses to the question "In your enterprise, who decides the pay of a worker who has just joined?" in the Enterprise Survey Questionnaire support the above conclusion. "The township government" was the answer in 42 per-

Figure 14-4. *Average Monthly Incomes in Agriculture, Industry, Sample TVPs, and State Enterprises, Nanhai*

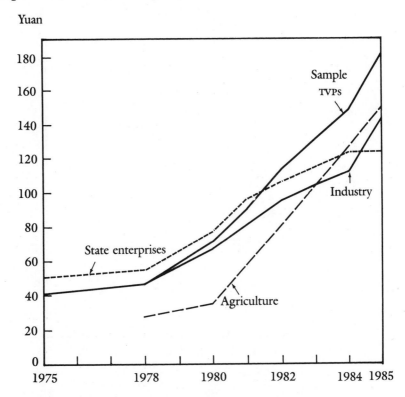

Sources: Enterprise Quantitative Questionnaire and information from fieldwork.

cent of the responses in Shangrao, 31 percent in Wuxi, 21 percent in Nanhai, and 17 percent in Jieshou (table 14-4).

From interviews we learned that community governments in Jieshou and Nanhai rarely interfere in their firms' decisions on employees' pay. Under such circumstances the high correlation between the average income of TVP employees and that of local farmers naturally indicates the influence of labor supply and demand on wages. But in Shangrao community governments not only interfere in enterprises' decisions on setting wages but have also adopted the principle that the salary level in TVPs should be a little lower than that in state enterprises rather than being set according to labor supply and demand. (See the discussion below.)

Supply of and Demand for Labor of Different Qualities

According to the theoretical model of a totally competitive labor market, if the quality of labor is disregarded and labor moves freely, labor should have

Figure 14-5. *Average Monthly Incomes in Agriculture, Industry, and State Enterprises, Jieshou*

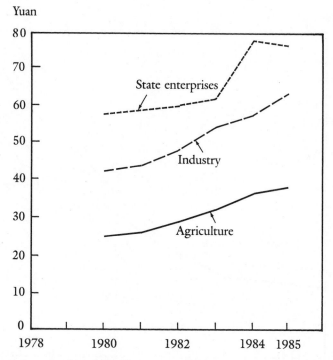

Source: Information from fieldwork.

a unitary price in labor markets at the same level (interregional, intercommunity, or interenterprise). It seems that the above analysis of the data and the conclusions we have reached contradict the theory. For instance, in Nanhai, which has the greatest mobility of labor at the intercommunity and interenterprise levels, wage differences are large at both levels. But the differences are very small at both levels in Wuxi, where almost no flow of labor can be found. Realities are much richer than theories, and many things that can be neglected in theoretical analysis are of great significance in practice. Here the crucial factor is the quality of labor.

The industrial composition of Nanhai's TVPs features strong local specialization. For example, Xiqiao town is the county's textile center; hardware and machine-building enterprises are concentrated in Pingzhou town; Danzao is the producer of pottery; Heshun has a relatively advanced building materials industry; and labor-intensive industries such as garments, toys, and electronics are mostly located in relatively backward areas like Guanyao. Local specialization in industrial structure is a principal factor in the big differences in salaries among communities.

Figure 14-6. *Average Monthly Incomes in Agriculture and Industry, Shangrao*

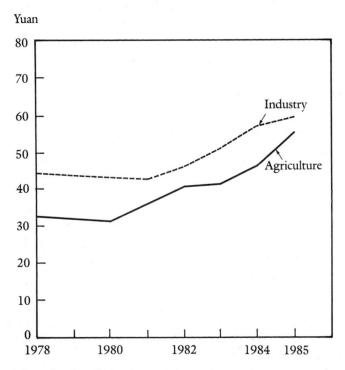

Source: Information from fieldwork.

Industries at differing levels of technical development have different requirements for labor quality, and hence the price of labor varies. Since learning complicated techniques is more costly and the supply of people who command such techniques is scanty, the price of highly trained workers will naturally be higher than that of workers who know only simple techniques. In addition, some techniques can be applied universally, whereas specialized techniques can be applied only in limited areas. Workers who have specialized techniques take a bigger risk in looking for jobs than those who know commonly used techniques. The higher price that specialized laborers enjoy is actually a kind of compensation for the employment risks they face.

The big differences in pay among enterprises within Nanhai's communities are caused mainly by differences among industries. The survey results show big wage differences among enterprises within communities. This is because the survey results do not take into account enterprise scales and do not include firms other than TVCEs. For instance, in Yanbu district wages in electrical appliance, hardware, and toy factories were evidently too low (an average

Table 14-4. *Who Decides the Salary for Newly Recruited Employees in Sample Enterprises*
(percent)

County	Village or township government	Government and enterprise jointly	Enterprise, but approved by government	Enterprise itself	Other
Wuxi	31.2	9.4	34.4	25.0	0.0
Jieshou	16.7	8.3	19.4	52.8	2.8
Nanhai	20.8	4.2	20.8	33.3	20.8
Shangrao	42.1	10.5	15.8	31.6	0.0

Source: Enterprise Survey Questionnaire.

Y1,223 a year in the six sample factories), whereas in machine-building and food-processing factories they were too high—Y2,222 a year in the eight sample factories.

The same factors also explain the small wage differentials in Jieshou. Industrial structure in the county is less diversified, and TVPs are involved mainly in agroprocessing, production of construction materials, brickmaking, and food processing. As a result, all communities and enterprises in Jieshou need workers of similar quality. Since wage levels are determined mainly by labor supply and demand, wage differentials are small. The wage level in Wuxi is not determined by labor supply and demand, so the small wage differences there cannot be explained in the same way as in Jieshou. Finally, the main reasons for big wage differences among Shangrao's communities are lack of mobility of labor, backward processing industries, and uneven distribution of natural resources such as minerals and water.

The Impact of Systemic Variables on Wages in Wuxi County

The wage level in Wuxi is lower than in Nanhai, the income of TVP employees has become lower than that of farmers in recent years, and wage differences at the intercommunity and interenterprise levels are small. These characteristics cannot be explained by labor supply and demand.

In Wuxi the wage determination mechanism is totally different from that of the market. TVCEs account for the overwhelming majority of all TVPs in the county, and all of their assets belong to the communities. In principle this means that the assets belong to every member of the community, but in reality they do not belong to any individual; instead, they are owned by the community government and are held and used by the enterprises. Each TVCE employee has the ambiguous status of an enterprise owner. This has made TVCEs a special kind of cooperative without clearly defined property rights. In such firms the only way benefits can be shared fairly is through income distribution. Therefore within the enterprise there is a strong motive to maximize average per capita income. But since enterprise assets are actually owned by the community government, the management of the enterprises is not allowed to depart too far from community goals. Thus firms' goal of maximizing employees' average income is partially offset by the community goal of maximizing (and balancing) the average income of community members. This is one of the main reasons that TVP wages in Wuxi are relatively low even though the county is suffering from a labor shortage. During our survey we learned that when in 1984 the county introduced a contract system and lifted wage ceilings for enterprises, the average wage soared by 28.8 percent. In 1985, after community governments restored controls, annual wage growth was reduced to 10.5 percent.

The community's desire to equalize average incomes within the community can be traced to its ownership of enterprise assets. Every community member is supposed to enjoy the same status as owner of these assets as well as equal rights to employment and income distribution. This requires community governments to adopt an egalitarian policy in distribution of income between industrial and agricultural laborers. Before 1983 most TVPs in Wuxi handed wages over to workers' production teams and the workers shared in the distribution of production team income. After the introduction of the PRS, community governments began to use profits remitted by enterprises to subsidize farmers. In recent years, with the emergence of a labor shortage, fewer and fewer people are willing to engage in painstaking agricultural production. To stop the dwindling of the local agricultural sector, community governments have been using profits from industrial TVCEs to supplement the incomes of agricultural laborers so that their incomes can catch up with or even surpass those of TVP workers.

The relatively small wage differences among enterprises in Wuxi's communities also reflect community governments' policy of egalitarian income distribution among community members. Community governments have adopted flexible policies for enterprises in different situations. For instance, firms that earn fat profits may be required to hold down workers' pay, whereas those in the red may try to raise employees' incomes by delinking the payroll from profits and linking it only to output value. Moreover, keeping wage differentials among enterprises low is a way of restraining labor flows and maintaining stable development of enterprises. The small wage differences among Wuxi's communities can also be attributed to this consideration. As labor is in short supply, to keep workers it is necessary for each community to prevent its wages from sliding much lower than those in other communities.

What should be stressed here is that egalitarian income distribution among community members in Wuxi has not had too adverse an impact on the economic efficiency of TVPs. This may be attributed to the employment, wage, and profit-sharing systems. The fundamental difference between TVP employees and state enterprise employees is that the former face less certainty in their employment. State enterprise employees can never lose their jobs and the related salary, welfare, and benefits, but a TVP employee will lose his job and will have to go back to the fields if the firm is closed. Thus the basic interest of TVP employees is tied to that of their firms.

Although community governments try to reduce income gaps, such gaps persist to a certain extent. TVCEs in Wuxi have generally adopted the piece-rate wage system, which has clarified the profits made by each individual within an enterprise and has offset the ambiguity in the relationship between profits of different enterprises. These tangible incentives have stimulated workers' enthusiasm. The practice of linking part of the payroll to enterprise profits also gives employees a limited share in profits and some incentive.

Understanding Wage Increases in Nanhai County

In the previous section we analyzed the great difference in wage levels between Wuxi and Nanhai counties from the perspective of Wuxi, where community goals restrain enterprises' motives to increase average income. But does this mean that the present high wage level and high wage growth in Nanhai are related to the cooperative nature of its enterprises and community governments' inability to restrain them?

It should first be noted that TVCEs behave similarly in Nanhai and in Wuxi and that community governments in Nanhai also like to control the ever rising level of wages in their firms. But in Nanhai individually run enterprises and partnerships account for a large proportion of the total number of TVPs, and these firms usually pay their employees higher wages than TVCEs. This not only compensates for the greater uncertainty in employment but also sharpens competitiveness in the labor market. In addition, agricultural production in Nanhai has reached a high level of development. In recent years more and more Nanhai farmers have turned to raising flowers, vegetables, and farm animals, and the county is enjoying a high commercialization rate and sharp growth in incomes. Agriculture there can no longer be regarded as a traditional sector; it has already become part of the commodity economy with profit-making as its management goal. Farmers in Nanhai have much higher incomes than those in Wuxi. In 1985 a person whose main occupation was agriculture, forestry, animal husbandry, or fishing had an average income of Y1,132 in Wuxi but Y1,786—58 percent higher—in Nanhai.

With labor in short supply, community governments and TVCEs in Nanhai are under pressure from both the agricultural sector and private firms. If they cannot keep their workers by offering high wages, the normal development of TVCEs will be threatened. Under such circumstances community governments in Nanhai allow TVCEs to set wages according to labor supply and demand. In the final analysis the high level of wages in Nanhai is a normal reflection of market regulation when labor is in short supply.

Nanhai data on wages are for 1985, however, whereas the data on labor flows reflect the situation in March 1987. The great influx of outside laborers into Nanhai started only at the end of 1985 and the beginning of 1986. We should not assume that the price of labor continued to rise sharply after that. An article in *Nanhai Nongcun* [Rural Nanhai] of February 1987 points out that in 1986 the number of rural laborers in the county engaged in farm production increased by 3.0 percent over the previous year, while the number engaged in industrial production dropped by 4.9 percent. The main reason was that some TVCEs had been contracted out to individuals, and the contractors had gradually replaced local employees with lower-paid workers from other regions. As a result, some local people returned to farming. Thus the inflow of laborers from other regions has to some extent held down wages of local workers.

Labor Market Development and Its Influence on TVPs

The description and analysis of labor mobility and wage determination in the four counties have shown the following.

- Although development of TVPs is highly advanced in both Wuxi and Nanhai, the two counties show sharply contrasting patterns. Labor flows at the interregional, intercommunity, and interenterprise levels are very low in Wuxi, and wages are not determined by the labor market but by community governments that strive to equalize local per capita incomes. Enterprises have little freedom to choose workers, and workers basically have no choice of profession. In Wuxi the labor market, as defined earlier in this chapter, does not exist.

- Among the four counties Nanhai has the greatest mobility of labor. Wages are determined mainly by labor supply and demand. Although community governments have various regulations that restrict the freedom of long-term TVCE workers (20–30 percent of the county's total TVP labor force) in choosing jobs, plentiful opportunities for employment and the great attraction of big salary differentials have countered community governments' efforts to control this 20–30 percent of the labor force. The labor market in Nanhai is the most developed among the four counties.

- If we regard Wuxi and Nanhai as two extremes of labor market development in the more industrialized areas, Jieshou and Shangrao can be seen as two extremes in the backward areas. Although mobility of labor is only slightly better in Jieshou than in Shangrao, workers and firms in Jieshou have much more freedom in choosing each other than in Shangrao. In areas that have substantial surplus labor, freedom of choice reflects the degree of development of the labor market more than does labor mobility. TVPs in Shangrao suffer from great interference by community governments in wage determination. Community governments there try to make TVPs imitate the fixed salary systems, retirement systems, welfare regulations, and even salary adjustment mechanisms of state enterprises. In a word, wage determination has nothing to do with supply and demand in the local labor market. In general, community governments in Jieshou do not interfere in enterprises' decisions on wages—even those of TVCES. Hence the small differences in wages at the intercommunity and interenterprise levels indicate that the market price of labor has already been formed.

The earlier analysis has also shown that at present China does not have a unitary labor market between urban and rural areas and that interregional rural labor markets remain at a low level of development. Despite the inexhaustible supply of labor nationwide, labor costs in some rural areas have skyrocketed and even surpassed the salary level in local state enterprises (see figures 14-3 and 14-4). Obviously the low level of development of interregional labor markets is harmful to the development of China's TVPs. Although most rural areas still have a labor surplus, some advanced localities have already seen a sharp rise in labor costs because of the shortage of labor. The advantages that an inexhaustible supply of labor hold for development are gradually disappearing in some rural areas of China.

Because of the restricted interregional flow of labor, some areas have already resorted to changing output mix, updating technology, and adjusting other factors of production. Industries and enterprises with different levels of technology usually have different capital-labor ratios. A firm's production scope and technology determine the level of labor costs that it can afford. If labor costs keep rising, the enterprise will have to choose a new capital-labor ratio or switch its production scope and technology level. In developing countries with relatively well-functioning labor markets, the flow of labor from underdeveloped to advanced areas will curb the rise of labor costs in the latter. As a result, enterprises in such areas can enjoy a long period of stable development after they have chosen the industry they will engage in and the level of technology they will pursue. But under present conditions in China's rural areas, TVPs in the advanced areas have to switch to other industries and technologies to counteract the rapid rise in labor costs caused by immobility of labor.

We saw many instances of this. In Yanbu town, Nanhai, a factory that produced mosquito repellent incense has switched to producing liquefied gas cylinders, and a furniture factory is now producing aluminum materials. In Pingzhou town a knitting mill had to suspend production because of high labor costs, and its machines now sit idle. A plastic products factory in Shatou town has transferred its technology, equipment, and capital to Sichuan Province because of the high cost of labor in Shatou. These frequent adjustments will inevitably lead to some waste of investment and will have an adverse impact on enterprises' stable development. Similar cases can be seen in Wuxi. Qianzhou township, for instance, once signed a contract with the Shanghai Foreign Trade Bureau to produce and export plush toys, but because of high local labor costs, the contract yielded no profits to the township. The township therefore later transferred the contract to a TVP in Taixing County in northern Jiangsu Province, where labor costs were only 50 percent of those in Qianzhou.

Flows of any factors of production inevitably call for some investments and risk taking. By comparison, the flow of labor needs less investment, and the risk involved is shared. The transport, dismantling, and installation of other factors of production can be much costlier than flows of labor, and the enterprise alone shoulders all the risk. Therefore flows of other factors are often less economic than labor flows. There is no doubt, however, that changes in product structure, improved technologies, and flows of other factors can partly compensate for the immobility of labor.

Because of the underdevelopment of interregional labor markets, local labor markets have different impacts on TVPs at different stages of development. In the initial stage of development of TVPs and when there is an inexhaustible supply of labor, the existence of a labor market helps enterprises choose a suitable amount of labor in accordance with the needs of their own development, and it can also help curb the rise in wages. But community interference in the allocation of labor and in wage determination can cause personnel redundancy in enterprises and lead wages to surpass the appropriate level based on supply and demand. This is because communities strive to expand local employment and increase local per capita incomes, and they regard the enterprises as a means of achieving their goals.

When the development of local TVPs reaches a relatively advanced stage and labor is in short supply, the existence of a local labor market facilitates rapid wage increases and has an adverse impact on the development of TVPs. Before 1985, when the interregional labor market had not yet opened up, wages in Nanhai soared with the growing shortage of labor. If community governments can interfere in setting wages, they will limit wage growth to further general community goals. For example, in 1985 community government controls reduced the growth rate of wages in Wuxi from 28.4 to 9.8 percent. (Such controls can slow the speed of wage increases to a certain extent but they do not curb the growth of total payrolls, since one of the principal goals of community governments is to increase local per capita incomes.) Furthermore, if there is no competition among workers for employment, wages will be highly inflexible.

The solution to the problems of wage inflation and inflexibility is the opening up of interregional rural labor markets. In 1986 Nanhai was able to coax local laborers to return to farming by bringing in cheap industrial labor from other regions. On the premise of an inexhaustible supply of labor in China, the opening up of rural labor markets will certainly create a more favorable climate for the development of TVPs. The analysis in this chapter has shown that labor mobility is related to the ownership and management systems of TVPs. Hence, system reform is a leading issue in the development of TVPs.

Table 14-A1. Cultivated Area and Labor Requirements for Crop Cultivation in the Sample Counties

Item	1975	1978	1980	1981	1982	1983	1984	1985
Crop area (mu)								
Wuxi	919,100	915,800	912,900	912,600	908,400	908,400	900,000	877,800
Jieshou	648,000	644,700	642,300	642,300	642,200	642,200	641,900	641,800
Nanhai	680,600	654,900	655,700	653,700	649,700	645,000	641,400	630,100
Shangrao	n.a.	n.a.	471,200	471,000	471,100	471,400	470,700	n.a.
Labor requirements for crop cultivation (workers)								
Wuxi	116,955	116,662	116,293	116,255	116,140	115,720	115,490	111,822
Jieshou	86,397	85,953	85,646	85,628	85,624	85,632	85,585	85,571
Nanhai	106,339	102,328	102,455	102,141	101,513	100,785	100,218	98,596
Shangrao	n.a.	n.a.	n.a.	n.a.	n.a.	n.a.	73,546	n.a.

Source: Information from fieldwork.

Appendix. A Method of Calculating Labor Supply for TVPs

To facilitate the calculations we assume that there is no surplus labor in forestry, animal husbandry, or fisheries. As the proportion of TVP employment in these activities is small and the potential surplus is even smaller, they can be neglected.

The great amount of potential surplus labor in China's agricultural sector determines the supply of labor to TVPs. Surplus labor in agriculture is calculated by deducting the labor needed for crop growing, forestry, animal husbandry, sideline production, fisheries, scientific research, education, public health, and other activities from the total labor force in rural areas. For the entire survey and the methods of calculation, see China Rural Development Research Group (1985), nos. 1 and 2.

The amount of labor needed for crop growing can be calculated by dividing the actual sown area in a region by the per capita crop-growing capacity of local farmers. Owing to different climatic conditions, types of crops planted, soil conditions, and levels of agricultural mechanization, farmers' crop-growing capacity differs among regions. During 1979–83 the Development Research Institute of the State Council Rural Development Research Center conducted a detailed survey on per capita crop-growing capacity among farmers in Ji'an Prefecture in Jiangxi Province, Fengqiu County in Henan Province, and Chuxian County in Anhui Province. The results of the survey are shown in the following table.

	Survey results	Theoretical figure	Average
Ji'an	6.28	6.45	6.4
Fengqiu	7.01	7.97	7.5
Chuxian	7.75	7.95	7.85

Ji'an has two crops of rice and one of wheat each year and devotes large areas to rice growing; Chuxian grows one crop of rice and one of wheat every year; and Fengqiu usually grows one crop of cotton and one of wheat or two crops of wheat a year. The crop-growing situation in Jieshou is similar to that in Fengqiu, that in Wuxi is similar to that in Chuxian, and that in Nanhai and Shangrao is similar to that in Ji'an. We can therefore use the averages of theoretical figures and survey results to derive a rough estimate of the crop-growing capacity per farmer in each of the four counties (see table 14-A1).

From the total labor force of each county, we subtract, in order, the amount of labor needed for crop cultivation (based on the crop-growing capacity per farmer as calculated above), actual labor used in forestry, animal husbandry, and fisheries, and employment in scientific research, education, culture, and government. We are left with estimates of the potential surplus labor from agriculture available for employment in TVPs.

Notes

1. Since statistics classified by township were not available for Jieshou, the analysis of the situation there is based on data from sample enterprises in that county and supplementary quantitative tables in the three communities of Jieshou town, Hebei township, and Jinzhai township.

2. Data on Dongjiang township are from government statistics on TVCES in Dongjiang. Data on Jieshou town are from the Enterprise Quantitative Questionnaire filled out by twenty-two enterprises in the town. Data on Yanbu district are from statistics provided by the TVP bureau in Nanhai County. No comparable data were available for Shangrao County.

15

Noneconomic Determinants of Workers' Incomes

Wu Quhui, Wang Hansheng, and Xu Xinxin

Analysis of the distribution of personal incomes can focus on actual income distribution or on the opportunity structure for maintaining and increasing incomes. The latter is more significant because it determines future income distribution. Opportunities for labor are related to the extent of free competition and reflect the social structure of a community. According to the economic theory of pure competition, the price of labor is decided by the relationship between market supply and demand, which in turn determines the opportunity structure of the selling and purchasing sides. But this theory is based on the premises that the supply and demand sides of the labor market have a simple trading relationship on a legally equal footing and that both sides pursue economic gain with no consideration of noneconomic factors such as social status. The wage-setting principle is marginal productivity, and the price of labor depends solely on its economic returns. Obviously this situation of pure greed competition is a theoretical construct that is rarely found in practice. The social structure and systemic environment confronted by TVPs in China's rural communities are far from the scenario given by this theory.

China's TVPs generally face a more complete market environment than do state enterprises. TVPs are much less controlled by state plans, they enjoy greater access to the labor market than state enterprises, and, in general, local labor supply and demand have a stronger influence on their wages. Wages in TVPs are directly linked to the enterprises' economic returns (see chapter 13). Community governments, however, exercise varying degrees of control over their firms, and their recognition of community members' economic rights and freedom also varies, both in content and in degree (see chapter 7). Even if two communities have similar labor markets, their governments may exercise different forms of noneconomic control over TVP employees' incomes.

The relationship between TVP owners and their employees depends on the form of ownership. China's TVPs fall largely into five categories of ownership: township enterprises, village enterprises, production team enterprises, partnerships, and individual firms. The first three are owned by community governments at various levels, while the latter two are private enterprises. The township government is the owner of its subordinate enterprises, and it also exercises administrative functions. As the government of a community, it protects the interests of community members, improves their living standards and social welfare, and adjusts income distribution among different social groups to achieve general parity within the community. But the township government, as requested by higher authorities, must also ensure a steady growth of agricultural production. Accordingly, it has to perform multiple functions and make a proper allocation of resources, including labor, within the community. In pursuit of such goals, township governments can utilize administrative means, but they may also use township enterprises to reduce unemployment and regulate income distribution. In contrast, private enterprises rely more on the market for labor. As a result, the relationship between owners and employees is simpler, and workers' incomes are determined more by economic laws.

Given the state of labor supply and demand, the ownership pattern determines the extent of market competition for labor. When township enterprises enjoy absolute superiority and competition from private enterprises is weak, the township government is likely to exercise stricter control over employment and wages of township enterprise workers to fulfill its objectives. For example, to ensure adequate labor for farming to boost food production, the township government may impose limits on the incomes of those engaged in industrial activities or simply use part of enterprises' profits to subsidize agriculture. But if there is fierce competition from private enterprises, township governments have to relax noneconomic control over wages in township enterprises.

Since the 1970s and particularly in the past few years there has been a big upsurge in the development of TVPs in China's rural areas. This has turned the originally simple rural society of farm laborers into a pluralistic society with diverse trades and strata—a transition that has profoundly affected income distribution between workers and farmers, among enterprises, and among individuals. Exactly what are these new income distribution patterns? What relationship do they have to the community opportunity structure? What roles do community governments play in income distribution? And finally, what have been the consequences of these patterns for incentives, equity, and efficiency?

In this chapter we focus on government intervention in the determination of personal incomes in TVPs in three counties: Wuxi, Nanhai, and Jieshou. (Shangrao was excluded from the analysis because some key data could not be obtained there.)

The Opportunity Structure and Sources of Labor

The ratio between total employment in TVPs and surplus agricultural labor in a community reflects labor supply and demand. In 1985 there were 323,800 TVP employees in Wuxi, or 80.5 percent of its surplus agricultural labor force. In Nanhai TVP employees numbered 206,839, or 86.5 percent of the county's surplus farm laborers. But in Jieshou TVP employees numbered only 28,900—15.0 percent of the surplus agricultural labor force—and the labor supply situation for TVPs was thus more favorable than in the other two counties (see chapter 14). As a result, TVP workers' average monthly income in Jieshou was Y66, compared with Y100 in Wuxi and Y178 in Nanhai.

Despite a similar labor market situation, there is a big difference between average incomes in Wuxi and Nanhai counties. Of course, this gap can be attributed to economic factors such as industrial structure, technical capacities, and product prices. But we have every reason to believe that different degrees of control by community governments over income levels have been an important factor. As can be seen from table 15-1, workers in private enterprises in Wuxi accounted for only 3 percent of total TVP employment, whereas the figure was 22 percent in Nanhai and 55 percent in Jieshou. Private enterprises usually shoulder much less responsibility for improving the living standards and social welfare of all community members, and they do not have administrative control over their employees. Their motive is simply to make profits, and they pay their workers mainly according to labor supply and demand. Township governments' control over the incomes of workers in township enterprises is weakened when there is fierce market competition for laborers from private enterprises and when supply is short. The result is a stronger role for market supply and demand.

Community opportunity structure is determined by the distribution of enterprises with different forms of ownership and by the mobility of community members. When all TVPs in a community are owned by its government, which strictly forbids mobility, community members' choices in employment and pay are limited and the community government is in a favorable position. But when there are many private enterprises and community members enjoy a high degree of mobility, the opportunity structure favors individuals,

Table 15-1. *Employment Structure of TVPs*
(percentage of total in TVP sector)

Type of enterprise	Wuxi[a]	Jieshou	Nanhai
Township	47.1	32.0	23.9
Village	50.0	13.4	53.6
Partnership	2.9	24.5	22.5
Individual		30.1	

a. Includes only industrial TVPs.
Source: Information from fieldwork.

Table 15-2. *Composition and Origin of the TVP Labor Force*
(percentage of total sample employees)

Item	Wuxi	Jieshou	Nanhai
Type of employee			
Long term	91.2	75.8	40.2
Temporary	8.5	18.1	59.8
Seasonal	0.3	6.2	0.0
Origin of employee			
Same village	94.0	79.9	50.9
Other villages in county	3.0	12.7	33.8
Other counties in province	1.6	4.8	14.2
Other provinces	1.4	2.8	1.1

Source: Enterprise Quantitative Questionnaire.

and their employment and incomes depend more on market supply and demand. Table 15-2 demonstrates the differences in mobility of community members in the three counties. Nanhai has the greatest intracommunity and intercommunity mobility, Jieshou is second, and Wuxi is last. Therefore in Wuxi the opportunity structure favors community governments, in Nanhai it favors community members, and in Jieshou the situation is in between. It is particularly worth noting that many so-called township enterprises in Jieshou are really private; only a few firms are truly run by township governments. The labor force in Jieshou enjoys fairly high mobility, but actual opportunities for choosing employment are far smaller than in Nanhai because labor supply exceeds demand.

As a result of varied social opportunity structures, workers join firms in drastically different ways in the three counties. The percentage of employees designated by community governments is substantially higher in Wuxi than in the other two counties. In Nanhai more workers are employed through the fairly well-developed labor market, and there are fewer government-designated employees. Unlike the situation in Wuxi, community governments are not able to compensate the unemployed or balance incomes of workers in firms with different economic returns and working conditions. In Jieshou too, workers are recruited by enterprises directly instead of through community governments, but the labor market is not as developed as in Nanhai. Many people are recommended by their relatives or friends, and consequently there are strong blood relationships within firms. TVP employees in Jieshou have a deep sense of belonging to their enterprises. They would accept wage cuts rather than desert their firms. They also have a strong desire to reinvest profits in their enterprises and are content with their present incomes. One reason is the difficulty of finding jobs in other firms.

A more unified ownership pattern also makes it possible for township governments to maintain control over the incomes of directors and managerial personnel. In Wuxi community governments are in a favorable position, whereas in Nanhai, where the ownership pattern is more diversified, directors and managerial personnel are attracted to private enterprises by higher pay, and they enjoy more employment choices and greater mobility (see table 15-3).

Community Balancing Mechanisms in Wage Determination

The community opportunity structure normally determines the extent of community government control over the incomes of TVP employees. Such control is designed to redistribute economic benefits among different groups within the community. The chief goals of township governments are to raise the general level of welfare and to balance the incomes of individuals in different social groups, and the governments use every possible means—usually administrative—to achieve these objectives. The higher the share of township enterprises' economic returns in total community income, the easier this is to do. As we have seen, township governments in Wuxi are in a more favorable position to exercise such control.

Balancing Incomes of Workers and Farmers

The average monthly income of township enterprise workers in Wuxi is Y110 and that of agricultural laborers is Y108. In Nanhai the figure for township enterprise workers is Y190. We do not have data on farm laborers, but their incomes could not be lower than those of TVP workers because many of the latter are now returning to farming. In Jieshou the figures are Y60 and Y40, respectively. There is little difference between average incomes of TVP workers and of farmers in Wuxi. The latter is probably a little higher than the former in Nanhai, and in Jieshou the average monthly income of workers is 1.5 times that of farmers.

In contrast to Nanhai, part of the income of Wuxi farmers comes from redistribution of industrial profits. In 1985 township governments in Wuxi set aside Y12.7 million to compensate farmers, whereas in Nanhai such com-

Table 15-3. *Origins of TVP Managers*
(percentage of sample total)

Origin	Wuxi	Nanhai	Jieshou
Same village	93.1	53.5	78.1
Other villages in county	0.6	39.7	16.5
Other counties in province	0.5	5.6	2.3
Other provinces	5.9	1.2	3.2

Source: Enterprise Quantitative Questionnaire.

pensation was only Y6.6 million. Average compensation per farmer was Y66.40 in Wuxi and Y37.40 in Nanhai. Moreover, actual compensation in Nanhai is probably less than 20 percent of the figures on the books. In Jieshou compensation for farmers accounted for 17 percent of the profits enterprises turned over to the state, or only Y40,000.

Enterprises' economic returns are diverted to farmers in different ways in the three counties. In Wuxi the main channel is community government subsidies for pig raising, grain production, and cultivation. The Dongjiang township government, for example, pays farmers Y10 for the first pig and Y20 for the second. For every half kilogram of grain sold to the government farmers receive a subsidy of Y0.06, and those who are willing to cultivate more than 10 mu of land receive Y12 in subsidies. Farmers also get similar subsidies from village governments. In Nanhai subsidies are seldom issued to individual farmers.

Another way to balance incomes is through a community pension system. Township governments in Wuxi stipulate that people who have worked in township enterprises for more than three years are entitled to pensions of at least Y15 a month. Agricultural workers enjoy preferential pension treatment, however. Specialized farming households receive the same pensions as TVP workers, but the retirement age for male farmers is five years earlier than for workers. Pension systems in Nanhai are available only to employees of township enterprises, and they differ among enterprises. No communities in Jieshou have established pension systems. The money farmers get from redistribution of TVP profits and the pension system are in fact entitlements for being community members which allow them to benefit from the economic returns of TVPs. People not employed in TVPs can be compensated through these "membership incomes."

In Wuxi substantial amounts of TVCEs' returns have been used to increase farm laborers' incomes and welfare. Township governments there feel a great responsibility for balancing the welfare of all community members. Moreover, under the county's agricultural policy, township governments are expected to ensure a steady growth of grain production at the same time as they develop TVPs. In fact, the original reason for establishing TVPs there was to promote agricultural production and ensure reinvestment in agriculture (see chapter 7). From the land contracts signed between township governments and farmers we can see the importance Wuxi has attached to grain production. In Dongjiang township, for example, land contracts contain strict stipulations on the crop varieties to be grown on contracted farmland; they encourage grain production, limit cash crops, and forbid leaving arable land idle. But in Nanhai farmers can grow any crops they wish as long as they fulfill state grain quotas, which they can do by buying grain from other localities. In Wuxi farmers must fulfill quotas with their own grain production. This continuing emphasis on grain production has led to a shrinkage in the acreage of cash crops. Historically Wuxi was an important silk producer, but since the 1960s its mulberry acreage has been declining, from 100,000 mu in 1962 to 80,000 mu in 1975, 70,000 mu in 1980, 60,000 mu in 1984, and only 35,000 mu in 1986.

Balancing Incomes among Enterprises in a Community

Communities also seek to balance wage incomes among TVPs. Differences in average wage income among firms are smallest in Wuxi, largest in Nanhai, and in between in Jieshou. Different factors are responsible for these gaps in the three counties.

In Wuxi township governments have exercised stricter control over wages and bonuses in enterprises. Firms' total wage bills must be approved by township governments, and taxes are levied on enterprises when wages surpass a stipulated standard (Y80 per month in Dongjiang township, for example). Township governments in Nanhai exercise indirect control over workers' incomes through their control over the personal incomes of those who have contracted to run enterprises. Since the contractors' incomes are linked to enterprise profits, higher wages for workers mean lower profits and reduced bonuses for directors, who thus have an incentive to hold down wages. Township governments in Jieshou have basically no control over TVP wages, which are set by enterprises themselves and largely reflect labor supply and demand on the market.

Township governments in Wuxi can achieve an income balance among community members through financial compensation for farmers, improvements in social welfare, and control over wages. Such influence is weaker in Nanhai and weakest in Jieshou. Not only do township governments exercise more control over wages in Wuxi; community members have less choice of jobs and rely more on community governments to improve social welfare.

In Nanhai, in contrast, private enterprises are more important, employees of private enterprises are recruited through market competition instead of being designated by community governments, and all job hunters have equal opportunities. Township governments therefore have less influence than in Wuxi. Moreover, reducing the wages of township enterprise employees and transferring part of township enterprise profits for redistribution to other community members would lead to unequal opportunities because employees of private enterprises are not affected by such wage limits. And since community members have more choices in employment, they are less dependent on community governments for bettering their welfare.

Community governments in Jieshou do not have much influence on TVPs because many township enterprises are actually run by individuals. In this situation the market plays a more significant role in determining wages, and the balancing function of community governments is limited.

Income Differences within Enterprises

In Wuxi individuals' living standards are strongly related to the general community living standard, which means that the realization of individual interests depends mainly on the community. But this does not mean that there are no income differences among classes of employees within an enterprise. On the contrary, differences in the human capital of management personnel and workers make it impossible to attain an income balance among directors, other managerial personnel, and workers and at the same time maintain the motivation of managers. In Nanhai and Jieshou, where not every community member shares equally in the increased overall welfare of their communities, individuals' welfare depends on the profits of their firms, but employees may or may not share equally in enterprise profits.

Information from the sample shows that income disparities within firms vary in the three counties. The ratios of average monthly wages, with workers as 1.00, are 1.74 for sales staff, 1.91 for technicians, and 2.07 for directors in Wuxi. In Jieshou the figures are 1.40 for sales staff, 1.96 for technicians, and 1.47 for directors. Income differences within enterprises in Nanhai are larger than in Wuxi, although accurate information is not available. Most TVP workers in Nanhai receive piece rates, the norms for which are set by the enterprises themselves. Usually there are no limits on the income disparity between directors and workers, but directors' incomes depend on enterprise profits. For example, the incomes of enterprise directors in Pingzhou town are made up of a basic monthly salary of Y66; a monthly position salary of Y70; a bonus in proportion to the enterprise's profits, divided into eight grades that range from Y60 to Y240 a month; and bonuses for above-quota profits, innovative activities, and above-quota sales.[1] According to local officials some enterprise directors could earn as much as Y30,000 a year under these regulations, but the highest actual income of a township enterprise director in Pingzhou in 1986 was Y5,000. Many township governments in Nanhai stipulate that enterprises can retain 30 percent of their profits as bonus. Of this, 70 percent is divided among workers and the rest among managers. For instance, managers of the Luocun Gloves and Hides Factory could earn Y10,000 in 1986, and workers received an average monthly salary of Y120 plus a monthly bonus of Y30. These figures show that income disparities within firms are bigger in Nanhai than in Wuxi and Jieshou.

The factors responsible for income differentials vary among the three counties. First, there are different contract management systems. In Wuxi twenty-five of twenty-nine sample township enterprises have adopted the collective contract system. In Jieshou 46 percent were contracted by individuals. In Nanhai there are no reliable data on the number of contracted firms, but case investigations indicate that most are contracted by individuals. Under the collective contract system, management and workers shoulder risks together and hence have common interests. But under the individual or director contract system, risks are shouldered by individuals, and their personal interests are divorced from those of the workers to some extent. This explains why there are different community government regulations on income distribution in Nanhai and Wuxi. In Wuxi's Dongjiang township the basic and position wages of top managers are fixed, but their floating wages are decided by production quotas and by the average level of workers' floating wages. Moreover, the maximum total incomes of directors are determined by the average income level of workers. (They are generally about twice the latter.) Income increases for directors hence depend on income increases for workers. Township governments in Nanhai usually set the relationship between directors' incomes and enterprise profits, leaving workers' incomes to be decided by directors. Obviously this puts the director in a more favorable position in income distribution than workers and other managers. Moreover, the director's personal income will decrease if he raises workers' incomes.

Decisionmaking on income distribution has much to do with opportunity structures. In Nanhai the existence of different ownership forms creates a competitive environment that is intensified by the shortage of labor. At the same time, the mobility of labor and managers is great. These two factors create more opportunities for workers and managers and make it difficult for township governments to exercise control over incomes of township enterprise employees. Inasmuch as the evaluation of enterprises is based on their profits and factory directors have the power to limit workers' wage increases, there are wide income differences within enterprises.

Township governments in Wuxi occupy a more favorable position. Community ownership of firms and weak labor mobility enable township governments to keep a rough balance of average individual incomes among enterprises and between TVP workers and farmers. They are also able to exercise direct control over income differences among types of employees within enterprises by controlling enterprises' total wage bills, linking incomes of directors and other managers with those of workers, and setting a maximum percentage difference between the two. Township governments thus ensure that directors enjoy no more favorable opportunities and rights than ordinary workers, and the incomes of directors and workers fluctuate synchronously. This certainly strengthens the workers' status as de facto owners of their firms.

Although as in Nanhai township governments in Jieshou do not have control over TVP wages but instead let directors make income distribution decisions, income differentials within enterprises are small. A possible explanation is that many of the county's township enterprises used to be private firms and have maintained many of their old methods. Some remain fundamentally private enterprises. It is possible to keep workers' wages low when there is heavy pressure from surplus agricultural labor. Enterprise directors also hold down their own nominal wages to keep the gap between their incomes and workers' wages narrow and thus help restrain the latter. This does not mean that the actual incomes of directors are low. They cover up their actual incomes because backward regions lack the concept of private property ownership and proprietors dare not claim their own enterprises. During fieldwork we met many people who refused to admit that their enterprises were their own property and regarded them as being owned by township governments.

Wage Determination

Table 15-4 lists the shares of various forms of worker income. "Other" includes welfare benefits offered by enterprises to all of their employees equally in the form of money, that is, membership incomes of employees. This type of income is nonexistent in Jieshou and minuscule in Nanhai, but it accounts for as much as 14 percent of monthly income of sample TVP employees in Wuxi. The appraisal of income distribution hence emphasizes enterprise membership in Wuxi but not in Nanhai and Jieshou. Income parity among employees in Jieshou is realized through equal distribution of basic wages and bonuses instead of through welfare benefits.

In Wuxi the income of managerial personnel is composed of basic wages, position wages, floating wages, and annual bonuses based on a work-point system. In Dongjiang township, for example, position incomes of chief managerial personnel are divided into two grades with three classes in each according to work load, responsibilities, and enterprise size (see table 15-5). Township governments decide to which grade an enterprise belongs. Floating wages depend on six indexes divided into 100 points, with noneconomic aspects (such as Communist party affairs, military recruitment, security, civil mediation, family planning, and office administration) accounting for 20 percent of the total. Annual bonuses are decided by the total annual profits of the community's township enterprises and by the increase in profits. Although bonuses are related to enterprise performance, the relationship is not completely fixed but rather is decided through comparison with income levels in other enterprises. As a result, the amount of annual bonuses is completely determined by township governments, and horizontal comparisons generate competition among directors of different firms, which forces them to go after production targets set by the township government. Since the floating wages of managerial personnel usually equal the average wage level of workers, in-

Table 15-4. *Composition of Monthly Income*
(percentage of total monthly income)

Item	Wuxi	Nanhai	Jieshou
Basic and piece-rate wages	67.5	78.5	92.7
Bonuses	18.8	20.6	7.3
Other	13.7	1.0	0

Source: Enterprise Quantitative Questionnaire.

Table 15-5. *Managerial Pay, Dongjiang Township, Wuxi County*
(yuan)

Occupation	Grade one	Grade two
Party secretaries and directors	50	36
Deputy Party secretaries and deputy directors	36	24
Accountants	24	14

Source: Information from fieldwork.

come differences between the two are reflected in managers' basic wages, position wages, and annual bonuses.

Incomes of managerial personnel in Nanhai are composed of basic wages, position wages, bonuses for profits and above-quota profits, and sales bonuses. Unlike the situation in Wuxi, the determination of these items is explicitly stipulated at the beginning of the year. Except for basic and position wages, the components of income are directly related to enterprise performance. For instance, in Xiqiao the township government stipulates that incomes of management personnel consist of basic wages, food subsidies, and bonuses, with no position wages or other living subsidies. The bonuses of directors and Communist party secretaries are divided into six classes, which are directly linked to the annual profits of their firms (see table 15-6). Bonuses of deputy directors are set at 90 percent of directors' bonuses, and bonuses for other managers are decided by directors according to certain ratios. In comparison with Dongjiang township, incomes of managers are more directly linked to the economic returns of enterprises, which are independent from each other in income distribution. The larger income gap among enterprises in Nanhai shows that wages indeed are directly decided by economic returns.

The determination of managerial incomes is simpler in Jieshou, where they are composed of basic wages and bonuses for overfulfilling profit targets. As in Nanhai, township governments make explicit stipulations beforehand and interfere little afterward.

The determination of workers' incomes also varies widely in the three counties (see table 15-7). As in the case of managers' compensation, incomes of workers in Wuxi are decided by township economic commissions. Although total wages are linked with enterprise profits, monthly pay of workers, even in village enterprises, has to be approved by the commissions. In fact, 3 percent of firms still determine wages according to a unified work-point system with farmers, a continuation of the past method. This also reflects the emphasis in income distribution on community membership, owing to lack of employment competition. Another interesting feature is that in Wuxi 18 percent of TVPs use work-point systems whereby workers' incomes are based not only on working time, work load, and product quality but also on attitudes, seniority, and other noneconomic factors.

Table 15-6. *The Relationship between Directors' Bonuses and Enterprise Profits, Xiqiao Town, Nanhai County*

Annual profits (thousands of yuan)	Monthly bonuses (yuan)
50	200
51–100	230
101–150	260
151–200	290
201–250	320
251–300	350

Source: Information from fieldwork.

In Jieshou workers' incomes basically consist of fixed wages, piece-rate wages, and bonuses, which are usually decided by directors. Since wage differences among enterprises within a community are relatively large and income gaps within enterprises are narrow, we can say that in Jieshou wages are based on economic returns of enterprises and that enterprises rather than individuals are the basic units.

In Nanhai 75 percent of workers' income is from piece-rate wages and the remainder consists of supplementary incomes, chiefly bonuses and extra piece-rates. Since there are wider income gaps among employees within enterprises, we can conclude that incomes in Nanhai are based on individual performance.

Conclusions

As discussed earlier, forms of ownership and individual mobility vary in the three counties. When township enterprises account for a large percentage of TVPs and labor mobility is restricted, individuals' choices are limited. The more opportunities for individuals are restricted, the more they have to rely on community governments to raise their living standards. Our analysis indicates that different opportunity structures in the three counties have led to different degrees of noneconomic intervention in the incomes of TVP employees by community governments.

In Wuxi there is virtually no labor market, and community members are mostly assigned to enterprises by community governments, which take into account not only the quality of laborers but also their economic conditions and family burdens. The result is that individuals depend on community governments for employment. Because of government intervention, income disparities between TVP workers and farmers are not large. These two factors have contributed to the development of a community consciousness that is much stronger in Wuxi than in Nanhai and Jieshou, as we can see from table 15-8. In Wuxi 10 percent of sample workers would prefer that most of their

Table 15-7. *The Composition of TVP Workers' Incomes*
(percentage of total number of enterprises)

Wage system	Wuxi	Jieshou	Nanhai
Primary			
Time rates	9.1	29.7	16.7
Piece rates	66.7	64.9	75.0
Enterprise work-points	18.2	0	8.3
Community work-points	3.0	0	0
Secondary			
None	12.1	34.3	30.0
Piece rates	72.9	60.0	55.0
Bonuses	79.1	2.9	5.0
Dividends	9.1	2.9	5.0
Other	6.0	2.9	10.0

Source: Enterprise Survey Questionnaire.

enterprises' profits be used for rural construction, but in Nanhai only 4 percent and in Jieshou 3 percent have such a wish. Wuxi community governments are placed in the delicate position of balancing equality and efficiency. They must, on the one hand, try to develop a sense of equality among different trades and social groups and, on the other, maintain sufficient incentives to stimulate the work initiative of all community members.

Community governments in Nanhai and Jieshou have a lighter burden in this respect. They intervene less in income redistribution among different social groups in the community, and workers' incomes are determined by enterprise performance. In Nanhai there is a relatively developed labor market through which most individuals seek employment. Wages are determined by enterprise efficiency and by labor market trends. This has led to marked income disparities between workers and farmers, among enterprises, and among different types of TVP employees. Individuals obtain economic benefits through labor market competition instead of government intervention. As a result, individualism is stronger and the sense of community interests much weaker than in Wuxi. Fifty-three percent of Nanhai sample employees would prefer that more enterprise profits be allocated as individual incomes, compared with only 27 percent and in Wuxi and 7 percent in Jieshou. In Jieshou as many as 89 percent of sample workers want their enterprise's profits to be used for reinvestment, but only 57 percent of the workers in Wuxi and 36 percent of those in Nanhai have such a desire (see table 15-8). This strong sense of identification with firms in Jieshou can be attributed to scarce job opportunities, the blood relationships common among employees, and the narrow income gaps within enterprises.

Distribution relationships within a community cannot but have an impact on the incentives of TVP employees. In Wuxi the incentive role of wages has been weakened and has been replaced by the pursuit of job reputation, social

Table 15-8. *Employees' Preferences Concerning Use of Enterprise Profits*
(percentage of total sample employees)

Use	Wuxi	Jieshou	Nanhai
Individual incomes	27.0	6.8	53.4
Expansion of production	57.3	88.8	35.6
Rural construction	10.1	2.7	4.0
Other	1.5	1.0	0.8

Source: Worker Survey Questionnaire.

status, and higher grading of enterprises. TVP employees in Wuxi prefer to remain workers rather than go back to farming, even if they would earn less. They would also prefer to be employed by state enterprises, even at lower pay than in their current jobs. TVP employees in Nanhai and Jieshou, however, care more about their incomes. In Nanhai and Jieshou there are marked differences among wage levels in different enterprises owing to lack of government intervention. As a result, incomes are more of an incentive than in Wuxi. Workers in the two counties would be farmers if they could earn more, and they would stay with TVPs for the sake of higher incomes instead of going to state enterprises. This tendency to pay more attention to incomes may have a significant effect on enterprise performance and the development of rural industry.

We also analyzed the relationships among different social groups within enterprises in the three counties. In Wuxi factory directors and workers commonly share risks. Community governments impose a ceiling on income differences between directors and workers and control firms' overall wage bills by levying a bonus tax. As a result, there are only small gaps among wage levels in different firms and between incomes of directors and workers. As there is a relatively developed labor market in Nanhai, workers obtain incomes through the market mechanism on the basis of their human capital, and relationships among social classes are based on economic division of labor rather than on noneconomic factors. In Jieshou the strong blood ties that often exist among employees are cemented by the scarcity of job opportunities, and there is no visible class polarization within an enterprise. When their enterprises face serious financial deficits, 84 percent of sample employees in Jieshou would prefer to stay even if their wages were cut by half. The ratios in Nanhai and Wuxi are 47 percent and 64 percent respectively. When they see other employees shirking, 70 percent of Jieshou sample workers will directly remind them that they should improve their behavior. In Nanhai only 52 percent and in Wuxi 51 percent of sample employees are willing to do this.

All these observations indicate that employees in Nanhai demonstrate the strongest individualism. They regard firms as arenas for economic activities and sources of their individual benefits. They also have a strong desire for labor mobility and rely on themselves instead of on government intervention to obtain incomes through market competition. Jieshou is another extreme example; enterprises are like big families in which individuals equally share economic interests, have a deep feeling toward their firms, and exert a strong influence over each other's behavior.

The three counties will face different problems in their future development. Wuxi will have to deal with the problem of efficiency. Employees should be encouraged to care more about their enterprises' performance through greater economic incentives instead of higher social status. Perhaps only systemic reforms could solve this problem. Nanhai will have to concentrate on the problem of economic equality. The experience of other developing countries shows that with industrialization the gap between rich and poor will further widen unless government intervenes. In a country like China where egalitarianism predominates, the size of income disparities that the masses will accept and the disparities that are most conducive to economic efficiency may differ, and further study of this issue is needed. The priority for Jieshou is to strengthen the organizational aspect of TVPs and weaken the existing blood relationships. It is true that family and other close personal relationships help to develop employees' identification with firms and encourage participation in the management of their enterprises. But we still have to ascertain whether employees' full identification with enterprises can change the nature of enterprises as economic organizations and whether the equal sharing of economic benefits will weaken the incentives of employees.

Note

1. In the Huada Electric Fan Factory, for example, the director is entitled to a bonus of Y240 out of every Y10,000 of above-quota profits, Y480 for every Y10,000 of profits arising from innovative activities, and Y360 for every Y10,000 of profits from above-quota sales.

Part V

The Role of Community Governments

Rural community governments—townships, villages, and to a lesser extent production teams—have had a profound impact on the nature, speed, direction, and accomplishments of rural industrialization in China. They established and own the community enterprises that are responsible for the bulk of the industrial output of the TVP sector. Moreover, where private firms have developed rapidly, they have done so with the encouragement and often the active support of community governments. Thus an analysis of the roles, motivations, and behavior of community governments and their leaders is essential for an understanding of China's TVP sector. The two chapters in this section look at this topic from somewhat different perspectives.

In chapter 16 Song Lina and Du He analyze the role of township governments in rural industrialization. The authors argue that the most fundamental linkage between township governments and their enterprises is in the realm of public finance: the enterprises provide the revenue needed to run the government and improve social welfare in the community. China's state budgetary system and the extrabudgetary funds that are so important at the local level are briefly described.

Song and Du then look more specifically at the public finances of township governments. Townships rely on revenue from community property to finance their operations, and rural industrialization carried out by township enterprises offers a potentially productive and easily tapped source of funds. The production responsibility system (PRS) further strengthened the public finance motivation for rural industrialization by removing agricultural land and related assets from the control of community governments.

The authors next discuss the bifurcated role of township governments—as property owners and as local governments—and the problems engendered because the two roles tend to weaken and compromise each other. They assess the direct participation of township governments in the operations of township enterprises as manifested both in preferential treatment for township enterprises and in restrictions imposed on them by township governments.

Factors that generate differences in the behavior of township governments—including natural resource endowments, the level of development, employment pressures, and the quality of the labor force—are then reviewed, and the impact of township governments on local industrialization is analyzed. In all four counties township governments have considerable control over township enterprises, but the focus and orientation of this control varies. Township governments in Jieshou and Nanhai regard the key levers of power to be control over personnel (through appointment of enterprise leaders) and investment. In Wuxi investment is first, followed by production planning, and in Shangrao control over production planning is considered the most important, with personnel second. The authors provide plausible explanations for this variation.

In the concluding section Song and Du argue that the present pattern of direct control by township governments over township enterprises will continue for some time and that rash attempts to change the system radically will fail. What is needed is a proper balance in the roles of township governments and avoidance of vicious cycles in financial flows between township enterprises and township governments.

In chapter 17 William Byrd and Alan Gelb analyze the motivations and incentives behind community governments' involvement in the TVP sector and their support for TVP development. The analysis is based on the assumption that Chinese community governments and their leaders can be viewed as self-interested and at least somewhat autonomous entities that pursue their own benefits, as distinct from the social welfare of the community as a whole. This basic postulate of public choice theory, which is usually applied to nation-states, has some interesting implications for rural communities in China.

Some key features of the rural economic and institutional environment are identified: population and factor immobility; the resulting spatial inequality in rural incomes and industrialization; the ineffectiveness of the fiscal system in redistributing income among localities; compressed income differentials within communities and TVPs; and the need for community governments to rely largely on the resources of their own communities in developing TVPs.

The authors go on to describe the flows of funds between TVPs and the local community and to review the strong linkages between TVP development and the community economy and government. These consist of fiscal linkages, income and employment linkages, and rewards to community government leaders—salaries and formal incentives, informal incomes and consumption, and promotions. It is argued that community government leaders in virtually all Chinese rural communities have strong incentives to develop the local TVP sector. The personal incentives for township leaders, however, are somewhat less than those for leaders of villages and production teams because the former are state cadres paid under a unified national system.

Byrd and Gelb then look at patterns of community government involvement in the TVP sector. These include successful development of community enterprises in certain areas that are better endowed with financial and human resources and have easy access to urban markets; fiscal predation against the community enterprise sector by community governments in poorer, more backward areas; creation of a general policy environment conducive to development of private enterprises; and more active and direct financial and personal support of larger, more successful private enterprises by community and county leaders. These patterns are leading to a situation in which ownership in the TVP sector is becoming increasingly correlated with the level of development: localities with successful community enterprises may or may not allow the private sector to flourish, but the backward, hitherto unsuccessful, areas are forced to turn toward developing private enterprise.

Fiscal predation occurs when community governments' regular revenues are insufficient to cover their large, virtually fixed expenditures for local public and social services and for their own payrolls. Governments are forced to milk their enterprises for funds regardless of whether the firms are earning profits. Unprofitable community enterprises respond to fiscal predation by "eating" their capital stock (that is, by using their depreciation funds for remittances to community governments) or by borrowing from banks. The latter case, in which community governments obtain indirect deficit financing from the local banking system, is especially detrimental.

The concluding section suggests that spatial imbalances in rural industrialization and TVP development are likely to persist as long as population and factor mobility continues to be restricted. Fiscal predation exacerbates the problems of backward areas. The dual role of community governments as both local governments and business corporations leads to severe conflicts in the backward areas that suffer from fiscal predation, and the government role commonly squeezes out the business role. Although local measures such as election of factory directors and contracts between directors and community governments can ameliorate fiscal predation, more fundamental solutions may be required. These might involve reducing the size of governments in backward areas (especially the number of people on community government payrolls) and financing through the state budget certain essential social and public services that are presently paid for with community governments' extrabudgetary funds. Another, narrower recommendation is for explicit bonus systems, tied to local economic performance, for township leaders.

16

The Role of Township Governments in Rural Industrialization

Song Lina and Du He

As the study of nonagricultural activities in China's countryside deepens, an increasingly clear picture of the external environment, business operations, and internal systems of rural industrial enterprises is emerging. China's rural industrialization is based on small rural communities, and the interests of these communities have a direct bearing on the behavior and goals of rural enterprises. Community governments not only have all the administrative functions of local government, but they also have some actual autonomy and represent to a great extent the common interests of their members. In this chapter the behavior of township governments is selected as the key variable for study, and its impact on rural industrialization is analyzed.

Public Finance and the Functions of Township Governments

China's highly centralized public finance system dates back to 1950. In March of that year the Central Committee issued two resolutions containing detailed regulations for the state financial management system. Except for some local taxes and a few small income items that could be retained by local governments to offset certain expenditures, all income was concentrated in the hands of the central government. Similarly, all outlays (except local supplementary expenditures) were included in the state budget. The financial outlays of local governments and state enterprises were all to be included in their budgets and had to be reported to and approved by the central government. In subsequent years this "uniform income and outlay" system underwent several changes, but it was not until 1980 that China began to break away from overcentralization and excessively strict control and to offer more financial autonomy to local governments and state enterprises.

Even under the centralized system, some government funds were mobilized and utilized outside the budgetary controls. At first these extrabudgetary funds included only a few items and were very small. Some townships, villages, and departments of local government tried to use their own production and business operations to help finance rural education, cultural activities, administrative expenditures, and the like. In 1953 extrabudgetary funds in China as a whole were equivalent to only 4 percent of the state budget, but the figure climbed to 8.5 percent in 1957 and to 20.6 percent in 1960. Readjustments by the state caused the figure to drop to 14.5 percent by 1966, but it then rose again and reached 35.6 percent in 1977. As economic reforms and decentralization of authority took hold, the figure jumped to 60 percent in 1981 and to more than 80 percent in 1985.

In the public finance structure at the county level there are both budgetary and extrabudgetary revenues. Budgetary revenues are allocated by the next higher level of government and must be used for specified purposes, in accordance with the uniform income and outlay system. Extrabudgetary revenues include supplementary industrial and commercial taxes, supplementary agricultural taxes allowed by the central government, and some other revenues from the county's operations and production activities. The four counties we surveyed had some extrabudgetary funds, but these were generally not high in comparison with total budgetary funds. The figures below, obtained from fieldwork, show the percentage shares of industry and agriculture in the extrabudgetary revenues of the four counties.

	Wuxi	Jieshou	Nanhai	Shangrao
Agriculture	0.0	27.4	0.0	49.0
Industry	100.0	72.6	100.0	51.0

The share of agriculture is zero in the two most industrialized counties, it is relatively low in Jieshou, and it is relatively high (nearly half of the total) only in Shangrao.

The uses of extrabudgetary funds in the sample townships of the four counties are shown in table 16-1. Townships in Wuxi and Nanhai spend considerable shares of their extrabudgetary funds on enterprise development, whereas those in Shangrao spend little for this purpose.

Table 16-1. *Extrabudgetary Expenditures in Sample Townships in Three Counties*
(percentage of total)

Type of expenditure	Wuxi	Nanhai	Shangrao
Enterprise development	30.5	22.1	1.4
Aid to agriculture	18.3	6.0	4.6
Community development	35.0	38.5	79.7
Monetary rewards for government employees	4.9	14.5	0.0
Administrative expenses outside the budget	11.3	18.9	14.3

Source: Township Leader Questionnaire.

Township Government Operations

Township governments are the grass-roots apparatus of the Chinese government. Their effectiveness is basically determined by the degree of their control over the public wealth of rural communities. In a sense they have some of the characteristics of small nation-states (see chapter 17). Through the township government public wealth is accumulated, multiplied, drawn into the income and outlay system, and distributed to every interest group and individual in the community.

Township governments are supposed to regard the overall interest of their communities as their ultimate goal. In fact, however, they have many, not necessarily compatible, tasks—promoting economic development, expanding employment, fostering industrialization, and improving local living standards—and they tend to favor those groups that can best quench their thirst for revenue. As a result, they cannot give fair treatment to every group and individual, and their control over public wealth can never be integrative and uniform.

In line with the dramatic changes in rural areas brought about by the production responsibility system (PRS), the township was made an independent level in the government financial system in 1984. Townships are now allowed to retain part of the tax revenues collected in the area under their jurisdiction. They have control over disbursements from this retained portion of revenue, but other budgetary expenditures are still determined and allocated by the county government. Extrabudgetary funds remain separate accounts under the control of township governments and are not subject to budgetary supervision.

The revenue of township governments thus falls into two categories. Budgetary revenue belongs to the government fiscal system and is generally used for specified purposes such as salaries of state employees, administrative expenditures, and operating expenses. Extrabudgetary revenue, which is generated by the business operations and other activities of township governments, is at the disposal of the township government. As the state budget can only provide subsistence to township governments, extrabudgetary revenue becomes the guarantee for their effective functioning.

THE INITIAL SITUATION. There is a widespread refusal to acknowledge that township public finances existed before the gradual establishment of the formal system in recent years. This may be correct theoretically or legally, but not in reality. Township public finances were brought into being by the inadequacy of funds allocated by the central government from its budget. The state invested much less in agriculture than in the urban industrial system and put only nominal amounts into rural communities. Therefore, even if the township government (called the people's commune at the time) refrained from ambitious public undertakings, it could hardly make ends meet with the funds allocated by the state.

During the people's commune period and even earlier, the community government collected funds locally for the central government. In return, the central government allocated budgetary funds to the community government through a top-to-bottom process. In this sense the township government could not be regarded as having independent finances and budget. But it was, after all, a grass-roots organ of state power, and if it did not have some discretionary resources at its disposal, it could not function effectively. So, during the prereform period the township government always controlled some resources for meeting local needs, and it used them for exchanges with lower-level communities—brigades and production teams. This kind of exchange brought the township government some financial income outside the state budgetary system.

Some exchanges were in kind rather than in money. For instance, when the local community wanted to build a road or dig an irrigation canal, the township government might offer its sponsorship, and the lower-level community groups would provide the labor. When the township government convened a meeting, it usually called on production teams to provide food for the participants. The township government gave not money but the time and energy for organizing projects, and the lower-level groups contributed inputs to undertakings that would advance their own development. But this primitive financial relationship could hardly meet the needs of ambitious township governments, which strove to organize production themselves or to control some profitable entities.

THE TRANSFORMATION TO MONETARY FORM. In their efforts to transcend the primitive financial relationship, township governments did not have many choices. Most township governments had to rely on income from agricultural production for primitive accumulation, but agriculture earned relatively low financial returns and could provide only limited financial support for the development of rural communities. Capital accumulation in rural communities was adversely affected by the state monopoly on the purchase and marketing of farm produce, by low prices for agricultural products, and by the segregation of the rural and urban economies.

The need to make up for the low income from agricultural production gave rise to repeated impulses for rural industrialization. By 1977 Wuxi, after experiencing three failures, was achieving the best results of any of China's 2,100 counties in running commune and brigade industries, and the income from these enterprises became the chief source of funds for the county's rural communities. During 1971–78, Y148 million in profits from these firms went into agricultural machinery, bridges and power stations, field terracing, and other agricultural investments. Rural industrialization was obviously the best

way for township governments to make up for the deficiencies in their revenue and to change the primitive financial relationship based on the exchange
of labor and goods into a monetary relationship based on the profits of commune and brigade enterprises.

Township Property

After 1949 the property system for rural communities underwent a series of
changes—land reform, the cooperative movement, and, in 1958, the people's commune movement. Under the people's communes, the land of rural
communities (including private farm plots and farmers' housing plots), as
well as large agricultural equipment, became the property of the three levels
of rural community government, with the commune at the top. (Farm tools,
household necessities, and farmers' houses were exempted from communal
ownership.) Since agricultural accumulation was too slow and could not meet
the demands of rural development, even in the earlier days of the people's
communes some nonagricultural assets came to be included in the public
property of rural communities—that is, in the assets of commune and brigade
enterprises. But although communities strove to develop rural industry, macroeconomic conditions prevented a wave of rural industrialization from occurring.

When the PRS was adopted, the property of the people's communes was
divided. The right to use land was accorded to farm households, and in most
areas agricultural fixed assets and large farming implements formerly owned
by the collectives were dispersed.

Table 16-2. *Fixed Assets of Industrial Enterprises, Wuxi, 1975–86*
(millions of yuan)

Year	County enterprises	Township enterprises	Village enterprises
1975	50.18	27.18	21.03
1976	43.46	41.87	29.47
1977	72.41	57.32	40.96
1978	80.87	77.82	52.34
1979	92.78	102.15	64.45
1980	105.22	133.61	85.73
1981	119.95	171.96	106.10
1982	138.05	194.25	129.31
1983	167.72	231.83	161.05
1984	203.07	280.40	191.53
1985	225.36	459.17	347.95
1986	262.62	613.10	479.50

Note: Assets are valued at original purchase prices.
Source: Information from fieldwork.

The share of commune and brigade enterprises in the assets of rural communities, however, did not decrease but increased to varying degrees. The original value of the fixed assets of township enterprises in Wuxi was Y27 million in 1975, but by 1986 the figure had risen to Y613 million, a nearly twenty-three-fold increase. In 1985 the fixed assets of township enterprises in Jieshou were worth Y9.8 million—1.9 times the 1980 figure of Y5.2 million. After 1979 the value of fixed assets of township enterprises in Wuxi exceeded that for county industrial firms, and by 1985 the fixed assets of industrial village enterprises had overtaken those of county firms (table 16-2).

The Impact of Changes in Community Property

The growth of agricultural productivity and the rapid transfer of surplus farm laborers to nonagricultural activities as a result of the PRS paved the way for rural industrialization by making available the necessary factors—labor, capital, and land. The changes in the composition of community property had several consequences for township governments.

First, most township governments did not control much industrial property, and when agricultural property was dispersed under the PRS, they experienced a short-term "anemia" in their extrabudgetary finances and a weakening of their administrative functions. For example, when we visited Wenzhou Prefecture, Zhejiang Province, in 1983, nonagricultural activities were booming, income per capita was rising rapidly, and capital accumulation in rural communities was high. But since the communities' old property had been dispersed and their new property was not yet properly organized, there was a great deficit in government finances. The result was that township governments became impotent in performing their administrative functions, and their managerial functions were greatly reduced. At that time, basic facilities and public works in the townships of Wenzhou Prefecture were rather backward, considering the rate of capital accumulation. Farmers were building three- and four-story houses with kitchens and bathrooms, but their kitchen slops were running in the streets for lack of sewers. Cultural, public health, and other public undertakings were lagging behind other areas. Township governments could not even organize projects but had to entrust the task to popular businessmen and venerable elders.

Second, the PRS altered the composition of property under the township governments' control, and their behavior changed accordingly. Their terms of reference shifted from agriculture to industry. The enlarged proportion of industrial wealth in township property further increased the financial power of rural communities. In 1985 in the sample townships of Wuxi the average value of output of industry was 11.3 times that of agriculture. Even in Jieshou, where industries were launched rather late, the value of output of industry was 2.8 times that of agriculture. The share of industry in township government revenue increased with the rise in the share of industrial property. Income from industrial production is now the chief source of township revenue in most areas, and income from agriculture accounts for only 19.1 percent of sample townships' extrabudgetary revenues, on average.

These consequences, although totally different, are both related to the general trend toward industrialization. The introduction of the PRS was a necessary precondition for rural industrialization and opened up prospects for development; the increased proportion of industrial property in the assets of local communities affected the form of industrialization and the degree of community government involvement in the process.

After property relationships in local communities have taken their initial shape and the industrialization process has been launched, it is necessary to protect community public finances. In the absence of a strict tax system, the township government can safeguard public finances only by participating directly in the management of firms—that is, by owning a portion of the community's property, independent of any interest group. Otherwise, community public finance becomes an empty word.

Rural communities benefit financially from industrialization in two ways. First, township government revenue is increased by the taxes paid by the enterprises, which are at least in part retained by township governments for their own use. Second, the township government draws income directly from enterprises under its control. Under China's specific conditions it is not feasible for township governments to meet all their financial needs from taxes on enterprises, and most township governments own and manage enterprises so that they will have a direct source of income.

The Bifurcation of Township Government Functions

In the process of rural industrialization the township government took on a twofold role—as community administrator and as enterprise owner. Whether the township government can function effectively in the first role depends largely on the level of revenue at its disposal. Township governments own certain assets as a means of achieving the objectives of community public finance. Hence the dual function of township governments inevitably affects rural industrialization.

The behavior of every township government leader has a twofold motive: to discharge government duties and to further personal interests. This does not mean that most township government leaders promote rural industrialization merely for personal gain. Rather, personal and public motivations are intertwined. One reason for this has been the past overemphasis on personal sacrifice and the neglect of deserved material rewards for grass-roots officials. Another reason is the relative decline in the regular incomes of these officials in recent years. When their pay was based on work-points in their home production teams or came from extrabudgetary revenue, their incomes were generally higher or more stable than those of ordinary commune members. But as rural industrialization and economic development have progressed, officials' incomes have not kept pace with those of most local residents. In general, the salaries of township government officials are lower than those of village cadres, and those of village cadres are lower than those of township enterprise employees.

The Focal Point of Township Governments' Work

Analysis of sample townships shows that most township governments give primary attention to the enterprises they run. This is because the relationship between the governments and their enterprises is one of broadly based interdependence. In our sample, direct and indirect investment by township governments accounted for more than 30 percent of the startup funds for township enterprises. The profits handed over by township enterprises in the sample counties constitute more than 38 percent of township government revenues. As administrators of rural communities, township governments also obtain revenue through taxation. In the sample, remittances by township enterprises account for 43.6 percent of township revenues and tax payments by enterprises under other forms of ownership for 14.3 percent.

Since the township government owns the assets of its enterprises, it has the right as well as the duty to manage this property. Moreover, governments must participate directly in management to realize the goals of their investment in the enterprises. The township government hence has a status similar to that of a board of directors but without all of its functions.

The Difficulties of Balancing Roles

The township government's role as not only the organizer and manager of rural industrialization but also a participant in it can distort its discharge of government functions. A good township government must play different roles simultaneously. Not only does it have to adjust the relations between its enterprises and other interest groups in the community, but it must also straighten out relations among its enterprises (for usually there is more than one firm directly under the township government) and among the owners, managers, and workers of each enterprise.

The administrative functions of the township government are greatly weakened by its status as owner and beneficiary of rural community property. Township governments have only indirect control over private enterprises, since they have no share in the firms' assets and cannot expect much revenue from them. As long as these enterprises pay taxes according to regulations and abide by the law, township governments exercise little authority over them. There is thus a difference in the degree of protection and control within the community.

For example, 79 percent of the sample township enterprises in Wuxi could

obtain raw materials at below-market prices through the township government, but only 5 percent of the private enterprises could. In the Jieshou sample, low-priced raw materials were distributed only to township enterprises.
Township enterprises in the Wuxi sample received 21 percent of their total
capital as allocations by township governments, whereas other enterprises received none; in the Jieshou sample, such allocations constituted 26 percent
of township enterprises' total capital, but other enterprises received none.

Township Governments' Influence on Township Enterprises

The township government protects and strictly controls its own enterprises
because it depends on them to a great degree. The dual functions of township
governments are mirrored in the twofold character of local protectionism.
Protection of private enterprises is motivated by the township government's
role as government administrator. The township government adopts protective measures for private enterprises only when these firms come into conflict
with entities from outside the community or when their development is hindered by unfavorable policies of higher levels of government. But its protection of township enterprises is motivated not only by its administrative role
but also by its status as owner.

Preferential Treatment

Since township enterprises are launched with financial assistance from township governments, these firms enjoy advantages from the beginning. In the
samples, township enterprises exceed other types of firm in the TVP sector
in capital, fixed assets, and number of employees and thus have higher productive capabilities. Their average value of output per worker is 1.64 times
that of village enterprises, 2.93 times that of partnerships, and 2.86 times
that of individual firms. Moreover, township governments give their enterprises priority in obtaining materials in short supply.

Township governments also provide township enterprises with an intangible resource—the use of the governments' credibility. Because of their close
association with township governments, township enterprises enjoy higher
status in the eyes of specialized branches of government (such as banks, industrial and commercial administrative bureaus, and tax and supply departments) than enterprises under other forms of ownership.

Restrictions

Despite these advantages, the efficiency of township enterprises is lower than
or at least no higher than that of other kinds of TVPs (see chapter 18). There
are several reasons for this, related to control by township governments.
First, township governments' dependence on township enterprises for income

increases the enterprises' management costs. In addition to paying taxes, township enterprises bear part of the governments' consumption expenses. As the "purse" of the township government, the enterprises have to receive guests, send presents, and pay expenses for meetings, travel, and visits on behalf of the government. Although no detailed data on these expenditures are available, the seriousness of this problem was evident from our talks with township enterprise leaders.

Second, since township enterprises are the chief means by which the township government attempts to achieve the comprehensive goals of the community, maximization of enterprise profits has rarely been pursued wholeheartedly. Almost all township governments seek to use rural industrialization to employ surplus labor from agriculture. Because of the stability of township enterprises, rural residents prefer to work in them, as is shown by responses to the Worker Survey Questionnaire. The township government usually decides the number of workers to be recruited by township enterprises, and enterprise directors cannot cut personnel at their own discretion even though they are aware that overstaffing adversely affects efficiency. In interviews in Wuxi many township enterprise directors admitted that there was overstaffing, in some cases as high as 50 percent (see chapter 14 for some examples).

Third, since the overall development objectives of rural communities have largely been shifted onto the shoulders of township enterprises, many of these firms cannot accumulate very well. This is especially true in Wuxi, where in 1986 industrial income was nearly ten times that of agriculture. To stimulate agriculture, township governments demanded that enterprises subsidize farmers. In Dongjiang township in 1986 more than 20,000 mu of land received a subsidy of Y12 per mu at the expense of township enterprises.

Moreover, township industrial corporations (TICs) under Wuxi's township governments strictly control the operations of township enterprises, especially their distribution of profits. TICs have the right to make plans for the development of all township enterprises, to adjust the reinvestment rate, and to launch new firms. They plan investments to establish new township enterprises and renovate old ones. Some enterprises may have to wait a long time to obtain the funds needed to increase production or to switch from products in little demand to other lines. These firms will witness further deterioration in their capabilities for accumulation and production.

Fourth, the impersonal character of property ownership in township enterprises means that management is kept at a low level and financial control is lax. Although government leaders are not permitted to derive personal monetary profit from the enterprises, the township government's right to participate in the management of its enterprises may become an opportunity for corruption. Officials may encroach on the property of township enterprises in nonmonetary ways to meet their personal needs.

Most directors of township enterprises have a strong desire to develop their firms, but they are under the control of the township government and wield no all-round management power. Understandably, they lack the attitude of the master, and the result can be serious waste. For instance, in Wuxi the waste rate for materials is worse for township enterprises than for village enterprises. The practice of workers' showing up but not doing much work is far more serious in township enterprises than in private enterprises and greatly increases the former's costs.

Reasons for Differences in the Behavior of Township Governments

Even under the same macroeconomic and policy circumstances, township governments in different localities behave quite differently. Several exogenous factors influence the behavior of township governments in different areas.

• *Natural resource endowment.* Shangrao is rich in natural resources, which exceed those of the other three counties in amount and variety. The county has deposits of coal, barite, lead, zinc, silicon dioxide, sulfur, limestone, and other minerals. In Wuxi mineral deposits in sample townships amount to only 450 tons, or 0.38 kilograms per capita. Jieshou and Nanhai have scarcely any mineral resources, but Jieshou does have fairly abundant agricultural resources; in sample townships arable land per capita is much larger than in Wuxi, and average forest coverage is 2.86 times Wuxi's. Arable land per capita is 0.3 mu in sample townships of Wuxi, 1.1 mu in Jieshou, 0.9 mu in Nanhai, and 1.1 mu in Shangrao. Thus, Shangrao has the best mineral resources of the four, and Jieshou has better agricultural resources than Wuxi and Nanhai. Yet Wuxi and Nanhai are far more developed economically than Shangrao and Jieshou.

• *The level of economic development.* Regional differences in economic development are shown by the income per capita of the rural population, which is a relatively comprehensive index. In Wuxi in 1985 the figure was Y754, in Nanhai Y1,029, in Jieshou Y285, and in Shangrao Y322. Our investigations confirmed these differences; the standard of living for typical households was highest in Nanhai, with Wuxi second and Shangrao and Jieshou trailing behind.

• *Employment pressure.* A rough indication of employment pressure is arable land per member of the agricultural labor force: the average is 6.1 mu in Wuxi, 2.9 mu in Nanhai, 2.6 mu in Jieshou, and 4.0 mu in Shangrao. But these numbers mask differences in the stages of development of rural industrialization and consequent differences in the degree to which agricultural workers have moved into industry. For instance, the figure for arable land per farmer in Wuxi is high because large numbers of rural population have already shifted to nonagricultural employment. A more accurate measure of employment pressures and requirements in rural communities is the annual percentage change in the industrial and agricultural labor forces, shown here for 1978–85. (The data are derived from fieldwork.)

	Wuxi	Jieshou	Nanhai	Shangrao
Industrial labor force	18.8	32.4	12.6	12.3
Agricultural labor force	−12.9	−10.5	−12.7	2.5

These figures indicate the capacity of rural industry to absorb agricultural workers. All counties except Shangrao have managed to shift labor from agriculture to industry at a fairly rapid rate. In Shangrao the agricultural labor force actually increased between 1978 and 1985.

• *Quality of the labor force.* Some characteristics of the rural population in the four counties were mentioned in chapter 4. The figures below, from the Enterprise Quantitative Questionnaire, show the average number of technical personnel and supply and marketing staff in sample firms. The much higher numbers of the latter in Wuxi and Nanhai are striking, as is, in particular, the low ratio of supply and marketing to technical personnel in Shangrao.[1]

Type of personnel	Wuxi	Jieshou	Nanhai	Shangrao
Technical	0.53	0.19	0.21	0.66
Supply and marketing	1.15	0.30	1.0	0.21

The differences in microenvironments and in conditions for industrialization reviewed above inevitably affect the decisions and behavior of township governments and thus the development of rural industries.

The Impact of Township Government Behavior on Local Industrialization

The ability of township governments to realize communal targets—conditioned partly by the factors discussed in the last section—affects their behavior and to a certain extent determines regional approaches to rural industrialization. In this section we examine broad differences in township governments' participation in management and control of township enterprises.

Management and Control

According to responses to the Township Leader Questionnaire, township governments in all four counties are deeply involved in the management of TVPs, especially township enterprises. The index of participation in management by sample township governments is 0.95 in Wuxi, 0.80 in Jieshou, 0.90 in Nanhai, and 0.78 in Shangrao. We see such participation in management as a positive concept—as assistance, not as predatory meddling. In Wuxi and Nanhai, known for their advanced economic development, the degree of participation of township governments in local enterprises is higher than in Jieshou and Shangrao.

The average degree of control over township enterprises exerted by township governments is 0.39 in Wuxi, 0.44 in Jieshou, 0.38 in Shangrao, and 0.39 in Nanhai. The high figure for Jieshou, which boasts a traditional, full-fledged system of political mobilization, tallies with other evidence that TVP industrial development there relies mainly on government mobilization and instructions. The county government in Shangrao has also had an important role in local industrialization, but it has been ineffective because of the poor quality of township officials: the low degree of control over township enterprises is not a rational choice but a situation the government has found no way to avoid. In Wuxi TVCE industries were launched much earlier, and a set of regulations governing the relationship between township governments and their enterprises has already taken shape. Hence the responsibilities, powers, and interests of the government and the enterprises are clearly defined. Of the four counties, Nanhai has the most characteristics of a free economy. There is a balanced ownership structure in the local TVP sector, firms rely more on the market than on the township government, and township governments have allowed more autonomy to enterprise management.

Management Priorities

The ranking in the Township Leader Questionnaire of respondents' priorities in supervising enterprises reflects the patterns of township government management (or control) in the four counties.

Priority	Wuxi	Jieshou	Nanhai	Shangrao
First	Investment	Personnel	Personnel	Production planning
Second	Production planning	Investment	Investment	Personnel
Third	Personnel	Production planning	Production planning	Investment

In analyzing the above choices, the stages of development in the four counties should be kept in mind. For example, sample township governments in Wuxi put personnel in third place, but this does not mean that they pay little attention to the appointment of township enterprise leaders. A complete set of procedures and standards for appointing and dismissing enterprise leaders has already evolved there, and staffing is no longer the focal point of the township government's work. Now enterprises are vying for power over investment and production, and township governments have had to strengthen their control in these areas. In Jieshou, sample township governments put personnel in first place, which reflects the county's reliance on cadres to push TVP development. This situation in Jieshou can be regarded as rational, since in the early stages of rural industrialization the township government has to control enterprise personnel to make its strength felt. The stress on personnel may be typical for localities that are latecomers in the drive for rural industrialization.

Sometimes township governments' priorities for supervision of township enterprises are simply illogical. When an area has just begun to see the need for local industrialization and is still in the experimental stage, the behavior of both the township governments and local enterprises may be confused, and their choices of priorities may be irrational. For instance, in Shangrao, sample township governments put power over production planning in first place. But in reality township governments in Shangrao are more concerned about personnel issues than about production planning, and in any case strict control over the latter is not really a good management method.

A common feature of the four counties is that, of fifteen indexes for appraising managerial behavior listed in the questionnaire, most township leaders focus on three: personnel, investment, and production planning. Hence township governments are concerned with some aspects of enterprises' internal management and decisionmaking but give little attention to marketing or sales. As chief owner of the assets of township enterprises, the township government, as part of its function, should oversee the operational behavior of the enterprise in the same way as boards of directors in Western countries do. Township governments and their enterprises do appear to have appropriate relations with regard to duty, power, and interest. But close examination reveals that governments' duty to their enterprises is motivated by their own financial needs and by the pursuit of wider community goals.

Power over personnel most determines relations between township governments and their enterprises, as responses to the Enterprise Director Questionnaire show. Since profit maximization by the enterprise conflicts with payment of taxes to the township government, the township government commonly restricts the actions of enterprise management through its power over personnel, and enterprise managers thus become a part of the government administration to a certain degree. Control of production plans by the township government is equivalent to controlling the value and quantity of output and thus achieving income targets for the enterprise and the township government. Control over investment can restrict enterprise expansion and direct resources toward other targets of the community and the township government.

Internal control of township enterprises by the township government may restrain the enterprises' expansion and development because the government frequently sacrifices township enterprises' interests for the sake of other goals. But since the realization of community goals must be based on the development of local enterprises, township governments find themselves in a dilemma. How township governments, influenced and limited by the specific conditions of their areas, deal with this dilemma affects the development of rural industries.

Development Patterns

Sample township governments have been able to secure for their enterprises some raw materials that are in short supply. In Wuxi 55 percent of sample township governments received allocations of raw materials from supply departments at the county level or above. The other 45 percent were able to secure raw materials on their own. Only 20 percent of the raw materials allocated to township governments in Jieshou came from rural communities; the rest were allocated by the county government. In the sample in Nanhai the county government allocated raw materials to only two township governments, which passed them on to township enterprises. In Shangrao 78 percent of the township governments received inputs from the county government, while the remaining 22 percent had to secure raw materials and other inputs on their own.

Township governments in Nanhai exercise control over the management of their enterprises, but local resources are limited, and the governments do not have ample materials to trade with township enterprises. For this reason TVPs, including township enterprises, chiefly depend on the market for survival.

TVPs in Wuxi are mostly TVCEs. Township governments exercise control through rough planning, and enterprises depend for their survival partly on the market and partly on planning.

In Jieshou agriculture predominates, and even now a large proportion of local revenue comes from that sector. Local industrialization bore the stamp not only of political mobilization but also of obvious spontaneity. This can be seen from the ownership of local TVPs. In the Jieshou sample a large number of TVCEs are actually individually run, but because individual enterprises have difficulty in requisitioning land and for other reasons, a number of them display the signboards of township enterprises. They do not have close relations with township governments, but they can be taken over by the local government once they grow to a certain scale. (For a detailed analysis see chapter 7.)

Shangrao has a weak industrial base and underdeveloped rural communities. Township governments strictly control the amount of profits kept by township enterprises, causing great difficulties for the firms' development. To make up for enterprises' losses, township governments trade local resources for materials in short supply and allocate to the enterprises raw materials bought at preferential prices from county supply departments. But since the capital accumulation of the communities is at a low level and township governments cannot cut down their expenses, the profits delivered by township enterprises are used to a large extent for the expenses of township governments or are passed on to other community interest groups. Only two sample township governments in Shangrao reported spending part of the income from township enterprises to expand the firms. In Wuxi, by contrast, sample township governments returned, to varying degrees, profit remittances from township enterprises so that the latter could keep reinvesting and developing.

Conclusions

Through descriptions of the behavior of township governments in different microeconomic environments, this chapter has illustrated the roles of township governments in rural industrialization. In addition, it has examined how the desire of township governments to increase their financial revenues has become one of their main motives for promoting rural industrialization.

Some observers hold that township governments should cut down their management and control of local township enterprises and develop a new relationship with them through shareholding. But this view neglects the basic fact that once local enterprises are divorced from township governments, local communities will not be able to achieve their goals. The township government—the main force in achieving local community goals—will not function effectively because it will lack funds; revenue from taxation can never be enough to meet the overall development needs of the community. In addition, the tax system in China has never been perfect, and tax evasion by enterprises will further reduce its effectiveness.

Therefore, for quite a long time it will be necessary for township governments to directly control some enterprises and to realize community goals through concerted efforts with enterprises. But township governments must maintain a proper balance between their roles as government administrators and as owners and operators of enterprises, to prevent a vicious cycle in the circulation of community wealth as a result of excessive levies on enterprises to meet community public finance needs.

Note

1. The higher average number of technicians in Shangrao sample firms probably reflects a looser definition of this category and the predominance of township enterprises in the sample. Correspondingly, the low number of technicians in Wuxi firms in relation to their size and industrial structure may be attributable to relatively narrow criteria for classifying employees as technical personnel.

17

Why Industrialize? The Incentives for Rural Community Governments

William A. Byrd and Alan Gelb

Local community governments at all levels—townships, towns, villages, and sometimes production teams—have played a crucial role in stimulating and supporting the rapid growth of China's TVP sector. Enterprises owned by these governments account for the bulk of TVP industrial output (see chapter 9), and where private firms have flourished, it has been with community governments' support and encouragement. Without the deep involvement of community governments, China's TVP sector could not have grown nearly as rapidly as it did in the late 1970s and early 1980s.[1] The incentives and motivations of community government leaders have impelled them to establish and finance community enterprises and in many areas to provide support for private enterprises. Where TVP development has not been successful, this has often been despite the best efforts of many community government leaders and officials. The short-term and long-term implications of reliance on local communities by the most dynamic part of Chinese industry must be considered when evaluating the future prospects of the TVP sector.

In this chapter we analyze Chinese community governments and their leaders as self-interested entities whose actions are geared toward maximizing their own benefits. This approach is applied to community governments, which can be viewed as interest groups with integrated, consistent objectives, and to individual government decisionmakers. The assumption that the government has its own independent interests that it strives to further is one of the key postulates of public choice theory.[2] This perspective contrasts sharply with the traditional view of mainstream Western economics that government is benevolent and that the main issue is designing and implementing economic policies that are optimal for the nation as a whole—assumptions shared by the neoclassical and Keynesian schools, among others, despite their different policy prescriptions.

Although we borrow one of the main postulates of public choice theory, in many respects our conclusions differ, owing to our subject. We look at rural communities with populations of sometimes only a few thousand people and always fewer than 100,000. Chinese community governments function in an environment of population and factor immobility and with a certain degree of independence in economic policy. They are thus akin in many ways to nation-states, albeit tiny in size. But they differ in fundamental ways from national governments: they have virtually no discretionary authority to tax, and they cannot print money or borrow. One of their main economic policy instruments is the establishment and development of community enterprises. In contrast, government ownership of enterprises in industrialized market economies is typically limited to a few sectors or is the result of historical accidents.

The Main Characteristics of the TVP Sector's Environment

We start by outlining some key features of the environment in which China's TVP sector functions. These include population and factor immobility, spatial inequality in rural incomes and industrialization, ineffective redistribution of income through the fiscal system, and compressed personal income differentials within communities and within TVPs themselves. The lack of mobility of factors and funds forces community governments to rely largely on their own resources in developing the TVP sector.

Population and Factor Immobility

The bulk of China's rural population is rooted in local communities, with little prospect for permanent migration elsewhere. Tiny numbers of students who are successful in their university examinations leave and usually end up in the cities; more important, increasing numbers of rural people go to the cities for "temporary" jobs in construction and other service activities. In some rural areas such as Nanhai there is an open labor market that attracts temporary migrant workers from poorer rural areas. In Jieshou successful farmer-entrepreneurs are allowed to move their production facilities and residences into town, switching their household registration status to that of "long-term urban resident." But both rural-urban and rural-rural mobility remain limited, and for many analytical purposes it is reasonable to assume complete population immobility.

Labor is somewhat less immobile than population because of opportunities for temporary employment in cities and in other rural areas. Nevertheless, mobility is restricted, and most jobs in the TVPs are still filled within the rural community. Capital is also immobile across rural communities, especially townships. Financial flows through the banking system are limited by the "gap" system of credit planning and the widespread perception that financial resources mobilized in a rural community should be used for investment within that community (see chapter 9). Flows of funds through the fiscal system are far from sufficient to offset imbalances in the financial resources of different localities, and flows of capital outside the banking and fiscal systems are still small. Finally, movement of managerial, entrepreneurial, and technical human resources in rural areas is limited. Although technical personnel can be attracted from other localities by high salaries and benefits, entrepreneurs are even more immobile than ordinary labor, since it is administratively much easier for them to locate their factories in their home communities than elsewhere (see chapter 9).

This all adds up to an environment in which flows of goods are relatively free (see chapter 5) but flows of key factors of production and of population are restricted. The policy instruments at the disposal of community governments, particularly at higher levels (townships and towns), create an economic situation that resembles a group of ministates under a free trade regime with factor immobility and fixed exchange rates. (An alternative but not inconsistent perspective is to view each rural community as a fixed-membership cooperative firm, with the added complication that lower-level communities are "nested" within higher-level ones.)

Dimensions of Spatial Inequality

Under these circumstances and given the tremendous imbalances in material, financial, and human resources among localities and regions, substantial inequality in factor rewards, particularly in personal incomes, is to be expected. Although it is beyond the scope of this chapter to analyze this phenomenon in detail, summary statistics illustrate the magnitude of spatial inequality in rural incomes.

Table 17-1 shows the variation in average income per capita among U.S.

Table 17-1. *Spatial Income Inequality among Provinces of China and U.S. States*

Area	Year	Highest (percentage of mean)	Lowest (percentage of mean)	Coefficient of variation (percent)[a]
China urban[b]	1983	137	75	13
China rural[c]	1980	194	70	28
China rural[c]	1985	195	62	31
United States[d]	1981	134	72	14
United States[d]	1986	140	70	17

a. Standard deviation divided by mean.
b. Average per capita income of urban residents in the capital cities of each of the twenty-nine provinces, based on household surveys.
c. Average per capita income of rural residents in each province, from household surveys.
d. Average per capita income by state.
Sources: State Statistical Bureau (1985c), p. 62; (1986b), p. 202; (1987c), p. 204; U.S. Government (1983); *Washington Post*, August 21, 1987, p. C2.

states and, separately for urban and rural areas, among provinces in China. China's state wage system holds down income inequality among cities to levels no higher than state variations in the United States, but rural income inequality among provinces is considerably greater than variations among U.S. states. Regional income inequality in the United States has declined greatly in the past fifty years as a result of improvements in transport and a great increase in interregional mobility.

Table 17-2 presents similar statistics for counties in two Chinese provinces and in several U.S. states. Inequality among counties in the United States is somewhat greater than among states; the amount and quality of public services that local governments provide varies, and the "Tiebout hypothesis" (Tiebout 1956, 1961) suggests that richer people congregate in localities that provide valued public services. Moreover, county data pick up differences between the rich suburbs of large cities and poorer rural areas. In Jiangsu and Anhui provinces there is relatively little spatial inequality in urban wages, but rural income inequality is substantial—only slightly less than cross-provincial income inequality and greater than inequality among U.S. states.

Income inequality within Chinese counties is usually much less severe than inequality among counties in a province. For example, in Nanhai in 1985 income per capita for the rural population in the richest township was 108 percent of the mean for all townships; in the poorest township it was 84 percent of the mean; and the coefficient of variation was only 7 percent. Inequality is lower within counties because resource endowments for communities within a county are generally more equal and because county governments try to hold down the gap between leading and lagging townships.

Table 17-2. *Income Inequality in Selected Chinese Provinces and U.S. States, by County*

Area	Year	Highest (percentage of mean)	Lowest (percentage of mean)	Coefficient of variation (percent)
Anhui urban[a]	1984	128	87	8
Jiangsu urban[a]	1985	127	85	10
Anhui rural[b]	1984	163	49	23
Jiangsu rural[c]	1985	164	62	23
Michigan	1981	164	60	17
Mississippi	1981	163	65	16
Oregon	1981	137	81	12
South Dakota	1981	183	39	21

a. Average wage per member of the urban work force.
b. Average per capita income for the rural population.
c. Average gross value of agricultural output (GVAO) per member of the rural population.
Sources: Anhui Jingji Nianjian 1985; Jiangsu Jingji Nianjian 1986; U.S. Government (1983).

Ineffective Redistribution Mechanisms

The degree of spatial income inequality in China's rural areas is especially surprising given China's strong ideological commitment to equality and the powerful redistributional instruments available to the state. But whereas government influence over urban wages effectively limits inequality in urban incomes, there is at present no comparable instrument for smoothing differences in rural incomes.[3]

Considerable redistribution of income does occur through the fiscal system. Richer, more developed provinces generate tax revenues in excess of expenditures and turn over surpluses to the central government, which provides subsidies to provinces in which local revenues fall short of expenditures. Similar fiscal redistribution occurs within provinces. Although substantial flows of resources are involved, they are far from sufficient to offset the underlying differences in resource endowments and levels of development. Table 17-3 shows variation in average per capita budgetary revenues and expenditures among provinces in China and among counties in Anhui and Jiangsu provinces. Variation in expenditure per capita, although much less than in revenue per capita, remains substantial, and there is significant correlation between the two at both the provincial and the county levels. If the three provincial-level cities of Beijing, Shanghai, and Tianjin are excluded, the coefficient of variation of expenditures per capita becomes even higher than that for revenues, and correlation between the two remains high. This suggests that there is little if any fiscal redistribution between rich and poor "mainstream" provinces in China. (Data were not available for Xizang, a case that probably also involves considerable fiscal redistribution.)

In any case, budgetary statistics do not reflect the large share of local public and social expenditures financed from extrabudgetary sources. Such spending is far greater in the richer, more developed localities. Moreover, a large part of budgetary spending, particularly at the lower levels, merely supports the government apparatus and pays for basic social services rather than directly raising rural incomes or financing TVP development. Finally, there is much anecdotal evidence that money transferred to the poorer areas through the fiscal system is not used with maximum effectiveness.

Egalitarian Income Distribution within Rural Communities

Somewhat counterbalancing the high degree of spatial inequality of income is the tendency toward compressed pay and income structures within rural communities and TVPs. Other things being equal, the smaller the community involved, the greater is this compression. In localities such as Wuxi the township government uses administrative controls to hold down variation in pay among TVPs within the township. Income variation among communities and compression within them is shown by data from the Worker Survey (see

Table 17-3. *Average Per Capita Budgetary Revenues and Expenditures*

Item	Highest (percentage of mean)	Lowest (percentage of mean)	Coefficient of variation (percent)	Correlation coefficient (R) for revenues and expenditures
Among provinces				
China, 1985				
Revenues	869	28	169	} 0.72
Expenditures	251	40	65	
China, 1985[a]				
Revenues	248	56	44	} 0.69
Expenditures	222	49	48	
Among counties				
Anhui, 1984				
Revenues	1,264	25	152	} 0.58
Expenditures	239	53	46	
Jiangsu, 1985				
Revenues	391	17	86	} 0.69
Expenditures	176	63	24	

a. Excludes Beijing, Shanghai, and Tianjin municipalities and Xizang

Sources: *Anhui Jingji Nianjian 1985; Jiangsu Jingji Nianjian 1986;* State Council Economic, Technological, and Social Development Research Center (1986).

chapter 13). About 60 percent of the variation in pay among sample workers is explained by firm dummy variables, which may be picking up intercommunity differences. This is especially striking given the deliberate oversampling of higher-paid employees (technicians, middle-level managers, and the like).

Egalitarianism within communities is the result of a combination of factors. Tightly knit communities with fixed memberships (often cemented by family and clan ties) would probably tend toward compressed personal income structures under almost any circumstances, and this tendency is strengthened by socialist ideals and policies. In the past the work-point system of collective distribution virtually ruled out significant inequalities in personal incomes within the communities where such distribution occurred (production teams and sometimes brigades). Moreover, in many areas wages of TVP workers were paid to their communities and were given to the workers themselves only in the form of community work-points, which prevented the industrial labor force from earning much higher incomes than agricultural workers. But probably the most important factor that limits intracommunity income inequality in rural areas today is the relatively egalitarian initial distribution of the main factor of production, land, under the production responsibility system (PRS). Egalitarian distribution of job opportunities in TVPs has also contributed to compression.

An assessment of trends that affect income distribution within Chinese rural communities would require a separate study. Ideological constraints against high personal incomes appear to be gradually eroding—for example, the permissible gap between the pay of directors and workers in community enterprises is generally rising. Specialized households and private entrepreneurs can earn even higher incomes. But in some areas, functioning labor markets may hold down differentials between agricultural and industrial incomes and reduce spatial inequality. Movements of labor may in part explain the considerable apparent reduction in rural income inequality among counties in Anhui Province between 1981 and 1984.[4]

Whether relatively equal income distribution within rural communities offsets the effect of spatial inequalities is a question for research. From the perspective of this chapter, the different patterns within and among communities are more important than the net result. As shown below, TVP development is a crucial determinant of communal development levels and living standards. Compression within communities means that the incomes of leading community members (government leaders and enterprise directors) depend at least to some extent on the average income levels in the community.

Self-Reliance in TVP Development

Factor immobility and ineffective redistribution force communities to rely on their own resources (broadly construed) to develop the TVP sector. Hence TVP development is likely to be highly uneven among regions and localities, owing to their unequal resource bases. Table 17-4 provides some indication of the striking spatial inequality in the development of industrial TVPs. Any analysis of the motivations and incentives behind community government support for TVP development must come to grips with these huge gaps, for understanding the anatomy of failure is just as important as assessing the reasons for success.

Flows of Funds between TVPs and Community Governments

Figure 17-1 shows the financial flows among township firms and township and county institutions. Township enterprises pay direct and indirect taxes to the township tax collector; they pay management fees (in effect, a tax, not a payment for services) to their supervisory agency, the township industrial corporation (TIC); and they generate after-tax profits, part of which are reinvested and part of which are turned over to the TIC. Remitted township enterprise profits flow upward through the system and are an important source of funding for township government salaries and overhead as well as for discretionary spending. Budgetary flows are relatively large, but appropriations are mostly earmarked for fixed costs (wages and overhead) and for specific projects. Management fees pay for the administrative support structure for TVPs at township, county, and higher levels. The main sources of funds for

Table 17-4. *Variation in Per Capita Value of Rural Industrial Output*

Area	Highest (percentage of mean)	Lowest (percentage of mean)	Coefficient of variation (percent)
Among provinces			
China, 1980[a]	691	4	142
China, 1985	531	2	133
Among counties			
Jiangsu, 1984[b]	554	8	119
Jiangsu, 1985[c]	414	18	97
Anhui, 1984[c]	1,100	17	161
Among townships			
Wuxi, 1984	362	42	61
Nanhai, 1985	235	22	63
Shangrao, 1985	474	30	104

a. Based on 1980 gross value of industrial output (GVIO) and 1981 rural population figures by province.

b. TVCEs only.

c. GVIO for county as a whole.

Sources: Anhui Jingji Nianjian 1985; Jiangsu Jingji Nianjian 1986; State Statistical Bureau (1987c), p. 14; and information from fieldwork.

investment in township enterprises are retained profits, remitted profits used by the TIC for reinvestment, and bank loans.

Township governments now retain for their own discretionary use a portion of above-quota budgetary revenue collected in their communities. This allows them to tap into part of the budgetary revenues generated by TVP development. Where the public finance system is in place at the township level, this revenue-sharing system has been formalized: townships in Wuxi are allowed to retain 8–12 percent of above-quota tax collections, and in Shangrao they keep 50–100 percent. In Nanhai the township public finance system has not been formally established, but townships are allowed to retain 1.5 percent of revenues collected locally within the plan and 20 percent of above-quota revenues.

Salaries and benefits of township government officials come from three main sources: budgetary allocations for salaries and for part of the overhead for the township leader and a few other cadres; profits remitted from township enterprises; and the shared portion of above-quota tax revenues. The latter two sources are used for the wage and overhead costs for collective (as opposed to state) cadres in the township government. Figure 17-1 also highlights the circular financial flows among enterprises, their employees, and banks: township enterprises pay wages and bonuses to workers, who then deposit money in banks, which then have more loanable funds, the lion's share of which is lent to local TVPs.

Figure 17-1. *Township Revenue Flows and Community Enterprises*

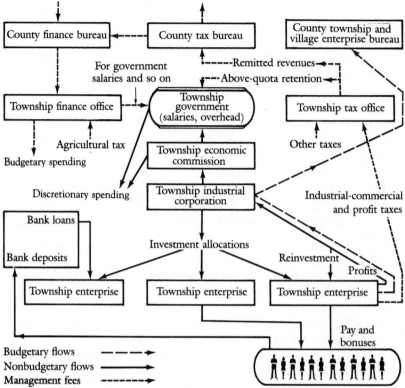

Table 17-5 shows financial flows between community enterprises and community institutions in two very different townships. Township A in Wuxi is the most industrialized township in China as measured by per capita gross value of industrial output (GVIO). Township B in Shangrao is one of the poorest and least industrialized townships visited during fieldwork. The composition of flows as well as their absolute magnitudes differ sharply.

Most of the large amount of tax revenue collected in township A is remitted to the county and is passed upward through China's fiscal system. In township B, not only does the township keep virtually all tax revenues collected, but it receives a large allocation from the county for budgetary expenditures. Profits and management fees from township enterprises constitute an important source of township government funds in township A, where sales revenue of TVCEs alone totaled more than Y200 million, but they are very small in township B. The burden on township B's enterprises, however, is paradoxically greater than in township A. Township B's firms lost nearly Y14,000 in 1986 but still had to remit a considerable amount of money to

Table 17-5. Government Income and Expenditure in Two Townships

Item	Township A (Wuxi, 1985)		Township B (Shangrao, 1986)	
	Amount (yuan)	Share of total (percent)	Amount (yuan)	Share of total (percent)
Sources of income				
Tax revenues	13,428,000	56.4	193,500	46.4
Used for quota budget spending	450,000	1.9	185,000	44.4
Retained by township (discretionary)	—[a]	—	6,800	1.6
Remitted to county	12,978,000	54.5	1,700	0.4
Additional budget allocation by county	—	—	209,800	50.4
Remittances by township enterprises	10,390,000	43.6	13,200[b]	3.2
Profits	8,320,000	34.9	n.a.	n.a.
Management fees	2,070,000	8.7	n.a.	n.a.
Retained by township	1,035,000	4.4	n.a.	n.a.
Remitted to county	1,035,000	4.3	n.a.	n.a.
Total	23,818,000	100.0	416,500	100.0
Available township resources	9,805,000	41.2	414,800	99.6
		Percentage of resources		Percentage of resources
Income				
Tax revenues	450,000	4.6	191,800	46.2
Remittances from township enterprises	9,355,000	95.4	13,200	3.2
County budgetary allocations	—	—	209,800	50.6
Expenditures				
Investment in township enterprises	6,720,000	68.5	19,300[c]	4.6
Support to agriculture	900,000	9.2	26,000	6.3
Public and social services	1,050,000	10.7	285,700	68.9
Administrative expenditures	138,000	1.4	70,800	17.1
Unidentified (residual)[d]	1,097,000	11.2	13,000	3.1
Total[d]	9,805,000	100.0	414,800	100.0

(Notes are on the following page.)

368   WILLIAM A. BYRD AND ALAN GELB

Notes to Table 17-5

n.a. Not available.

— Not applicable.

a. In 1985 the township public finance system had not yet been established in township A. In 1986 township A was to retain 3.7 percent of tax revenues collected within the quota and 8 percent of above-quota tax collections.

b. Since township B's enterprises had net losses totaling Y13,759 in 1986, these remittances were financed by additional bank borrowing and by drawing from depreciation allowances (in effect "eating" the enterprises' capital stock).

c. This is probably an overestimate, since it was assumed that all budgetary expenditure "in support of production" other than items clearly specified as agricultural was for investment in township enterprises.

d. Total expenditures are assumed to be exactly equal to total township revenue resources, with the unidentified portion of expenditures then derived as a residual.

Source: Information from fieldwork.

the township government. They accomplished this by incurring additional bank debt and by using their depreciation funds, thus "eating" enterprise capital.

On the expenditure side, too, there are striking differences. Perhaps the most important is that in township A nondiscretionary spending for salaries, overhead, social services, and the like constitutes only a small proportion of total spending (about 12 percent). In township B, by contrast, education and health alone account for more than 60 percent of total expenditure and salaries and overhead for close to 20 percent. The absolute level of township government spending on reinvestment in township enterprises is nearly 350 times as large in township A as in township B.

These differences in flows of funds reflect a huge gap in economic development and industrialization (see table 17-6). Differences in industrialization

Table 17-6. *Economic Indicators for Two Townships*
(yuan, except as indicated)

Indicator	Township A (Wuxi, 1985)	Township B (Shangrao, 1986)	(percent) A/B
Population (number)	18,779	23,396	80
Average per capita income of rural population	907	131	692
GVAO per capita	399	197	203
GVIO per capita	11,268	17	663
Sales income of township enterprises per capita	5,846[a]	14	418
Local revenue per capita[b]	1,268	9	14,089
Expenditure per capita	522	18	2,900

a. Industrial township enterprises only.

b. Includes both budgetary and nonbudgetary revenues but not additional budgetary funds provided by the county for quota budget expenditures.

Sources: Table 17-5 and information from fieldwork.

and in community government financial resources are far greater even than the large difference in average per capita income, which is roughly 7 to 1. Fiscal redistribution hardly makes a dent in resource inequality at this level. Although these tremendous differences are extreme by Chinese standards, they graphically portray the high degree of spatial inequality in rural industrialization and fiscal capacity as well as in incomes.

Financial flows are somewhat simpler for private enterprises, although there is great variation among localities and enterprises. Figure 17-2 shows some strong community-firm linkages. Private enterprises pay tax to the township tax office, typically on sales income (often 5 percent in industrial-commercial tax plus a certain amount, usually 2 percent, in lieu of the profit tax, which is generally not collected). Management fees are paid to the township industrial and commercial administrative management office, which is in charge of enterprise registration, and sometimes also to the community government. Finally, part of enterprise surplus goes directly to the commu-

Figure 17-2. *Flows of Funds between Private Firms and the Local Community*

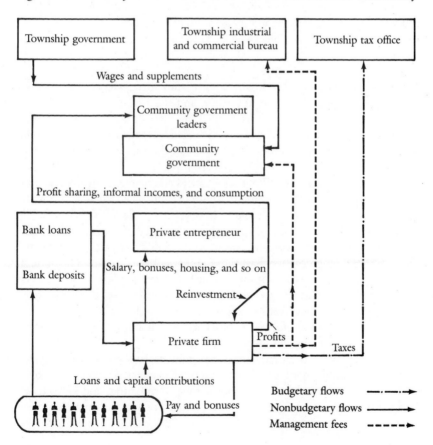

nity government and its leaders, sometimes as explicit profit remittances, profit sharing, or salary payments to community government leaders, but also in the form of informal payments, gifts, banquets, and so on.

Owners typically do not provide additional capital to a private enterprise once it is established on a sound footing; indeed, the seed capital they put in at founding is often repaid to them quickly. Subsequently, the private entrepreneur typically does not withdraw a large proportion of after-tax profits but instead reinvests profits in the firm. (Of course, he can appropriate some enterprise surplus in the form of wages, bonuses, other benefits, housing, and the like.) Private enterprises may obtain significant amounts of capital directly from employees and local community members. Larger and more successful private enterprises may also be able to obtain loans from banks (see chapter 9).

Linkages between the TVP Sector and the Local Economy

We are now ready to discuss the main linkages between TVPs and rural communities. These consist of fiscal linkages, income and employment linkages, and various rewards for community government officials.

Fiscal Linkages

The importance of TVP development for community government revenues is apparent. TVPs generate tax revenues, and the township gets a share of the taxes collected in excess of its quota. The share of tax revenues retained by townships varies greatly. The more advanced localities retain a lower share of taxes than do poor localities, but because of their rapid economic growth it is easier for them to exceed the collection plans, which are set largely on the basis of past collections. Profit remittances and management fees of community enterprises are important in the more advanced areas and are the main source of discretionary community government funds. TVPs, especially community enterprises, are highly visible profit centers that make convenient sources of government revenue. Moreover, indirect tax rates on industrial production are much higher than those on agricultural output. The agricultural tax (really a form of taxation on land) is frozen at a low level and even so is hard to collect in the poorer areas. Collection of taxes and levies from individual households is frowned on in Chinese rural communities. It is an embarrassment to local officials if they need to rely on such sources, which in any case would not yield much revenue.

The fiscal linkage is all the more important because community governments face a rather hard budget constraint. Deficit financing by any level of government below the center is not permitted in China, and lower levels of government do not have the right to establish new tax instruments or set tax rates.

Given the increasingly close link between community revenue and expenditures and the importance of the TVP sector in increasing revenues, TVP development is the single most important determinant of a local community's spending capacity. This is particularly true of resources for discretionary spending—those not required to meet the community government's payroll and overhead. Since discretionary community government funds are mainly used for investment in new or existing community enterprises, TVP development (or lack thereof) can easily become self-reinforcing. Localities such as Wuxi that have achieved successful TVP development generate large flows of discretionary resources, the lion's share of which is used to promote further TVP development. The more backward areas, such as parts of Shangrao and Jieshou counties, must use almost all of their locally mobilized revenues and their grants from higher levels of government to meet their virtually fixed expenditures on payroll, overhead, social services such as education and health, and so on. Since so few discretionary resources are available for community enterprise development, it never gets off the ground, and this perpetuates the shortage of discretionary resources for TVP development.

The fiscal linkage is important to community government leaders for a number of reasons. In the first place, it is reasonable to assume that like government bureaucrats anywhere, they are budget maximizers (see Niskanen 1968). Community government leaders interested in maximizing their fiscal resources have a strong incentive to promote TVP development. A related benefit is the enhanced fiscal autonomy for community government leaders who can draw on discretionary resources from TVPs. In addition, the pay of community government leaders and officials comes largely from revenues from TVPs; government personnel below the township level are collective rather than state cadres and hence are paid entirely from nonbudgetary revenues. Whether they receive any income at all from their positions depends to a large extent on TVP development.

Income and Employment Linkages

The level of TVP development is an important, if not the primary, determinant of rural per capita incomes. The correlation (R) between the value of rural industrial output per member of the rural population and average income per capita in China's provinces was 0.91 in 1985. Similar relationships hold among counties in the same province and, to a lesser extent, within counties. TVPs have been critically important in generating employment and raising living standards in rural areas. Both township leaders and factory directors, in their responses to questionnaires, overwhelmingly cited increasing employment and raising local living standards as the primary motivations for establishing new firms. In a situation of factor and population immobility, the sharp increases in agricultural productivity brought about by the PRS could not have been translated into higher incomes without TVP development, as rural surplus labor could not have found more productive employment anywhere else.

In the more developed localities such as Wuxi and Nanhai there has been a wholesale shift in the labor force from agriculture to industry in the past several years. These areas have been so successful in generating nonagricultural employment opportunities that they are experiencing a labor shortage (Wuxi) or significant temporary in-migration (Nanhai). In Shangrao, where the TVP sector has not developed rapidly, there is still a large surplus of rural labor that cannot and should not be employed in agriculture.

Rewards to Community Government Officials

The incentives created by the more general fiscal and economic linkages noted above are important to community government officials and leaders and in many cases may outweigh any explicit personal financial incentives. Carrying on community government business and dealing with superiors in the county government must be much easier and pleasanter when revenue constraints are eased, community members are fully employed in high-paying jobs, and the local economy is booming.

But the personal rewards and career prospects of community government leaders also depend greatly on income, employment, and revenue mobilization in their communities. These personal benefits can be divided into three main categories: pay increases and bonuses associated with TVP development and other indicators of community economic progress; informal sources of income and consumption generated by TVP development; and prospects for promotion and the related improvement of social status. The first set of benefits can be described in a fairly precise manner, but there is considerable variation among localities and among the township, village, and production team levels. Only anecdotal, largely qualitative evidence is available on the second category. The third category is important in poorer parts of the country but is actually a negative incentive in better-off areas.

PAY. Community government leaders' pay varies significantly with the degree of TVP development in the community, and this variation tends to be greater for villages and production teams than for townships and towns. There is an implicit but powerful linkage between average income per capita in communities and the maximum socially or administratively permissible level of pay for community government leaders and for directors of community enterprises. The margin by which their pay can exceed the average income of community members (or of enterprise workers in the case of directors) varies among localities and has been increasing, but everywhere and at all times there appears to be at least some fuzzy limit that cannot be transgressed.

In Wuxi the pay of a factory director is generally limited to no more than twice the average pay of employees in his factory. Nominal pay and supplements for leaders of a village are also about twice the average pay of employees of the village's enterprises.[5] Since workers' wages are linked to enterprise profits, there is an indirect relationship between community government leaders' incomes and the profitability of community enterprises. The current reward system reflects measures by the county to limit differentials between community government leaders and factory directors on the one hand and ordinary workers on the other after community government leaders and especially factory directors received what were deemed excessively high incomes in 1984.[6]

In Jieshou it is harder to discern a clear pattern, but in the private enterprises surveyed, owners (who are also directors) often appear to be able to earn high salaries only by paying their workers much higher wages than warranted by local labor market conditions. Informal incomes of both township and village officials are closely related to community enterprise profits and to incomes of community enterprise employees. When average incomes are relatively low, the fixed portion of community government leaders' compensation looms more important, especially at the township level.

In Nanhai township leaders' pay is typically two to three times the average income per worker in their communities. A similar relationship holds at the village level; since variation in average income per capita among villages is typically greater than variation among townships, village leaders' pay tends to differ much more than that of township leaders. Leaders of successful villages can earn far more than their superiors in the township government; leaders in one township earn about Y2,500 a year in the formal pay structure, whereas incomes of village leaders range from Y2,000 to Y6,000 a year. Incomes of village officials are linked directly to the profits of "their" community enterprises, unlike the situation in Wuxi.

In Shangrao there is also some linkage between local income levels and community government leaders' pay, but the variation may be considerably less, and hence the incentive effects are weaker. The reason is the low general level of incomes and the influence of state wage scales, which for township leaders set a lower limit on compensation that is high by local standards. Moreover, since the community enterprise sector in most townships has an abysmal profit performance, there is little if any linkage between community enterprise profits and leaders' pay.

Income determination differs as between township leaders and leaders of lower-level communities. The former are government cadres on the state budget payroll and are subject to a national salary scale. The official salary of a township leader is roughly Y1,000 a year and is largely invariant across localities and regions with widely differing per capita incomes. If the state salary scale were strictly adhered to, township leaders in advanced localities such as Wuxi and Nanhai would earn considerably less than ordinary TVP workers. Incentive problems are aggravated because—unlike leaders of lower-level communities—township leaders, as government cadres, are forbidden to engage in business activities on the side, which can be potentially lucrative.

The richer areas have added supplements to the compensation package of township leaders to make their total pay reasonably competitive. These supplements must be financed from nonbudgetary funds, primarily remittances from community enterprises. They do raise township leaders' income levels substantially, but the room for variation according to TVP performance and other economic indicators is still limited. In the poorer areas there is no scope for variation at the lower end, since the base pay of township leaders forms a floor. In Shangrao township leaders' pay does not go below about Y1,000 a year, and the maximum for those whose townships perform well is not much more than Y1,500. This may significantly dampen the extent to which leaders suffer for the poor economic performance of their townships, although they would still be adversely affected through the nonpecuniary linkages mentioned above.

Village and production team leaders are not under the state wage system, and their pay is free to vary across localities in line with local income levels. The top pay of such people in Nanhai can reach as high as Y15,000 (in a village where workers received about Y5,000), and at bottom it can be Y2,000 or even less. The main determinant of village leaders' pay is the profits of village firms. In Shangrao village leaders' pay reportedly ranges from Y1,000 to Y2,000 a year.

A good example of the strong incentives for village leaders is Xiqiao town in Nanhai, which in 1986 promulgated a detailed incentive pay system for leaders of subordinate villages. Village leaders get Y55 a month of base position pay. A large floating wage component that depends on the achievement of economic and social targets is paid annually. Up to Y500 a year can be earned for meeting village targets for state grain procurement, tax revenue, and treasury bond quotas (Y150), family planning (Y100), military recruitment and militia work (Y100), and financial and contract management activities (Y150). Subordinate production teams in each village can earn up to Y600 a year for fulfilling various targets. Finally, a gradually falling percentage of the profits of community enterprises goes to the village leader and his coworkers. The profit-sharing rate ranges from 8 percent for profits of less than Y50,000 to 1 percent for profits of Y2 million–Y3 million. Conceivably, a village leadership group could earn as much as Y57,000 a year through this reward mechanism.[7] With annual base wages at only Y660, the possibility of earning up to Y1,100 for meeting various targets and perhaps Y10,000 or more on the basis of community enterprise profits creates strong incentives for village leaders in Xiqiao to develop community enterprises. Similar incentives are in place elsewhere in Nanhai.

The income of production team leaders is, if anything, even more closely linked to the performance of community enterprises. Under the PRS the administrative role of production teams has been sharply circumscribed, and those without successful enterprises have become largely vestigial organizations whose leaders have no opportunity to earn high incomes. Production team leaders have thus been driven to develop team enterprises (of which they often are concurrently director) or to establish their own firms. In Jieshou one former team leader bought his team's edible oil-processing plant, which had previously been operating inefficiently under his management, and turned it into a large and successful diversified enterprise that produced machinery as well as food products. Some team leaders in Nanhai get large explicit payments (sometimes more than Y10,000 a year) from production team firms even though they are not directly involved in management.

It is impossible to gauge the magnitude of community government leaders' informal incomes with any precision, but rewards of this type are an important part of their total compensation. Outright bribery may not be common and in any case involves risks for the recipients. Much more prevalent is consumption of community government or enterprise resources, from cigarettes to banquets to housing construction. Since more funds are available for such uses in the more developed areas, community government leaders undoubtedly have an additional incentive for stimulating TVP development. Whereas formal pay incentives generally are related closely to the performance of community rather than private enterprises, private enterprises are as good a source of informal incomes as community enterprises and are sometimes even better.

PROMOTION AND OTHER CAREER INCENTIVES. These work quite differently in different parts of the country. In Wuxi and especially in Nanhai successful community government leaders are generally unwilling to be promoted to the next higher level. Production team leaders do not want promotion to village cadre status; village leaders, in particular, do not want to become township leaders; township leaders do not want to be county government cadres; and county officials reportedly try to avoid promotion to the provincial level. This phenomenon is the result of the relatively low government wage scale (in relation to local incomes in the richer areas) and the prohibition against government cadres' engaging in private business on the side. The impact of these negative incentives may not be serious and indeed may have some benefits—leaders without promotion opportunities may well be more concerned about the long-term welfare of their communities.

In the poor, backward areas promotion incentives are much more potent. Not only is there little if any loss of income for promoted community government leaders, but the change in household registration status from rural to urban residency for those promoted to the township or county level is of incalculable value. In Jieshou and especially in Shangrao, lower-level community government leaders actively strive for promotion to state cadre status. Criteria and decisions concerning promotion may be somewhat subjective, but undoubtedly the economic performance of the community for which the leader is currently responsible carries great weight.

Despite the variations in personal incentives for community government leaders among regions and localities and among community levels, it is clear that everywhere and under almost any circumstances community government leaders have strong incentives to develop the TVP sector. This is broadly true even where TVP development has lagged or failed. Thus the main forces that differentiate TVP performance among regions and localities are not related to the personal incentives of community government leaders but rather to the prevailing patterns of constraints and their interactions with these incentives.

Patterns of Community Government Involvement in the TVP Sector

In relatively prosperous areas the relationship between community governments and their enterprises tends to be mutually beneficial. But in poorer areas governments are forced to exploit their enterprises, to the long-term detriment of both firms and community. This section examines the reasons behind these dramatically different outcomes and also discusses the conditions that lead to encouragement of private enterprise.

Support for Community Enterprises in Well-Endowed Areas

In better-off areas such as Wuxi and Nanhai that have a strong base of existing community enterprises, most community governments are in a relatively comfortable financial situation. Budgetary revenues far exceed minimum budgetary expenditures, and some above-plan revenues can be retained for the discretionary use of township governments. Large nonbudgetary revenue flows from community enterprises greatly exceed public expenditures not covered by the budget. The bulk of these funds, and the substantial profits retained by community enterprises, are therefore available for reinvestment to expand the community enterprise sector. Finally, these areas also have high personal incomes and bank deposits, which can be used for loans to local TVPs (see chapter 9). All this means that mobilizing resources for public expenditures is relatively easy: basic expenditures as well as numerous extras can be financed from a small part of the profits remitted by community enterprises, leaving adequate funds to support the continued development of the enterprises. All of the linkages discussed in the previous section reinforce the incentives of community government leaders to promote the development of community enterprises.

Important policy changes in recent years have strengthened the incentives and increased the opportunities for community governments in the better-endowed areas to promote community enterprise development. The linkages in the fiscal and financial systems between local mobilization and funds available for investment in TVPs were put in place only recently. Variation in the pay of community government officials probably has become significant only since the late 1970s. The PRS increased both the pressures and the incentives to generate additional employment by developing community enterprises. The removal of political restrictions on rural industrialization and the weakening of ideological opposition to raising rural personal incomes were also important.

Fiscal Predation in Backward Areas

The same set of linkages can have an adverse impact on community enterprise development in backward areas with low incomes and a weak or nonexistent base of TVP development. The incentives are basically similar to those in the more advanced areas, but the opportunities for developing community enterprises in the traditional pattern are much more limited. Moreover, the difficult financial situation of community governments impels them to draw funds from community enterprises for public expenditures, regardless of the enterprises' profitability and ability to pay. Even when the firms are losing money, they still have to make payments to community governments, which they do by using their depreciation funds (in effect "eating" their capital stocks) and borrowing from banks and rural credit cooperatives. Fiscal predation thus occurs because community governments are forced to appropriate the funds of community enterprises to meet urgent and largely fixed public expenditure needs.

The basic problem is that the minimum necessary public expenditure requirements of community governments (as determined by their responsibilities and payrolls) are at least somewhat inelastic with respect to local income per capita, development, and industrialization. In the advanced areas minimum public expenditures are small in relation to local capacity to mobilize resources. In the poorer, more backward localities mobilization capacity is much lower, since it declines more or less in line with incomes and industrial production. Yet the number of community government employees may not be that much smaller, and the governments are expected to provide and largely finance a full array of education, health, and other social services that may not be much worse in quality than those in more developed regions.[8]

The need to meet largely fixed expenditures forces community governments in poorer areas to exploit community enterprises in ways that harm their long-term development potential. Community enterprises are starved for development funds, and because their credibility with banks is severely strained, they find it hard to obtain loans even for genuine business investments. In this way a vicious cycle arises. Since community enterprises lack the investment funds needed for healthy development, the fiscal situation of community governments remains tight, which in turn means that community government leaders are forced to continue milking community enterprises, and so on.

A related form of fiscal predation occurs when community governments require their enterprises to take on excessive numbers of workers and managers.[9] The latter are often former village and production team officials who were moved out to make room for younger replacements or whose jobs were eliminated as a result of the PRS. Excessive payrolls further squeeze the funds available to community enterprises and make it more difficult for them to achieve self-sustaining development. Local political considerations sometimes lead to the appointment of inexperienced and even incompetent officials to decisionmaking positions in community enterprises. This not only reduces efficiency but may also have a severe effect on workers' morale. Padding of payrolls and intervention by community governments in the day-to-day operations and management of community enterprises appear to be more pervasive in poorer, less industrialized localities such as Shangrao.

Fiscal predation harms the long-term prospects for TVP development and hence, through the linkages described earlier, the long-term interests of community governments. Although the practice is shortsighted, it is understandable, given the short-term pressures on community governments. Fiscal predation can be viewed as an attempt by community governments in backward areas to get around their hard budget constraint in the short run by obtaining indirect deficit financing from the banking system. The linkages and incentives that work so well in generating TVP development in better-off areas turn against it in more backward areas that lack an established, viable TVP base. Healthy TVCEs have no trouble generating employment, remitting profits to the government, and obtaining bank financing for their operations—indeed, these things come naturally. But these same activities are deadly to the viability and development prospects of community enterprises if they are forced on them from outside.

As in the success stories represented by Wuxi, institutional and policy changes in recent years have affected community government involvement in the more backward areas. Before the PRS, paying for government salaries, overhead, and social expenditures must have been a considerable burden on the poorer rural communities, but it was spread over the entire community through the work-point system and collective income distribution. Although this undoubtedly hampered development potential in the more backward areas, consumption may have been affected more than investment. In any case, how the impact was handled was to a large extent the choice of the community government.

The PRS made agriculture and the community population as a whole much more immune to fiscal predation and left only rural industry as a source of financing for nonbudgetary expenditures. This provided a strong incentive for community officials to promote TVP development. But where the development of community enterprises has not reached the take-off, or self-sustaining, stage, community governments have been tempted—even compelled—to milk their enterprises. In contrast to the prereform situation, predation mainly consists of using investment funds (community enterprise depreciation allowances and bank loans obtained by the enterprises) to finance the consumption expenditures of community governments.

The fiscal predation evident in relationships between community governments and their enterprises in backward localities raises doubts about the strategy of self-reliance in the provision and financing of social services in rural areas. Self-reliance was highly successful in the past; it has allowed China to reach unprecedentedly high levels of rural education and health with only modest budgetary expenditures. A comprehensive and all-encompassing rural government and Communist party network was also financed largely from local resources. But fiscal predation and unsuccessful TVP development in backward areas show that self-reliance has severe disadvantages and high costs.

Insulating Community Enterprises from Fiscal Predation

Government officials in Shangrao, particularly at the county level, are only too aware of the harmful pattern described above. A number of measures have been taken, particularly in a few of the more successful townships and towns, to insulate and protect community enterprises from fiscal predation. Sometimes the community government itself has taken the initiative in this respect, realizing that its longer-term interests lie in keeping intervention and profit levies to a minimum and allowing community enterprises to develop.

The best example of a community in Shangrao that has avoided fiscal predation and seems to be on the way to self-sustaining TVP development is Shaxi town. Shaxi has certain advantages: it was a traditional commercial center; it has a fairly solid base of TVP development; there are long-standing commercial ties between Shaxi firms and enterprises in Shanghai; and the large profits earned from ramie cultivation and trade in 1984–86 provided a source of funds for TVP development. (This money was tapped by requiring new employees of community enterprises to contribute Y100–Y5,000 in capital.) Nevertheless, before strong measures were taken to combat fiscal predation, the TVP sector was not developing rapidly.

In 1984 Shaxi instituted measures to strengthen the management of community enterprises and improve incentives. A contracting system was established between factories and the TIC as well as between the TIC and the town government. Factory directors are now elected by the workers, not appointed by the town government, and they have broad authority in decisions on personnel and employment, the use of funds, payment of bonuses, and business operations. Permanent workers were converted into contract workers with renewable terms of one year. Finally, piece-rate wages were instituted in all factories. Only 40 percent of after-tax profits within the plan and 20 percent of profits above the plan are remitted by factories to the TIC and the town government.

Election of factory directors seems to be effective in helping to stem government intervention and fiscal predation. Elected directors may be in a better position to resist the tendency toward inflated managerial staffs and excessive levies of funds by community governments. Changes and reductions in management teams have occurred after new factory directors were elected. Given the personal ties between community officials and appointed community enterprise managers, it is easier for elected factory directors under contract with the community government to get rid of people who are not needed. An elected director is also in a better position to resist pressures from the community government or from his own friends and relatives to pad the payroll. Under the election system the director derives part of his legitimacy from workers, who are also community members. This gives him a more secure position and somewhat greater independence and makes it more likely that an arm's-length contractual arrangement with the community government will work well.[10]

Worker election of factory directors and the associated contract system are not primarily an attempt to institute greater worker participation for its own sake or to improve employee incentives and morale, although they may have these effects. Instead they serve as a built-in mechanism, devised by community governments in their own long-term interests, to limit fiscal predation and excessive government intervention in enterprise operations, especially in personnel decisions. Election may not be the optimal method of selecting enterprise directors, but at least it prevents community leaders from giving in to the temptation to choose unsuitable or incompetent persons.

These methods, which seem to have worked well in Shaxi, may not succeed everywhere in Shangrao or in other backward areas. Townships in worse financial straits may not be able to exercise the requisite self-discipline even when dealing with firms with elected managers and contractual arrangements. A principal factor behind Shaxi's success was probably its reasonably good financial situation, which allowed it to meet public expenditure requirements relatively easily. In other townships a weak base of entrepreneurial and managerial skills makes it difficult for community enterprises to achieve healthy profitability in the first place. Although the measures implemented by Shaxi represent an admirable attempt to come to grips with the problems of fiscal predation and excessive government intervention, the situation will remain precarious until TVP development becomes self-sustaining and the revenue crunch has been eased.

General Indirect Support for the Development of Private Enterprises

Some community and county governments, both in more developed areas and in backward regions, have chosen to create an administrative and regulatory environment conducive to the development of private enterprise. Where there is a modicum of entrepreneurial spirit and experience in the population (even from forty years ago), relaxation of restrictions on private enterprises in itself usually stimulates substantial development. This has benefits for the community economy and the community government whether or not the community enterprise sector is dynamic.

In Nanhai government authorities had a relatively permissive attitude toward private enterprises even in the prereform period, and there was a burst of private enterprise development after the Central Committee Document No. 1 of 1984 officially sanctioned such development. At present, private enterprises are allowed to flourish, but most are not permitted to take out bank loans above certain limits, and an exodus of community enterprise employees to go into business on their own has been partly stemmed by administrative measures. There are some large private entrepreneurs in the county who got into business early or took advantage of their access to bank loans when these were not restricted. Many of them seek to protect themselves by establishing joint ventures of various kinds with community governments (see chapter 9). Most private enterprises, however, are very small. In Shangrao private enterprises have expanded their share in total TVP sector industrial output, apparently even in the absence of strong measures to encourage them. Private enterprises, particularly small ones established without the assistance of community governments, may be in a better position to resist fiscal predation than are community enterprises. Moreover, these enterprises raise local incomes, increase employment, and provide small amounts of revenue for the community government through management fees and tax payments.

In the more advanced areas, local authorities can choose whether to let the private enterprise sector flourish, but in any case they would be foolish not to actively promote the continued development of the traditional community enterprise sector. Wuxi has chosen to restrict private enterprises, Nanhai to let different forms of ownership coexist. In areas in which community enterprise development has not been successful, a permissive attitude toward private enterprises has important benefits for community governments and their leaders, although these are less direct than the fruits of successful development of community enterprises. If the latter is difficult or impossible to achieve, development of private enterprises may provide at least a second-best solution and help community government leaders meet some of their plan targets. Without explicit positive actions by community governments, however, private enterprises are likely to remain relatively small.

Personal and Financial Sponsorship of Large Private Enterprises

Community and county authorities sometimes go a step farther and provide direct personal and financial support to large private enterprises. In Jieshou and the surrounding counties, leading county officials personally sponsor a small number of successful private entrepreneurs. Sponsorship facilitates private enterprises' dealings with local administration and red tape and provides ideological and administrative protection without which the firms would feel vulnerable, given their size and visibility. This close personal relationship between private enterprises and their community government sponsors is accompanied by a relaxed attitude toward the enterprises' access to community resources such as bank loans. Community government officials may also gain personal advantages from sponsorship of private enterprises, but the magnitude of these benefits is hard to gauge.

In some Jieshou townships the community government provides entrepreneurs with funds and other support to develop firms that may be private in theory but that are under loose administrative supervision by the community government. In one township, Jinzhai, four of the seven "township-run" industrial firms are of this semiprivate nature. This approach may be superior to traditional community enterprise development in that enterprise directors may be somewhat insulated from the community government, while at the same time the firm has access to community resources. But there are numerous ambiguities and potential problems because property rights are not well defined. Some large private enterprises in Jieshou town have been collectivized, a step facilitated because many of them registered as collective firms when they were established in the early 1980s.

A similar strategy that works from the other side of the TVP spectrum is contracting or leasing community enterprises to private management. Usually what happens is that money-losing community enterprises are contracted out to avoid their being a drain on community resources. At the very least, contracting insulates community enterprise management from petty interference by community officials and other agencies. A good example is Shaxi town, where enterprise directors and employees may receive somewhat higher rewards, but directors do not have complete independence and are not residual claimants. Stronger forms of contracting can fall just short of outright sale to private ownership; in both Jieshou and Nanhai contracting has often been a prelude to such sales.

The benefits to community governments and their leaders from active promotion of private enterprises (particularly large ones) are in many respects similar to those from TVPs in general, but there are some differences. The scope for informal payments and personal benefits is probably greater for private than for community enterprises, but flows of budgetary and non-budgetary funds to the community government itself are smaller. Direct involvement by community governments in larger private enterprises leaves a legacy of confused property rights that may pose problems for successful private enterprises in the future.

Implications and Policy Issues

Uneven Development and Ownership Patterns

Concern about the problems of backward areas, some of which have failed to establish a self-sustaining TVP sector, should not distract us from the highly successful development and performance of the TVP sector as a whole. The strong incentives for community governments to promote TVP development undoubtedly have been crucial to the success of the sector. But tremendous inequality in the economic resource base[11] and limited population and factor mobility have led to highly uneven patterns of TVP development that are likely to continue as long as imbalances in endowments and immobility of factors remain unchanged. Under these circumstances community governments that are striving to establish and develop TVPs are largely left to their own devices and resources. Where these are inadequate, progress is bound to be slower.

Imbalances are exacerbated by fiscal predation, which may well be the most severe obstacle to TVP development in backward areas, such as parts of Shangrao, that have poor endowments of material and human resources. Fiscal predation is the result of a confluence of factors, including poor resource endowments, a precarious fiscal situation, surplus labor and cadres, and the hard budget constraint of community governments. The inelasticity of basic public expenditures with respect to levels of income and development is a fundamental cause of fiscal problems in poorer areas and thus of fiscal predation. Although local and community authorities may be able to ameliorate fiscal predation somewhat, significant changes in national policies may be required to achieve substantial improvements in the situation (see below).

As a result of fiscal predation and other factors, ownership is becoming correlated with the level of development. The backward areas are being forced to turn away from a traditional community enterprise development strategy and actively encourage or at least permit the emergence of a large private enterprise sector that sometimes includes sizable firms with assets exceeding Y1 million and with more than 100 workers. The better-endowed areas have a greater degree of choice with respect to the private enterprise sector, but in any case they will continue to develop the traditional TVCE sector. Whether the turn to private ownership will allow backward areas to catch up with the front-runners is an open question, but resource inequality and continuing factor immobility make such an outcome unlikely except in a handful of exceptional cases.

Conflicts between Government and Ownership Roles

The dual roles of township and village governments as conventional local governments and as business entities in charge of community enterprises do not conflict severely in advanced areas such as Wuxi, where traditional community enterprise development has been highly successful and is now self-sustaining. In fact, in Wuxi the two roles are institutionally separated to some extent. The TIC directly exercises ownership and other economic roles with respect to township enterprises. Its primary relationship with the township economic commission (TEC) is to turn over to it part of the profits remitted by township enterprises. The TEC has a dual role, but it is not directly responsible for supervising enterprises. Finally, the township government is considerably removed institutionally from the community enterprise sector, although undoubtedly township leaders become involved in important decisions on investment projects, the creation of new enterprises, and the like. But in the backward areas where fiscal predation occurs, there are severe conflicts between the two roles of community governments, and the government role commonly squeezes out the business role.

From this perspective, the issue of how to avoid fiscal predation is akin to the question of how to avoid conflicts in the dual roles of township governments. Institutional separation is one alternative, but it runs the risk of diluting community government incentives to promote TVP development (although this does not appear to be a problem with the limited degree of separation in Wuxi). Another possibility is to enforce a greater degree of independence for community enterprises with respect to the community government so that, for example, community enterprises are required to remit funds to the community government only if they make a profit according to a strict accounting definition. Although this alternative would protect individual community enterprises from fiscal predation and prevent community governments from using firms to soften their hard budget constraint, it might also weaken risk bearing and financial intermediation by the community government. (Since in backward areas the community government has not been able to play any risk-bearing or intermediary role anyway, this may not be a severe weakness.) Greater independence for the local community banking system might prevent community governments from using it as a means of "deficit financing." Still other alternatives would require nationwide policy changes that are explored below.

The Need for Greater Pay Incentives for Township Leaders

A primary issue in the area of personal incentives and rewards to community government leaders is the uniform nationwide pay scale for township magistrates, who, unlike leaders of villages and production teams, are considered state cadres and are under the state pay system financed from the budget. Supplements and subsidies from nonbudgetary revenues are necessary to ensure an adequate salary for township leaders in areas such as Nanhai. Despite these supplements, township leaders in better-off areas are paid less than many village leaders, and variation with TVP performance and other economic indicators is generally less than for village leaders. A large part of township leaders' rewards may come from informal income and benefits, but this opens the door to corruption.

Considerations of scale, risk pooling, and resource mobilization would suggest that in most parts of the country the optimal size of rural community for community enterprise development is the township (see chapter 9). But township leaders' personal income incentives for TVP development are weaker than those for village and production team leaders. It would be desirable to institute for township leaders an explicit bonus system linked to township employment, output, profitability, and related indicators. To be effective, the bonuses would have to be potentially large in relation to base pay, and both components should vary according to the level of personal incomes in the locality. Bonuses could be linked to future as well as current TVP development and profits, perhaps through performance-based pension benefits. Similar incentive schemes could be instituted at the county level, where variation in pay is even smaller than at the township level.

Methods of Preventing Fiscal Predation

Unchecked fiscal predation will lead to stagnation of the community enterprise sector in some areas and to a turn toward rural development strategies based on private enterprise. This pattern may not be welcome ideologically or politically beyond a certain point, and in any case there are many unresolved problems and inconsistencies concerning private enterprises, especially large ones (see chapter 9). Thus, avoiding or at least ameliorating fiscal predation is an urgent policy issue, but it is by no means easy, as the experience of Shangrao shows.

Some specific measures that are within the scope of authority of township governments themselves (and were actually instituted by Shaxi town) have been discussed above. But these may not work everywhere and, as in Shangrao, they seem most efficacious where community resource constraints are at least temporarily eased by inflows of funds. The question arises as to whether there are any nationwide policy changes that could help the situation. There are, but they would represent a sharp departure from past practices and may require substantial commitments of resources.

The fiscal problems of backward townships are related to two of their structural characteristics. In backward areas the government and its activities are too big (in particular, the number of people on the community government payroll is too large) in relation to the resources of the community. Moreover, grass-roots rural communities have borne, by default, much of the financial burden of providing basic services, regardless of their ability to pay.

The problem of fiscal predation therefore needs to be attacked from two different angles. First, the size of community governments and in particular the number of cadres (including those who are "placed" in community enterprises for lack of anything better to do with them) must be reduced to correspond better to local community resources. Backward areas cannot afford and probably do not need the full government administrative structure and staffs that may be necessary in the more advanced areas where economic activity is much greater.[12] Although retrenchment may be difficult and gradual, the objective should be clear.

Second, the relative importance of the social expenditures now being taken care of outside the budget at the township level should be evaluated, and activities that are truly important to national objectives should be included in the state budget. If such activities as primary education (now partly financed outside the budget) are neglected in the more backward areas, the existing inequality in resource endowments, living standards, and development prospects will become even worse. Putting essential public and social services under the state budget would require additional budgetary resources, but it would ease rural communities' financial constraints and hence reduce the need for fiscal predation.[13] If community public expenditures can be met from budgetary allocations, levies on community enterprises can be limited and profits remitted by them can be used primarily for reinvestment in the TVP sector.

Finally, because of factor immobility, solving the problem of fiscal predation may not by itself greatly reduce spatial inequality in TVP development. But if fiscal predation ceases, community enterprises and their government supervisors will at least be in a better position to acquire the crucial missing factors—managerial skills, marketing ability and contacts, and technical knowledge and capabilities—from outside.

Notes

1. Rural development programs and industrialization efforts have often failed in other countries because local governments had no incentives to ensure their efficiency. See chapter 19 for a discussion of Tanzania.

2. There is now a large and growing literature on public choice (see Buchanan 1975 and Mueller 1976). Public choice theory can be used to derive some powerful results concerning the harmfulness of government intervention, the need for constitutional restrictions against excessive government spending, and so on.

3. In the past, restrictions on high personal incomes may have helped lessen variations in incomes among localities. These restrictions have been weakened as rural reforms have progressed.

4. Migration does not reduce the population of poorer areas but rather increases residents'

incomes by allowing them to take higher-paying temporary or seasonal jobs in richer areas.

5. In the early 1970s a general principle was that the income of a brigade (now village) leader in Wuxi should be about 30 percent above the income of a relatively hard-working agricultural laborer. Later, brigade leaders' incomes were more closely linked to the pay of brigade industrial workers. In addition, the allowable differential has widened.

6. Contract systems for factory directors, introduced in 1984, at first linked rewards to enterprise performance indicators rather than to workers' incomes, and this allowed great pay differentials.

7. Although the earlier rewards mentioned are given to individual village leaders, the pay drawn from enterprise profits is so large that it must be split among the leadership group and perhaps among other village cadres as well.

8. Shangrao's educational system is renowned for its quality and for the number of its high school graduates who pass examinations for admission to universities.

9. One township-run hydropower station in Shangrao, for example, had more than 100 employees when 60 were sufficient for the job. Nearly all of the workers were "placed" through personal or work-unit connections.

10. The question then arises as to what to do with superfluous management personnel, who are often unable to perform other economic tasks adequately. Lingxi township has rediscovered the "golden handshake" as an effective way of getting rid of superfluous and incompetent cadres both in the government and in the enterprises.

11. This includes human resources. Because of China's strong basic education system, the quality of ordinary labor does not differ greatly among regions and localities, but for a variety of reasons entrepreneurs, managers, and technical personnel are unevenly distributed.

12. In Shangrao the separation of Shangrao city from the county exacerbated the problem by creating two separate and comprehensive government structures where probably only one was necessary.

13. Where budgetary funds are limited or if it is decided to give such a reform a more decidedly "redistributional" character, inclusion of these expenditure items in the budget could be instituted only for townships below a certain threshold of poverty and backwardness.

Part VI

Comparative
Perspectives

Most of the earlier chapters in this volume have involved comparative analysis, but primarily within the TVP sector. Chapters 18 and 19 attempt systematic comparisons between TVPs and relevant examples from outside the sector. Chapter 18 compares township firms and the state enterprises that most closely resemble them—small state enterprises administered by counties or municipalities. Chapter 19 looks at analogies to China's TVP sector elsewhere in the world.

In chapter 18 Song Lina examines township enterprises and local state enterprises (LSEs), noting that these are the two most closely comparable types of firm in the TVP and state sectors. The study is based on data from sample township enterprises and from questionnaires completed by a small number of LSEs and their employees in Nanhai and Shangrao counties. Song's main hypothesis is that convergence between township enterprises and LSEs is occurring and that the two types of firm are becoming more and more similar in organization and behavior. The chapter documents this phenomenon and proposes explanations.

Song first points out the structural similarities between townships, on the one hand, and counties or small cities ("urban communities"), on the other. Despite their vastly different sizes, both types of community are characterized by broadly based economic sectors, increasingly similar labor force compositions, a variety of firms, and recruitment of employees mainly from within the respective communities.

The analogous relationships between the two categories of firms and their owners (township governments and county or city governments) are seen as a principal factor in convergence. In particular, both types of firm have a similar position within their respective communities and provide significant revenues to their governments. Both have better access to inputs and other forms of preferential treatment within their communities, which partly offsets the burden of high profit remittances. Township enterprises and LSEs are both under quasi-planning systems established by their respective community authorities. The control mechanisms exercised by community governments over township enterprises and LSES are broadly similar.

Song goes on to look at managers of both kinds of enterprise and finds that both sets of directors had surprisingly similar motives for taking their present posts. The directors tend to be outstanding people in their communities, although LSE directors have considerably higher educational qualifications than township enterprise directors. Criteria for assessment of their performance are broadly similar. Township enterprise directors internalize community goals to a much greater extent than do LSE directors, however. In both types of firm directors lack meaningful decisionmaking autonomy.

Both township enterprise and LSE workers are primarily recruited from within the local community, and their educational levels are broadly similar. Both sets of workers have shifted their primary occupation from agriculture to industry to varying degrees, but they retain strong ties to the land. One important difference is that compensation packages for township enterprise workers tend to be much more closely tied to performance than those of LSE workers. Welfare benefits for LSE employees are extensive, whereas those mandated for township enterprise workers are minimal, but some township authorities are striving to provide benefits similar to those in LSES. Finally, workers' attitudes toward risk, participation, status, and so on are fairly similar.

The author compares the economic performance and efficiency of township enterprises and LSES and finds that both tend to be less profitable than other types of firm in their respective communities but that township enterprises earn substantially higher economic returns than LSES. Some reasons for the latter phenomenon are suggested: weaker accounting and bookkeeping systems in township enterprises, with much less external auditing and control; lower production costs in TVPS because of tax exemptions, much lower welfare expenditures, use of low-cost or substandard materials, higher labor productivity (owing to performance-based wage systems), and lower capital requirements; and possible differences in the subsectoral composition of industry.

The chapter closes with some comments on the future prospects of LSES and township enterprises. Song asserts that LSES will stagnate for the foreseeable future, whereas township enterprises will continue to grow rapidly. Existing differences between township enterprises and LSES will be reduced as convergence continues.

In chapter 19 Alan Gelb and Jan Svejnar compare Chinese TVPS with a wide range of local public enterprises, worker cooperatives, and private firms in other countries. Comparators were selected for maximum similarity to TVPS, at least with respect to key aspects of their institutional structure. This meant that many interesting firm types were not included in the analysis. Although some illuminating similarities emerge, in general there are great differences between TVPs and even this select group of comparators, giving grounds for caution in drawing lessons.

The chapter starts by looking at two types of firm in Eastern Europe: collective farms, which are often organized as producer cooperatives and engage in diversified activities outside of agriculture, and Yugoslov labor-managed firms. The former are similar in many respects to Chinese TVPs, but they have not developed nearly as rapidly. Furthermore, their role in the economy is much less important, perhaps because Chinese community governments have actively supported TVP development and because Chinese TVPs can compete more easily with the inefficient state sector. Another public ownership comparator, small-scale rural manufacturing in Tanzania, is briefly analyzed, and it is suggested that one reason for the poor performance of these firms has been their limited fiscal and other linkages with local governments.

The authors then turn to international comparators under private ownership. The Mondragon group in Spain's Basque region has some important similarities with China's TVP sector. Gelb and Svejnar argue that Mondragon represents an alternative path for regional development and rural industrialization that may become more relevant for China if the TVP sector moves toward more private and autonomous, yet still group, ownership patterns in an environment of continuing labor immobility. Other, in certain respects more remote, examples include U.S. company towns, regulation of firms by Swiss cantons, and Japanese-type Z-firms. The last, as noted in chapter 13, share many characteristics with Chinese TVPs and may be highly relevant for China.

Gelb and Svejnar then look at tendencies for firms to change ownership forms. In market economies dominated by capitalist ownership, many successful worker cooperative firms eventually are sold to private ownership because it is impossible to find new workers with sufficient capital to replace the membership shares of those who retire or leave. The opposite transition, from capitalist to worker ownership, can be triggered in a number of ways, including bankruptcy and sale to employees, benevolent voluntary transfers by owners, and transfer of stock to employees for the sake of tax advantages or to mobilize capital.

The last part of the chapter assesses the ability of firms to adjust to adverse changes in economic conditions, looking in particular at whether enterprises respond to a downturn by cutting employment or reducing wages. There is some evidence from international experience that communal and Z-firms tend to cut wages rather than employment. Mondragon is a notable example. The response of Chinese TVPs to adversity cannot yet be fully assessed, but it may well be that community enterprises will prefer wage reductions and that private enterprises will engage in other responses, depending on such factors as the number of persons from outside the local community in the work force.

18

Convergence: A Comparison of Township Firms and Local State Enterprises

Song Lina

Urban-rural dualism in China's economic structure is disintegrating, and industrial developments in urban and rural areas are complementing and infiltrating each other. The factors that affect urban industrialization also affect rural industrialization, directly or indirectly. As extensive commercial relations are established between urban and rural industrial systems, separation or semiseparation between urban and rural economies is breaking down.

In a sense, rural industrialization in China has taken the urban industrial system as its model. Since their emergence TVPs have found themselves in a relatively open "market" environment. Yet this is not a market mechanism based on the principles of fair competition and equal opportunity. Although the situation has improved, discrimination by government agencies, the market, and the public still exists, and industrial TVPs therefore seek protection. On the one hand, they have to struggle against an unfair economic structure, the consequence of the traditional planned system; on the other, they long to be admitted into the planned economy and to come under government protection. These characteristics are particularly prominent in firms administered by township governments.

Urban state enterprises, by contrast, have begun to feel the weakening of government protection that has followed the relaxation of control through central planning. Disturbances in the newly emerging markets have affected them from time to time, and they want to turn to new norms of behavior, but administrative restraints limit their choices. TVPs, which are freer from administrative restraints and more responsive to the market, offer a model for the reform of state enterprises.

Both township and state enterprises react ambivalently to their environments. They are aware of the barriers to their development and wish to overcome them through reform, but they also have a habit of dependence on the old institutional frameworks and administrative environments. As they seek new paths, they may look to each other's behavioral patterns for norms lacking in their own systems but conducive to development. The consequent cross-pollination between the behavior of state and township enterprises is leading to a convergence of systems. We hypothesize here that state and township enterprises are becoming more and more similar in operations and structure.

This chapter compares the environments, goals, operations, and efficiency of two types of enterprises—industrial township enterprises and local state enterprises (LSEs) in small cities and in counties—with a view to explaining their recent evolution. For the sake of a more scientific and persuasive comparison, only LSEs in the same localities as our sample township enterprises have been chosen for this study. This helps eliminate structural variations and noncomparable elements of regional development and local traditional culture.

The data on LSEs are primarily from the industrial statistics of Wuxi city, Shangrao city, Foshan city, and Jieshou County. In addition, ninety Worker Survey Questionnaires were distributed to workers in county-administered LSEs in Nanhai and Shangrao, and eighty-one were retrieved. The Enterprise Survey Questionnaire and the Enterprise Director Questionnaire were also distributed to LSEs in the two counties. Case study materials and interviews are another important source of information.

Structural Similarities between Urban and Rural Communities

Superficially, a city differs greatly from a township. For example, the population of Shangrao city is 142,500, 6.3 times the average population of sample townships in Shangrao County (22,800). The original value of the total fixed assets of LSEs in Shangrao city is Y101 million, 5.7 times the average for sample townships in Shangrao County (Y18 million). In 1985 city-administered LSEs in Shangrao city paid Y13 million in taxes, profits, and fees, 317.5 times the average (Y40,000) for the township sample. The gross social output value of Shangrao city was Y153 million, 21.5 times that of the average township (only Y7 million). But despite these differences in size, urban and rural communities in China are surprisingly similar.

The Composition of Economic Sectors

Even the smallest community generally includes the five principal sectors—industry, agriculture, commerce, construction, and transport—but the shares can vary. Table 18-1 covers two pairs of proximate communities. In Wuxi city and Wuxi County industry has an overwhelming weight as measured by gross value of output. In the sample townships of Shangrao County, agriculture has a substantial share. All sectors, however, regardless of their relative weights, are generally represented in each community.

Table 18-1. *Composition of Economic Output, Wuxi and Shangrao, 1985*
(percentage of total)

Community	Industry	Agriculture	Construction	Communications and transport	Commerce
Wuxi city	89.3	1.0	3.9	1.4	4.3
Wuxi County, sample townships (average)	82.9	7.4	5.8	0.9	3.1
Shangrao city	64.3	3.4	11.4	6.6	14.2
Shangrao County, sample townships (average)	40.3	31.0	18.7	3.8	7.6

Sources: Township Leader Questionnaire and information from fieldwork.

Ownership and Administrative Structures

As the outline below shows, there is a parallel structure of enterprise owner-ship in cities and townships.

City	Township
LSES	Township enterprises
Big collective enterprises	Village enterprises
Small collective enterprises	Partnerships
Private industrial and commercial enterprises	Private enterprises

The administration of enterprises under different forms of ownership also exhibits common characteristics. For instance, small collective and private enterprises in cities, like rural private enterprises and partnerships, are under the supervision of local industry and commerce administrations. Both LSES and township enterprises are directly subordinate to the responsible depart-ments of the respective community government. (Whereas in other chapters, community government refers to rural governments at the township, village, and production team levels, in this chapter it also includes county and small city governments.) Big collective enterprises in cities are on the same level as village enterprises; both are partly under the administration of government departments but maintain relative independence in property relations. They are thus less subject to government influence than are LSES.

Labor Composition

Cities and townships still differ greatly in their urban-rural population mix. For example, 79 percent of the population in Shangrao city is urban and only 21 percent is rural, whereas, on average, only 7 percent of the population of sample townships of Shangrao County is urban and 93 percent is rural. This contrast, however, is no more than a matter of household registration. Agricultural labor has been rapidly shifting to nonagricultural activities as rural industrialization proceeds (see table 18-2), and the populations and labor compositions of rural communities are gradually becoming more like those of urban communities.

Kinship and Native Ties

It is generally believed that traditional ties of kinship, clan, and village are much more important in TVPs than in urban enterprises. But this is not entirely true. Table 18-3 shows the original homes of workers in sample TVPs. The survey of LSE workers indicates that 27.1 percent are from other counties, cities, or provinces, while the rest are residents of the city or county in which their firm is located. Most enterprises in China recruit their workers in the vicinity, and LSEs and TVPs are no exception. We will define local, or native, TVP workers as those who come from within the township and local employees of county LSEs as those who reside within the county. Under these definitions natives account for 80.4 percent of sample TVP workers in Wuxi, 70.8 in Nanhai, and 90 percent in Shangrao; in the sample of county LSEs 72.9 percent of the workers are natives, which is not significantly different from the percentages in TVPs.

Furthermore, TVPs have begun to extend their recruiting spheres. Many TVP leaders noted in interviews that because workers recruited among kin and friends could become difficult to handle, they were considering recruiting workers from outside the community. Although doing so would cost the enterprise more in expenditures on shelter and meal facilities for workers, the TVPs would profit by bringing together productive factors from larger areas. The localist and clannish character of TVPs may be weakened by this trend.

Enterprises in urban communities have evolved in a different direction. In the past few years unemployment among urban youth has been serious, and many state enterprise workers have retired to vacate places for their sons and daughters. In addition, many state enterprises have established affiliated enterprises ("labor service companies") to create employment for the grown children of their workers (see Byrd and Tidrick 1987). Consequently it is common in urban communities for several family members to work in the same firm.

Table 18-2. *Changes in the Labor Force, 1978–85*
(annual percentage change)

Sample townships, by county	Industrial	Agricultural
Wuxi	18.8	−12.9
Jieshou	32.4	−10.5
Nanhai	12.6	−12.7
Shangrao	12.3	2.5

Source: Township Leader Questionnaire.

Table 18-3. *Original Homes of TVP Workers*
(percentage of total sample workers in each county)

County	Same village	Other village, same township	Other township, same county	Other county	Other province
Wuxi	58.6	21.9	8.8	5.2	5.4
Nanhai	53.0	17.8	16.5	9.7	3.0
Shangrao	67.1	22.9	3.6	2.1	4.3

Note: Percentages may not add up to 100 owing to rounding. Corresponding information for Jieshou is not available.
Source: Worker Survey Questionnaire.

In sample LSES in Nanhai and Shangrao counties each factory director has an average of 1.25 relatives working in the firm; for township enterprises in the same counties the average is 1.54. Urban unemployment has put pressure on the recruiting system of state enterprises. When the government cannot solve the problem of employment, enterprises and families have to do it. In rural communities reliance on enterprises and family connections to provide employment for surplus labor began earlier, with the adoption of the PRS. Thus, as the employment mechanism shifts from government control to local absorption, cities and townships are becoming more alike.

The Influence of Ownership Systems on Convergence

The patterns of relationships between community governments and enterprises under various forms of ownership are similar in counties and townships. A sort of father-son relationship exists between the county government and its subordinate LSES, as well as between the township government and its subordinate enterprises, but both governments have relatively remote connections with other types of firm. This is because both have ownership rights over the assets of their subordinate firms and depend on them for revenue.

Although community governments do make startup investments in subordinate enterprises, the amount of capital they put up is not necessarily large. They also often provide intangible assistance. For example, they may use their influence to help firms obtain bank loans and business licenses. They also requisition land, recruit workers, secure scarce raw materials, and find technology and markets for their enterprises.

Interdependence

Even if county and township governments do not invest much in enterprises, they are still dependent on them. Their relations with enterprises center on revenue sharing (see chapter 16); a large share of their revenues comes from taxes and profits turned over by subordinate enterprises. For example, revenues from subordinate LSEs and administrative departments accounted for 71.5 percent of Shangrao city's extrabudgetary revenue in 1985, up from 63.9 percent in 1984. The bulk of the extrabudgetary revenues of sample township governments also were from enterprises, primarily from taxes, fees, and profits remitted by township firms.

Communities began industrialization at different times and are at different levels of development. This affects community governments' orientation toward the use of extrabudgetary revenues. In Wuxi sample townships spend, on average, 30.5 percent of these revenues on township enterprises, directly or indirectly, but the figure is only 22.1 percent in Jieshou. Similar spending patterns can be found in city governments. For instance, Shangrao city spends 35.1 percent of its extrabudgetary revenues on enterprises.

Management

When enterprises turn over to community governments more in taxes, fees, and profits than the amount returned by the governments, the enterprises may have trouble accumulating capital and may find themselves at a disadvantage in an increasingly competitive market. But community governments, as owners of these firms, may also protect them. In this sense, city and township governments have functional similarities in the management of subordinate firms.

County and township governments are at different administrative levels and have different privileges in the hierarchy of the centrally planned economy. This situation existed earlier and is continuing in the reform period. In all activities, from the central financing of lower levels of government to the planned distribution of needed inputs among state enterprises, the amounts always decrease progressively down the hierarchy, and very little trickles down to township governments from the provincial, city (or prefectural), and county governments.

The reforms have, however, substantially reduced the control of state enterprises through central planning. The number of materials directly under state control has been cut from 256 to 20 categories; the number of state-controlled industrial goods was reduced from 123 categories in 1980 to 66 in 1986; the coverage of the value of industrial output by the state mandatory plan has been reduced to 20 percent; and depreciation allowances are beginning to be totally at the disposal of state enterprises. Revenue-sharing systems in public finance have given lower levels of government more discretionary funds and hence more flexibility, provided that they meet revenue targets.

Quasi-Planning Systems

The increased funds at the disposal of community governments and the weakening of central controls have created a foundation for the establishment of local protective quasi-planning systems. These systems provide benefits for enterprises, particularly those established by community governments, so that they can be counted on to turn over taxes, fees, and profits. In a sense a quasi-planning system operates like a traditional planning system: it tries to infiltrate every link in the operations of the enterprise, from personnel, finances, and materials to production, supply, and marketing. But community governments can no longer impose inflexible administrative restraints on enterprises, for the extent to which they can control or support them is limited by their own capabilities. Regulation by the community government's quasi-planning system is effective only where the administrative system is highly developed (as in Shangrao) or where the community government is skillful in organizing the economy (as in Wuxi). The administrative capabilities of township governments vary greatly, and so can their quasi-planning systems.

In a macroenvironment where supplies of and demand for inputs and energy are not balanced, community governments' desire for goods and materials is a clear indication of their concern for the development of their enterprises. Both county and township governments draw on two sources—the central planning system and local efforts—to build up a reservoir of inputs needed by enterprises. Inputs from the central planning system—including even college graduates assigned through personnel departments—can increasingly be obtained by monetary means; only the prices (based on cost) vary.

In recent years the materials supply departments of city and county governments have often obtained needed inputs through exchange. The materials bureau of Wuxi County is outstanding in this regard. Of the materials sold through the purchase and sales companies of the bureau in 1985, only 5 percent were from the state planning system. The rest were obtained by exchanging materials with or investing in units that produce goods in short supply, such as steel and electricity. In the first half of 1986 the bureau did a business of Y400 million, more than fifty-seven times that done by its counterpart in Jieshou. Although raw materials obtained through exchange or investment are more expensive than those assigned by the state plan, the prices are no higher than on the market, and the supply is more regular. Therefore firms under various forms of ownership try their best to be admitted into the quasi-planning systems.

Although it is almost impossible for township governments to get inputs from the central planning system, they can obtain some materials through their subordinate departments (industrial companies or administrative offices for TVP administration), through multilateral exchanges or investments, or even through personal relationships. In addition, township governments can obtain from the county materials department medium-price raw materials—inputs priced between the market price and the state plan price.

In the distribution of low-price materials, city and county governments give priority to subordinate LSEs and big collective enterprises. Similarly, township governments give priority to their subordinate enterprises. Responses to the Township Leader Questionnaire show that township governments provide extremely few materials to partnerships and none at all to individual firms, whereas significant amounts are made available to TVCES.

Means of Control over Enterprises

The supply of favorably priced inputs by community governments to subordinate firms is a means of compensating for overtaxation and creating a more favorable environment for them. But community governments need additional control measures if they want their enterprises to keep bringing in revenues and at the same time to have good prospects for development.

At present, inputs to China's state enterprises provided through state planning account for only an estimated one-third of the total value of needed inputs, and two-thirds come from the market. Meanwhile, local governments have gradually reduced their planning control over LSEs. Ten LSEs in Shangrao and Nanhai reported that they no longer depend on state planning for needed raw materials and that state mandatory plans cover only one-eighth of their total output. Local governments, however, have not relaxed

Table 18-4. *Decisionmaking in Sample LSEs and Township Enterprises*
(percentage of sample)

Type of decision	Made by factory		Not made by factory	
	LSEs	Township enterprises	LSEs	Township enterprises
Appointment of factory director	30	13.3	70	83.3
Formation of management team	50	50.0	50	40.0
Worker recruitment	30	28.8	70	71.9
Wages	10	18.8	90	62.5
Large production-related expenditures	0	87.5	100	12.5
Production planning	80	50.0	20	18.8
Product pricing	40	n.a.	60	n.a.
Proportion of profits to be retained	0	19.4	100	71.9

n.a. Not available.

Note: Since not all enterprises responded to all parts of the question, the percentages do not always add up to 100.

Source: Enterprise Director Questionnaire.

their supervision of enterprises correspondingly (see table 18-4). Except for production plans, LSES do not seem to have much decisionmaking power. Community governments impose strict control over LSES through their authority over personnel and financial matters to make sure that due amounts of taxes, fees, and profits are remitted. For instance, in LSES under the Nanhai County government, cadres ranking above section chief (that is, factory leaders) are officially appointed by the county government, whereas cadres from section chief down are appointed by responsible county departments. Although production plans are made by enterprises, decisions on products and output are made by the county economic committee or its subordinate industrial companies. The sale of products is also controlled by superior departments, and only products in excess of the quota are marketed by the enterprises themselves. When it comes to important investments, government departments represent LSES in negotiations with banks and financial departments. Decisions on selecting projects or changing products are made by government departments.

The core of the relationship between LSES and local governments is the proportion of profits remitted. Although governments own the assets of LSES, they cannot avoid adversely affecting the accumulation of enterprise assets in the exercise of their functions. County governments do not behave like independent asset owners; they are concerned not only with increasing the value of enterprise assets but also with carrying out their government functions with the help of revenues from enterprises. The consequent conflict between enterprise development and government activities is manifested in arguments over the amount of profits to be turned over by LSES. Most of the LSES we studied bargained with government departments over profit retention. This suggests that the functions of community governments undermine the integrity of management of LSES. Township enterprises face the same problem; the decisionmaking power of sample township enterprises is curtailed by township governments and their subordinate departments (see table 18-4), sometimes to an even greater extent than in LSES.

County and township governments have fundamentally similar ownership relations with their subordinate firms. These two types of firm enjoy high positions in their respective communities, receive considerable government protection, and are the main sources of revenue for community governments. Therefore LSES and township enterprises have essentially similar relations with their superior community governments, and their behavior is similar or is becoming more so.

Similarities among Managers

There are many parallels between managers of LSES and township enterprises. This section reviews similarities in perceived responsibility to the government and to the firm, the characteristics of managers, the criteria by which managers are evaluated, management objectives, and problems stemming from managers' lack of real authority.

Responsibility

The ownership of LSEs and township enterprises is currently rather vague. It is difficult to distinguish or quantify the assets generated by the initial or backup investment by the community government and those attributable to reinvested profits or self-accumulation. As managers of the enterprises, factory directors cannot represent only the owners or the enterprises; they must look after the interests of both sides. Their actions therefore exhibit clear traces of conflict.

Directors' strong sense of identification with the government-owner can be inferred from the way in which they come to their positions. In sample township enterprises of Nanhai and Shangrao 88.3 percent of factory directors were directly engaged by the township government, and very few were elected by the workers or hired under contract. In sample LSEs of these two counties 70 percent of factory directors were appointed by the government; few came to their positions in other ways.

Almost all directors of sample LSEs see themselves as responsible first to government departments and only secondarily to the workers. The majority (85.7 percent) of directors of sample township enterprises took the same view. Managers cited "submission to assignment" as their main motivation for taking the position (table 18-5).

Characteristics of Factory Directors

The differences between directors of LSEs and of township enterprises are not very significant. Directors of sample LSEs have more education (see table 18-6), but township enterprise directors are generally experienced people with a rich knowledge of nonagricultural activities and are not so different from their counterparts in LSEs. In any case, a middle school education can be enough for daily management work in TVPs.

Table 18-5. *Motivations for Becoming a Factory Director*
(percent)

Motivation	LSEs	Township enterprises
Submission to assignment	88.9	86.7
Sense of social responsibility	88.9	73.3
Interest in the work	33.4	66.7
Improvement of social position	22.3	66.7
Improvement of economic position	0.0	10.0
Greater freedom	0.0	0.0

Source: Enterprise Director Questionnaire.

Table 18-6. *Educational Levels of Factory Directors*
(percent)

Educational level	LSE directors	Township enterprise directors
College graduate	55.6	0.0
High school graduate	11.1	23.3
Middle school graduate	22.2	56.7
Primary school graduate	11.1	20.0

Source: Enterprise Director Questionnaire.

In our samples the ages of the two groups of factory directors fall basically in a normal distribution between 30 and 50 years. Directors of LSEs have, on average, 14.9 years of work experience and a cadre career (including as factory director) of 13.3 years. Directors of township enterprises are less experienced; they have, on average, 8.8 years of work experience, and their average cadre career is 7.8 years. But 90 percent of the latter group have served in the military, been purchasing agents, or done business before. These experiences undoubtedly influence their present work and make them no less capable than their counterparts in LSEs. They are outstanding people in their own communities.

Criteria for Assessing Factory Directors

Township governments use several criteria to evaluate township enterprise managers. Managers must be able to expand the firm (an indication of managerial ability); they must be conscientious and honest in their work (personality); they must be popular and supported by workers (ability and personality combined); and they must turn over a set amount of revenues to the township government (the core relation between firm and government). The criteria used by county governments with respect to LSE directors are basically similar.

In our investigations we also learned how the two groups of factory directors assess their own abilities. Their selections of desirable personal attributes overlapped on four items: sense of responsibility and drive, technical ability, management ability, and understanding of the market. But directors of LSEs chose decisionmaking ability, innovative ability, and democratic ideas as important characteristics, whereas their counterparts in township enterprises chose sense of principle and competitive spirit.

Management Objectives of Factory Directors

Differences emerge in the choices of management goals by factory directors (see table 18-7). The first three management targets chosen by directors of LSEs center on the self-interest of the enterprises, although they do not over-

Table 18-7. *Managerial Objectives*

Rank (1 = most important)	LSE directors	Township enterprise directors
1	Promote stable and long-term development of enterprise	Promote prosperity of township
2	Produce brand-name goods to raise credibility	Improve internal management
3	Maximize profits; improve internal management	Increase financial income of township
4	Increase financial income of locality	Maximize profits

Source: Enterprise Director Questionnaire.

look contributions to the finances of the locality. The choices made by directors of township enterprises, however, include some community government goals: promoting the prosperity of the township and increasing the financial income of the township were ranked first and third in importance, whereas maximizing profits was only fourth.

Township enterprise leaders have internalized the goals of community governments to a greater extent than have LSE directors. The comparatively centralized exercise of governmental functions by city and county governments is closely related to stable financial income and better methods of taxation. Municipal and county governments are therefore able to engage in much more orderly and standardized management of subordinate firms. Instead of interfering directly, leaders usually make contacts with factory directors through government departments.

In rural communities, although such institutions as township economic commissions and industrial offices do exist, township governments are involved more directly in management of township enterprises, for several reasons.

- Township communities own fewer enterprises than do county governments. If the leaders of county governments directly handled the affairs of every enterprise, their workloads would be unmanageable.
- To establish an orderly and regular management system takes time. In rural industries a complete reporting system has not yet been established. The "farmers' style" of management that has evolved in agriculture over several thousand years is a chronic problem that must be overcome.
- The smaller the community, the more conspicuous the community interest, and thus the closer the agreement between the factory director and the community government. In townships, the contribution made by township enterprises to the community is obvious, and the township

enterprise director has an important position locally. The factory director not only has to manage the operations of his own firm but also shoulders the heavy task of community development.

In urban communities relations between LSE directors and community governments are much simpler. Directors only have to stick to fixed targets and regular financial channels, and they do not usually have to assume many other burdens. Their contribution to the development of their communities is made through tax payments. Unlike township enterprise directors, they seldom have to be entangled in trivial matters.

The Lack of True Management Authority

Although the managers of the two types of enterprises face different financial environments, their powers are similar and are basically limited to choosing the management team of the enterprise and deciding on the annual production plan. They cannot do much actual decisionmaking, but they are often partly responsible for enterprise risks. Under the traditional socialist mode, managers, in the basic sense of the word, did not even exist. Enterprise directors were administrative officials who were appointed by government departments.

As far as LSE and township enterprise managers are concerned, the mixture of enterprise property rights and management rights naturally leads to divided self-interest. They have to conform with the wishes of their superior community governments, but they also have to ensure the development of their enterprises.

In the sample, only one LSE director felt he would not face punishment for enterprise bankruptcy caused by improper management, whereas the figure is as high as 13.3 percent for directors of sample township enterprises. Most directors of both types of firm face penalties from community governments—loss of bonuses, reduction of salary, or even dismissal—if they cause losses. Despite the harsh restrictions on their personal interests, managers have power in name only, and they are not able to take effective control of firm operations.

Workers' Characteristics

Township enterprise workers are former (or even current part-time) farmers, whereas LSE workers are urban residents. But in general, differences between the two sets of workers are not as great as might be imagined. This section examines the workers' relationship to the land, their personal characteristics, wage systems and benefits, and attitudes, including the intensity of their desire to participate in enterprise decisionmaking.

Ties to the Land

Unlike workers in most urban communities, employees of township enterprises are farmers who have just left the land or have not yet completely broken away from agricultural production. In county LSEs located near rural communities a sizable portion of employees also are fresh from the farm, and some workers' families still live in rural areas. These employees therefore share some similarities with TVP workers.

The average household size for sample LSE workers in Nanhai and Shangrao is 4.1, whereas the figure is 5.8 for households of TVP workers in the two counties.[1] The number of household members engaged in nonagricultural production averages 2.2 in the former and 2.7 in the latter. Factory wages are the main income for 92.6 percent of the households of sample LSE workers. Most TVP workers (77.3 percent) also consider income from industrial activities to be the main income of the family.

Although the economic position of LSE and TVP workers is closely linked to industrial production, it is still, to different degrees, under the influence of the land. In the sample, families of workers in county LSEs hold, on average, 1.0 mu of contracted land; the corresponding figure for TVP workers is about 3.3 mu. Only 27.2 percent of LSE workers' families till their own land; most families employ hired hands or subcontract the land to other people. The majority (84.1 percent) of TVP workers' families still take care of their own land, and households that have contracted all their land to other people account for less than 5 percent. Despite these differences, the number of workers who personally take part in agricultural production is small in both types of firms: 7.4 percent for LSEs and 10.0 percent for TVPs.

Table 18-8. *Educational Levels of Workers in Nanhai and Shangrao*
(percentage of sample)

Educational level	LSE workers	TVP workers
No schooling	0.0	2.1
Primary school	2.5	23.9
Higher primary school	13.6	17.8
High school (secondary vocational school)	38.3	39.3
Senior high school	25.9	17.5
Higher education and technical and vocational training schools	11.1	8.9

Note: Since not all workers responded to this question, percentages do not add to 100 percent.
Source: Worker Survey Questionnaire.

Personal Characteristics

Among sample LSE workers in Shangrao and Nanhai, 76.5 percent are male and 23.5 percent female; in TVPs 48.8 percent are male and 51.2 percent female. The average age of sample TVP workers is 27.8 years; in LSEs it is 35.7. LSE workers had an average of 1.3 jobs before their present employment; TVP workers had 1.2. The average length of service in the firm is about 11.0 years for LSE workers, and their total experience in industrial activities averages 15 years. The average length of service in the present job for TVP workers is 5.5 years, and their total experience in nonagricultural activities averages 8 years. The educational level and professional qualifications of sample workers in TVPs are only a bit lower than those of LSE workers (table 18-8).

The Wage System

Sample TVP workers earn Y1,434 a year, whereas sample LSE workers earn Y1,302 a year. (According to Nanhai County officials the wages of LSE workers are generally about 20 percent lower than those of local TVP workers.) The gap may well reflect the different wage systems adopted by LSEs and TVPs. Among sample LSE workers 55.6 percent are on a fixed salary system and only 6.2 percent have piece-rate wages. In contrast, only about 8 percent of sample TVP workers are paid by the hour, and the rest are subject to some form of piece-rate payment.

Generally speaking, piece rates effectively mobilize the enthusiasm of workers, and as a result TVPs can attract workers employed by LSEs. Many state enterprise workers, especially technicians, would like to work in TVPs. In the state-owned Nanhai Silk Factory alone, 15 workers, mostly skilled technicians, quit their jobs to work in TVPs during January-February 1987; 143 people left the factory in 1986. One-third of the current employees, including some managers, have part-time jobs in TVPs. According to the factory director, the wage rate for workers in local TVPs in the textile industry is Y0.12–Y0.28 per meter of cloth, as against only Y0.06 per meter in LSEs. An ordinary worker in a state textile firm could see his pay rise from Y100 to Y300 a month if he became a TVP director.

Although the wage system in LSEs is not as flexible as in TVPs, many state enterprise directors are beginning to consider the reform of the wage system. But since not all problems can be solved by an enterprise director, real change depends on the improvement of macropolicies. As the high-salary attraction exerted by TVPs has caused a labor shortage for LSEs in some professions, the LSEs have had to recruit workers from regions where rural industry is underdeveloped. An LSE in Nanhai hired more than 2,000 temporary workers from Guangxi Province—equal to the number of local staff. The factory has the right to give these temporary workers piece-rates. Eventually, piece-rate systems may replace fixed wages or payment by the hour in LSEs.

The Welfare System

Although the wages of workers in LSEs are on the low side, their welfare treatment is generous. In the sample 60.4 percent of TVP workers are not entitled to housing and subsidies from the enterprise, 41.0 percent of the workers do not receive financial aid for medical care, 52.3 percent are not covered by insurance on the job, 53.9 percent do not get pensions on retirement, and 58.4 percent cannot have their children replace them. By contrast, workers in sample LSEs are entitled to all of these benefits. Some township governments are trying to provide state enterprise–type welfare treatment for their TVP employees. The government in Lingxi township, Shangrao County, has implemented a series of welfare measures for its eight subordinate enterprises. Workers are classified as permanent employees, appointed by the township government, or temporary employees. Permanent employees are entitled to free medical care and pensions and cannot be freely dismissed from their jobs.

Workers' Attitudes

Differences between workers in county LSEs and in TVPs are not as large as people imagine. Their similarities are especially evident in their attitudes.

WORKERS' SENSE OF STABILITY. Among sample TVP workers in Nanhai and Shangrao, only 13 percent fear that they might lose their present jobs, while the rest have considerable confidence in the stability of their jobs. Among sample LSE workers in the two counties, 6 percent believe it is possible for them to lose their jobs.

ATTITUDE TOWARD RISK. About 64 percent of sample TVP workers have never planned to run or jointly run a factory with other people. Among sample LSE workers in the two counties, the figure was 59 percent. Only 6–7 percent of sample workers in both types of enterprises actually plan to run or jointly run a factory.

ATTITUDE TOWARD THE STATUS OF TVP WORKERS. Among sample TVP workers 16.5 percent agree with the statement that they are one rank lower than state enterprise workers. Among sample LSE workers 19.8 percent hold that opinion, but most do not agree.

PARTICIPATION BY WORKERS. TVP workers show a weak desire for and a low degree of participation in enterprise management. The actual degree of participation by workers in LSEs is also low. The proportion of sample LSE workers who take part in decisions on appointment and dismissal of enterprise leaders accounts for only 16 percent, and they have even less power in other respects. LSE workers, however, hope to have power in some spheres such

Table 18-9. *LSE Workers' Desires for Participation*

Item	Total frequency	Precedence
Appointment or dismissal of firm leaders	43.2	1
Development of new products	12.3	2
Use of profits kept by enterprise	9.9	3
Dismissal of workers	6.2	4
Decisions on wages and bonuses	6.2	4
Distribution of work within the factory	2.5	6
Recruitment of workers	0	—
New investment	0	—

— Not applicable.
Source: Worker Survey Questionnaire.

as appointment or dismissal of enterprise leaders. Table 18-9 shows how workers rank their desire for participation in specific areas. These choices indicate that LSE workers' desire for actual participation is low because they think that a good and reliable enterprise management team will run the firm in such a way as to promote their interests.

Comparison of Economic Benefits

Comparisons of the economic efficiency of the two types of firms suggest that they are the enterprises with the lowest efficiency in their respective communities and that township enterprises are more efficient than LSEs. This section probes into possible reasons for the latter phenomenon, with specific illustrations from the textile industry.

Efficiency

National statistics on output-capital and profit-capital ratios in state enterprises and urban collective industrial firms are shown in table 18-10. The ratios are much lower for state enterprises than for urban collective firms. The labor productivity of industrial state enterprises, however, is Y15,198 per person, whereas the figure for urban collective enterprises is only Y8,206 per person. Similarly, the economic benefit index of sample township enterprises in the four counties is lower than that of firms under other ownership systems. (See chapter 10 for detailed statistics.)

Owing to similarities in ownership relations and in external environments, the behavior and systems of LSEs and township enterprises tend to converge. In general, both kinds of firm have relatively low efficiency in their respective communities. This conclusion is supported by statistics on industrial firms in Wuxi (see table 18-11).

Table 18-10. *Profitability in State and Urban Collective Enterprises, 1985*

	State enterprises		Urban collective enterprises	
Type of industry	Output value per Y100 of fixed assets	Profit per Y100 of fixed assets	Output value per Y100 of fixed assets	Profit per Y100 of fixed assets
Heavy	66.9	10.7	204.2	26.7
Light	209.2	19.4	321.0	21.0
Total	95.0	12.4	269.6	23.5

Source: State Statistical Bureau (1987b).

Why Township Enterprises Are More Efficient than LSEs

Table 18-12 shows that the economic benefits of township enterprises are higher than those of state enterprises at the national level. Analysis of economic benefits in industrial enterprises in Wuxi reveals the same phenomenon: output-capital and profit-capital ratios in township enterprises are higher than in county LSEs (table 18-11). Why are there substantial differences in economic benefits between LSEs and township enterprises even though their environment, operations, and internal systems are converging? Several possible reasons are discussed here.

ACCOUNTING SYSTEMS. The accounting system in TVPs is much weaker than in state enterprises because bookkeeping in TVPs is accountable only to the owners. Leaders of township governments will not severely punish their firms for cheating and giving false accounts to government agencies such as the tax, industrial and commercial, and statistical departments; indeed, they often support such actions. Moreover, not all of the income and expenditures of TVPs have to go through banks, and the enterprises gain considerable extra scope for their activities because they can pay less tax and evade banks' restrictions on the use of cash.

The bookkeeping activities of state enterprises are controlled by a uniform nationwide accounting inspection system that covers almost every link in the operations of an enterprise, from the wages of employees to expenses for business trips and from production expenses to nonproduction expense items. Hence accounting management in state enterprises limits the scope of enterprise activities. Many state enterprises have begun to set up their own small "banks" in recent years, but they are still far less flexible than TVPs.

The purchasing and marketing agents of TVPs have sufficient cash and are allowed to offer some individuals gifts, meals, commissions, and the like in return for materials in short supply or for sales opportunities. TVPs can also easily manipulate their business accounts to lower their taxes or to increase

Table 18-11. *The Relative Efficiency of Different Types of Industrial Firms in Wuxi, 1984*
(yuan)

Item	County LSEs	County-owned collective firms	Township enterprises	Village enterprises
Total output value created by Y100 of capital	202.1	232.8	228.7	277.4
Total profit created by Y100 of capital	23.4	23.7	25.9	33.0
Total tax and profit created by Y100 of capital	31.7	31.6	37.7	45.1

Source: Information from fieldwork.

total wages without incurring, for example, a bonus tax. If a state enterprise were to do these things, it would run great risks because of the restrictions under the existing system and the accounting controls that have been written into the country's laws. These are a great deterrent to everyone in state enterprises, and only a few dare to defy the law.

COST STRUCTURE. Many TVPs have lower costs than state enterprises, as is illustrated by a comparison of costs in the silk industry in Nanhai County (see table 18-13).

There are several reasons for these cost differences. First, TVPs (including township enterprises) enjoy tax exemptions during the first several years of operation. Some firms, mainly private enterprises, announce bankruptcy as the tax exemption period draws to an end and then set up again under a new name. According to estimates by tax officials in Rongcheng County, Hebei Province, TVPs in that locality have hidden at least 30 percent of their profits.

Second, the welfare system for workers in state enterprises is quite comprehensive. State enterprises at all levels offer such benefits as payment of medical expenses (sometimes including part of the medical costs for family members), insurance on the job, subsidies for heating in winter and cold drinks in summer, and pensions. One factory director estimated that workers' welfare expenses amounted to 11 percent of the factory's total wage bill and the trade union fee to 2 percent. Workers in TVPs can never hope to catch up with state enterprise workers in welfare benefits, but these benefits do increase production costs for state enterprises.

Third, management costs are higher in state enterprises than in TVPs, by about 50 percent according to table 18-13, mainly because of overstaffing and complicated managerial structures in state enterprises. The director of an LSE in Nanhai noted that the factory has ten sections and offices and that none can be abolished because they correspond to those in the responsible govern-

Table 18-12. *Economic Efficiency in State and Township Enterprises, 1985*

Type of industry	State enterprises		Township enterprises	
	Output value per Y100 of fixed assets	Profit per Y100 of fixed assets	Output value per Y100 of fixed assets	Profit per Y100 of fixed assets
Heavy	66.9	10.7	176.5	19.6
Light	209.2	19.4	256.2	18.5
Total	95.0	12.4	207.1	19.2

Source: State Statistical Bureau (1987b).

ment departments. An LSE does not have control over which internal department-ments to set up. As a result, managerial personnel account for about 10 per-cent of the total number of employees in the enterprise. By contrast, TVPS spend very little in this area and have not built up a managerial hierarchy. Often the owner and manager are the same person, and the entrepreneur takes on many duties. Furthermore, according to the director of an LSE silk factory in Nanhai, management fees for LSES are higher than those for TVPS, especially private enterprises.

Fourth, LSES make higher interest payments to banks than do TVPS, mainly because they take out more loans. In the latter half of 1984 the Agricultural Bank in Nanhai County inaugurated stricter measures to control the huge amount of loans demanded by partnerships and individual enterprises, and the amount of lending to them declined. Perhaps more important, the total amount of capital required by TVPS per unit of output (including working cap-ital and fixed assets) is lower than for state enterprises.

Fifth, TVPS often use low-cost or substandard raw materials. For instance, when TVPS use polyester-cotton blended yarn instead of pure cotton yarn, the price difference can well be more than Y2,000 a ton. For some other such substitutions, the price difference is as much as Y4,000 a ton.

Sixth, labor productivity in TVPS that produce silk textiles is about 10 per-cent higher than in LSES because the comparatively higher wages in TVPS stimulate workers' enthusiasm. Pay for TVP workers is about Y0.16–Y0.18 per meter of cloth, whereas the figure is only Y0.06 per meter for LSE workers. Many LSE workers have to moonlight, which affects their performance on their primary job.

INDUSTRIAL COMPOSITION. National statistics show that the profit created by every Y100 of fixed assets in township enterprises is Y6.8 higher than in state enterprises (see table 18-12). In light industry profitability in township enterprises is slightly lower than in state enterprises, but in heavy industry it is much higher. Further studies are needed to analyze this matter in more detail.

Table 18-13. *Textile Production Costs in LSEs and TVPs in Xiqiao Town, Nanhai*
(yuan per meter of cloth)

Item	LSEs	TVPs	Difference
Tax	0.64	0.28	0.36
Welfare (including pensions)	0.16	0.00	0.16
Management fee	0.10	0.05	0.05
Interest paid to banks	0.20	0.10	0.10
Materials	n.a.	n.a.	0.20
Labor efficiency	n.a.	n.a.	0.12

n.a. Not available.
Source: Information from fieldwork.

Conclusions

What are the prospects for county LSEs and rural township enterprises? Owing to the limitations of the sample surveyed, especially the insufficient materials on LSEs, it is difficult to provide convincing statistics, much less a reliable conclusion about future trends. But a hypothesis can be put forward for future investigation: for a long time to come, the growth rate of county LSEs will not be very fast. Generally speaking, these firms were founded much earlier than township enterprises and have made a considerable contribution to the community and the community government. Precisely for these reasons, their accumulation cannot be very high, and their pace of development suffers. At present, and for some time to come, county LSEs will probably experience a fairly painful period as they evolve from leading firms in their communities to backward firms with poor economic benefits.

Although township enterprises also suffer from various restrictions, they are in a burgeoning and rapidly growing stage. But since it will take time for the entire industrial system to become an organic whole in the vast rural areas of the country, township enterprises may have a long period of heavy responsibilities.

Note

1. The statistics concerning TVP workers used here include workers in enterprises under all ownership systems and thus cannot completely represent township enterprises. But in general, workers in enterprises of different ownership do not exhibit obvious differences (see chapter 13).

19

Chinese TVPs in an International Perspective

Alan Gelb and Jan Svejnar

The rapid growth of China's industrial TVP sector in the 1980s naturally raises questions about its economic behavior and its significance for the Chinese economy. Other chapters in this volume discuss the institutional and behavioral features of TVPs. This chapter compares TVPs with similar firms in other countries in the hope of improving our understanding of TVP behavior and our ability to formulate meaningful policy conclusions. The emphasis is on the ownership and management structure of TVPs and on the relationship between TVPs and local government.

Principal Features of the Chinese TVP Sector

China's TVP sector has evolved within a state-owned economy, with virtually no markets for land, capital, and labor, with heavily regulated product markets, and with a very even distribution of income and wealth, at least locally. Township and village authorities have conditioned the development of the sector to a great extent. Commercial and corporate law remains undeveloped in China. Although most TVPs, especially the larger ones, are owned and controlled by community governments, there are significant variations in ownership.

There are three broad categories of TVPs: community enterprises, partnerships, and individual proprietorships. The latter two categories are referred to as private firms. Many TVPs fall into an intermediate category: they are heavily influenced by community governments but may have substantial managerial autonomy and mixed ownership. Because of low labor mobility and the prevalence of bonus systems, it could also be argued that complex "implicit labor contracts" exist between firms and their workers. The most distinctive feature of TVPs, however, is the strong connection between firms and community governments. Even private firms are subject to considerable government influence, and all TVPs need permission from the community government to undertake such basic activities as acquiring land and buildings and taking out bank loans.

Implications for Comparators

Because of the close relationship between TVPS and community governments, we have to choose as international comparators locally owned public and private firms the operations of which are considerably influenced by local authorities. This particular form of ownership and control is not observed in many countries. Government ownership of industry, when significant, is usually more centralized and corresponds more closely to the Chinese state enterprise system. The most similar cases are found among labor-managed and private Yugoslav firms and collective farms and producer cooperatives in Eastern Europe. A few other countries, such as Tanzania, have made limited moves toward this pattern. Some similarities can be found in capitalist economies where there are close links between firms and communities; the powerful role played by Swiss cantons and township authorities in regulating the operation of firms is an example. Prototypical company towns in the United States and Canada have demonstrated considerable overlap between the interests of local governments and of enterprises, although in these cases, a large firm "owns" the community rather than the reverse.

It is also important to stress the differences between TVPS and some types of firms that at first sight might seem to resemble them closely. TVPS evolved within a state-controlled economy, not out of a capitalist or colonial background. They have been motivated by economic objectives, and the political orientation of local authorities has usually determined only the dominant structure of property rights and management. TVPS should therefore not be compared with politically motivated experiments with communal ownership—for example, the enterprises run by workers and local communities under Peru's 1984 Law of Social Property Firms. (Experience with this initiative has been disappointing; see Scott 1979.) Other examples are found in Jamaica, which converted substantial areas of foreign-controlled sugar land into producer cooperatives (Richards and Williams 1982); Algeria, which initiated a policy of autogestion, or workers' self-management, for farms and rural industries vacated by French proprietors; and Great Britain, where the Labour government initiated several cooperative experiments in 1974. The results of these initiatives were not inspiring (see Mallarde 1975 and Bradley and Gelb 1983b), but the political environment must be borne in mind when considering their performance.

The sugar and dairy cooperatives of India are interesting, but as agro-processing cooperatives they are not comparable with manufacturing cooperatives (see Attwood and Baviskar 1987 for a review). Some Israeli kibbutzim have substantial industry, but their idealistic origins render them a distinctive case.

There is some merit in comparing TVPS with collectively owned firms, such as producer cooperatives, that are established and operated for economic reasons. In small communities with extensive family ties the distinction between TVP members and the rest of the community may be blurred, and these TVPS may resemble a cooperative of the whole community. This is especially true in south China. It is also worthwhile to note the similarities between TVPS and capitalist firms that follow the "Japanese" system of long-run labor contracting and worker-firm identification.

Comparisons with Socially (Publicly) Owned Enterprises

The main comparators in this category are in Eastern Europe and Yugoslavia, but some analogies are also found in Tanzania's local state enterprises.

Eastern Europe

The activities of collective farms and producer cooperatives in many Eastern European countries resemble those of Chinese TVPS. Nonstate enterprises operate alongside traditional state enterprises. Many and often all of their activities are outside the central plan, their product prices are to a large extent market determined, and they concentrate on goods that are not supplied effectively by state enterprises. They thus select market niches in which demand and potential monopoly rents are high, and they often supply high-quality products at unusually high prices. These activities are tolerated and even encouraged by the authorities because the firms or farms reduce social discontent by supplying products that are in demand and would not otherwise be available. Economically, their existence depends in part on the pent-up demand for commodities, which is a systemic feature in Eastern Europe.

On the supply side the shift in terms of trade in favor of agriculture has provided many collective farms in countries such as Czechoslovakia with the resources needed for investment and for diversification into nonagricultural activities. In this respect, too, there is a parallel with China's experience.

Slusovice, a Czech collective farm, is perhaps an extreme example, but one that clearly illustrates these points. Since 1968 this farm has extended its membership to include technicians, engineers, economists, managers, computer specialists, and marketing professionals. It has radically mechanized, automated, and reduced its agricultural activities, which it maintains, even though it does not have a comparative advantage in them, because it has to fulfill planned delivery targets. At the same time, it has focused on specialized industrial production, high technology development and applications, and services. Slusovice's success in the relatively uncompetitive Czech system has been so marked that the government has used it as a showpiece for foreign visitors and dignitaries. The farm has also reorganized its management structure (it now has a vice president for public relations), and although in principle it is under the local government's jurisdiction, it is, in effect, under the patronage of the central government.

Other examples abound. For instance, Eastern European nonstate enterprises, particularly collective farms, are very successful in bidding for government contracts for the renovation of historical buildings in direct competition with the understaffed and inefficient state enterprises.

A significant difference between Chinese TVPs and Eastern European nonstate firms is that TVPs comprise a substantially larger share of the total market. Although no reliable statistics exist on the Eastern European firms, there is no doubt that so far they are relatively insignificant operations with high visibility and high social value. A related difference is that Chinese TVPs have begun competing with state enterprises, but the comparable Eastern European firms have done so only rarely and have focused instead on unexploited and highly profitable market niches. Chinese TVPs have therefore evolved beyond the stage of their Eastern European counterparts. This is attributable both to the more active role of Chinese community governments in fostering TVP development and to the greater ease with which these firms, even at small scale, can penetrate China's relatively less-developed industrial market. State enterprises in China may also be less forbidding competitors than those in Eastern Europe.

Yugoslavia

Yugoslav industrial firms fall into two broad categories: labor-managed firms (LMFs), which are part of the social property sector, and private firms, which operate independently alongside them. These two types of firms strongly resemble Chinese community enterprises and private enterprises (especially individual firms), respectively.

LMFs are in principle controlled and run by workers, but in practice managers and local as well as regional authorities determine their policies to a large extent (see Prasnikar and Svejnar 1987). Yugoslav private firms are more autonomous than LMFs, but they too have to comply with the rules and regulations set forth by authorities. In LMFs the capital is owned socially (rather than by individual workers or by the labor force of the firm as a whole), and in this respect LMFs resemble community enterprises in China. Capital in Yugoslav private firms may be owned by individuals, families, or groups of individuals—a situation parallel to that in Chinese private firms.

Both LMFs and Chinese community enterprises are required by the authorities to reinvest a sizable part of their income. In both cases authorities stress growth, employment generation (if unemployment or underemployment is a serious problem), and social goals such as equality of worker incomes as important objectives for enterprises. The authorities also ensure that some resources are transferred from successful firms to firms in need of funds for development. In China this is usually done by the authorities directly, through reallocation of community enterprise profits. In Yugoslavia it is accomplished by pooling resources among LMFS.

Finally, labor markets and utilization of labor by enterprises show important similarities. In both countries the appointment and promotion of managers is strongly influenced by local authorities and the Communist party. The size of the labor force often exceeds the level of maximum profitability in Yugoslavia and is known to do so in China in some cases. Layoffs are rare, as exogenous shocks are absorbed primarily by changes in income rather than through adjustment of the labor force. The labor pool from which firms draw their workers is local or at most regional, since labor mobility is limited in both systems. There is more worker participation in the management of Yugoslav LMFS than of Chinese TVPS.

In sum, in Yugoslavia as well as in China, local authorities act in many respects as a holding company that influences important decisions of firms and acts as a risk-sharing institution for the regionally immobile residents of the area.

But Yugoslav firms and Chinese TVPS also exhibit important differences. First, although local authorities are influential in Yugoslavia, the republican (that is, regional) and federal (central) governments decide some issues that are within the purview of local authorities in China. TVPS are on average much smaller than LMFS, and whereas TVPS were often spearheaded and are still controlled by local authorities, LMFS are usually large enough to be of regional and sometimes nationwide importance. The size of LMFS and their strategic role in the economy make them analogous to Chinese state enterprises in some ways.

The social ownership of LMF capital implies ownership by Yugoslav society as a whole, whereas Chinese community enterprises are owned by the township or village. This crucial distinction means that in Yugoslavia laws and regulations relating to the required reinvestment of firm income and pooling of resources with other firms often come from the republican or federal level. In China the transfer of resources to other TVPS takes place within the community; in Yugoslavia sharing of capital often transcends regional boundaries and is in effect a form of subsidization of less developed by more developed regions.

The influence of higher-level authorities over LMFS also explains why these firms are much larger than TVPS and why they face softer budget constraints, tend to be less flexible, and avoid bankruptcy in circumstances in which TVPS might not. LMFS are large because the Yugoslav government wanted to create sizable firms able to compete with large foreign corporations on the world market and because of the desire of LMFS themselves to grow to monopolistic proportions in the presence of the peculiar capital market features discussed below. The size of LMFS and their close relationship with higher-level authorities make the latter more willing to forestall bankruptcy by providing subsidies. This in turn reduces the incentives for LMFS to improve their efficiency and respond rapidly to a changing economic environment. The resulting "lethargic" behavior of many LMFs resembles that of Chinese state enterprises more than that of TVPs, which cannot rely on the resources of higher-level authorities and are closely monitored by local officials.

This difference in observed behavior is partly attributable to the weaker incentives offered to workers in LMFs and the greater constraints on their incomes. In particular, most workers in Yugoslav firms are paid salaries, and income differentials are limited by government controls, but most TVP workers are on piece rates or other, often profit-related, incentive schemes.

In the financial sphere, banks in China may be heavily influenced by local governments, but not by TVPs. In Yugoslavia banks are effectively controlled by their firm-clients. Interest rates are set, for ideological reasons, well below the shadow price of capital and are usually negative in real terms. Since each firm's control over the bank depends on the size of its deposits and loans, the Yugoslav system gives firms an extreme incentive to borrow excessively, grow in a capital-intensive way, and strive to capture as large a share of the capital and product market as possible.[1] Demand for bank loans by TVPs in China is also voracious, especially in periods of high growth, and local governments may influence the behavior of local bank branches, but direct ties between firms and banks are much less pronounced.

Finally, although Yugoslav LMFs share power with managers and authorities at various levels, their workers clearly influence enterprise policy more than do their counterparts in Chinese community enterprises. This means that Yugoslav LMFs probably pursue the welfare of their worker-members (as distinct from that of the local community as a whole) to a greater extent than do most Chinese community enterprises.

Tanzania

State enterprises dominate Tanzania's industry; private firms and joint ventures, sometimes with foreign partners, are next in importance. Beginning in the early 1970s district development councils (DDCs) were established with foreign assistance, with the development of small-scale local industry as one of their goals. The Small Industries Development Organization (SIDO) was founded in 1973. The available information indicates that the results of these initiatives were discouraging. Employment in small manufacturing rose by less than 2 percent a year up to 1978 and declined during 1978–82 as the economy entered a severe recession. The use of installed capacity and of common facilities that had been set up to promote industry was low (see Havnevik, Skarstein, and Wangwe 1985).

One reason for this poor performance seems to have been the limited linkage between these initiatives and local governments. The latter had no fiscal or other incentives for ensuring that the ventures were profitable. This left the way open for other objectives, notably patronage, which sometimes resulted in gross overmanning of the few potentially viable firms. Tanzania has begun to rethink such policies as the prohibition of private industrial ventures in its 8,000 *ujamaa* villages.

Comparators under Private Ownership

The main private comparators are the cooperatively owned Mondragon enterprises in Spain, company towns in the United States, the Swiss cantonal system, and the "Japanese-type" or Z-firm model.

The Mondragon Group

In 1956 a priest in the Basque village of Mondragon, Spain, inspired a group of unemployed technicians to buy out a bankrupt firm and start an experiment in worker ownership. The venture grew rapidly, and other cooperatives followed, initially in Mondragon itself and then in neighboring towns and cities. The cooperatives established a bank (the Caja Laboral Popular—CLP), a social security system, and technical research and training cooperatives. By the 1980s the Mondragon group had almost 20,000 worker-members, 85 affiliated industrial cooperatives, and a number of other cooperatives in agriculture and services. It has encouraged the formation of numerous cooperative schools and housing associations and has become a significant force in regional development. The performance of the Mondragon group over the past three decades is considered to have been very good (see Bradley and Gelb 1983a; Thomas and Logan 1982 provide an extensive description and assessment).

Mondragon's firms differ from Chinese community enterprises in that they are autonomous and are owned solely by their employees. It is also misleading to equate the CLP with a holding company or a township industrial corporation. Representatives from the industrial firms sit on the CLP's board; the bank may have an equity stake in new firms and in firms that have run into serious difficulties; and it provides management and promotional services that help firms overcome some of the disadvantages of their relatively small scale.[2] It also helps to pool the risks involved in new starts, which are usually funded jointly by the founding individuals, the CLP, and interested cooperatives, usually those of the founding members. But under normal circumstances the CLP has no say in the operation of industrial firms or in their use of surplus.

Mondragon's firms are owned partly as indivisible "socialized" capital but mostly in the form of individual accounts of their worker-members. The accounts receive allocations of surpluses and losses based on a distribution formula that emphasizes the share of the member in the "wage" bill (wages are anticipations out of profits). Departing members must be bought out with the savings of new and remaining workers, so there is a strong incentive to grow and to hire more labor. This incentive system is suitable for the objec-

tive, so important at the start of the Mondragon experiment, of creating employment in the repressed, war-damaged Basque provinces, especially as pay
levels are constrained within a differential of about 3 to 1. This range appears
comparable with that seen in community enterprises in China, but such sophisticated ownership systems are absent in the Chinese TVP sector.

The strength of the links between Mondragon firms and their local communities depends on the location of the firms and, in particular, on whether
the community is small and isolated (as many Basque villages are) or is a
large city. In Mondragon itself, now a town of 30,000, the cooperatives are
extremely important to the community in providing employment, incomes,
and local facilities—10 percent of the profits of all cooperatives go to a social
fund used for local facilities and services. A small cooperative in a large center would have far less influence. But the relationship between communities
and firms is more or less an arm's length one, in that firms are considered
commercial entities operating in a market economy rather than extensions
of the community.

Because firms are owned by their members, Mondragon's arrangements for
control differ substantially from those of most Chinese TVPs. Members elect
a board that appoints the management. Workers have an alternative channel
of communication, the social council—a form of workers' council—to air
grievances. There seems to be little demand for trade union representation
in addition to this channel.

To sum up, Mondragon suggests a different path toward regional development from that of the Chinese community enterprise sector. Its organizational arrangements may not be ideal in all circumstances; in particular,
the ownership system is difficult to reconcile with a mobile labor force.
Mondragon nevertheless offers rich lessons for the possible development of
the TVP sector toward private and more autonomous, yet still group, ownership patterns.

The Company Town and Cantonal Systems

In the United States as well as in other capitalist countries, individual firms
(or a small group) may create a community or dominate it economically. In
these "company towns" employment, the local tax base, and property values
all depend on the activities of the firm, which in effect "owns" the town
rather than the reverse. The company may even influence the selection of
public officials. These cases are therefore the opposite from what happens
in community enterprises.

Some communities that have suffered from departures of firms or that recognize their vulnerability to important company decisions have attempted to
attract and develop industry on a community basis. The Jamestown Labor-
Management Committee in upstate New York, for instance, was formed in
1972 to rejuvenate the town in the face of the exodus of private capital from

the area. The role of the committee was to build a partnership of interests among investors, labor organizations, and government organizations to reverse the process of industrial decline. This effort met with considerable success. New industries were established or attracted to the area, and a long period of industrial decline was arrested (see Jamestown Labor-Management Committee 1977).

Successful worker and community mobilizations of this type yield economic benefits and give the community greater control over local businesses. In unsuccessful cases the community may actually become worse off. Local savings contributed by workers and residents are often lost in the attempt to save failing or abandoned firms. For example, Rath Meatpacking in Waterloo, Iowa, was unable to compete in the depressed meatpacking industry and declared bankruptcy despite wage cuts, layoffs, and local investments.

Local communities or larger units such as states often compete to attract industry with the aim of maintaining or creating jobs and maximizing the tax base. The competitive approach requires open capital and entrepreneurial markets, as well as skill in negotiating with firms. New York State has attempted to attract high technology industry into the Ithaca and Rochester areas, with only limited success. In contrast, the town of Auburn in upstate New York has, through its own initiative, attracted Japanese capital. Access to good technical facilities appears to have been important in the location of certain industries—for example, in the Research Triangle area of North Carolina and in New England. It may thus make sense for communities to pool resources with the aim of creating a good environment for "footloose" private firms.

The decentralized system in Switzerland provides another example of close interaction between local authorities and business. Cantonal, township, and communal authorities approve and regulate many aspects of enterprise behavior. The rules and regulations concerning, for example, zoning and taxes are usually clearly defined, but such issues as the national or local composition of the labor force may be subject to negotiation. Unlike American company towns, Swiss political and social units usually predate the firms, and in that respect firm-community relationships are more akin to those of Chinese TVPs.

"Japanese-Type" Firms (Z-Firms)

Firms operating in the "privileged third" of the Japanese economy create an enriched employment relationship, sometimes referred to as the "paternalism–lifetime commitment" model (see, for example, Dore 1973). Key elements of this model include a long employment horizon, a strict seniority system, benefits that tie workers to the firm, measures to increase workers' involvement, and a substantial bonus element in total pay, so that pay, rather than number of workers, absorbs the impact of changing business conditions. Although the cultural heritage of Japan may be a factor in the prevalence of this model, Ouchi (1982) has pointed out that some of the most successful U.S. firms (Z-firms) practice similar principles. Z-firms often derive from strong identification between firms and communities; many originated in small isolated towns and were started by owners with strong ethical principles.

Z-firms, although perhaps not direct comparators, are of considerable interest because they present an alternative to the Taylorist "hire and fire" archetype for private firms. The Z-firm model may be of great relevance for China because of the degree of community identification and the low labor mobility there. A very high proportion of respondents to the Worker Survey Questionnaire expected to stay with their firms for a long time, and the analysis in chapter 13 suggests that Chinese private firms are closer to Z-firms than to Taylorist ones.

Changes in the Form of Firm Ownership

The structure of ownership and control of firms is not static but responds to economic and political imperatives. For example, the transition from family firms to corporations coincided with a need to exploit economies of scale and at the same time to diversify against risk through the introduction of limited liability. Some large and well-known U.S. firms, notably Amana (air conditioners) and Oneida (silverware), began as firms owned and run by small religious communities and gradually evolved into typical shareholder-owned firms. The recent and current privatization waves in countries as diverse as Great Britain, France, and Chile have important economic and political dimensions. In this section we consider the economic factors that tend to shift enterprises from worker ownership to private ownership and the reverse.

From Worker to Private Ownership

The transition from worker to private ownership in capitalist countries can involve successful firms or failing firms. The latter case is analogous to the acquisition of bankrupt private firms by a new owner and is therefore not of special interest here. The transition of successful worker-owned firms, however, has an important systemic underpinning that affects the operation of these firms and our evaluation of them.

The factors that determine the likelihood of transition in the successful cases are the nature of worker ownership and the time horizon of the current worker-members. When each member of the collective has a clearly defined share in ownership that can be sold to current or incoming members at market value, the tendency toward private, noncollective ownership is not very pronounced. This is the case in Mondragon. When, however, a significant number of members would like to sell their shares but cannot find new or current members who are willing to purchase them at the market price, the incentive to sell to outsiders may become strong. If the market value of the firm is particularly high and worker-owners do not expect to stay with the firm for long, the incentive to sell becomes even more pronounced.

A tendency to sell a worker-owned firm to private outsiders also exists when ownership by worker-members is collective rather than individual. In this case workers are not assigned individual shares in enterprise assets and therefore cannot individually sell their capital holdings, but if the entire firm is sold to an outside bidder, the workers will divide the proceeds. Collective ownership hence provides an important incentive for older workers to sell the firm, and it often pits older cohorts of members against younger ones.

The above set of factors, often referred to as the generational or worker horizon problem, has been responsible for the transformation of many successful worker-owned firms into private ones. Examples in the United States include the Plywood Cooperatives in the Pacific Northwest, the Vermont Asbestos Group, and U.S. News and World Report. If the promotion of worker collectives or communal ownership is considered desirable, these factors are seen as negative. If growth of employment and output are the goals, the transition may have a negative or a positive effect. Finally, in the debate about the relative performance of worker-owned and private capitalist firms, it is important to remember that the measured performance of worker-owned firms is biased because some of the best-performing ones are no longer worker owned.

From Capitalist to Worker Ownership

The transition from capitalist to worker ownership usually follows one of four patterns.

1. A benevolent or enlightened capitalist-owner decides to pass his firm on to the labor force. This is a rather special case, but some well-known worker-owned firms originated this way—for example, the John Lewis Partnership (which has 30,000 members), Scott Bader, and Baxi Heating, all in Great Britain.

2. Capitalist firms give or sell workers shares in the firm to generate capital, to attract workers with special skills, or to elicit greater identification with the firm and hence better performance. The firm remains traditional in structure, and the share of total capital owned by workers is typically rather small. Widespread employee shareholding of this type is a new development, although stock option plans for management have long been commonplace.

3. A capitalist firm closes down and becomes bankrupt, and the community or the workers take over to save the local economy. Private capital is usually unwilling to step in, and this reluctance may signal serious problems that cannot be overcome even under worker ownership. (An example is the case of Rath Meatpacking, noted above.). But—as in the case of the Library

Bureau, a subsidiary of Sperry Rand—the decision of the parent company to close the firm may simply be motivated by low profitability, and worker-owners can still earn reasonable incomes.

4. As a result of recent tax legislation, capitalist firms in the United States have found it advantageous to introduce employee stock ownership plans (ESOPs) that enable workers to acquire company shares either directly or indirectly, through their pension plans. The General Accounting Office estimates that in 1986 there were approximately 5,000 U.S. corporations with active ESOPs. Great Britain too has introduced incentives to encourage transfer of shares to employees. As in case 2, in most instances ESOPs have not shifted the structure of power significantly. Often workers have not obtained any voting rights, and sometimes ESOP incentives have been used to favor the interests of owners at the expense of workers.

The Debate on Efficiency

Although many observers believe that private ownership has an edge over public ownership in industry, the relative merits of conventional capitalist ownership and worker ownership are still hotly debated. Recent econometric studies indicate that the effect of individual worker ownership on productive efficiency (total factor productivity) is positive or insignificant and that of collective ownership is zero or negative (see, for instance, Jones and Backus 1977, Cable and Fitzroy 1980, Jones and Svejnar 1985, and Defourney, Estrin, and Jones 1985). Case studies suggest that the particular form of ownership, the way in which it was introduced, and the accompanying decision-making rights may influence the effect of ownership on productivity.

Systemic Flexibility and Adjustment

The ability of TVPs to adjust to changing conditions and their flexibility in relation to state enterprises depend in large part on institutional arrangements that constrain or stimulate their performance. As recent Chinese and, to a lesser extent, Eastern European experience indicates, nonstate firms in a socialist planned economy tend to expand rapidly on the upswing of the economy. This is primarily attributable to their ability to fill niches left by state enterprises and to expand investment rapidly. Their behavior in the more mature phase (when niches have been fully exploited) is harder to predict.

Comparative international experience provides some support for the proposition that communal firms, as well as those organized on the Japanese model, tend to respond to economic downturns by reducing incomes rather than by shedding labor, in contrast to "conventional" firms in a market economy. Japan's success in avoiding unemployment is notable (although it may be partly attributable to the existence of a large "unorganized" sector of firms that subcontract work from large firms and so act as a cushion). Among collectives the clearest example is perhaps the reaction of the Mondragon group to the severe downturn in the Spanish economy after 1979 (see Bradley and Gelb 1985). Layoffs were minimized, and incomes were reduced to the extent needed to preserve capital. At the same time, the search for new products was intensified, and resources were pooled to permit promising new starts. The performance of the Mondragon cooperatives was considerably better than that of the rest of the Spanish economy during the recession. In the economy at large, hiring ceased and labor was laid off despite regulations that limited dismissals. The result was a sharp segmentation of the labor force according to age as unemployment rose for all age groups, but especially for younger workers. Wage increases began to moderate only when unemployment became severe.

The behavior of Chinese TVPs during a downswing has not yet been fully observed. Given their flexibility during other parts of the cycle, however, they can be expected to display considerable readiness to adjust. The degree and form of adjustment will depend on the severity of the downturn, the availability of alternative products or markets, and the role of local authorities who act as both risk sharers and enforcers of social values. One would expect adjustment to take place primarily through reductions in incomes rather than through layoffs. In this sense TVPs resemble Yugoslav LMFs, Japanese and Z-firms, and the Mondragon cooperatives. They differ from Swiss firms, many of which lay off foreign workers during recessions, as well as from firms in capitalist economies that rely on temporary layoffs rather than wage fluctuations to absorb the impact of shifts in demand. Like the Japanese, Yugoslav, and Mondragon firms, community enterprises would probably emphasize flexible labor use within the firm and an active search for new markets.

It is more difficult to assess how Chinese private firms that hire wage labor from outside the community will behave during a downturn. Many may rely on labor adjustment, like their counterparts in other countries. Others may adjust like Z-firms, cutting pay and bonuses and trying to maintain employment. The outcome would depend on the relative power of entrepreneurs and community authorities and on the way in which private property rights, which are still rather fragile in China, are interpreted and exercised.

Notes

1. Greater capitalization leads to greater control over the bank, whereas a greater share of the product market guarantees greater control over product prices. Both allow the LMF to raise worker incomes, collective consumption, or both more than it otherwise could.

2. Mondragon decided, after a strike at the largest cooperative in 1974, to try to limit maximum firm size to about 500 members to preserve the cooperative spirit; the largest firm now has about 2,500 members.

References

Anhui Jingji Nianjian 1985 [Anhui Economic Yearbook 1985]. Hefei: Anhui Jingji Nianjian Bianyuan Weiyuanhui.

Attwood, D. M., and B. S. Baviskar. 1987. "Why Do Some Cooperatives Work But Not Others? A Comparative Analysis of Sugar Cooperatives in India." *Economic and Political Weekly* 22, no. 26:38–56.

Bradley, Keith, and Alan Gelb. 1983a. *Cooperation at Work: The Mondragon Experience.* London: Heinemann.

———. 1983b. *Worker Capitalism: The New Industrial Relations.* London: Heinemann.

———. 1985. "Mixed Economy vs. 'Cooperative' Adjustment: Mondragon's Experience through Spain's Recession." World Bank, Development Research Department Discussion Paper 122, Washington, D.C.

Brown, James N., and Orley C. Ashenfelter. 1986. "Testing the Efficiency of Employment Contracts." *Journal of Political Economy* 94(3), pt. 2 (June):S40–S87.

Buchanan, James M. 1975. "Public Finance and Public Choice." *National Tax Journal* 28, no. 4 (December):383–94.

Byrd, William A., and Gene Tidrick. 1987. "Factor Allocation and Enterprise Incentives." In Gene Tidrick and Chen Jiyuan, eds., *China's Industrial Reform.* New York: Oxford University Press.

Cable, J., and R. Fitzroy. 1980. "Cooperation and Productivity." *Economic Analysis and Workers' Management* 14:163–80.

China Economic Yearbook Editorial Board. 1981. *Zhongguo Jingji Nianjian 1981* [China Economic Yearbook 1981]. Beijing: Zhongguo Jingji Guanli Zazhishe.

———. 1985. *Zhongguo Jingji Nianjian 1985* [China Economic Yearbook 1985]. Beijing: Jingji Guanli Chubanshe.

China Rural Development Research Group (ed.). 1985, 1986. *Nongcun, Jingji, Shehui* [The Rural Areas, Their Economy, Their Society]. Irregular serial. Nos. 1–3 (1985) and 4 (1986). Beijing: Zhishi Chubanshe.

Defourney, J., S. Estrin, and D. Jones. 1985. "Effects of Worker Participation on Enterprise Performance." *International Journal of Industrial Organization* 3:197–217.

Development Research Institute. 1986. "Lun Nongcun Feinong Chanye de Fazhan"

[On the Development of Rural Nonagricultural Activities]. *Jingji Yanjiu* [Economic Research] 8 (August):9–24.

Domar, Evsey. 1966. "The Soviet Collective Farm as a Producer Cooperative." *American Economic Review* 56, no. 4 (September):734–57.

Dore, Ronald. 1973. *British Factory, Japanese Factory*. London: Allen and Unwin.

Enos, J. L. 1984. "Commune- and Brigade-Run Industries in Rural China: Some Recent Observations." In Keith Griffin, ed., *Institutional Reform and Economic Development in the Chinese Countryside*. London: Macmillan.

Fuss, Melvyn A., and Vinod K. Gupta. 1981. "A Cost Function Approach to the Estimation of Minimum Efficient Scale, Returns to Scale, and Suboptimal Capacity." *European Economic Review* 15:123–35.

Griffin, Keith, and Kimberley Griffin. 1984. "Commune- and Brigade-Run Enterprises in Rural China: An Overview." In Keith Griffin, ed., *Institutional Reform and Economic Development in the Chinese Countryside*. London: Macmillan.

Halvorsen, R., and R. Palmquist. 1980. "The Interpretation of Dummy Variables in Semilogarithmic Equations." *American Economic Review* 70, no. 3 (June):474–75.

Havnevik, K., R. Skarstein, and S. Wangwe. 1985. "Small-Scale Industrial Sector Study, Tanzania." Report to the Minister of Finance, October 1985. Dar es Salaam.

Hayek, Friedrich A. 1948. *Individualism and Economic Order*. Chicago: University of Chicago Press.

Hebert, Robert F., and Albert N. Link. 1982. *The Entrepreneur: Mainstream Views and Radical Critiques*. New York: Praeger.

He Jiacheng. 1987. "Zhuazhu Tuopin Zhifu de Sange Guanjian Huanjie" [On Three Key Links in Letting Poor Areas Prosper]. *Jingjixue Dongtai* [Trends in Economics] no. 5 (May).

Ho, Samuel P. S. 1986. *The Asian Experience in Rural Nonagricultural Development and Its Relevance for China*. World Bank Staff Working Paper 757. Washington, D.C.

Institute of Economics, CASS. 1987. *Zhongguo Xiangzhen Qiye de Jingji Fazhan yu Jingji Tizhi* [The Economic Development and Economic System of China's TVPs]. Beijing: Zhongguo Jingji Chubanshe.

Jamestown Labor-Management Committee. 1977. "Commitment at Work: The Five-Year Report of the Jamestown Labor-Management Committee." Jamestown, N.Y.

Jiangsu Academy of Social Sciences. 1981. *Collected Papers on the Experiences of Jiangsu Commune and Brigade Enterprises* (in Chinese). Nanjing: Jiangsu Renmin Chubanshe.

Jiangsu Jingji Nianjian 1986 [Jiangsu Economic Yearbook 1986]. Nanjing: Jiangsu Renmin Chubanshe.

Jones, D. C., and D. Backus. 1977. "British Producer Cooperatives in the Footwear Industry." *Economic Journal* (September):488–510.

Jones, D. C., and J. Svejnar. 1982. *Participatory Firms: Evaluating Economic Performance*. Lexington, Mass.: Lexington Books, D. C. Heath.

———. 1985. "Participation, Profit Sharing, Worker Ownership and Efficiency in Italian Producer Cooperatives." *Economica* 52 (November):449–65.

Kalai, Ehud. 1977. "Nonsymmetric Nash Solutions and Replications of Two-Person Bargaining." *International Journal of Game Theory* 6(3):129–33.

Kirzner, Israel M. 1973. *Competition and Entrepreneurship*. Chicago: University of Chicago Press.

Knight, John B., and Richard Sabot. Forthcoming. *Education, Productivity, and Inequality: The East African Natural Experiment*. New York: Oxford University Press.

Krueger, Anne O. 1968. "Factor Endowments and Per Capita Income Differences among Countries." *Economic Journal* 78 (September):641–51.

Lewis, W. Arthur. 1954. "Economic Development with Unlimited Supplies of Labor." *Manchester School of Economic and Social Studies* 22, no. 2 (May): 139–91.

Lin Qingsong and others. 1987. "Gongren Gufen Suoyouzhi de Qiye Zhidu: Guowai Feiquxing Qiye Zhidu de Kaocha he Sikao" [Observations and Reflections on Atypical Enterprise Systems in Other Countries]. *Jingjixue Dongtai* [Trends in Economics] 6 (June):31–37.

Little, Ian M. D., Dipak Mazumdar, and John M. Page, Jr. 1987. *Small Manufacturing Enterprises: A Comparative Analysis of India and Other Economies*. New York: Oxford University Press.

Lu Mai and Dai Xiaojing. 1987. "Xian Jieduan Nonghu Jingji Xingwei Qianxi" [An Elementary Discussion of the Economic Behavior of Rural Households at Present]. *Jingji Yanjiu* [Economic Research] 7 (July):68–74.

Luo Hanxian. 1987. *Zhongguo Jingji Tizhi Gaige: Nongcun—Zhongguo Nongcun Fazhan Shehuixue* [Economic System Reform in China: Rural Villages— Development Sociology in China's Rural Villages]. Hong Kong: Guangjiaojing Chubanshe.

Mallarde, E. 1975. *L'Algerie Depuis*. Paris: La Table Ronde.

Ministry of Agriculture. Various years. *Zhongguo Nongye Jingji Ziliao* [Statistical Materials on China's Agricultural Economy]. Beijing: Nongye Chubanshe.

———. 1986a. *Zhongguo Nongxuyuye Tongji Ziliao 1984* [China Agriculture, Animal Husbandry, and Fishery Statistical Materials 1984]. Beijing: Nongye Chubanshe.

———. 1986b. *Zhongguo Nongxuyuye Tongji Ziliao 1985* [China Agriculture, Animal Husbandry, and Fishery Statistical Materials 1985]. Beijing: Nongye Chubanshe.

Mueller, Dennis C. 1976. "Public Choice: A Survey." *Journal of Economic Literature* 14, no. 2 (June):395–433.

Nanhai Nongcun [Rural Nanhai]. Periodical.

Niskanen, William A. 1968. "Nonmarket Decision Making: The Peculiar Economics of Bureaucracy." *American Economic Review* 68, no. 2 (May):293–305.

Ouchi, W. 1982. *Theory Z: How American Business Can Meet the Japanese Challenge*. New York: Avon.

Perkins, Dwight H., and others. 1977. *Rural Small-Scale Industry in the People's Republic of China*. Berkeley: University of California Press.

Prasnikar, J., and J. Svejnar. 1987. "Enterprise Behavior in Yugoslavia." *Advances in the Economic Analysis of Participatory and Labor-Managed Firms* 3.

Reynolds, Lloyd G. 1982. *Labor Economics and Labor Relations*. 8th ed. Englewood Cliffs, N.J.: Prentice-Hall.

Richards, V., and A. Williams. 1982. "Institutional and Economic Aspects of the Jamaican Sugar Cooperatives." In D. C. Jones and J. Svejnar, eds., *Participatory Firms: Evaluating Economic Performance*. Lexington, Mass.: Lexington Books, D. C. Heath.

430   REFERENCES

Riskin, Carl. 1978a. "China's Rural Industries: Self-Reliant Systems or Independent Kingdoms?" *China Quarterly* 73 (March):77–98.

———. 1978b. "Political Conflict and Rural Industrialization in China." *World Development* 6, no. 5 (May):681–92.

Roth, Alvin E. 1979. *Axiomatic Models of Bargaining.* Lecture Notes in Economics and Mathematical Systems 170. New York: Springer-Verlag.

Schumpeter, Joseph A. 1934. *The Theory of Economic Development.* Cambridge, Mass.: Harvard University Press.

Scott, C. D. 1979. "Agrarian Reform and Agricultural Labor Markets." University of East Anglia Occasional Paper 2. Norwich, U.K.

Sigurdson, Jon. 1977. *Rural Industrialization in China.* Cambridge, Mass.: Harvard University Press.

State Council Economic, Technological, and Social Development Research Center. 1986. *Zhongguo Jingji Nianjian 1986* [China Economic Yearbook 1986]. Beijing: Jingji Guanli Chubanshe.

State Statistical Bureau 1982. *Statistical Yearbook of China 1981.* Hong Kong: Economic Information and Agency.

———. 1983. *Statistical Yearbook of China 1983.* Hong Kong: Economic Information and Agency.

———. 1984. *Statistical Yearbook of China 1984.* Hong Kong: Economic Information and Agency.

———. 1985a. *Statistical Yearbook of China 1985.* Hong Kong: Economic Information and Agency.

———. 1985b. *Zhongguo Gongye Jingji Tongji Ziliao 1949–84* [Statistical Materials on China's Industrial Economy 1949–84]. Beijing: Zhongguo Tongji Chubanshe.

———. 1985c. *Zhongguo Shehui Tongji Ziliao* [China Social Statistical Materials]. Beijing: Zhongguo Tongji Chubanshe.

———. 1986a. *Statistical Yearbook of China 1986.* Hong Kong: Economic Information and Agency.

———. 1986b. *Zhongguo Nongcun Tongji Nianjian 1985* [China Rural Statistical Yearbook 1985]. Beijing: Zhongguo Tongji Chubanshe.

———. 1986c. *Zhongguo Tongji Nianjian 1986* [China Statistical Yearbook 1986]. Beijing: Zhongguo Tongji Chubanshe.

———. 1987a. *Statistical Yearbook of China 1987.* Hong Kong: Economic Information and Agency.

———. 1987b. *Zhongguo Gongye Jingji Tongji Ziliao 1986* [Statistical Materials on China's Industrial Economy 1986]. Beijing: Zhongguo Tongji Chubanshe.

———. 1987c. *Zhongguo Nongcun Tongji Nianjian 1986* [China Rural Statistical Yearbook 1986]. Beijing: Zhongguo Tongji Chubanshe.

———. 1987d. *Zhongguo Nongcun Tongji Nianjian 1987* [China Rural Statistical Yearbook 1987]. Beijing: Zhongguo Tongji Chubanshe.

Svejnar, Jan. 1986. "Bargaining Power, Fear of Disagreement and Wage Settlements: Theory and Evidence from U.S. Industry." *Econometrica* 54, no. 5 (September):1055–78.

Thomas, Henk, and Chris Logan. 1982. *Mondragon: An Economic Analysis.* Winchester, Mass.: Allen and Unwin.

Tiebout, Charles M. 1956. "A Pure Theory of Local Expenditures." *Journal of Political Economy* 64, no. 5 (October):416–24.

———. 1961. "An Economic Theory of Fiscal Decentralization." In National Bureau of Economic Research, *Public Finances: Needs, Sources, and Utilization*. Princeton, N.J.: Princeton University Press.

Tidrick, Gene, and Chen Jiyuan. 1987. *China's Industrial Reform*. New York: Oxford University Press.

Todaro, Michael P. 1969. "A Model of Labor Migration and Urban Unemployment in Less Developed Countries." *American Economic Review* 59, no. 1:138–48.

U.S. Government. *U.S. County and City Data Book, 1983*. Washington, D.C.: Government Printing Office.

Vanek, Jaroslav. 1970. *The General Theory of Labor-Managed Market Economies*. Ithaca, N.Y.: Cornell University Press.

Wang Xiaoqiang, and others. 1983. "Nongcun Shangpin Shengchan Fazhan de Xin Dongxiang—Wenzhou Nongcun Jige Zhuanye Shangpin Chanxiao Jidi de Kaocha Baogao" [New Trends in the Development of Rural Commodity Production—Report on an Investigation of Several Rural Production and Marketing Bases in Wenzhou]. Reprinted in *China Rural Development Research Group* no. 3:69–93.

Ward, Benjamin. 1958. "The Firm in Illyria: Market Syndicalism." *American Economic Review* 48, no. 4 (September):566–89.

Williamson, Oliver E. 1985. *The Economic Institutions of Capitalism*. Cambridge, Mass.: Harvard University Press.

Wong, Christine. 1979. "Rural Industrialization in China: Development of the 'Five Small Industries.'" Ph.D. dissertation. University of California, Berkeley.

World Bank. 1984. *World Development Report 1984*. New York: Oxford University Press.

———. 1988. *China: Growth and Development in Gansu Province*. A World Bank Country Study. Washington, D.C.

Wu Xiang. 1986. *Zhongguo Nongcun Gaige* [Rural Reforms in China]. Beijing: Guangming Ribao Chubanshe.

Xinhua Yuebao [New China Monthly Digest]. Beijing.

Zhou Qiren and Huang Zhuangjun. 1987. "Zhongguo Xiangzhen Gongye Qiye de Zichan Xingcheng, Yingyun Tezheng Jiqi Hongguan Xiaoying—Dui 10 Sheng Daxing Xiangzhen Gongye Qiye Chouyang Diaochade Fenxi" [Asset Formation, Operational Features, and Macroeconomic Impact of China's Township and Village Industrial Enterprises—An Analysis of a Sample Survey of Large Township and Village Industrial Enterprises in Ten Provinces]. *Zhongguo Shehui Kexue* [Social Sciences in China] no. 6 (November):41–66.

Zhu Tonghua. 1985. *Xiangzhen Gongye yu Xiaochengzhen* [Township and Village Enterprises and Small Towns]. Beijing: Zhongguo Zhanwang Chubanshe.

Index

ment and, 124; expenditures of, 342, 343, 344, 364–70, 370–71, 377, 383, 386; factor immobility and, 359–60, 386; grants by, 87, 89; income distribution and, 324, 360–61; industrial structure and, 105–06; investment and, 349, 351; labor immobility and, 359–60; market interactions and, 87–88, 100, 102, 107, 109; officials in, 365, 370, 372–76; operation of, 344–46; ownership and, 5, 6, 351, 383–84; profit remittances and, 15, 364, 366, 370, 378; profits and, 124, 125, 227, 345, 351, 357, 365, 366, 369, 374; public finance and, 342–50; revenues of, 342–43, 344, 347, 348, 350–51, 364–70, 370–71; status hierarchy analysis and, 162–64; TICs and, 226; township property and, 346–47; TVCES and, 5, 227, 349, 350–52; TVP development and, 5, 6, 62, 63, 226–29, 272–73, 358–59, 365, 368, 377, 382; TVP financial flows and, 364–70; TVP relations and, 376–83

Township industrial corporations (TICS), 226, 351, 384

Township Leader Questionnaire, 24, 31, 33, 227, 353, 399

Townships: defined, 3; TVP data set and, 25–27

Township and village community enterprises (TVCES): bank loans in Wuxi and, 158, 159; capital and, 200–01, 208, 213; community governments and, 5, 227, 349, 350–52; comparative analysis and, 393–400; defined, 3–4; economic reform and, 272; economies of scale and, 239–42; efficiency and, 247; farm labor income and, 328; firm size and, 239; growth and development of, 11–13, 69–71, 139–45, 264–65; income and, 69, 71; in Jieshou, 144–45, 146, 156, 356; leading industrial subsectors (by re-

gions) and, 261–64; money-losing, 225; in Nanhai, 141–43, 151–54, 159–61; ownership and, 124, 125, 195, 196, 197, 324; penalties for leaving, 150; poor performance by, 154–56, 207; private enterprise and, 175, 177, 185; production teams and, 149, 151; profit distribution and, 229–32; regional imbalances and, 260–61, 264, 267–68; in Shangrao, 143–44, 154–56; status hierarchy analysis and, 148–51; structural reform and, 123–27; in Wuxi, 138, 139–41, 148–51, 152, 157–59, 166, 356. *See also* Brigade industries; Commune industries

Township, village, and private enterprises (TVPS): accounting systems and, 409–10; adaptability and, 167–68; adjustment and, 92–94, 98–102, 108–09; agriculture and industrial development and, 48–55, 113–17, 222–23; bank loans and, 78, 223–26; capital and, 51–52, 61; capital productivity and, 233–42; communal model of, 281, 283; community governments and, 5, 6, 62, 63, 226–29, 272–73, 358–59; compared with other types of firms, 414–15; competition and, 90, 92–98, 107–08; cooperation of TVCES with, 97; cost structure and, 410–11; defined, 3; development patterns and, 81–83; description of, 413–414; Eastern European state enterprises compared with, 415–16; efficiency and, 243, 245–47, 250–53, 247–50, 254; employment and, 62, 372; entrepreneurship and, 189–90, 191–95, 195–97, 198, 199–203, 208, 209–12; equipment and, 54–55, 62; financial flows among, 364–70; firm size and, 88; future prospects for, 169–70; gross output and, 65–66; historical background on, 9–11; industrial composition comparison and, 411; institu-

The backlist of publications by the World Bank is shown in the annual *Index of Publications*, which is available from Publications Sales Unit, The World Bank, 1818 H Street, N.W., Washington, D.C. 20433, U.S.A., or from Publications, Banque mondiale, 66, avenue d'Iéna, 75116 Paris, France.

DATE DUE